Natures of Africa

Ecocriticism and Animal Studies
in Contemporary Cultural Forms

Natures of Africa

Ecocriticism and Animal Studies in Contemporary Cultural Forms

Edited by
F. Fiona Moolla

WITS UNIVERSITY PRESS

Published in South Africa by:
Wits University Press
1 Jan Smuts Avenue
Johannesburg 2001

www.witspress.co.za

Compilation © F. Fiona Moolla 2016
Chapters © Individual contributors 2016
Published edition © 2016 Wits University Press

First published by Wits University Press in 2016

978-1-86814-913-1 (print)
978-1-86814-916-2 (PDF)

All rights reserved. No part of this book may be reproduced or transmitted in any form or by any means, electronic or mechanical, including photocopying, recording or by any information storage and retrieval system, without written permission from the Publisher, except in accordance with the provisions of the Copyright Act, Act 98 of 1978.

Cover image: *Scion* by Gerhard Marx (2011). Bronze, 70 x 100 x 30cm, Edition of 5 + 1AP Image courtesy of the artist and Goodman Gallery.

Copyedited by Mark Ronan
Proofread and indexed by Margaret Ramsay
Original jacket design by Fire and Lion
Typeset by MPS Limited, Chennai, India

TABLE OF CONTENTS

FOREWORD vii

INTRODUCTION 1

1. **'HERE IS SOME BAOBAB LEAF!':** *SUNJATA*,
   FOODWAYS AND BIOPIRACY 27
   Jonathan Bishop Highfield

2. **SHONA AS A LAND-BASED NATURE-CULTURE:**
   A STUDY OF THE (RE)CONSTRUCTION OF SHONA
   LAND MYTHOLOGY IN POPULAR SONGS 49
   Mickias Musiyiwa

3. **THE ENVIRONMENT AS SIGNIFICANT OTHER:** THE GREEN
   NATURE OF SHONA INDIGENOUS RELIGION 77
   Jacob Mapara

4. **ANIMAL ORAL PRAISE POETRY AND THE**
   SAMBURU DESIRE TO SURVIVE 97
   James Maina Wachira

5. **THE PARADOXES OF VOLUNTOURISM:**
   STRATEGIC VISUAL TROPES OF THE NATURAL
   ON SOUTH AFRICAN VOLUNTOURISM WEBSITES 118
   Reinier J. M. Vriend

Table of contents

6. **TOWARDS AN ECOCRITICISM IN AFRICA:** LITERARY AESTHETICS IN AFRICAN ENVIRONMENTAL LITERATURE 141
   Chengyi Coral Wu

7. **CRITICAL INTERSECTIONS:** ECOCRITICISM, GLOBALISED CITIES AND AFRICAN NARRATIVE, WITH A FOCUS ON K. SELLO DUIKER'S *THIRTEEN CENTS* 166
   Anthony Vital

8. **NAVIGATING GARIEP COUNTRY:** WRITING NATURE-CULTURE IN *BORDERLINE* BY WILLIAM DICEY 187
   Mathilda Slabbert

9. **NEGOTIATING IDENTITY IN A VANISHING GEOGRAPHY:** HOME, ENVIRONMENT AND DISPLACEMENT IN HELON HABILA'S *OIL ON WATER* 212
   Ogaga Okuyade

10. **HUMAN MASKS?** ANIMAL NARRATORS IN PATRICE NGANANG'S *DOG DAYS: AN ANIMAL CHRONICLE* AND ALAIN MABANCKOU'S *MEMOIRS OF A PORCUPINE* 235
    Wendy Woodward

11. **NATURE, ANIMISM AND HUMANITY IN ANGLOPHONE NIGERIAN POETRY** 257
    Sule Emmanuel Egya

12. **ANIMALS, NOSTALGIA AND ZIMBABWE'S RURAL LANDSCAPE IN THE POETRY OF CHENJERAI HOVE AND MUSAEMURA ZIMUNYA** 276
    Syned Mthatiwa

ABOUT THE AUTHORS 305

ACKNOWLEDGEMENTS 307

NOTES 309

INDEX 323

FOREWORD

Byron Caminero-Santangelo

In her introduction, Fiona Moolla suggests that an African ecocriticism must be informed by specific material and cultural conditions on the continent, and not simply draw on a supposedly more universal postcolonial framework. As she notes, there have been regrettably few book-length ecocritical studies focused on Africa and, much of the time, 'African environment and animals have been considered in monographs and edited volumes in a general postcolonial context together with criticism of other world literatures'. Moolla rightly insists on the need for close consideration of how 'the natural world and animals have been active agents in African cultural forms' and 'fundamentally constitutive of the worldviews and lifeways that have created [African] cultural "texts"'. In this sense, the importance of *The Natures of Africa* is embedded not just in the individual chapters of the book, but also in how the collection as a whole points to common issues and concerns that can ground productive dialogues about African cultural production in the context of the environmental humanities.

At the same time, the collection is very much connected to postcolonialism through its focus on decolonising knowledge and representation. Such counter-discursive work need not engage directly with the historical experience of colonialism in Africa or even explicitly with what Derek Gregory (2004) terms 'the colonial present'. However, it does challenge ways of perceiving and conceptualising the world rooted in the perspectives of those empowered by imperial modernity and serving to reproduce forms of domination. This intellectual project has two components. The first is to illuminate how dominant ways of processing the world have been shaped by colonial discourses of identity and geography, how they suppress or render invisible other (unsettling) forms of knowledge and perception, and how they reinforce uneven political relationships. The second path to decolonising knowledge entails the articulation of marginalised cultural perspectives and forms of knowledge that might enable resistance to imperialism and alleviate its violent effects. Although *The Natures of Africa* is engaged with both aspects of perspectival decolonisation, its links with the second, often more difficult, component are particularly striking.

In general, what has come to be known as postcolonial ecocriticism emphasises the generative relationships among mainstream environmental discourse, originating in and centred on the West and colonial power. This discourse all too easily separates nature and its defence from systemic inequality among humans and suggests that, through an awareness of the truths of ecology, and appreciation and care for nature, one can escape the influence of socio-economic positioning. Such a perspective cannot be separated from notions of objectivity and universality underpinning colonial knowledge production (DeLoughrey and Handley 2011; O'Brien 2007; Vital 2008). For example, colonial power was enhanced by the notion that, lacking a basis in proper ecological knowledge, 'local systems of resource use threatened nature' (Adams 2003: 30). This idea all too often still informs 'contemporary thinking on conservation' (Adams 2003: 19).

Central to the decolonising work of *The Natures of Africa* is its challenge to the *particular* position assigned to Africa in relation to nature in colonial discourse. In imperial mapping of geographical difference, Africa has been defined by its embodiment of timeless and dangerous wilderness. Africans fit into this picture either as human manifestations of Africa's wild essence or by being erased from the picture altogether. Approached from an instrumental perspective on untransformed nature, such representations all too easily position Africans and African places as having no intrinsic value, and as ripe for exploitation through resource extraction and 'development' driven by the interests of the privileged and powerful. If the safari image of Africa seems to contradict this positioning by representing parts of the continent as pastoral places where tourists, settlers and experts can establish an identification with a magnificent wildness, and can serve as its stewards, it still reinforces imperial relationships and the commodification of African nature (Brockington 2002). The chapter on voluntourism by Reinier Vriend draws attention to one pernicious effect of such discourse in contemporary Africa. As he argues, in the efforts to 'sell' voluntourism to a Western audience, businesses draw on images of 'wild Africa' even though the work of the volunteers rarely focuses on 'wild' or even on rural areas. In the process, both Africa and volunteerism all too easily become commodified, the imperial centring of the volunteers as purveyors of 'development' gets reinforced, and the communities they supposedly come to help get disempowered.

Safari discourse is closely tied to imperial 'wisdom' about environmental change in Africa, which constructs Africans as lacking the proper environmental sensibility and knowledge to take care of the continent's biodiversity, and suggests that conservation efforts in Africa need to be conceived and led by Western experts (Fairhead and Leach 1996; Leach and Mearns 1996; Neumann 2005). This construction has been, and still is, closely tied to imperial forms of control over natural resources. For example, in regard to scientific forestry, it underpinned the creation of forest reserves and powerful forestry departments that enabled the state to seize vast areas of forest already in use by indigenous peoples. At the same time, while imperial conservation in Africa was apparently intended to prevent unrestrained exploitation of natural resources for short-term gain, it also worked closely with capitalist development, often with disastrous ecological results. In response to Western 'wisdom' underpinning conservation in Africa, African writer-activists have sought to decolonise environmental discourse by emphasising, on the one hand, the ecological benefits of indigenous cultures and, on the other hand, the violence done to African places and peoples as a result of (neo)colonial representation and practice. A number of chapters in *The Natures of Africa* contribute to this project through analysis of the values and knowledge embedded in orature and other popular cultural forms from South, East, and West Africa. James Wachira argues that Samburu animal praise poetry contributes to the safeguarding of a community's survival both through its inscription of ecological knowledge of animals and by formulating an environmental ethics rooted in a strong sense of interconnection between human and animal life. Mickias Musiyiwa examines the politically ambivalent relationship between anticolonial nationalism in Zimbabwe and the appropriation in popular song of a Shona land mythology enabling a 'ritually directed ecosystem' in which ecological health is maintained and which is undermined by the instrumental vision of land entailed by colonialism. Jonathan Highfield examines the ways that accessing the knowledge and values embedded in representations of food and foodways in orature and its adaptation in popular culture enable resistance to socio-ecological threats posed by (neo)colonial practice. Specifically, he uses different versions of the *Sunjata* epic to explore the significance of the baobab in precolonial West Africa, and the ways they concomitantly point to the need for food sovereignty and for a reinvigoration of indigenous food practice in the face of biopiracy and the allure of unhealthy Western foodways.

A number of chapters in *The Natures of Africa* explore the significance of animism as a basis for ecologically healthy cultural practice and as a means to understand the link between indigenous ecological sensibility and African literature. According to Sule Egya, an animist sensibility underpins Nigerian poetry in two important ways: it has encouraged poets to turn to non-human components of specific places for inspiration and it has offered them an important means to thematise critical political concerns. In turn, it grounds the poetry in a sense of community that includes spiritually charged flora, fauna and natural phenomena, and, as a result, can encourage a sense of ethical responsibility to them. In discussing what he calls a Shona 'green' religion, Jacob Mapara references the importance of taboos embedded in animistic belief that enable effective environmental regulation (an issue also raised by Syned Mthatiwa). Mapara even uses the example of the spiritual value ascribed to fig trees, which echoes Wangari Maathai's (2006) discussion of the benefits of Gikuyu animistic belief in her memoir, *Unbowed*. She remembers her mother's warnings not to disturb wild fig trees, sources of streams and centres of biodiversity that were protected by communal taboo: 'The reverence the community had for the fig tree helped preserve the stream', and the trees 'held the soil together, reducing erosion and landslides. In such ways, without conscious or deliberate effort, [the community's] cultural and spiritual practices contributed to the conservation of biodiversity' (Maathai 2006: 46). More generally, Maathai represents hope as rooted in traditional communal identity and culture formed by a close relationship with the soil, embodying an ideal ecological wisdom. Many of Africa's current problems, according to Maathai, stem from the denigration of these cultures by colonialism and the spread of a capitalist outlook, encouraging a narrow instrumentalisation of nature and its rapid transformation for the sake of profit and economic development (Maathai 2006, 2009).

In her writing, Maathai draws on an anti-colonial pastoral vision that depicts indigenous environmental cultures enabling the maintenance of healthy ecosystems and foregrounds the corrupting effects of colonial modernity, including destruction of an effective accommodation between humans and nature. Given the success of the Green Belt Movement, Maathai's use of a pastoral sensibility suggests it can be an effective strategy for those engaged with struggles for environmental justice. It helped connect environmentalism with anti-colonial struggle and encouraged Kenyans to rally around the protection of the soil and biodiversity as a marker of counter-hegemonic collective identity.

Yet, at the same time, as many of the contributors to *The Natures of Africa* suggest, the use of an anti-colonial pastoral vision as a means to promote environmental justice in Africa is potentially problematic in its re-inscription, if inversion, of a delimitation between nature and culture and/or between tradition and modernity. While arguing for the value of Zimbabwean poets' use of the pastoral for decolonising ecological sensibility and knowledge, Syned Mthatiwa also points out its possible limitations. For example, he notes that an uncritical celebration of animism can gloss over the ways that it potentially renders some parts of nature valuable at the expense of others and that a perpetuation of a country–city divide in African writing can elide the ways that the rural has been transformed by modernity. Approaching the limitations of an anti-colonial pastoral vision from the perspective of animal studies, Wendy Woodward considers the ways that two African novels, Patrice Nganang's *Dog Days: An Animal Chronicle* and Alain Mabanckou's *Memoirs of a Porcupine*, subvert the 'high seriousness' of mythic belief in a connection between African nature, particularly animals, and 'sacred wisdom'. Such belief, she argues, is represented by the novels as reinforcing divisions between tradition and modernity, nature and culture, and animal and human, which can enable the naturalisation of neocolonial authority and disable a sense of ethical responsibility to animals. Taking a somewhat different approach, Anthony Vital suggests that the pastoral impulse can short-circuit attention to the complex socio-ecological conditions in Africa shaped by imperial histories and relationships, and to the ways that human desire, including pastoral desire, is both part of these conditions and hampers an understanding of them. He advocates a form of ecocritical reading that draws attention to the complexities of urban ecologies, of the relationships between nature and cities, and the ways they have been shaped by modernity. Such reading, he argues, necessitates bringing together the insights into 'the drama of human need and desire' enabled by literary criticism and an awareness of natural and social processes offered by 'other specialist languages, those of the social and natural scientists'.

As Rob Nixon has so eloquently established, representing how socio-ecological conditions in Africa have been shaped by uneven imperial relationships requires disrupting engrained ways of seeing and conceptualising violence. Nixon is concerned with what he terms the 'slow violence' of environmental catastrophe, an attritional 'violence of delayed destruction ... that is typically not viewed as violence at all' and with the 'strategic and representational' challenges posed by such violence to those trying to bear witness to it, including the 'perceptual habits that downplay' it (Nixon 2011: 2–3, 10, 15). Ogaga Okuyade's chapter on Helon Habila's novel *Oil on Water* brings attention to the ways that fiction can bring to consciousness aspects of slow violence that are not made visible in other kinds of discourse. Okuyade argues that Habila depicts how oil extraction and exploration in the Niger Delta have not only led to a vast environmental refugee crisis, but have also created the devastating impact of mass displacement on peoples' consciousness and sense of identity. Representing such violence cannot only be rendered by stories of international flows and forces, but it also requires, as Okuyade notes, local stories about and perspectives on the psychic damage resulting from the destruction of communities and ecological homes. Similarly, Mathilda Slabbert argues that William Dicey's Orange River travel narrative, *Borderline*, reveals the ways that conditions along the river can be understood only in terms of the intersection of a regional history of displacement and toxic slow violence with (trans)national imperial history. This aspect of *Borderline*, she argues, necessitates a foregrounding of marginalised knowledge and stories that decentre the privileged narrative voice and undermine the sense of mastery so often embedded in imperial travel writing. It also entails an interdisciplinary orientation, a willingness to take into account the value of different kinds of expertise and discourse to understand and represent slow violence.

In her introduction, Fiona Moolla suggests that there are some parts of the continent (in particular, North Africa), some genres (drama), and some themes and critical approaches (posthumanism and ecofeminism) that are missing from *The Natures of Africa*. However, addressing the full range of possible geographical perspectives, genres and issues that could be pertinent to African ecocriticism would be a nearly impossible task, especially given the relatively nascent state of the field. What is most important at this juncture is the kind of groundbreaking work achieved by the collection in terms of the range of voices from Africa, the prominence of orature and animal studies, the interplay of genres and the careful attention to oft ignored issues, such as African cities, uses of African nature in advertising on the web, the history of environmental criticism from Africa and environmental refugees.

More generally, the collection draws attention to perspectives rooted in African cultural texts and socio-ecological experience that are crucial for the formulation of what Anthony Vital refers to in this volume as 'an ecocriticism within and for Africa' based on 'all that makes African worlds distinct'. As I have argued elsewhere, such a focus can serve to highlight 'regional alterity that cannot be subsumed by a more universal imperial or postcolonial condition' (Caminero-Santangelo 2014: 9). In this sense, it is crucial that an African ecocriticism be theoretically informed by African writing and orature, and not simply entail applying critical models developed in and for other cultural contexts to African texts. This project includes legacies of environmental writing from Africa that have previously been ignored in ecocriticism – in part because they do not fit with the predominant environmental sensibilities of the West. In her chapter, Coral Wu makes an important contribution in this regard by exploring an unrecognised history of environmentally oriented literary criticism by African scholars.

At the same time, as Vital notes, the formulation of an 'ecocriticism within and for Africa' necessitates that we take into account the 'points at which Africa participates in global realities'. Such 'realities' include processes of (often uneven) exchange and transformation, which can trouble cultural delimitation based on geographical categories, as can differences within supposedly unified, bounded spaces. In other words, an African ecocriticism needs to be understood relationally: it is part of more 'global' fields – for example, postcolonial ecocriticism – even as its identity relies precisely on the way that it cannot simply be subsumed by that field and, at the same time, it is itself constituted by a play of internal connection and difference. *The Natures of Africa* implicitly embraces such an understanding in that, viewed collectively, the chapters explore often very different cultural traditions, socio-ecological conditions and authorial perspectives; they are written by scholars working in very different contexts inside and outside of Africa; and they use frameworks based on a wide range of influences, from inside and outside of Africa, from different disciplines, from different theoretical traditions and with different scalar emphases. Yet the contributors also focus on making connections across the continent and point to the possible ways that their conclusions might inform an 'African ecocriticism'.

References

Adams, William. 'Nature and the colonial mind', in William Adams and Martin Mulligan (eds), *Decolonizing Nature: Strategies for Conservation in a Post-Colonial Era*. London: Earthscan, 2003.

Brockington, Dan. *Fortress Conservation: The Preservation of the Mkomazi Game Reserve, Tanzania*. Oxford: James Currey, 2002.

Caminero-Santangelo, Byron. *Different Shades of Green: African Literature, Environmental Justice, and Political Ecology*. Charlottesville: University of Virginia Press, 2014.

DeLoughrey, Elizabeth and Handley, George (eds). *Postcolonial Ecologies: Literatures of the Environment*. Oxford: Oxford University Press, 2011.

Fairhead, James and Leach, Melissa. *Misreading the African Landscape: Society and Ecology in a Forest-Savannah Mosaic*. Cambridge: Cambridge University Press, 1996.
Gregory, Derek. *The Colonial Present*. Oxford: Blackwell, 2004.
Leach, Melissa, and Mearns, Robin (eds). *The Lie of the Land: Challenging Received Wisdom on the African Environment*. Portsmouth, NH: Heinemann, 1996.
Maathai, Wangari. *Unbowed: A Memoir*. New York: Anchor, 2006.
Maathai, Wangari. *The Challenge for Africa*. New York: Pantheon, 2009.
Neumann, Roderick. *Making Political Ecology*. New York: Hodder Arnold, 2005.
Nixon, Rob. *Slow Violence and the Environmentalism of the Poor*. Cambridge, MA: Harvard University Press, 2011.
O'Brien, Susie. '"Back to the World": Reading ecocriticism in a postcolonial context', in Tiffin, Helen (ed.), *Five Emus to the King of Siam*. Amsterdam: Rodopi, 2007.
Vital, Anthony. 'Toward an African ecocriticism: Postcolonialism, ecology and *Life and Times of Michael K.*' *Research in African Literatures* 39, 1 (2008): 87–106.

INTRODUCTION

F. Fiona Moolla

This book emerged out of a conviction that environment and animals are vital to an all-encompassing flourishing – where the word 'vital' suggests more than just 'important' but, retrieving its deeper etymological root, where environment and animals are 'vita'– they are life itself. This book emerged out of a conviction, and not much else: there has been no funding or major conferences behind it. These facts about the coming into existence of the volume have had paradoxical consequences. On the one hand, the individual members of the community that has been established through the volume, for the most part, have never physically met except through the conversations conducted in cyberspace beneath the tree of knowledge of our project site. The conviction that has inspired the volume has therefore not imposed a massive carbon cost on the environment it is moved to respect but, instead, has relied on 'clean' technologies. One might say that it has translated theory into praxis. However, the 'clean' technology that has allowed the digital cultural communion of the contributors could not have emerged without just over three centuries of dirty industrialisation, and its concomitant global social, cultural and economic cost to people, animals and environment.

This book has been motivated by the instinct that recognition of the life of animals and the significance of the natural world are not foreign to continental Africa, but are deeply constitutive of the cultures that together create a strategically essentialised Africa in the postcolonial period. This intuition could not be verified because the scholarship, with the regional exception of South Africa and its strong focus on literary culture, for the most part does not exist. Mention must be made here, however, of the publication of the papers presented at a conference titled 'Literature, Nature and the Land: Ethics and Aesthetics of the Environment', which was convened at the University of Zululand, South Africa, in 1992. The conference proceedings include papers on several African writers, including Ayi Kwei Armah, Kofi Awoonor, Wole Soyinka, Es'kia Mphahlele and Mazisi Kunene, among others.

Cheryll Glotfelty, in the introduction to *The Ecocriticism Reader* (Glotfelty and Fromm 1996), identifies 1993 as the year in which ecocriticism emerged as a clearly defined critical school in the Anglo-American academy. The Zululand ecocritical conference of the Association of English Teachers of South Africa (mentioned above), which indexes significant interest and scholarship in the area of culture and environmental studies, therefore pre-dates the crystallisation of Anglo-American ecocriticism. Furthermore, Chengyi Coral Wu's chapter in this volume makes a strong case for the existence of an African environmental criticism in the 1980s, which emerged around a number of key essays. In the past few years, a body of Nigerian ecocriticism has emerged, catalysed largely around eco-activism in the Niger Delta, again with a predominantly literary focus. But, for the most part, African ecocriticism has, to this point, largely existed as a subset of postcolonial ecocriticism, which, itself, has only fairly recently come into existence as an area of research. This is surprising given the fact that the environment, certainly to a greater extent than animals, has been on the radar for a number of years now. In 2010 the 36th annual conference of the African Literature Association had an ecocritical focus. The conference was titled 'Eco-Imagination: African and Diasporan Literatures and Sustainability', which is also the title of the conference proceedings published in 2014, and edited by Irène d'Almeida, Lucie Viakinnou-Brinson and Thelma Pinto. Similarly, environment was a significant focus of a number of panels at the 2014 African Literature Association conference, which celebrated the 40th anniversary of the association. In 2015 the conference of the Association of English Teachers of South Africa returned to its 1992 ecocritical land focus with the theme 'Environment, Race and Land Use', this time within the borders of South African cultural expression. To date, however, for the most part, questions of African environment and animals have been considered in monographs and edited volumes in a general postcolonial context, together with criticism of other world literatures, the most significant of which are surveyed below.

Probably the best-known eco- and zoocritical book is Graham Huggan and Helen Tiffin's *Postcolonial Ecocriticism: Literature, Animals, Environment* (2010), which draws on a number of works by African writers treated broadly thematically, rather than individually. The intersection of the art and activism of Ogoniland's Ken Saro-Wiwa, who was executed in 1995 at the behest of dictator Sani Abacha, is generally considered in the context of postcolonial resistance to predatory oil exploitation. The fiction of Nadine Gordimer and J. M. Coetzee is analysed in a section that unpacks the politics of the pastoral, and Coetzee features again, together with Zakes Mda, in the zoocritical section of that book.

Published in the same year as the book by Huggan and Tiffin is Laura Wright's *'Wilderness into civilized shapes': Reading the Postcolonial Environment* (2010), which considers Ngũgĩ wa Thiong'o's *Petals of Blood* and Mda's *Heart of Redness* for cultural representations of relations with the natural world, which simultaneously invent precolonial tradition. There is also a chapter on animal–human relations in the novel *Disgrace*, by J. M. Coetzee, a writer who, unlike many African writers and those of the African diaspora, often seems to transcend national and continental location and definition. Wright also considers less canonical writers, like Flora Nwapa and Sindiwe Magona in particular, with a focus on women's connections with the land from which they have been displaced.

A third book published in 2010, which considers environment and animals from the perspective of the global South, is Bonnie Roos and Alex Hunt's *Postcolonial Green: Environmental Politics and World Narratives* (2010). This edited volume foregrounds Africa in chapters by Sheng-Yen Yu, Jonathan Bishop Highfield (who has also written a chapter in the present volume) and Neel Ahuja, which consider apocalypticism in Coetzee's *Waiting for the Barbarians*, foodways, as presented in Bessie Head's novels, and international primate-conservation discourses, respectively.

Postcolonial Ecologies: Literatures of the Environment, edited by Elizabeth De Loughrey and George B. Handley (2011), features a chapter by Allison Carruth dedicated entirely to animals in Coetzee's recent novels, a full chapter by Byron Caminero-Santangelo on Mda's *The Heart of Redness* and part of a chapter on marine-mammal communication by Jonathan Steinwand, which looks at Mda's *The Whale Caller*, among other international writers. Rob Nixon's chapter, 'Stranger in the eco-village', foregrounds African ecotourism, but will be considered in more detail in the context of Nixon's own book, to be surveyed next.

In *Slow Violence and the Environmentalism of the Poor*, Nixon (2011) examines a range of African fiction and non-fiction in the broader context of world literatures. Nixon briefly alludes to Tsitsi Dangarembga's *Nervous Conditions* (1988), which dramatises in ecological terms the transition to a divided modernity of its protagonist, Tambu. Nixon contrasts the symbolism of the aesthetic pleasures of the garden at the mission with the mealie fields of the homestead. The heroine of Dangarembga's *Bildungsroman*, he concludes, 'will belong forever to two earths: this second soil of luxurious self-expression but always just beneath it her childhood soil, fraught with survival's urgent chores' (Nixon 2011: 28). But that division is even more complex than Nixon suggests. If the non-modern Zimbabwean land is identified with back-breaking (female) labour, it is also identified in the novel with the individual and social pleasures of childhood trips to the Nyamarira River, Tambu's 'flowing, tumbling, musical playground' (Dangarembga 1988: 59), whose privacy is intruded upon by roads built for trucks, markers of global capitalist penetration of the Zimbabwean land.

In the present volume, the chapter by Syned Mthatiwa on the work of Chenjerai Hove and Musaemura Zimunya reflects some of the insights and tensions of Dangarembga's novel of development – in this case, through the genre of Zimbabwean written verse. In the work of both these poets, Mthatiwa identifies a pastoral, precolonial element, represented by the Nyamarira in Dangarembga's novel, and the rigours of survival in a cosmological context where the environment is a significant and challenging actor in the drama of human existence.

There are two chapters in *Slow Violence* that consider the social and ecological consequences of the global dependence on fossil fuels.

In one of these, the effects on continental African are highlighted. Nixon exposes, through the life work of Ken Saro-Wiwa, the brutal consequences of politics and aesthetics, which transcend literary debate and, through the autobiography of Wangari Maathai, reveals the complexities of the intersection of gender and ecocritical activism. In 'Stranger in the eco-village', referred to above, Nixon also explores the African tourism industry through a literary journalistic essay by Njabulo Ndebele, and wildlife conservation in a short story by Nadine Gordimer. In the current volume, Reinier J. M. Vriend takes questions of nature and tourism further by exploring the role of nature and African charismatic megafauna in the photographic images employed in internet advertising of the highly paradoxical enterprise of African voluntourism.

The most recent addition to the growing number of books on postcolonial ecocriticism is Roman Bartosch's (2013) strongly theoretical point of entry into the field, *Environmentality: Ecocriticism and the Event of Postcolonial Fiction*. This monograph focuses on works like Amitav Ghosh's *The Hungry Tide* and, in an African context, the novels of J. M. Coetzee and Mda, which have become fairly canonical in the context of ecocriticism from formerly colonised parts of the world. Bartosch's angle on these novels highlights the ways in which nature and animals in the cultural production of the global South unsettle, through their rifts and tensions, the universality of Western social constructions of nature and environmental responses. Bartosch highlights the potential of literature, in this book represented only by the novel, to 'address problems and aporias of environmental ethics in a globalised world' (Bartosch 2013: 14).

To date, there have been six special issues of journals that consider cultural representations of environment and animals, predominantly in a South African context. The first of these is a 2006 issue of *Current Writing: Text and Reception in Southern Africa*, with the title 'Animal presences, animal geographies'. This special issue adopts an interdisciplinary approach to the area, with analyses of non-fiction, novels, poetry, maps and documentary film. In 2007 Alter*nation: Interdisciplinary Journal for the Study of the Arts and Humanities in Southern Africa* published a special issue that looked at wilderness and forests, mainly in a South African context but with excursions into Malawian poetry by Syned Mthatiwa (whose essay on the environmentalism of two Zimbabwean poets is anthologised in the present volume) and the Nigerian novel, represented in a comparative piece on Chinua Achebe and Ben Okri. More recently, a 2013 issue of Alter*nation* focused on 'Coastlines and littoral zones in South African ecocritical writing'. This issue features analyses of a wide range of southern African fictional and non-fictional oceanic texts, with one exception, which explores the Niger Delta poetry of Tanure Ojaide.

A 2010 issue of *Safundi: The Journal of South African and American Studies* is devoted entirely to animal studies and ecocriticism, with articles that cross the boundaries of disciplines, media, genre and modes, including a concluding essay by Jennifer Wenzel, which critically reflects on the voices brought into conversation in the issue.

A 2014 issue of *Scrutiny 2: Issues in English Studies in Southern Africa* features a themed section with articles on poetry and novels, again in a South African context. South Africa is also the focus of a 2014 special issue of the *Journal of Literary Studies* edited by Wendy Woodward and Erika Lemmer, titled 'Figuring the Animal in Post-apartheid South Africa'. This draws on the papers presented at the third human-animal studies colloquium held at the Centre for Humanities Research at the University of the Western Cape in 2013. (The focus of the third colloquium reflects the South African focus of the first colloquium held in 2011, while the topic of the second colloquium in 2012 was 'Animal vulnerabilities'.)

A number of seminal essays on African ecocriticism deserve mention here, some of which will be explored and evaluated further in the chapter in this book by Chengyi Coral Wu. These are William Slaymaker's 'Ecoing the other(s)' and Byron Caminero-Santangelo's 'Different shades of green' in *African Literature: An Anthology of Criticism and Theory*, edited by Tejumola Olaniyan and Ato Quayson (2007). Slaymaker and Caminero-Santangelo present controversially contrary views on the rootedness of a literary environmental ethos and/or its burgeoning in Africa. In 'Shifting the center', an earlier essay in *Environmental Criticism for the Twenty-first Century*, edited by Stephanie LeMenager, Teresa Shewry and Ken Hiltner (2011),

Caminero-Santangelo makes a case for the origins of an African literary environmental consciousness that significantly pre-dates the 2005 award of the Nobel Peace Prize to Wangari Maathai, co-founder of the Green Belt Movement. Here Caminero-Santangelo considers East African ecocritical precursors to Maathai in Okot p'Bitek's *Song of Lawino* (1966) and *Song of Ocol* (1967), and Ngũgĩ wa Thiong'o's *A Grain of Wheat* (1967).

Dan Wylie's 2011 essay, 'Literature and ecology in southern Africa', anthologised in *SA Lit: Beyond 2000*, is part of a volume that highlights the transition from the 'post-apartheid' to a literature that is significantly transnational. For Wylie, the transnational moment seems to be one especially productive of what he terms 'infiltration' – an approach to interpretation attuned to the multiple exchanges between 'places, levels and cultures', which simultaneously 'captur[es] ... both material and symbolic interconnectivities' (Wylie 2011: 354). This is a mode of reading that Wylie hopes might finally allow criticism to jettison the 'lingering binarisms of imperialism and apartheid' (Wylie 2011: 368). This hope, paradoxically, is belied by most of the essays in the present volume, where a prevailing environmental concern seems precisely to require a retrieval, in the broader African context, of the impact of colonial ecological mutations of lifeways, which, in the current historical moment, are drawn into globally complex, but perhaps fundamentally unequal, flows and networks.

To date, there have been only two edited volumes dedicated solely to African ecocriticism and one to South African debates on environmentalism. The sophisticated, epistemologically self-reflexive approach of *Environment at the Margins: Literary and Environmental Studies in Africa*, edited by Caminero-Santangelo and Garth Myers (2011), is succinctly captured in James Graham's review in a 2013 issue of *Postcolonial Text*.

> [The] contention made by *Environment at the Margins* is that [it] is not merely within iconic literary works or a given historical moment or movement that 'an African ecocriticism' (6) is to be discovered. Instead, the assembled essays range from critiques of colonial accounts of African peoples, landscapes and

animals ... to the writing of post-colonial anthropology and ecology *as* fiction ... The rationale here is to bring 'literary and environmental studies of Africa into robust interdisciplinary dialogue' (15), so that an 'African ecocriticism' might emerge performatively through such an encounter, rather than be prescribed as an addendum to a generic, first world-issued 'postcolonial ecocriticism' (10). (Graham 2013: 1)

The most recent anthology, *Eco-critical Literature: Regreening African Landscapes*, edited by Ogaga Okuyade (2013), who has written a chapter in the present volume, is a collection of criticism of African novels, non-fiction prose, poetry and film, some of which are relatively new to a continental African and international audience. The figure of the destructive human that emerges in Anglo-American environmentalism is interrogated in *Toxic Belonging? Identity and Ecology in Southern Africa*, edited by Dan Wylie (2008). The essays in that volume place South African literature and narrative non-fiction under an interdisciplinary lens. Interestingly, in the chapters that consider indigenous environmentalism in the present volume, the figure of the parasitic human does not appear to emerge.

There are only two monographs on environment and animals that focus on African literature. Caminero-Santangelo's (2014) book by the same name as the essay in Olaniyan and Quayson's anthology has recently been published. *Different Shades of Green: African Literature, Environmental Justice, and Political Ecology* again underscores the idea that emerges in postcolonial ecocriticism more generally that environment cannot be defended without engaging colonialism, capitalism and imperialism.

The only zoocritical book in an African context to date is Wendy Woodward's *The Animal Gaze: Animal Subjectivities in Southern African Narratives* (2008), which provides a panoramic view of the representation of animals across a wide range of southern African prose, both fiction and non-fiction, through a consideration of African indigenous knowledges and current theoretical debates in human-animal studies. Woodward widens her own geographical gaze in the present volume to analyse the use of animal narrators in two francophone novels set in central and West Africa.

Although ecocritical scholarship appears to be a research area that is just opening up, the natural world and animals have been active agents in African cultural forms for as long as these forms have existed. This is because environment and animals fundamentally constitute the worldviews and lifeways that have created these cultural 'texts'. African cosmologies, their *paideia*, or social education, their art and their entertainment could not exist without nature and animals. And these stories inform the print literatures that developed in the 20th century. Consider, as one example, the Yoruba creation myth that has Obatala descending from the heavens on a gold chain with a white hen, a black cat, some sand in a snail shell and a palm nut. Or consider the anti-consumerist ethical instruction behind the cautionary Ibo tale of the greed of the tortoise who tricked the birds out of a feast in the sky, which, when incorporated into the late Chinua Achebe's *Things Fall Apart*, creates a different, perhaps anti-consumerist, allegorical dynamic in a literary and capitalist-colonial context.

Similarly, the proverbs that constitute the philosophy of Africa cannot be conceived without the natural world and animals. It is no surprise, then, that nature and animals are not a deliberate and critically studied dimension of African cultural forms, as the themes of anti- and postcolonial resistance, individual alienation or the representation of women have been. Nature and animals are so fundamentally constitutive of African culture that they form an invisible backdrop that has required the frequent and prolonged droughts of the 20th century in the Sahara, the environmental ravages caused by oil and gas extraction in the Niger Delta, the threatened destruction of the rain forests of West Africa as a consequence of the extinction of forest mammals, and so on, as the focusing lens through which nature and animals are now seen. The lifeways of African cultures, through the active presence of nature and animals in their mythical understandings of the world, have maintained a healthy environmental democracy that has been broadly sustained over centuries. Thus, African cultures, and non-modern cultures more generally, articulate, using a different repertoire, the conviction voiced by Bruno Latour in *Politics of Nature* (2004) that contemporary post-Cartesian globalised societies must recognise that nature is not science but a social construct, and that a new collective needs to be composed that 'redistribut[es] speech between humans and nonhumans' (Latour 2004: 232).

Interestingly, the African trans-species and trans-animate collectivities discussed in a number of chapters in this volume do not, however, appear to heed Latour's injunction of radical indeterminacy. The distribution of speech among human and non-human African actors does not feel it needs to learn to *'be skeptical of all spokespersons'* (Latour 2004: 232, emphasis in the original). The current ecocritical agenda and, potentially but not necessarily, environmental response are being set by a global culture with which Africa has had a fraught relationship, and one that has fundamentally transformed African land, landscape and social relations among human and non-human actors over the last hundred years or so, but often in the space of just a few decades.

The catch-22 of African environmentalism, and how it is refracted in criticism of African cultural forms, is that, although the global environmental crisis is not a product of African lifeways, African lifeways have to acknowledge the crisis in their unavoidable engagement (or perhaps entry) into global culture. This idea is articulated by postcolonial historian Dipesh Chakrabarty, who uses a conceptual vocabulary that is startlingly simple but startlingly powerful. In 'The climate of history', an essay that appeared in *Critical Inquiry* in 2009, Chakrabarty proposes four theses. The first thesis is that the anthropocene era collapses the distinction between a subjective human history and an objective natural history. Chakrabarty identifies the beginning of the anthropocene era, or the age in which human activity has a global impact, with the Industrial Revolution of the last quarter of the 18th century, rather than with the 'invention' of agriculture, as is sometimes proposed by climate theorists. He adds that the impact of human activity speeds up in the second half of the 20th century. Chakrabarty suggests that the assumption held in common by historians up until the mid 20th century was that nature transformed, but so slowly that it was essentially just a 'timeless' backdrop for human activity, and therefore nature was not a subject for historiography at all. (In Chakrabarty's remarks we see a different version of nature as background from the one discussed in the context of African ecocriticism above.) Although nature has not been consciously foregrounded in African cultural forms because it is such an obvious actor that it is not even to be remarked upon, nature in the discourses of modernity faded into a utilitarian background as a consequence of social disembedding and the subject-object divide consequent to Cartesianism. European, and later American, romanticism challenged to a certain extent this disconnection, but in a framework established by the Enlightenment, against which it recoils. In recent decades, this conception changes where nature is re-identified and reconceptualised. In this new context, human beings, increasingly in scientific discourse, are revealed to be a geophysical force, in tandem with a renewed foregrounding of the environment. Jacob Mapara addresses precisely the rising prominence of environment from about the mid 20th century in the Anglo-American world in a chapter in this book, which uses Shona indigenous religion as a counterpoint.

Chakrabarty's second thesis is that the anthropocene necessitates a qualification of 'Humanist Histories of Modernity/Globalization' (Chakrabarty 2009: 207), since it compels a re-evaluation of the idea of a non-contextualised, universal freedom as an absolute virtue because 'the mansion of modern freedoms stands on an ever-expanding base of fossil-fuel use' (Chakrabarty 2009: 208). Chakrabarty goes on to ask the rhetorical questions, 'Is the Anthropocene a critique of the narratives of freedom? Is the geological agency of humans the price we pay for the pursuit of freedom?' (Chakrabarty 2009: 210).

The third thesis proposes that a postcolonial capitalist critique needs to engage the 'Species History' of humans, which is forced into existence by the anthropocene. The fourth thesis suggests that the articulation of individual and species histories created by modernity tests the limits of historical understanding.

In his essay 'Postcolonial studies and the challenge of climate change', Chakrabarty (2012) proposes a third figure of the human that must be acknowledged in contemporary environmental debates, which joins the figures of the human as individual disembedded subject and the human in terms of its species history. This third figure is the universalist rights-bearing subject, assumed by postcolonial-postmodern views but, in this case, endowed with what Chakrabarty terms the 'anthropological' differences of class, gender, and so on. The corollary of Chakrabarty's analysis fatalistically complicates the idea of a simple acknowledgment proposed by Latour of nature and animals in the collective democracy of humans, referred to above, since Chakrabarty ventures that man as a geophysical force lacks an ontological agency – and, hence, how can one call to the collective a non-ontological agency?

In some ways, Julia Martin's (1993) paper with the intriguing title 'New, with added ecology? Hippos, forests and environmental literacy', delivered at the 1992 Zululand conference referred to in the literature survey above, makes the same points that Chakrabarty has made more recently. Martin's analysis, sharpened as it was by apartheid iniquities, presents Chakrabarty's articulation of different scales of human history in rather more human terms, identifying the ways in which nature is more than just an 'eternal backdrop to human activity' (Martin 1993: 79). She suggests that her own eco-activism is

> motivated by the sense human beings may have reached an unprecedented moment in history, when ozone and rain forests are possibly crucial to the survival of our species. But living in South Africa makes it impossible to ignore the links between environmental crisis and the poverty and disempowerment of the majority. Future governments will be faced with the seemingly impossible task of addressing both the people's ultimately unsatisfiable desire for First World models of modernity, and the impact of development on an already degraded environment. (Martin 1993: 79)

In Martin's analysis here, one may identify Chakrabarty's human history in its Enlightenment-universalist, and anthropological and species forms.

Chakrabarty's (2012) essay on postcolonialism and climate change concludes with the observation that, 'Today, it is precisely the "survival of the species" on a "world-wide scale" that is largely in question. All progressive political thought, including postcolonial criticism, will have to register this profound change in the human condition' (Chakrabarty 2012: 15). Quite startlingly, Chakrabarty proposes on a global scale what James Maina Wachira's research into the animal praise poetry of the Samburu, presented in a chapter in this book, suggests on a very local scale, namely that the Samburu express in their praise songs to animals the desire to survive as a community. Global survival of the species seems paradoxically to collapse here into pretty much the same dynamic as the local survival of a community whose cultural expressions may all too easily be dismissed as idealised indigeneity.

It is precisely the need to widen the debate on environment and animals highlighted above that encouraged the formation of the African natures-cultures project, which reaches fulfilment in this volume. The project follows up on an intuition of an essential transdisciplinarity of approach, which may lead to a crossing of what Boaventura de Sousa Santos has referred to in 'Beyond abyssal thinking: From global lines to ecologies of knowledges' as the 'epistemological abyss' (De Sousa Santos 2007: 51) that separates contemporary global epistemologies from indigenous and non-modern epistemologies. The project was driven by a sense that the geographic scope of scholarship in an African context must be wider than its nodal points in South African and Niger Delta literatures, and that the genres engaged must be more representative. In the essay 'Shifting the center', referred to above, Caminero-Santangelo calls for the need to bring the tensions in African nature writing into debate by 'putting texts and authors in dialogue' (Caminero-Santangelo 2011: 161). It is fascinating that two of the texts he considers are Okot p'Bitek's *Song of Lawino* and *Song of Ocol*, which straddle the complicated divide between oral and print cultures, and share in the conceptual constructions of both. (One recalls here the production history of p'Bitek's text, where his oral-songstress mother asked him to sing his verse as if, in fact, it were a song.) Whereas Caminero-Santangelo argues for the need to bring literatures in English into dialogue, this volume attempts to bring genres into debate. For this reason, the ambit of this volume has been pushed beyond print literature circulated internationally, which has tended to produce only one, perhaps the globally dominant, social creation of nature.

Some of the areas that provided a productive point of departure for the project have included the following questions: are Africans 'in nature'? Is there a nature, or an African nature or African natures? Are there evolutionary roots for biophilia? Are we genetically programmed for the pastoral? Is there an African pastoral mythology? Is there a pastoral (or anti-pastoral) of the African tropics and of the desert? Are there aquatic pastorals/anti-pastorals that encompass the Indian and Atlantic oceans, the Great Lakes and great rivers? Is there wilderness in Africa? Is Africa the wilderness? Is there wilderness?

Environmentalism seems almost inevitably to mesh with spirituality and religion. In an African context, which may or may not reflect a global paradigm, one might ask whether the trajectory is one from the worship of gods, to God, to man and now to nature. Do African animisms reflect an inherent agency in nature that tends to prevent environmental collapse? By contrast, does the anthropocentrism of African animism, which many scholars compare unfavourably with nature-friendly indigenous American spiritualities, lead to an oppositional stance to environment? Does the stewardship model framed by African monotheisms represent the seeds of destruction? Does the idea of mother earth in many African ethnically based religions, which morphs into the idea of Mother Africa, especially in Négritude poetry, translate into African ecofeminism? Given the large-scale colonial land expropriation that took place throughout Africa, should land be given back to the people or back to the land? Does the experience of African urbanisation collapse the country–city dichotomy that emerges in the North Atlantic context? 'Techno-ecotopia': is there an African science and technology, and are they the answer? Where are the African cyborgs? How much should Africa consume? Do African community or ethnic cultures represent bioregionalism? Where these communities have been displaced, should a process of reinhabitation follow? How do host environments cope with the mass displacements witnessed as a consequence of climate change and conflict? How successful have African environmental movements, like Green Belt and Niger Delta activism, been?

These are some of the questions that could have also been addressed in the volume, and the essays that follow introduce a number of other fascinating ideas. It is quite revealing that a very strong voice in this volume belongs to research into oral cultural forms. This provides a welcome balance to the dominance of the analysis of print cultural forms in most of the previous scholarship on the topic. Two of the chapters in this volume represent pioneering research into new areas, namely Mickias Musiyiwa's essay on Zimbabwean popular songs and James Wachira's essay on Samburu animal praise poetry. To date, the only work done on environment and animals in African oratures has been broad, vague and generalised surveys that either suggest, positively, that indigenous African cultures are generally nature-centric, or that support the general view from outside Africa that African animisms have a combative attitude to nature.

Of the essays on literature in the volume, analyses of novels predominate, as opposed to poetry and non-fiction narrative; the genres of short stories and drama are not represented at all. Another highly original study is that of Dutch scholar Reinier J. M. Vriend, who analyses the use of website photographic images of African landscape and animals in the context of the phenomenon of 'voluntourism', which, itself, is a growing area of study.

The essays in this volume reveal interesting overlaps and dissonances when various expressive media are brought into conversation – for example, oral traditions, and print and digital cultures. But, as is generally the case, too sharp a focus on the various media and genres within media results in a blurring of the lines, suggesting a network of Wittgensteinian 'family relationships', rather than crisp definitions. For example, the oral-culture songs studied by Musiyiwa often rely on technology – in this case, the radio – for dissemination, so they could just as easily have been considered as an example of a techno-culture, especially as radio programmes frequently also exist as internet podcasts. Similarly, the *Sunjata* oral epic, studied by Jonathan Bishop Highfield, morphs quite unproblematically into film, so this research also straddles boundaries. The animal narrators in the two novels considered by Woodward are beings influenced by oral cultures. Therefore, this analysis could be considered from the points of view of both orature and literature. Within the boundaries of the various media, individual forms studied here, for example Dicey's *Borderline*, the travel narrative analysed by Mathilda Slabbert, cross generic borders, displaying features of both fiction and non-fiction.

Chapter outline

Canadian philosopher Charles Taylor, in *Sources of the Self* (1989), suggests that in non-modern understandings of the world the boundary between the human subject and nature is porous. In Chapter 1, '"Here is some baobab leaf!": *Sunjata*, foodways and biopiracy', the idea of the porous border is contemplated literally by Jonathan Bishop Highfield. The author considers that most intimate of communion with nature, which occurs when we ingest it. Highfield's study brings foodways studies into dialogue with ecocriticism in the context of the best-known African oral epic, *Sunjata*. This chapter foregrounds the baobab, that highly iconic African tree, whose profound symbolic and material value has gone entirely unnoticed in earlier studies of the West African epic. Highfield 'reads' the oral epic both for traces of the knowledge of the more than 2 000 indigenous food sources that were replaced by imported crops and for a 21st century repossession of local foodways.

Highfield highlights the way that, throughout the epic, the baobab operates at real and symbolic registers. This tree may store up to 10 000 litres of fresh water, its fruit is edible and its highly nutritious leaves may be dried and stored for months. The tree itself in the epic is also a symbol of power and the index of identity and home that summons the epic hero back from exile. Baobab leaves capture the talismanic power that allows the crippled prince, Sunjata, to rise from his ignominy, and the fruit is linked to Mande leadership. But, far from relegating the epic and the lifeways it symbolically captures to an archaic past, Highfield traces the ways in which the philosophical, cultural and social apprehensions of the epic have transitioned into the contemporary genre of film, among other media.

The focus in Chapter 2 is also on orature, but this time the study concerns contemporary popular Zimbabwean songs that bear a complicated relationship with the Shona mythologies on which they draw. Mickias Musiyiwa signals this complexity through the ambivalence of the title of his essay, 'Shona as a land-based nature-culture: A study of the (re)construction of Shona land mythology in popular songs'.

For Musiyiwa, contemporary popular Zimbabwean songs both capture and transform Shona land mythology in what could be considered a kind of reinvention of tradition, to use the concept given currency by Eric Hobsbawm and Terence Ranger. Musiyiwa highlights the contradiction that although the land expropriations of the Mugabe government had massive international coverage, very little is widely known about the ways in which Shona culture shapes both land apprehension and imagination. An understanding of this might help to explain why land invasions took place despite significant local criticism of the policy. Contemporary songs incorporate other genres of expression, like folk tales and legends, and centrally articulate the idea of Shona absolute dependence upon land. Through its association with the ancestors, land becomes embodied and inspirited, and Shona agricultural interactions with the land become ritualised. Musiyiwa refers to this as a form of 'ritually directed ecology' or 'religiously controlled ecological management'. Musiyiwa stresses, as M. A. Mohamed Salih has highlighted in *Environmental Politics and Liberation in Contemporary Africa* (1999), nearly two decades ago, that in a postcolonial context, environment is always a political concern. In Zimbabwe, the land mythology allowed disparate nationalist, guerrilla and peasant groups 'to harmonise their grievances and loyally articulate them'.

In Chapter 3, 'The environment as significant other: The green nature of Shona indigenous religion', Jacob Mapara also underscores the idea of a religious encompassing of questions of environment in a Zimbabwean context. This essay traces a history of the concept of 'green religion' in the North Atlantic, understanding the term to suggest human respect for nature expressed through the tenets of religious faith. This understanding is different, however, from the trend that has seen nature replacing God as an ontic source. The latter idea is variously challenged in an Anglo-American context by situating nature within a network, bush or mesh in the work of Donna Haraway (1991), among others, or linking nature to the idea of the inherent open orientation of art, as Mick Smith does in *Against Ecological Sovereignty* (2011).

For Mapara, the concept of reverence for nature may be new, but the approaches described in Shona cultural apprehensions are old. For this author, the bonds with nature are more deeply constitutive among African indigenous religions than they are in the monotheistic traditions. Shona religious understanding is captured in the cultural forms of proverbs, folk tales and songs. Through an analysis of some of these, Mapara traces the outline of a land ethic that has existed 'invisibly' since time immemorial, but which, given transformations in conceptualisation of land as a result of the colonial and capitalist integration of Rhodesia, and later Zimbabwe, into the global economy, now needs to be articulated. Mapara's comprehension of the links between human, animal and natural existence runs so deep that the Shona orientation towards encouraging life is extended from nature, unusually in an ecocritical context, to human life. Shona worldviews that shape human relations, such as the encouragement of marriage and the censure of abortion, are read as a fundamental part of a life ethic that encompasses all of nature. So, unusually in an environmental context, humans do not emerge as destructive of and parasitic upon nature, but instead are seen as an essential part of an ethic that values all life. Mapara reconceptualises a global ecocritical framework from an African perspective, fundamentally transforming the 'eco' of the others.

James Maina Wachira's research into the animal praise songs of the Samburu of Wamba County, Kenya, in Chapter 4, 'Animal oral praise poetry and the Samburu desire to survive', is another fascinating study of African oral forms – this time of a contemporary, coeval community whose customary, sustainable, environmentally respectful lifeways coexist with the wilderness sanctuaries of the modern Kenyan national state. Wachira's study is new and necessary. To date, apart from general overviews of African indigenous cultures alluded to above, there has been no scholarship that specifically considers this relationship with the natural world and animals in African oratures.

Wachira has collected and transcribed the animal praise poetry of the Samburu. Whereas praise poetry conventionally pays tribute to exceptional human beings, Samburu animal praise poetry combines respect for and awe of significant animal actors in the environment that allow the Samburu to survive. Wachira's findings are full of surprises. The animals that inhabit the land of Wamba County are not the companion species we have become familiar with in North Atlantic human-animal studies, but are instead seen as the allies of human beings in protecting and conserving a rugged environment, which both humans and animals regard as home. Wachira's research also underlines the idea that the relationship between humans and the natural world is not one where the line collapses entirely into the nature-cultures of contemporary posthumanism. His research suggests the idea mentioned above of a porous border between nature (including animals) and human culture.

The findings of Wachira's study remind us that Africans are not in nature, as ecotourist tableaux frequently present them to be. Without exception, the mythologies of African cultures suggest a 'golden age' where the intimate proximity of the natural world and animals and gods made human life easy. As a result of human misdemeanour, this closeness to other forms of existence is lost, setting up a boundary between humans and animals, and humans and gods, which at key charged moments may be breached. The Samburu also recollect through ancestral memory a time when humans and animals lived together, until animals abandoned human society in despair of and disappointment at human conduct. This connection is revived by singing the animal praises.

Chapter 5, by Reinier J. M. Vriend, 'The paradoxes of voluntourism: Strategic visual tropes of the natural on South African voluntourism websites' analyses the use of photographic images of nature and animals that appear on South African voluntourism websites. Paradox is the dominant mode uncovered by Vriend in voluntourism web-based advertising. Voluntourism is a subset of tourism, in which doing good is commodified. Voluntourists, predominantly from the global North, attempt to alleviate the poverty of the global South, channelled through the structures established by an international tourism industry, which, since the 1970s, has increasingly relied on a globalised understanding of nature outside of cultural specificities. Thus, although voluntourism activities are largely urban, natural rural landscapes and wildlife are used to promote the industry. Marketing voluntourism means poverty, social inequalities and social ills are unique selling points, which must be both visible and invisible. For voluntourism to grow and be more profitable, the poverty on which it feeds must grow. Foregrounding urban poverty, however, contradicts the South African tourism 'brand'. Agencies therefore use images of a globalised nature to render invisible the irreconcilable contradictions upon which this industry is based. In this context, therefore, the images of the natural world are the anodyne of an age of historically unprecedented national and global inequalities, which become ethically justifiable.

Chengyi Coral Wu's essay, 'Towards an ecocriticism in Africa: Literary aesthetics in African environmental literature' (Chapter 6), establishes the framework for the subsequent essays on literature, which include analyses of novels, travel narrative and page poetry. Wu's chapter underscores the idea implicitly emphasised in earlier essays in this book that African ecocriticism cannot be established upon conceptions of nature that present themselves as universal. African ecocriticisms furthermore reveal that relationships with land are always social and political. Wu's survey of the literature suggests that the African novels that wrote themselves onto the international literary scene in the 1950s and 1960s disclose an environmental sensibility and presciently foreshadow future environmental degradation. Wu makes the case that not only does African environmental literature pre-date formalised Anglo-American ecocriticism, but also that African eco-aesthetics forces a recognition of alternative tropes and themes to the dominant Anglo-American literary constructions of nature.

In Chapter 7, 'Critical intersections: Ecocriticism, globalised cities and African narrative, with a focus on K. Sello Duiker's *Thirteen Cents*', Anthony Vital deconstructs in the era of global warming the division between the country and the city, which ecocriticism, especially in its romantic and pastoral modes, implicitly assumes. For Vital, ecocriticism is most significantly a discursive practice that recognises that the African city is in nature, and linked to both the country and to other cities through complex networks of exchange. This recognition should not, in the universality of its approach, lose the cultural specificities of particular African cities in relation to other African and international cities.

In *Thirteen Cents*, K. Sello Duiker's novel set in Cape Town, the African city at the tip of the continent, Vital does not find any solutions to the nature-culture problems set in motion by global modernity. He does find, though, a range of productive tensions that highlight the potential of the novel to teach through the ways in which it textualises society and nature. Vital argues that, given the distortions of neoliberal individualism, the protagonist of *Thirteen Cents* develops a distinctive 'misreading' of the city-in-nature. The child protagonist therefore retreats from his subjection to exploitation and abuse as a consequence of a network of relationships of power to Table Mountain, where he can experience an ancestral nature in the form of non-modern culture. The apocalyptic strain in the novel is transcendent in closure where the boy in his solitude imagines nature as his only ally, destroying the corrupt city with a giant wave from the ocean. The boy's figuring of his experience, Vital argues, can be read productively alongside natural and social-scientific work on Cape Town in its environment.

With Mathilda Slabbert's essay, 'Navigating Gariep country: Writing nature-culture in *Borderline* by William Dicey' (Chapter 8), we shift genre from fiction to narrative non-fiction. William Dicey's Orange River investigative travel narrative, *Borderline*, dramatises its title in a number of ways. The Orange River is a fluid border that separates national territories, but is also a water body that, symbolically, through its flow, connects Africa with the Atlantic Ocean and with water masses further afield. The narrative also represents a borderline genre, straddling travelogue, novel, autobiography and investigative journalism, melding socio-environmental and aesthetic concerns with advocacy. Unlike in many of the earlier essays, Slabbert interprets the idea of nature-culture not through myth, but through history. She suggests that *Borderline* connects 'socio-environmental concerns with transnational and imperial histories to stimulate an awareness of Africa's extensively interwoven history of nature and culture'.

In 'Negotiating identity in a vanishing geography: Home, environment and displacement in Helon Habila's *Oil on Water*', which forms Chapter 9, Ogaga Okuyade alerts readers to a hidden cost of oil exploitation in the Niger Delta, which emerges through a consideration of details of the plot and vivid imagery of Habila's third novel. The narrative of *Oil on Water* dramatises the unique displacement of the riverine communities of the Niger Delta. Their displacement as a consequence of oil extraction is from homes that are literally disappearing since they are being submerged. The well-developed literature of exile, in the context of exodus from places that also constitute the culture and identity of people, acquires here an additional resonance, given that, in the Niger Delta, the places called home actually vanish with the flight of the people.

Wendy Woodward, in Chapter 10, considers two francophone African novels in 'Human masks? Animal narrators in Patrice Nganang's *Dog Days: An Animal Chronicle* and Alain Mabanckou's *Memoirs of a Porcupine*'. Woodward picks up here on an African dimension of a recent international trend towards the use of animal narrators in novels. For Woodward, the animal protagonists in these novels are wholly urban, political and linguistic beings who, nevertheless, allow the 'real animal to take precedence'. Through the dynamics of animal narration, the boundaries between the human and the non-human, the modern and the traditional, and fantasy and reality are collapsed. In this respect, these novels are in advance of African literary theory where animal lives remain occluded. Whereas Anthony Vital argues that an African ecocriticism should highlight the distinctiveness of the insertion of African cultural worlds into global culture, the trend Woodward identifies in these novels is towards a non-essentialised Africa that is fully absorbed into global culture. These novels do not validate themselves through local custom, but instead 'subvert the high seriousness of African mythology'. Entering into an exchange across genres, these novels present a contrasting view to the perspective offered in the oratures studied in earlier chapters, where animal subjectivity and agency were acknowledged and deemed essential to human survival through the mythologies that these novels are presented as satirically criticising.

In Chapter 11, Sule Emmanuel Egya presents an overview of ecocritical trends in the verse of Christopher Okigbo, Wole Soyinka, Niyi Osundare, Tanure Ojaide and Onookome Okome in his essay 'Nature, animism and humanity in anglophone Nigerian poetry'. Egya's analysis of the work of these poets suggests an African inflection of the idea of bioregionalism or place through the concept of animism. The animist view of the inspirited natural world and animals creates a spiritual link between the poets and the land, captured in the pervasive tone of yearning in the poetry to be bound to nature through place. The personal longing for organic connection is simultaneously political, in that these poets, 'mindful of the fact that the flora and fauna have a life of their own, … deploy them to make political statements about the condition of their nation'. Egya also animistically refracts Edward Said's concept of 'filiation', or forms of association based on patriarchy and biological descent, to suggest an alternative animist filiation, in which the poets desire, through their art, to be the disciples of the gods of nature and the gods in nature.

Syned Mthatiwa's essay, 'Animals, nostalgia and Zimbabwe's rural landscape in the poetry of Chenjerai Hove and Musaemura Zimunya' (Chapter 12), is a complex interpretation of the work of two Zimbabwean writers, which simultaneously engages ideas in a number of other chapters in this book. Mthatiwa draws on Dan Wylie's conception of a 'culturescape' to express the relationship of these writers to landscape and animals, which is constituted through a Shona mythological comprehension of the world.

Mthatiwa's analysis is subtle in its observation that the work of these poets may not necessarily embody the ethos of the Shona peasantry, but that the poetry is one lens through which this world may be glimpsed. The environmental ethic of both these poets is inflected through a personal development that has followed a trajectory from the countryside to the city, and a conflicted induction into colonial modernity and education. Personal development, ironically, has entailed a loss of the childhood pastoral mode, while colonial and postcolonial modernity has involved a 'spoil[ing]' by exploiting the relationships among human beings, animals and the land. Mthatiwa impresses upon the reader the fact that although the poetry is realistic in its description of the conflicts and hardships of rural existence, the pastoral remains the dominant mode through which nature is constituted in this cultural form. Again, this chapter underscores the way in which an African ecocriticism is necessarily social, historical and political.

What makes this volume especially revealing – and challenging – is the variety of views on the relationship between human beings, animals and the natural world, all of which emerge out of continental Africa and all of which demand engagement. The volume is also distinctive because of the ways in which the authors have taken up one another's ideas in conversations that run through the chapters. No attempt has been made to force a consensus, nor have significant approaches been excluded to present a particular, politically interested ecocritical perspective of continental Africa. Authors, genres and cultures have been brought into an exchange on environmental futures, which have not occluded environmental pasts and which are unanimous in the call for respect for the environmental present ... to ensure a shared future.

References

Bartosch, Roman. *Environmentality: Ecocriticism and the Event of Postcolonial Fiction*. Amsterdam: Rodopi, 2013.

Caminero-Santangelo, Byron. 'Different shades of green: Ecocriticism and African literature', in Tejumola Olaniyan and Ato Quayson (eds), *African Literature: An Anthology of Criticism and Theory*. Malden, MA: Blackwell Publishing, 2007.

Caminero-Santangelo, Byron. 'Shifting the center: A tradition of environmental literary discourse from Africa', in Stephanie LeMenager, Teresa Shewry and Ken Hiltner (eds), *Environmental Criticism for the Twenty-First Century*. New York: Routledge, 2011.

Caminero-Santangelo, Byron. *Different Shades of Green: Literature, Environmental Justice, and Political Ecology*. Charlottesville: University of Virginia Press, 2014.

Caminero-Santangelo, Byron and Myers, Garth (eds). *Environment at the Margins: Literary and Environmental Studies in Africa*. Athens: Ohio University Press, 2011.

Chakrabarty, Dipesh. 'The climate of history: Four theses.' *Critical Inquiry* 35 (2009): 197–222.

Chakrabarty, Dipesh. 'Postcolonial studies and the challenge of climate change.' *New Literary History* 43, 1 (2012): 1–18.

D'Almeida, Irène Assiba, Viakinnou-Brinson, Lucie and Pinto, Thelma (eds). *Eco-Imagination: African and Diasporan Literatures and Sustainability*. Lawrenceville: Africa World Press, 2014.

Dangarembga, Tsitsi. *Nervous Conditions*. London: The Women's Press, 1988.

DeLoughrey, Elizabeth and Handley, George B. (eds). *Postcolonial Ecologies: Literatures of the Environment*. Oxford: Oxford University Press, 2011.

De Sousa Santos, Boaventura. 'Beyond abyssal thinking: From global lines to ecologies of knowledges.' *Review*, XXX, 1 (2007): 45–89.

Glotfelty, Cheryll and Fromm, Harold. *The Ecocriticism Reader: Landmarks in Literary Ecology*. Athens, GA: University of Georgia Press, 1996.

Graham, James. Review of *Environment at the Margins: Literary and Environmental Studies in Africa*, edited by Byron Caminero-Santangelo and Garth Myers, http://postcolonial.org/index.php/pct/article/view/1664/1491.

Haraway, Donna. *Simians, Cyborgs and Women: The Reinvention of Nature*. London: Free Association Books, 1991.

Huggan, Graham and Tiffin, Helen. *Postcolonial Ecocriticism: Literature, Animals, Environment*. London: Routledge, 2010.

Latour, Bruno. *Politics of Nature: How to Bring the Sciences into Democracy* (translated by Catherine Porter). Cambridge, MA: Harvard University Press, 2004.

LeMenager, Stephanie, Shewry, Teresa and Hiltner, Ken (eds). *Environmental Criticism for the Twenty-First Century*. New York: Routledge, 2011.

Martin, Julia. 'New, with added ecology? Hippos, forests and environmental literacy', in Nigel Bell and Meg Cowper-Lewis (eds), *Literature, Nature and the Land: Ethics and Aesthetics of the Environment*. University of Zululand, 1993.

Nixon, Rob. *Slow Violence and the Environmentalism of the Poor*. Cambridge, MA: Harvard University Press, 2011.

Okuyade, Ogaga (ed.). *Eco-critical Literature: Regreening African Landscapes*. New York: African Heritage Press, 2013.

Roos, Bonnie and Hunt, Alex (eds). *Postcolonial Green: Environmental Politics and World Narratives*. Charlottesville: University of Virginia Press, 2010.

Salih, M. A. Mohamed. *Environmental Politics and Liberation in Contemporary Africa*. Dordrecht: Kluwer Academic Publishers, 1999.

Slaymaker, William. 'Ecoing the other(s): The call of global green and black African responses', in Tejumola Olaniyan and Ato Quayson (eds), *African Literature: An Anthology of Criticism and Theory*. Malden, MA: Blackwell Publishing, 2007.

Smith, Mick. *Against Ecological Sovereignty: Ethics, Biopolitics, and Saving the Natural World*. Minneapolis: University of Minnesota Press, 2011.

Taylor, Charles. *Sources of the Self: The Making of the Modern Identity*. Harvard University Press, 1989.

Woodward, Wendy. *The Animal Gaze: Animal Subjectivities in Southern African Narratives*. Johannesburg: Wits University Press, 2008.

Wright, Laura. *Wilderness into Civilized Shapes: Reading the Postcolonial Environment.* Athens, GA: University of Georgia Press, 2010.
Wylie, Dan (ed.). *Toxic Belonging? Identity and Ecology in Southern Africa.* Newcastle upon Tyne: Cambridge Scholars Publishing, 2008.
Wylie, Dan. 'Literature and ecology in southern Africa', in Michael Chapman and Margaret Lenta (eds), *SA Lit: Beyond 2000.* Scottsville: University of KwaZulu-Natal Press, 2011.

Chapter 1

'HERE IS SOME BAOBAB LEAF!': *SUNJATA*, FOODWAYS AND BIOPIRACY

JONATHAN BISHOP HIGHFIELD

Historian Felipe Fernández-Armesto writes that food is a 'linkage in the chain of being: the substance of the eco-systems which human beings strive to dominate. Our most intimate contact with the natural environment occurs when we eat it' (Fernández-Armesto 2001: xiii).

Food and foodways are the bridge between human culture and the natural environment. As Fernández-Armesto (2001: 5) puts it: 'Culture began when the raw got cooked.' The combination of the local ecosystem with the ways plants and animals were selectively bred, and the methods by which they were cooked create regional differences that become part of how people in those regions understand their culture. This chapter looks at the intersection of foodways studies and ecocriticism through one of the major oral epics of West Africa, *Sunjata*. Paying attention to food in African narratives – considering what is eaten and how it is grown or procured, and by whom – influences one's understanding of what is happening in the story. African storytellers, writers and film-makers use food and foodways as markers of independence, as symbols of cultural colonisation, and as signs of continued deprivations. Through foodways, one can glimpse famines, invasions and historical access to trade networks, and food can even serve as a vehicle for communication. Since the stories are not constructed in a vacuum, they can also reveal something about what food means in specific historical moments, in specific places and for specific populations.

In some respects, the diet of contemporary sub-Saharan Africa is remarkably similar across the region, despite the enormous differences in its bioregions. Much of this similarity emerged from colonisation, when European colonists attempted to turn most of the continent into vast plantations. To peel back the layers of colonial influence on the foods of the African continent, however, is difficult. Seamus Deane calls colonialism 'a process of radical dispossession' (Deane 1990: 10). Precolonial bioregionalism in agriculture was a victim of that dispossession. As Deane points out, a primary impulse after independence has been the attempt to repossess the history, cultures and languages stripped during the colonial era, because even if such attempts are futile, they are necessary steps out of the legacies of colonialism (Deane 1990: 11).

But how does such repossession happen with the foodways of Africa when over 2 000 species of indigenous grains, fruits, vegetables and roots were displaced by imported crops in the colonial era, and continue to be neglected in agricultural initiatives on the continent (*Lost Crops of Africa* 1, 1996–2008: xv)? Traces of precolonial foods remain in the oral epics and folk tales that pre-date the colonial era. In *Sunjata*, the oral epic of the Mande peoples, it is a tree that provides a glimpse into the relationship between humans and the natural environment, between foodways and culture, in a West Africa before the advent of the Atlantic slave trade and European domination of the region.

The baobab tree is one of the iconic images of Africa. The thick-trunked tree with bare limbs, which look like tree roots, is a common sight across much of the continent, with its territory bordered by the Sahara Desert to the north and the Kalahari Desert to the south (Watson 2007: 28). Laurens van der Post (1978: 13) writes that the baobab 'proclaim[s] the oneness of the Africa to which I belong'. The baobab is central in mythologies across Africa, and it receives near-universal protection (*Lost Crops of Africa* 2, 1996–2008: 75). Besides its mythological status, the baobab provides welcome shade in the savannah and alerts farmers that the planting season is near because its leaves bud just before the arrival of the rains (*Lost Crops of Africa* 3, 1996–2008: 48).

Swallowing the magic fruit: Baobab and *Sunjata*

The baobab holds a significant place in *Sunjata*, which tells the story of the founding of the great empire of Mali.[1] Since it is entirely orally transmitted, there is not a definitive version of the epic, and Stephen P. D. Bulman has compiled a list of 64 published versions of *Sunjata* between 1889 and 1992 (Bulman 1997: 71–94). Although there are differences among these versions, the same plot drives the narrative: two brothers, who are hunters, travel to the land of Dô, which is being terrorised by a buffalo. On their way, they meet an old woman, and because they share their meal with her, she reveals that she is the buffalo and gives them magic to defeat her when she is in her animal form. She also tells them that the king of Dô will offer them a maiden as a reward, and when he does so they must choose a hunchback because she will give birth to a mighty king. Everything goes as the buffalo woman said it would, but after receiving Sogolon, the hunchbacked maiden, from the king, the brothers find they cannot have sex with her because her magic is too strong. They gift her to the king of Niani, Maghan Kon Fatta, and she becomes his second wife. After a war of wills and magic, he impregnates her. When Sogolon Djata, or Sunjata, the promised son, is born, however, he is unable to use his legs and, when the king dies, his scheming first wife, Sassouma, persuades the council of elders to place her son, Dankaran Touman, on the throne instead of Sunjata. After Sassouma insults Sogolon, Sunjata dramatically takes his first step, uproots a baobab tree, and reveals that the prophecies of his greatness are true. Sogolon, concerned that Sassouma will kill Sunjata, leads her son into exile. They are accompanied by Sunjata's two sisters and Manding Bory, his half-brother. Sunjata's griot, Balla Fasséké, does not come with them because Dankaran Touman has sent him to negotiate with the king of Sosso, Soumaoro Kante. While in exile, Sunjata makes many allies, and on the eve of his mother's death, he hears from envoys from Niani that Soumaoro Kante has defeated Dankaran Touman. Sunjata creates an army from the allies he has cultivated, is reunited with his griot, rides south and confronts Soumaoro, defeating him in the Battle of Krina. Afterwards, Sunjata founds the empire of Mali, rewarding his allies with kingdoms of their own.

Narrated in this way, the story seems straightforward and predictable enough. A performance of the epic by a griot, however, is more elaborate and concerned with genealogy, with cementing Sunjata's legacy within a history of Islam in West Africa, and with following the stories of Sunjata's allies. The scholar Jan Jansen, for example, recounts that one particular performance that took place in Kangaba, Mali, 'lasted from 3 p.m. until 7 p.m. and – after a break for dinner – from 9 p.m. until 6 a.m. the next morning"' (Jansen 2001: 30), which hints at the density and narrative possibilities of the story. Among many other things, the *Sunjata* epic reveals the ways in which food defined identity and circulated across West Africa in the 12th century CE and afterwards. The baobab tree, and its fruit and leaves play a crucial role in the *Sunjata* story.

However, before I explore the role of the baobab in the narrative of the cripple who becomes king, I should put the *Sunjata* story into context. At its height, in the early 14th century CE, the empire of Mali covered a huge swathe of West Africa, stretching from the Atlantic Ocean, near what is now the border between Senegal and Mauritania, to the north-west border of present-day Nigeria, and from the edge of the Sahara in the north to the present-day border of Burkina Faso and Ghana in the south.[2] Its influence was greater than the extent of its territory, however, especially as the kings of Mali regularly made the 5 000-kilometre pilgrimage to Mecca (Davidson 1998: 37–42). Though the kingdom of Mali probably existed for 200 years before Sunjata came to the throne, the oral epic that bears his name tells the story of the ascension of Mali over another kingdom, Takrur, both of which were attempting to expand as the empire of Ghana collapsed (Davidson 1998: 34).

David Conrad points out that the various forms and versions of the *Sunjata* story are performed in many different ways:

> The *Sunjata* epic comprises a series of episodes, some of which form the core of the narrative and are the most frequently performed. These are more or less familiar to most people of

traditional Manding societies, and the basic storyline and characters have become known to the outside world through both popular and scholarly publications. Other, less familiar episodes of the epic are known to relatively few of even the most knowledgeable *jeliw* [a Mandinka term for griots], and these are rarely performed publicly. In any case, depending on the type of occasion, the time available and the make-up of the audience, most performances mention only a few of the episodes. At one end of the spectrum, in the course of a brief street performance, for example, a female *jeli* (*jelimuso*) might simply evoke the name of Sunjata, Fakoli, or another of the epic heroes in one of her songs. At the other extreme, *jeliw* have been known to narrate one episode after another for five hours or more without stopping, and to continue at that rate for several days. (Conrad 2006: 81)

Many things influence the performance of the *Sunjata* narrative. If it is performed to an audience with descendants from one of the characters in the story, the version recited will stress the importance of that ancestor in the epic. Because there is not a definitive written version, the *jeliw* wield enormous influence over the construction of the epic.

In *Griots and Griottes*, Thomas Hale (2007: 10) lists over 15 terms that are used for 'griot' in West Africa. Because of the different nomenclatures used in the various languages of West Africa and the numerous subcategories within each language, Hale uses the generic term 'griot' instead of choosing a word from any specific language group. Hale devotes an entire chapter to the various roles of the griot in society, which he summarises as

> recounting history, providing advice, serving as spokesperson, representing a ruler as a diplomat, mediating conflicts, interpreting the words of others into different languages, playing music, composing songs and tunes, teaching students, exhorting participants in wars and sports, reporting news, overseeing, witnessing or contributing to important life ceremonies, and praise-singing. (Hale 2007: 19)

The role of griots altered during the colonial era and their influence continued to wane after independence came to West Africa. Nevertheless, narrating the *Sunjata* story still has the power to have an impact on politics and societal relations today. As Manthia Diawara points out in a paper on how the *Sunjata* epic continues to resonate today, griots cite direct genealogical connections between contemporary politicians and the heroes (and villains) of the epic:

> The influence of a pre-colonial narrative like *The Epic of Soundiata* is evident not only in the novels of the colonial and post-colonial epochs, but also in contemporary politics and popular culture of countries like Mali, Guinea, Gambia, and Ivory Coast. In Mali, for example, the griots praised Modibo Keita, the country's first president, as the direct descendant of Soundiata Keita, Emperor of Mali. After the coup d'etat in 1969, however, the same griots hailed the new president, Moussa Traore, as the savior of the country, a parallel to Tira Maghan Traore, one of Soundiata's chief generals who conquered Gambia. (Diawara 1992: 157)

On the day of the coup by Traoré, the sign-on music on Radio Mali changed from the 'Sunjata fasa,' or praise song of Sunjata, to the 'Tiramagan fasa,' or praise song of the Traoré (Hale 2007: 24).

One can hear both the 'Sunjata fasa' and 'Tiramagan fasa' performed on the griot recording *An bè kelen* (We are one). These recordings offer an aural insight into the performance of the *Sunjata* cycle, as they feature vocal performances by three renowned *jeliw* from the village of Kela – Kumatigi (Master of the Word) Lansine Diabate, El Hadji Bala Diabate and El Hadji Yamuda Diabate – accompanied by singer Bintan Kouyaté and musicians on the ngoni, djembe, tjumba and guitar. The opening track on the disc is 'Sunjata fasa,' the praise song for Sunjata, also known as 'Hymn to the bow'. As Jansen points out in the liner notes accompanying the recording, 'Sunjata fasa' is the central melody in the griots' repertoire, and 'they are able to talk using this melody for hours!' (Jansen 1994: 6). Lansine Diabate and El Hadji Yamuda Diabate, who sing and recite on *An bè kelen*, also performed at the 1997 septennial *Sunjata* recitation held in Kangaba, which,

Jansen (2001: 33) contends, is the 'ultimate' version of the epic. Listening to them perform in the recordings on *An bè kelen*, therefore, gives one a sense of the rhythms and performative aspect of the oral epic.

For most audiences, however, the *Sunjata* story comes as a translated transcribed oral narrative. As Conrad points out, 'the prospect of trying to glean historical information from [oral epics] is not an encouraging one. But woven into the patchwork fabric of these narratives are infrequent threads bearing diminishing echoes of people and events of the distant past' (Conrad 1984: 35). One of those echoes recalls foods of the previous centuries.

Foodways across Africa began changing with trade from Asia and from Islamic-controlled Europe. Ancient Mali was very much tied into these trade routes, and mention of the movement of goods along these routes surfaces repeatedly in versions of *Sunjata*. Oral epics alter over time but, despite the changes in foodways and the retelling of the epic in a manner that speaks to a contemporary audience, the role of the baobab remains unchanged in the *Sunjata* story. In a Gambian version sung by Banna Kanute and transcribed by Gordon Innes, the fruit of the baobab is said to predict the next Mande ruler:

> A tall slender baobab tree grew within the town of Manding.
> This little baobab tree was round; it grew up,
> And produced a single fruit.
> When you say 'one single fruit',
> That means that it produced one fruit.
> As to that fruit, all the marabouts declared it,
> All the diviners by cowries declared it,
> All the diviners by stones declared it,
> The diviners by sand declared it,
> They predicted that whoever swallowed a single seed of the fruit of that baobab
> Would be in control of the town of Manding for sixty years.
> (Innes 1974: 149)

Fruit often plays an important role in folk tales and mythology. Eating the fruit from the tree of the knowledge of good and evil gets humanity kicked out of Eden in the Judeo-Christian creation myth. Pomegranates are a prominent feature of paradise in Islamic belief. In Norse mythology, Idunn's apples keep the gods from ageing. Loki uses the lure of even more wonderful apples to kidnap her, which causes Odin and the other gods to grow prematurely grey. Golden apples figure in one of the labours of Hercules and granting an apple in the Judgement of Paris leads to the Trojan War in Greek mythology. In a temple in Kanchipuram, in the Indian state of Tamil Nadu, is an ancient mango tree, the *sthala-virutcham*, which bears four different types of mangoes, one for each of the four Vedas. In Maori myth, the theft of poporo fruit leads to the great migration to Aotearoa from Hawaiki.

That so many different cultures would associate fruit with foundational stories seems obvious – fruit is not only nourishing, but it also holds the seed of the next generation. The fruit of the baobab is a hairy, nut-like pod, with fibrous, dry flesh. It is not obviously attractive, in the manner of the apples and mangoes that appear in the aforementioned tales. It is not the luscious red apple that tempted Snow White. But the fruit of the baobab is not the only part of the tree that is important in the *Sunjata* story: in nearly every version of the story it is the baobab leaf, or rather the lack of it, that signals the end of Sunjata's crippled state. Because Sunjata cannot walk, his mother, Sogolon, has no one to gather baobab leaves for a stew she is preparing. Niane renders the account of the griot Djéliba Koro as follows, with Sogolon declaring:

'Oh son of misfortune, will you never walk? Through your fault I have just suffered the greatest affront of my life! … Sassouma has just humiliated me over a matter of a baobab leaf. At your age her own son could walk and used to bring his mother baobab leaves.' …

'Very well then, I am going to walk today,' said Mari Djata. 'Go and tell my father's smiths to make me the heaviest possible iron rod. Mother, do you want just the leaves of the baobab or would you rather I brought you the whole tree?'

'Ah, my son, to wipe out this insult I want the tree and its roots at my feet outside my hut.' (Niane 1965: 19)

In Banna Kanute's version, while bringing his mother the baobab tree Sunjata swallows the fruit:

> Sunjata arose in this fashion:
> He grasped the eaves of his mother's house,
> He arose and stood up,
> He laid his hands upon the middle of the roof, high up;
> He called upon God three times,
> And he stretched out his hand.
> The baobab tree which stood in the middle of the town of Manding,
> And which slaves were guarding,
> And armed men were guarding –
> Sunjata seized that baobab tree and twisted it,
> And laid it at his mother's doorway.
> He split open the baobab fruit and swallowed it.
> To his mother he said, 'Here is some baobab leaf!' (Innes 1974: 191)

Some versions have Sunjata throwing the baobab tree in front of his mother's hut. I think the richest version, however, is the one related by Fa-Digi Sisòkò and translated by John William Johnson:

> [Sunjata] came forward.
> He planted the baobab behind his mother's house:
> 'In and about the Manden.
> From my mother they must seek these leaves!'
> To which his mother said, 'I do not think I heard.'
> 'Ah, my mother,
> Now all the Manden baobabs are yours.'
> 'I do not think I heard.'
> 'Ah, my mother,
> All those women who refused you leaves,
> They all must seek those leaves from you.'
> His mother fell upon her knees, *gejebu*! (Johnson 1986: 141–142)

The living tree becomes a reminder of Sunjata's ascension to power both for those living in his time and for future generations. The griot Mamadou Kouyaté uses landmarks still observable in his time to indicate the factuality of the Sunjata story: 'To convince yourself of what I have said go to Mali. At Tigan you will find the forest dear to Sundiata ... Go to Kirikoroni near Niassola and you will see a tree which commemorates Sundiata's passing through these parts' (Niane 1965: 83). The baobab tree becomes a striking reminder of Sunjata's strength and enduring legacy. It becomes both the reason Sunjata defeats the crippling disease that has plagued him from his birth and the magical talisman that confirms his destiny as founder of the empire of Mali.

The baobab is also the symbol that brings him back from exile to defeat the sorcerer king who has enslaved the Mande. While in exile in Mema, Sunjata's mother hears that there are merchants in town selling baobab leaves and *gnougou* (leaves from the *Moringa oleifera*): 'Sogolon took the baobab leaves and gnougou in her hand and put her nose to them as though to inhale the scent' (Niane 1965: 44). When smelling the leaves, she catches the scent of the foods she had left behind when she went into exile to ensure the fulfilment of her son's destiny. The traders carrying the baobab leaves are actually emissaries sent to petition Sunjata to return to lead Manding against its enemies. That they have chosen to find him by bringing foods from his homeland indicates that even in the 12th to 14th centuries it was clearly understood that foods from home signify identity. As Stanley Mintz points out in *Tasting Food, Tasting Freedom*, there are foods that carry with them more than just flavour: 'Such cherished tastes are rooted in underlying economic and social conditions, and they are surely far more than simply nutritive' (Mintz 1996: 24). The baobab leaf and the *gnougou* take on a much richer significance because of their absence while Sogolon and her family are in exile. Anthropologist David Sutton writes that 'there is an imagined community implied in the act of eating food "from home" while in exile, in the embodied knowledge that others are eating the same food' (Sutton 2001: 84). Sogolon will never return to Niani and the baobab that her son had procured for her, but in cooking and eating sauce made from the leaves she is distantly sharing a meal with the family and friends she left behind. As Sutton (2001: 102) writes, 'eating food from home becomes a particularly marked cultural site for the re-imagining of "worlds" displaced in space and/or time'. And the act of sharing a meal reflects hospitality, a central belief in African ethics (Gyekye 2013).

Translating the epic: Dani Kouyaté's *Keita! L'héritage du griot*

In *Keita! L'héritage du Griot* (1995), a filmed version of the *Sunjata* epic by the Burkinabé film-maker Dani Kouyaté, this act of sharing a meal occupies an important place in the narrative. Kouyaté specifically indicates his engagement with the role of the griot: 'We ought to try to understand the griot's techniques and adapt them to the new media' (Thackway 2003: 59) – and *Keita!* attempts to do that. Kouyaté, the son of a griot (actor, Sotigue Kouyaté), wrote and directed the film, which uses part of the *Sunjata* story as both a plot device and a metaphor for the confused adolescence of schoolboy Mabo Keita, himself a descendant of Sunjata.[3] *Keita!* tells the story of the griot Djéliba (played by Sotigue Kouyaté) and his attempt to initiate Mabo Keita into the story. On his website, Dani Kouyaté identifies himself as a griot and indicates that his cinematic art is an outgrowth of his calling: '*J'ai de la chance d'appartenir au siècle du cinéma, c'est un instrument fabuleux pour un griot*' (Frindéthié 2009: 88).[4]

That foodways are important in the film is indicated in the first scene of the *Sunjata* story that Djéliba relates to Mabo. A hunter comes to Maghan Kon Fatta and shares part of an antelope he has killed on the king's land. The king's griot indicates the importance of this gesture by telling the hunter that those who show respect for the customs of Mande are welcomed as if they were at home. That sharing of food is followed by another, when the two hunter brothers share a meal with the buffalo woman. Through these two shared meals, knowledge is exchanged: the hunter tells the king that the daughter of the buffalo, Sogolon, will give birth to his heir, and the buffalo woman tells the brothers how to defeat her and elicits their promise that they will leave the land of Dô with her daughter or wraith.

These foodways and their link to an African ethic emerge out of the story Djéliba tells Mabo. In the world where Mabo lives and that Djéliba visits, the African ethic of hospitality is countered by a neocolonial ethic that suggests that the community must be subordinated to the needs of the individual. In the film, sharing meals and the baobab tree are used by Kouyaté to emphasise the way that Mabo, and all intellectually curious young Africans, are caught between the twin desires of knowing the past and succeeding in the present.

An enormous baobab tree is one of the central images in Kouyaté's film and this image moves between the main story – the griot Djéliba's initiation of Mabo – and Djéliba's retelling of the *Sunjata* story, which serves as Mabo's initiation. In the film's present narrative, Mabo also tells his classmates the story of Sunjata uprooting the baobab for his mother. Mabo has clearly internalised the story, something that makes his mother, Sitan, and his teacher, Mr Fofana, uncomfortable. In Kouyaté's film, the importance of knowing this story, of remembering the past, is clearly juxtaposed with the knowledge imposed on Africans during colonialism and retained in the postcolonial classroom. Mabo needs to master the knowledge that Mr Fofana teaches, however, if he is to do well in his examinations, which is important not only to his parents, but to Mabo as well. When, towards the end of the film, Mabo declares that he wants to continue hearing the story but also to go to school, he asserts his desire to combine multiple types of knowledge.

Keita! suggests that personal connections to African genealogies and ethics have degraded in modern West Africa. To emphasise this, Kouyaté juxtaposes a scene in which Djéliba slowly and deliberately tells Mabo the *Sunjata* story with a scene from a wedding that Mabo's parents, Boicar and Sitan, attend. As they leave the wedding, the praise singer follows Boicar, singing his praises as Boicar indulgently tosses her money. Although praise singing is part of the griot tradition and is still expected at public functions, genealogical and historical teaching is the primary purpose of a griot. But by performing that genealogical function, Djéliba incurs the displeasure of Sitan and Mabo's schoolteacher. The sequence of scenes suggests the victory of individualism in West African society: there might be time for hurried praising of the rising middle class, but the time it takes to initiate a child into his own story no longer exists. To emphasise this, juxtaposing the image of Djéliba lounging in his hammock in a traditional boubou with that of Boicar rushing off to work in his bureaucrat's jacket offers insight into the priorities that define their lives.

There is one scene in *Keita!* where food is used to illustrate the gap between the world of Boicar and Djéliba. Eating at the Keitas' house, Djéliba is served what Sitan calls 'a white meal': spaghetti. The pasta, served without sauce and intended to be eaten with cutlery, is unfamiliar to Djéliba, who calls it 'sapaki'. After struggling with the knife and fork, Djéliba asks for a bowl of water and proceeds to eat the sapaki in the traditional way (with his hands) and with much slurping. After finishing, he belches contentedly.

There are several ways of reading this scene. The pasta is a food of convenience, served unaccompanied. Although it is clearly a middle-class dish because of the expense of importing it, nutritionally it provides only carbohydrates and, although a serving of enriched spaghetti is relatively nutritious, it does not contain the same variety of nutritional requirements as a traditional Burkinabé fish-and-vegetable stew. For the liberated Sitan, spaghetti offers convenience and a certain cachet as an 'exotic' food. For Djéliba, however, the 'sapaki' does not have those qualities. After setting aside the silverware, he eats the pasta with his hands, as he would millet dumplings, while telling Mabo that 'the empty belly has no ears'. In other words, food fuels the acts of storytelling and listening. In one of Sitan's few concessions to Djéliba, she tells him that the next evening she will serve something traditional and more to his liking. The film undercuts that gesture of hospitality somewhat, however, when Mabo reveals to Djéliba that Sitan never prepares meals and that all their food is cooked by a servant.

The film also juxtaposes Sitan's freedom from having to cook with Sogolon's pride in the preparation of food. In Kouyaté's film, when Sogolon asks Sassouma for some baobab leaves for her stew, Sassouma tosses an entire basket of them at her face with open contempt: 'Here! I've always got plenty of them. I never run out of them. My seven-year-old son procured them for me. Yours should do the same instead of continually crawling.' Sogolon leaves Sassouma's compound with an empty calabash, and leaves falling from her hair and shoulders.

It is Mabo who tells this story in the film. The camera pans from three backpacks discarded on the ground to a silk-cotton tree to reveal three boys in the branches. Two friends of Mabo's are listening intently to him telling the story. Kouyaté's use of the silk-cotton tree references a proverbial saying often repeated in versions of *Sunjata*:

> All of a sudden he looked up at the king and said, 'Oh king, the world is full of mystery, all is hidden and we know nothing but what we can see. The silk-cotton tree springs from a tiny seed – that which defies the tempest weighs in its germ no more than a grain of rice. Kingdoms are like trees; some will be silk-cotton trees, others will remain dwarf palms and the powerful silk-cotton tree will cover them with its shade. Oh, who can recognize in the little child the great king to come?' (Niane 1965: 5)

Mabo has taken on the role of storyteller, and the story, like the seed of the silk-cotton tree, is transported on the wind.

Though the silk-cotton tree appears in various versions of the *Sunjata* epic, it is anachronistic. An impressive part of the landscape of West Africa today, it is thought to have arrived only in the 15th century as part of the Columbian exchange – the movement of plants, animals, pathogens and cultures across the Atlantic in the years following the first European voyage to the Americas (Niane 1965: 87). So the presence of the silk-cotton tree represents the adaptable nature of orature, something that is crucial in the world in which Mabo lives.

The segment of the story that Mabo tells his friends also seems to insist on the importance of flexibility. After his mother is insulted, Keita decides he will learn to walk, so he sends his brother to the blacksmith, where a large iron bar has been forged by the smith's father, anticipating the day Keita will need it to help him rise to his feet. Three men transport the rod to Sogolon's compound, and Keita tries to use it to pull himself to his feet. His strength is too much for the forged iron, however; it breaks and Keita crashes back to the ground. As the crowd stands over the prostrate Keita, the hunter appears and tells Sogolon to fetch a 'branch of "sun-sun" ... 'He'll know what to do with it.' Keita pulls himself to his feet using the flimsy branch of the West African tree. Kouyaté's film suggests that the 'Hymn to the bow' in the *Sunjata* epic is about the branch of sun-sun that Keita uses to pull himself up. The film associates Keita with the magic of the hunter, rather than the magic of the blacksmith.[5] The presence of the hunter at the beginning and end of *Keita!* suggests the centrality of the knowledge of the natural world in the film, as do the termites in the opening sequence, the black bird that is Djéliba's totem, and, of course, the baobab tree.

As Mabo continues telling his story to his friends, the camera follows a crowd trailing behind Keita as he marches from the village to a massive baobab tree, with boys collecting leaves in its branches. As Keita strains to pull the tree from the ground, the scene cuts to Mabo and his friends sitting in the branches of the silk-cotton tree: 'Mabo: He tore it out. He uprooted it. He put it on his back. He brought it to his mother's hut.'

With the baobab tree in her compound, Sogolon now becomes the person who will share the leaves with the rest of the community. The smell of the leaves, which imaginatively transports her back to Niani from Mema is redolent then not only of homecoming but also of hospitality – something difficult to offer in exile.

After Mabo tells the other boys of Keita's uprooting of the baobab tree, they press him for more of the story:

Boy 1: And then?
Mabo: I don't know. Djéliba's going to tell me.

In the end, Djéliba cannot finish telling Mabo the story of his ancestor. The last part of the tale Djéliba tells in Kouyaté's film has an interesting twist: instead of going into exile, Keita and his family are expelled from Niani for threatening Dankaran Touman after he sends their griot away to the Sosso kingdom. The loss of the griot by Keita echoes Mabo's loss of Djéliba, who returns to Wagadu after Mabo gets into trouble at school and Sitan threatens to leave Boicar.

As Djéliba leaves the compound, Mabo chases after him. Outside he does not find Djéliba but the hunter. 'What are you doing here?' Mabo asks him. 'You were in the story.' The hunter is the only character who moves between the two worlds in Kouyaté's film. He appears in the beginning of *Keita!*, apparently placing the idea to initiate Mabo into the story in Djéliba's head, and then he appears to Maghan Kon Fatta and prophesies the birth of Keita. At the end of the film, the hunter leads Mabo to the base of a baobab tree and tells him, 'You will find other griots on your road,' echoing the unfilmed next segment of the story, where Keita gains knowledge and allies on his journey north. The film closes with a shot of Mabo looking at Djéliba's totemic bird circling in the sky. Mabo's face fills the screen and the ancient-looking wrinkled bark of the baobab serves as the background of the shot, linking Mabo with the tree his ancestor uprooted.

A tree like no other: Baobab and biopiracy

So, why the baobab? What is it about this tree that gives it distinction in the epic? The answer has to do with the centrality of the baobab tree in the myths and sustenance of West Africa. The editors of the *Lost Crops of Africa* series write that in 'overall utility, perhaps no tree on earth surpasses baobab' (*Lost Crops of Africa* 1996–2008, 2: 81). They add:

> Few plants engender so much respect. Millions believe each tree receives divine power through these 'roots' reaching toward heaven. Out of both regard and gratitude people maintain baobab near their houses. Indeed baobab often seems like some vegetative pet that moves in wherever it finds a friendly family (which in a way it does – sprouting from seeds thrown out in household food wastes). (*Lost Crops of Africa* 1996–2008, 3: 41)

Nearly every part of the baobab is useful. Its leaves are used as a green vegetable during the rainy season and are high in crude protein, important amino acids, calcium, manganese and other minerals, and protovitamin A (*Lost Crops of Africa* 1996–2008, 2: 79). The leaves dry easily without losing much of their nutritional value (*Lost Crops of Africa* 1996–2008, 2: 78). The protein in baobab leaf is so high that it can be used successfully to avoid kwashiorkor in newly weaned infants (*Lost Crops of Africa* 1996–2008, 2: 81). The fruit is equally impressive nutritionally:

> 100 grams of [dried baobab fruit pulp] provides protein (5 g), carbohydrate (30 g), energy (130 calories), and fiber. In terms

of daily nutritional needs, that same 100 g of dried baobab fruit pulp also supplies 25 percent of protovitamin A, 500 percent vitamin C, 34 percent thiamine (B1), 17 percent riboflavin (B2), and 106 percent vitamin B6. As to mineral requirements, it provides 33 percent of the calcium, 26 percent of the phosphorus, and 50 percent of the iron needed each day. (*Lost Crops of Africa* 1996–2008, 3: 43)

Baobab fruit pulp can be dried in a similar way to the leaves and stored away as nutrition for hard times:

Despite a disconcerting appearance, these leathery circlets have an immense importance because they can be stacked up like dinner plates and stored away for months or even years. Poor people in a dozen countries rely on this shelf-stable reserve for sustenance during droughts or other disasters when neither gardens nor markets yield enough. (*Lost Crops of Africa* 1996–2008, 3: 43)

In addition to its spectacular nutritional profile, the baobab earns its name of 'bottle tree' because a single tree can hold a reservoir of 10 000 litres of fresh, clean water, which will remain indefinitely potable 'as long as the hole in the trunk is covered to prevent outside contamination' (*Lost Crops of Africa* 1996–2008, 3: 54). The tree can therefore serve as both a food and water source during drought conditions.

For these reasons, the baobab – the deformed-looking tree that can sustain a village – is linked to the crippled boy who becomes king of the empire of Mali. Whether or not the historical figure of Sunjata existed, there is great metaphorical depth in the story of the epic battle between Soumaoro, the bringer of death dressed in human skins, and Sunjata, the deformed boy who, after eating a baobab fruit, rises up to destroy the death bringer.

The fruit of the baobab is ephemeral. The flesh within the fibrous pod melts away, leaving seeds and a strange astringency in one's mouth. And, although the *Sunjata* story still has resonance in parts of West Africa, it has not dispersed throughout the diaspora like trickster stories or West African religions. The role of the griot as historian and genealogist is similarly melting away. Robert C. Newton writes that in contemporary West Africa, griots are seen as

> irrelevant relics of past glories who have become transformed into contemporary wedding singers or recipients of the largesse of wealthy businessmen who would bestow lavish gifts upon them in exchange for having their virtues extolled on a national stage or in an international studio. On the other hand, they regain prominence when the national government or African Studies scholars appear as patrons and reward them handsomely for their unique contribution to projecting cultural identity. *Sunjata*, like other praise-songs and performances, goes to the highest or most respected bidder. (Newton 2006: 25)

Dani Kouyaté argues for the continued relevance of the griot in a world where colonial legacies still persist – because the griot can tell of the world before colonisation and resource extraction.

The story of Sunjata and the baobab is significant for the continent today. Baobab products have become big business for multinational drug and food companies, with numerous patents placed on its leaves and fruit (McGown 2006: 36).[6] As Andrew Mushita and Carol Thompson point out in *Biopiracy of Biodiversity*, the attempted stripping of foods from Africa is only the latest in a series of thefts that have weakened the infrastructure of the continent: 'First there was the theft of people. Second there was, and is, the theft of minerals. Third, Africans are now working to prevent the 21st century from becoming the theft of their biodiversity' (Mushita and Thompson 2007: 5).

Baobab is being touted as the new superfood (Haider 2013). But it is a superfood for the world's elite, and not for the people of Africa, who have enjoyed its many uses for millennia:

> Removal of plants is not simply the taking of a seed or seedling, but usurps local knowledge. Instead of working with local communities to adapt the plant or develop new uses, the bioresources are looted for the benefit of the pirates. The removal was not

exchange nor free trade, for the Europeans compensated neither the national government nor the traditional healers nor cultivators, for their knowledge or plant resource. The taking of plants could disrupt traditional relations and reduce the economic competitiveness of the communities that had provided the labor, scientific knowledge, and raw materials. (Mushita and Thompson 2007: 27)

To see how traditional relations and economic competitiveness might change in the case of the baobab, one merely needs to look at the recent situation with quinoa in the Andes. Long one of the most important staple foods in the Andean region, quinoa has become too expensive for the locals to eat. The desire for quinoa in the US and Europe is driving many Andean farmers into monocultural agriculture (i.e. producing quinoa for export) and forcing them to rely on imported processed products for their own food (Arellano Valdivia 2013; Blythman 2013; Romero and Shahriari 2011). As Bolivian anthropologist Mauricio Mamani Pocoaca writes:

Nuestra quinua formará parte de la comida chatarra y nosotros seremos los consumidores dependientes: razón por la que lloran los campesinos en silencio y saben que, en el futuro, nunca más serán los dueños de la semilla de quinua y además están conscientes que, en el futuro desaparecerán algunas variedades que desde su origen, tuvieron distintas aplicaciones en su uso. (Mamani Pocoaca 2013)[7]

Consumerist imperialism is continuing to alter the ecologies and cultures of the formerly colonised regions of the world for the pleasure and convenience of the world's elite. Foods that were once shared in times of both feast and famine have become mere commodities, their links to the hospitality that defined communal identity lost to the onslaught of global capitalism.

Sunjata tells the story of the son of a buffalo and a king who overcomes crippling disability with the aid of a baobab and his mother's encouragement to lead his people against an invading sorcerer king. It is a story with a form that can evolve to speak to different audiences at different places and different times. Thomas L. Cooksey (2009: 262) writes: 'Rather than representing an absolute past, the *Sundiata* represents the living expression of a living culture, a work that remains in service of the future'.

The epic suggests ways of seeing the world and ways of constructing communities that are still relevant in present-day West Africa. Today, as neocolonial theft of food resources threatens the continent, the 'Sunjata fasa' needs to be performed with as much amplification as necessary to make it heard over the chatter and allure of multinational advertising. *Sunjata* tells how people of different nations came together to oppose a conqueror who asserted his mastery over the natural world and the human societies inhabiting it. It is a story that insists upon the connections between the environment and human cultures. A new generation of storytellers needs to be educated to tell stories like *Sunjata* – stories that insist on cultural and ecological connections and argue for food sovereignty and local control of resources.

References

AmbrosiaLab, http://www.ambrosialab.com/mission.htm (accessed 4 August 2013).

Arellano Valdivia, Juan. '*Los dilemas del cultivo y el consumo de la Quinua en los Andes.*' *Globalizado: Blog de Juan Arellano*, 27 October 2013.

Austen, Ralph A. (ed.). *In Search of Sunjata: The Mande Oral Epic as History, Literature and Performance*. Bloomington: Indiana University Press, 1999.

Bird, Charles S. (ed.). *The Dialects of Mandekan*. Bloomington: African Studies Program, Indiana University, 1982.

Blythman, Joanna. 'Can vegans stomach the unpalatable truth about quinoa?' *The Guardian*, 16 January 2013.

Brooks, George E. *Landlords and Strangers: Ecology, Society, and Trade in Western Africa, 1000–1630*. Boulder: Westview Press, 1994.

Bulman, Stephen P. D. 'A checklist of published versions of the Sunjata epic.' *History in Africa* 24 (1997): 71–94.

Conrad, David C. 'Oral sources on links between great states: Sumanguru, servile Lineage, the Jariso, and Kaniaga.' *History in Africa* 11 (1984): 35–55.

Conrad, David C. 'Oral tradition and perceptions of history from the Manding peoples of West Africa', in Emmanuel Kwaku Akyeampong (ed.), *Themes in West Africa's History*. Athens: Ohio University Press, 2006: 73–96.

Cooksey, T. L. '"The man of the day to follow": Dani Kouyaté's *Keita!* and the living epic.' *Literature Film Quarterly* 37, 4 (2009): 262–269.

'Cosmetic preparations with an additive from the baobab tree – US 20090324656 A1', http://www.google.com/patents/US20090324656 (accessed 4 August 2013).

Davidson, Basil. *West Africa Before the Colonial Era*. London: Longman, 1998.

Deane, Seamus. 'Introduction', in Terry Eagleton, Frederic Jameson and Edward Said (eds), *Nationalism, Colonialism, and Literature*. Minneapolis: University of Minnesota Press, 1990.

Diawara, Manthia. 'Canonizing Soundiata in Mande literature: Toward a sociology of narrative elements.' *Social Text* 31/32 (1992): 154–168.

Fernández-Armesto, Felipe. *Food: A History*. London: Macmillan, 2001.

Frindéthié, K. Martial. *Francophone African Cinema: History, Culture, Politics and Theory*. Jefferson, NC: MacFarland, 2009.

Gyekye, Kwame. 'African ethics', in Edward N. Zalta (ed.), *The Stanford Encyclopedia of Philosophy*, fall 2011 edition.

Haider, Paul. 'Baobab fruit powder from Africa: A powerful new super food.' *OM Times*, http://omtimes.com/2013/01/baobab-fruit-powder-from-africa-a-powerful-new-super-food (accessed 4 August 2013).

Hale, Thomas. *Griots and Griottes*. Bloomington: Indiana University Press, 2007.

Innes, Gordon. *Sunjata: Three Mandinka Versions*. London: School of Oriental and African Studies, 1974.

Jansen, Jan. Liner notes. *An bè kelen*. Leiden: PAN Records, 1994.

Jansen, Jan. 'The Sunjata epic: The ultimate version.' *Research in African Literatures* 32 (2001): 14–46.

Johnson, John William. *The Epic of Son-Jara: A West African Tradition*. Bloomington: Indiana University Press, 1986.

Keita! L'héritage du Griot. Directed by Dani Kouyaté. California Newsreel, 1995.

Lost Crops of Africa (3 vols). Washington, D.C.: National Academy of Sciences Press, 1996–2008.

Mamani Pocoaca, Mauricio. '*Adiós con lágrimas a la quinua.*' *Todo sobre la quinua*. 21 April 2013, http://laquinua.blogspot.com/2013/04/adios-con-lagrimas-la-quinua.html.

Manfredini, Stefano. 'The health properties of baobab (*Adansonia digitata*).' Powerpoint lecture presented in Verona, 6 September 2002, http://www.baobabdirect.com/newsitems/2002_06_HealthPropertiesOfBaobab_UNIV_Ferrara.pdf.

McGown, Jay. *Out of Africa: Mysteries of Access and Benefit Sharing*. Edmonds, WA: Edmonds Institute, in cooperation with the African Centre for Biosafety, 2006.

McNaughton, Patrick R. *The Mande Blacksmiths: Knowledge, Power, and Art in West Africa*. Bloomington: Indiana University Press, 1993.

Mintz, Stanley. *Tasting Food, Tasting Freedom: Excursions into Eating, Culture, and the Past*. Boston: Beacon Press, 1996.

Mushita, Andrew and Thompson, Carol B. *Biopiracy of Biodiversity*. Trenton: Africa World Press, 2007.

Newton, R. C. 'Of dangerous energy and transformations: Nyamakalaya and the Sunjata phenomenon.' *Research in African Literatures* 37, 2 (2006): 15–33.

Niane, D. T. *Sundiata, An Epic of Old Mali* (translated by G. D. Pickett). London: Longman, 1965.

Romero, Simon and Shahriari, Sara. 'A food's global success creates a quandary at home.' *The New York Times*, 20 March 2011.

Sutton, David E. *Remembrance of Repasts: An Anthropology of Food and Memory*. Oxford: Berg, 2001.

Thackway, Melissa. *Africa Shoots Back: Alternative Perspectives in Sub-Saharan Francophone Film*. Bloomington: Indiana University Press, 2003.

'Use of parts of the baobab plant as animal food or as additive in animal food – US 20090258112 A1', http://www.google.com/patents/US20090258112 (accessed 4 August 2013).

Van der Post, Laurens. *First Catch Your Eland*. New York: William Morrow, 1978.

Watson, Rupert. *The African Baobab*. Cape Town: Struik, 2007.

Chapter 2

SHONA AS A LAND-BASED NATURE-CULTURE: A STUDY OF THE (RE)CONSTRUCTION OF SHONA LAND MYTHOLOGY IN POPULAR SONGS

MICKIAS MUSIYIWA

The land seizures in Zimbabwe that took place from 2000 onwards not only shocked the world and received condemnation because of the violence, injury, death and destruction of property involved, but they were controversial also because of their immediate national consequences. The result was Zimbabwe's economic collapse and increased political turmoil.

This characterises what is generally known about Zimbabwean land reform globally, but little investigation has been done into the (cultural) land beliefs and their impact on land imagination in Zimbabwe. To help elucidate why the land invasions took place and why land redistribution went ahead despite severe sanctions and criticism from the West, this chapter explores the Shona people's natural relationship with the land – a relationship enshrined in a historically celebrated land mythology. I have chosen Shona popular songs as the analytical entry into this mythology because, since time immemorial, Shona popular songs, among other Zimbabwean oral artistic forms and cultural practices,[1] have sustained the survival, celebration and popularisation of land mythology.

The Shona people have a total dependence on land, and theirs is a land-oriented culture. The Shona popular songs have provided an effective space for the construction and articulation of land mythology and, depending on emerging land interests, its reconstruction. I argue that these songs illustrate the existence of a highly influential land mythology that shapes the Shona imagination of, and interaction with, the land, as well as the ecological issues surrounding land.

Shona mythology and popular songs

There is an interesting correlation between popular songs and the land mythology that I analyse here. Many Shona popular songs, both recorded and unrecorded *chimurenga*[2] songs and folk songs, construct, and at the same time embody and express the Shona land mythology. Therefore, the songs constitute a communicative platform and a strategy for disseminating and popularising the land discourses embodied in the mythology. Although other modes of expression, such as oral and written literature, are also media for constructing the mythology, I contend that songs provide a more effective mode for constructing and communicating this mythology. They are not only a key genre of Shona ethno-aesthetics, and the most employed means of articulating, (re)constructing and celebrating this mythology but, as I will demonstrate, they also incorporate the mythology's other expressive modes (including myths and legends). Furthermore, as music, they have a much more powerful mobilisation effect. Songs deliver the mythology in a more memorable way than other communicative modes. Many scholars, including Sadomba (2011), Pfukwa (2008), Kriger (1992) and Pongweni (1982), have noted the critical role of *chimurenga* songs in the mobilisation, recruitment and politicisation of peasants and guerrillas during Zimbabwe's liberation war (Chimurenga) of the 1960s and 1970s. This was a period when land mythology was at its zenith and the same phenomenon was repeated from 2000 onwards during the farm invasions.

My aim of theorising Shona society as a land-based nature-culture is not only inspired by the fact that in Zimbabwe, Shona mythology is the oldest but, more importantly, because it has historically been the most influential in shaping land imaginings in Zimbabwe. The rise of modern Zimbabwean nationalism in the 1950s, and the subsequent armed struggle, and, later, the land seizures at the turn of the millennium owe their success to the mobilisation of this land mythology and its associated traditional beliefs.

Three concepts central to this chapter's argument – mythology, land and ecology – require clarification. Whereas the dictionary definition of land is that part of the earth's surface not covered by sea, as a concept, land has often been interpreted in different ways by societies and historical eras in terms of its value and the benefits that humans accrue from it. Hubacek and Van den Bergh (2002: 3) assert that land can be understood in terms of various functions, often divided into several categories, chief of which are 'the environment, economics, society and spirituality'. They elaborate on this explanation, stating that, environmentally, land is conceptualised as soil, which provides water and habitat for wildlife. In terms of the economic category, the land means economic productivity and 'provides aesthetic value and amenity services', as well as being 'a store of value and assets'. In terms of its social function, land ownership 'acts as a source of prestige and an organizing principle for socio-economic relationships'. And, spiritually, 'for some cultures, land is a deity that exercises control over its people' (Hubacek and Van den Bergh 2002: 1). As my discussion will illustrate, these various concepts of land are all enshrined in Shona land mythology, although the spiritual concept of land appears to be at the centre of the Shona people's framework of understanding land. The social, economic and environmental dimensions of land are derived and find justification from the central spiritual dimension.

The term 'ecology' requires explanation because, although it is a separate notion, it is closely linked with the concept of land because the various functions people attach to land determine their ecological behaviour. Ecology is the science concerned with explaining 'the relationship between living things and their environment' and 'the relationship between and among species' (Jackson and Steiner 1985: 180).

But what is mythology? Along with the related term, 'myth', mythology is associated with fluidity (see, for instance, Csapo 2005; Kirk 1974; Leach 1954). The fluidity arises from the fact that the concepts' meanings vary according to the sociocultural and historical contexts in which they are applied (Kirk 1974: 19). Therefore, explanations of these terms must be sensitive to the particular historical and sociocultural realities from which myth(s) or mythology are constructed because specific peculiarities shape the meanings of these terms. I offer, therefore, working definitions of the terms that are appropriate to Shona culture's mythological terrain. Whereas in its ordinary sense, the term 'myth' refers to something untrue, in a mythological milieu, where myths are traditional stories, they are 'true for those who use' them (Leach 1954: 6). Within a particular culture's history and traditions, a myth can be defined as a traditional story or narrative that comments on the sociocultural and physical phenomena of that society (Kirk 1974: 38). Walter Burket adds that myth often has a 'secondary, partial reference to something of collective importance' (in Bremmer 1987: 1). Although the term 'mythology' has various meanings, the sense relevant to my discussion conceptualises mythology as a body or corpus of myths that belong to a particular culture, and tell about heroes and heroines, and gods and other supernatural beings (Hirsch, Kett and Trefil 1988: 149). However, I argue that to fully understand mythology in the context of the Shona culture in particular and African cultures in general, there is a need to broaden this definition. In African mythology, besides myths, other traditional narrative forms, such as legends and folk tales, folk songs, verse, aphoristic sayings (such as proverbs) and some ritual practices, cohere to form a corpus that is referred to as mythology.

Notwithstanding the advent of literacy, which arrived with the Europeans at the end of the 19th century, it is important to emphasise that, by virtue of being a product of an oral culture, Shona mythology is primarily oral. Its orality should be taken into consideration because it has implications for its interpretation. As Kirk (1974: 18) asserts, the form, interpretation and function of mythology differ in oral and literate cultures.[3] This view has been elaborated by Ong, who argues that the thought patterns and their expression in oral cultures are characteristically different from those of writing cultures (Ong 1982: 31–77).[4] When

I speak of a Shona land mythology, I refer to cultural beliefs and practices about land that appear in traditional narratives, songs, verse and rituals, and which have historically shaped the Shona people's interaction with land. In my broad aim to illustrate Shona as a nature-culture, I analyse key motifs of the Shona land mythology and how they have been appropriated and reconstructed during the three land wars of 1896–97; 1966–79 and 2000, all known as Chimurenga. These motifs include the myths of *mwana wevhu* (child of the soil);[5] the *mapfupa angu achamuka* (my bones shall rise); the *tora gidi uzvitonge* (take a gun and liberate yourself); and *Zimbabwe ndeyeropa* (Zimbabwe is about blood).

The *mwana wevhu* myth

Shona land mythology is almost synonymous with the *mwana wevhu* myth, which is at the core of the tenets from which other myths were constructed. By definition, this myth refers to a Shona person in his or her ancestral land, distinguishing him or her 'from those [i.e. aliens who do not share the same totemic identity as him or her] whose links with the land are not so close' (Hodza and Fortune 1979: 14). The myth is such a key concept of the Shona relationship between people and the land that it encapsulates the Shona people's ontological and ecological relationships with land, and forms the basis for the construction of their superstructure (particularly religious and political beliefs).

Historically, and especially from the 1950s as African nationalism emerged, the *mwana wevhu* myth has been intertextualised in many folk and *chimurenga* songs to construct land discourses. It garnishes nationalist rhetoric and is often used as an honorific title to address every patriotic Shona person in a collective sense.[6] It imbues a Shona person with patriotism, which is reflected in the folk song '*Zimbabwe yanditora mwoyo*' (Zimbabwe has taken my heart) and Simon Chimbetu's 1980s hit '*Zimbabwe iyoyi*' (This Zimbabwe), in which he relives his journey to Mozambique to join the guerrillas and fight for land restoration:

Zimbabwe iyoyi yanga yanditora mwoyo (This Zimbabwe had taken my heart)

Hatinete kusvika tatora ivhu redu (We will not rest until we take back our land)

The *mwana wevhu* myth is a key tenet of the Shona philosophy of land and the people's belief that their existence is entirely regulated by or based on *ivhu* (the land). It embodies the central belief of the Shona concerning what land is, who owns it and how it should be managed.

It is important to point out from the outset that the fundamentals of the Shona philosophy of land, like the philosophies of many other African cultures with respect to natural resources (forests, rivers, lakes, etc.) on which people's lives are dependent, uses religion as the medium to construct and disseminate its fundamental notions, and to enforce or persuade people to adhere to and apply them. To speak of a Shona land mythology is therefore another avenue of entry into Shona religion. The term '*mwana wevhu*' comes from the Shona people's religious beliefs, which symbolically link the people with *ivhu* (soil/land). The origin of the myth can be traced back to the formation of chiefdoms in early Shona society. To speak of a Shona chiefdom or empire[7] is to refer to a specific territory. That territory belongs to the founding ancestors, usually a brother and a sister (see Musiyiwa 2011), who are the *sikarudzi* (the progenitors or creators of the tribe) (Hodza and Fortune 1979: 16). These were usually the first rulers of the chiefdom, or the empire's dynasty. From a Shona religious perspective, they would be the chiefly spirits, or lion spirits, called *mhondoro*,[8] remembered and respected in the chiefdom for their instructions on how the land should be managed. Because the ruling chief or emperor is a member of the ruling dynasty, he is also closely associated with the land's chiefdom. As Bourdillon (1987: 67) asserts, 'the land is intimately associated with the history of a chiefdom, with the ruling chief and with ancestral spirits who live on it'.

All the children born in the chiefdom took the totemic identity of their ancestors and were referred to as *vana vevhu* (children of the soil). This meant that they were ritually tied to the land that their ancestors found and ruled. They and the land were one and the same thing. Thus both the living and their ancestors are the *vene/varidzi vevhu* (owners of the soil)[9] (Hodza and Fortune 1979: 12–13). Besides being *vene/varidzi vevhu*, the ancestors (*vadzimu*) were also the embodiment of the very soil, hence they are referred to as *vari pasi* (those in the ground/soil). This means the land is understood by the Shona as the abode of the ancestors. The term *'vari pasi'* thus refers to the world of the ancestors whose abode is the very land.

Although the land belongs to the ancestors, and the living claim ownership of the land by virtue of it being bequeathed to them by their ancestors, ultimately the land belongs to Mwari, the Shona supreme being who created the universe and has 'ultimate dominion over all the country' (Bourdillon 1987: 69), and not the *mhondoro*, as Taringa claims (Taringa 2006: 196, 198).[10] Mwari, the creator of the universe and human beings, has the epithets Nyadenga (Owner of, or One who Dwells in the Sky) and Musikavanhu (The Creator of Humans).

Incorporating biblical concepts into their land mythology and likening themselves to the Israelites with respect to the land of Canaan, the modern Shona also claim that the land belongs to them because it is an ancestral birthright given to them by Mwari. There is a Shona myth that, besides validating the claim that land is their God-given birthright, also illustrates this importance of land to Shona existence. The myth goes as follows: Mwari decided to give gifts to two men. To the first he gave people and livestock, and to the second he gave only a handful of soil. The second man was able to claim ownership of all that grew, lay or walked on the land, including the other man and his people and livestock. The second man became the chief of the whole land, while the other man became his headman (Bourdillon 1987: 67; Posselt 1929: 57).

The symbolic meaning of this myth underscores the value of land to Shona ontology and the religious dimension of the relationship people have with the land. Because *vari pasi* are the owners, representatives and 'guardians of the land' (Schofeleers 1978), they determine how the land should be managed by their living descendants. They also provide rain and ensure the fertility of the soil.

Shona land mythology has a strong ecological dimension, a point that I will elaborate on later. At this juncture, it is important to emphasise that the association of the land with ancestors explains why in Shona culture the soil is personified. It is a being, a protagonist in the everyday drama of Shona life and ontological imagination. The living can invoke the soil (i.e. the ancestors) to address issues in their relationship with the land. This ritual is called *kumutsa ivhu* (awakening the soil). It is an appeal to the world of *vari pasi* to fight on behalf of the living, especially when the land, and hence their lives, are threatened. For instance, in the appropriation and reconstruction of the mythology by nationalists, peasants and guerrillas during the liberation struggle, the most famous territorial spirits among the Shona – those of Chaminuka, Nehanda and Kaguvi – were constantly evoked to inspire the struggle. As will be discussed later, this was despite the fact that the three were killed leading an anti-colonial resistance geared to ensure the land remained in their hands. Kaguvi and Nehanda led the 1896–97 anti-colonial resistance, now popularly known as the First Chimurenga in Zimbabwean nationalist discourses. Chaminuka was a powerful Shona chief who was killed by the Ndebele in 1883.[11] Dick Chingaira's *chimurenga* song '*Tinotenda midzimu mukuru*' (We are thankful to the great ancestors) expresses the whole mythological idea of *vadzimu* as the *varidzi vevhu*. In the song's structure below, and henceforth in all the songs that follow, 'L' stands for 'Leader' and 'R' for 'Respondents'.

L: *Hanzi daidzai vose veZimbabwe*
R: *Ivo Ambuya Nehanda*
L: *Vamiririre nyika vagoitonga iyo*
R: *Ndeyavo ivo Sekuru Kaguvi*

It is being said, call all the national ancestors of Zimbabwe
Herself, Grandmother Nehanda,
To represent and rule the country
It belongs to him, Grandfather Kaguvi[12]

In line 3 of this extract, *nyika* (the country, i.e. Zimbabwe) is said to be represented by Nehanda in the line *Vamiririre nyika* ... (So that she represents the country ...). Besides, she has to rule it: ... *vagoitonga* ... (... so that she rules it ...). The fact that the land belongs to the ancestors is projected in the last line of the extract – *Ndeyavo ivo Sekuru Kaguvi* (It belongs to him, Grandfather Kaguvi). These lines echo the Shona people's belief that territorial spirits, such as Nehanda and Kaguvi, 'remain powerful guardians of the chiefdom. They are believed to continue their rule through the chiefs, their successors, whom they protect and support' (Bourdillon 1987: 104).

The traditional nationalist song '*Nyika yamadzibaba*' (The fathers' nation), which celebrates Zimbabwe's attainment of independence in 1980, also expresses the idea that the ancestors are the owners of the land, although this song refers exclusively to male ancestors:

L: *He-e vakuru we-e musazokanganwa*	Hey, you elders, do not forget that we have taken Zimbabwe
R: *Nyika yemadzibaba, nyika yeZimbabwe*	The country of the fathers, the country of Zimbabwe

Another song expressing a similar point is '*Tondorwira nyika*' (We are going to fight for the country), which was sung during the nationalist struggle to mobilise young men and women to join the war effort. The following is an extract:

L: *Tondorwira nyika*	We are going to fight for the country
R: *Yamadzibaba*	Which belongs to the fathers

The way land is interpreted in these songs is politico-patriarchal because, traditionally in Zimbabwe, the political sphere was dominated by men. However, in the religious domain female spirits' roles are visible, as influential as those of men and recognised as such.[13] In the Mbare Chimurenga Choir song '*Hatibve muno*' (We will not leave [this country]), Chaminuka, Nehanda and Kaguvi are again cited as the owners of the land who died for it. Consequently, the singers feel that because they are bound together with their slain ancestors (and, metaphorically, with the land), the land is therefore theirs – '*Zimbabwe inyika yedu*' (Zimbabwe is our country) and swear to never go anywhere else:[14]

L: *Zimbabwe inyika*	Zimbabwe is a country
R: *Yedu isu hatibve muno*	It is ours, we will not leave it
L: *Nehanda akafira*	Nehanda died
R: *Muno*	Here

L: *Chaminuka akafira*   Chaminuka died
R: *Muno*   Here
L: *Kaguvi akafira*   Kaguvi died
R: *Muno achifira nyika yake*   Here fighting for his country

The intimate relationship between Shona life and land explains why, since the late Iron Age, the Shona economy has been dominated by agriculture. For this reason, periods of rain deficiency and drought are some of the most fictionalised and historicised in Shona folklore. Even today droughts are usually attributed to some disturbance, violation or conflict in the land–human relationship created by the Shona or by outsiders. Traditionally, this violation was seen as an infringement of the land *miko/zviera* (taboos) imposed by the territorial spirits. One of these was the observance of the *chisi* ([sacred] day of rest), when nothing relating to working on the land, such as ploughing, weeding, fetching firewood, cutting down a tree, or merely carrying a hoe or an axe, was allowed. This observance was enforced by the ruling chiefs and their subordinates in the chiefdom's administrative hierarchy. Those who violated the rest day were fined by the traditional authorities and severely warned not to do it again. The *chisi* day is still widely observed in Zimbabwe but the specific day of observance varies from one chiefdom to another. Jacob Mapara's chapter in this book (Chapter 3) also refers to the centrality of taboos in Shona religion.

Most of the taboos are ecological and concerned with 'rituals to counteract droughts, floods, blights, pests and epidemic diseases affecting cattle and man' (Schofeleers 1987: 2). To borrow Rappaport's phrase, "a ritually directed ecosystem" (1969), I may refer to land in the Shona land-human interaction as "ritually directed". In this system, the territorial spirits are believed to determine, through their spirit mediums, modes of productivity – which types of crops should be grown in preference to others – in times of ecological constraint, such as droughts. Ceremonies with an ecological bearing on the land were conducted at the chiefdoms, among clans and in the villages. Of particular note was the *mukwerera/mutoro* (rain-making ceremony). This would be conducted to ask Mwari and *vadzimu* for enough rain in the forthcoming farming season. Among the central and southern Shona people (the Karanga) and other ethnic groups in western Zimbabwe, Mwari's emissaries, called *manyusa* (rain-makers), who resided in the chiefdoms, would each year visit the Matopos Hills, where an elaborate Mwari cult was based. They would ask for rain and have their seeds for sowing in the planting season blessed for fertility (see Bourdillon 1979; Daneel 1970; Ranger 1985). As the rain fell, its importance as a life giver and fertiliser of the land was welcomed. People would ululate and utter the saying '*ngainaye pasi rive dovetove*' (let it [the rain] fall, so that the earth becomes a wetland), meaning that the life cycle of the land was beginning again. Naked children would dart into the pounding rain to have fun, singing, '*mvura ngainaye tidye makavhu*' (let the rains fall so that we can eat pumpkins), expressing hope for a forthcoming bumper harvest.

Agriculture, in turn, had an influence on Shona religion, which has been referred to as 'agro-ecological' (Sadomba 2011: 13). The religiously controlled, ecologically managed land–people relationship gave rise to a life of abundance, it was believed. This is nostalgically mythicised in Shona oral traditions known as *pasichigare*, a precolonial life akin to paradise (an idyllic existence similar to Arcadia in European pastoral narratives). In nationalist discourses that incorporate biblical land concepts, this idyll has been likened to the promised land, full of *uchi nemukaka* (milk and honey). For example, in Cde Chinx's song '*Maruza imi III*' (You have lost for the third time), the romanticised *pasichigare* life is evoked to rally the masses to support the government's fast-track land reform by chronicling the history of Zimbabwe's colonisation. According to the singer, the reason behind the (British) colonisation of Zimbabwe is that its land is '*izere uchi nemukaka*' (abundant with honey and milk):

Voti nanga-nangawo neZimbabwe	And now they relentlessly focused their attention on Zimbabwe
Izere uchi nemukaka	Abundant with milk and honey

In the Born Free Crew's celebratory song 'Ndatadza kukanganwa' (I have failed to forget), independence and the land reform of 2000 are said to have restored the abundant precolonial past because now 'todya uchi nemukaka' (we are eating honey and milk).

L: *Ndatadza kukanganwa kus-unungurwa kwatakaitwa*	I cannot forget how we were liberated
L: *Tawana kuzvitonga, todya uchi nemukaka*	We got our sovereignty, now we are eating honey and milk

Colonisation and the disruption of nature–human intimacy

The British colonisation of Zimbabwe in 1890 had land as its targeted key resource. Although Cecil John Rhodes was initially interested in minerals, hoping to find a second Rand, the importance of land to the newcomers is seen in the promises given to members of the Pioneer Column, a group of mercenaries whom Rhodes assembled to colonise Zimbabwe. Each member was promised 300 acres of land in Mashonaland and 15 gold claims. With their columns of horse-drawn wagons traversing the land, they were an awesome and ominous spectacle, signalling an arrival with far-reaching consequences for the land.

The *mbira* song '*Chemutengure*' captured the spectacle:

L: *Chemutengure, chemutengure*	That-which-carries, that-which-carries [i.e. the wagon]
R: *Chave chemutengure, vhiri rengoro*	It is now that-which-carries, the wheel of a wagon

The British 1890 entry into Mashonaland is interpreted in Shona folklore as a fulfilment of Chaminuka's March 1883 prophecy, *kuchauya vasina mabvi* (those without knees [i.e. Europeans] will come [into the land]). Four decades later, as the European population increased, the Land Apportionment Act of 1930/31 was enacted. The new law reallocated land using a racial criterion. The Shona and other groups were forcibly evicted from their ancestral lands and settled in infertile and sandy reserves. This set in motion the disruption of Shona as a land-centred culture. The disruption was captured with melancholy and pessimism in the Shona saying *'pasi papinduka'* (the land has been turned upside down).

The *mwana wevhu* land philosophy would not make sense after the people had been cut off from the land where the graves of a whole line of ancestors were located, the very ancestors who owned the land and symbolised it. With the passage of time, the ecological observances imposed by the *vari pasi*, which ensured a cordial and sustainable relationship between the land and the people, would become weaker and weaker as capitalist agriculture introduced new methods of land management. The settlerist ideology of the Rhodesian government's processes, such as colonial administration, education and Christianity (in short, Westernisation), combined to weaken the land–people relationship and its agro-ecological religion, ushering in a diametrically opposed notion of land and its management to that of the Shona. Mechanised agriculture dug deep into the soil, radically disturbing it. This was an infringement of land taboos tantamount to desecrating the graves of the ancestors and the soil they symbolised. The use of fertilisers, herbicides, pesticides and other soil chemicals went against the grain of traditional Shona fertilisation techniques based on the use of humus, manure and sacerdotal seed blessings. The development and expansion of urban, mining and commercial farming settlements further violated the land. The new settlements desecrated religious shrines that were critical to the well-being of the land–people relationship.[15] The giant plants of heavy primary and manufacturing industries, and the dams and boreholes constructed to provide water for the ever-thirsty commercial plantations and farms also breached the Shona people's land-based, ritually regulated ecology.

The *mwana wevhu* philosophy and Zimbabwean nationalism

As the relationship between people and the land was significantly undermined by colonisation, the old mythological ideas about lost land were kept alive in Shona popular folklore, captured in the collective memory through songs, folk tales, myths, legends, oral poetry and religious ceremonies, among other communicative modes. Now, since the land had been lost, their recital was always accompanied with intense emotions. These folkloric genres became important cultural capital in the construction of modern Zimbabwean nationalism and its primary goal of recovering expropriated land. Therefore, the First Chimurenga (1896–97), Second Chimurenga (1966–79) and the post-2000 Third Chimurenga can be conceptualised as land movements.

Severe land degradation in the reserves, which became especially evident from the 1950s onwards, clearly demonstrated that the harmonious ecological interaction between the Shona people and the land had been infringed. Pressure from the growing population in the reserves and numbers of livestock began to weigh far beyond the carrying capacity of the arid and sandy reserves, wreaking havoc on the pre-European stability of the ecosystem. Soil erosion and deforestation worsened. The severity of the ecological disaster caught the attention of the colonial government, which in 1951 intervened by enacting the Land Husbandry Act, a legal instrument to back land-conservation measures. Among the interventions were forced evictions, the digging of contours and destocking. These measures were very unpopular with villagers, as they entailed 'sweeping changes in tenure and land allocation procedures' (Ranger 1985: 151). The process aggravated black people's land grievances since the reserves in which they had been forced to live were not their ancestral lands. Their resentment is captured in the folk songs *'Nhamo yamakandiwa'* (The trouble of [digging] the contours) and *'Mombe mbiri'* (Two cattle). The former was a protest against the digging of contours and the latter against destocking in the reserves.

Zimbabwean nationalism, when it began to develop, capitalised on this popular land mythology, and it was used to drum up popular support for the armed struggle in the 1960s and 1970s. Nationalism also took advantage of the fact that in this period anti-white sentiment over land shortages had reached highly emotional levels. Explaining why in the 1970s the Weya Reserve became 'a haven of guerrillas' during the war, the district commissioner of Makoni district posed the rhetorical question: 'What better place was there for the seed of African Nationalism to germinate, grow and, as the 1960s were to display, flower?' (Ranger 1985: 151).

Mwana wevhu became a catch-phrase that was voiced during nationalist rallies as black politicians addressed the masses and resuscitated the land mythology. With nationalists evoking territorial spirits (particularly Chaminuka, Nehanda and Kaguvi, the legends of the anti-colonial First Chimurenga), the nostalgic sentiment of *kudzokera chinyakare* (a return to precolonial idyllic life) was whipped up to exhort the masses to the nationalist cause. As previously alluded to, Zimbabwean nationalism found fertile ground in the land mythology. The appropriation of this mythology would recur during the white commercial farm invasions that began in 2000. Peasants believed that they could return to their ancestral land and revive the *pasichigare* land-based life. After all, this was what their ancestors had attempted in 1896–97, fighting a land war with a retrogressive vision of driving Europeans off the land and resuscitating a disrupted life (Ranger 1967). Constructed through the emotive land mythology, the religio-cultural dimension of Zimbabwean nationalism explains why young men and women joined the armed struggle en masse to fight against the might of the Rhodesian Security Forces with only rudimentary military training and basic weapons.

Kumuka kweivhu (The rising of the soil)

The Shona belief that the land is and belongs to *vadzimu*, and that during the First Chimurenga the iconic religious figures Nehanda and Kaguvi were slain by the British in defence of their land and sovereignty gave rise in Shona folklore to the construction of the inspirational myths *tora gidi uzvitonge* (take the gun and liberate yourself) and *mapfupa angu achamuka* (my bones shall rise). The latter is said to derive from Nehanda: as she faced the guillotine moments before her execution, Nehanda told her tormentors that after her death her bones would rise. This prophecy meant that being an ancestor (and a territorial spirit), and thus embodying the land that the white man had seized, the land was feeling the pain and embarrassment of being oppressed and would turn against its oppressors. The living people, the *vana vevhu*, with their ancestors as symbols of their land, would eventually rise against the white settlers, demanding the restoration of their birthright. The white settlers were blamed for all the unprecedented misfortunes that afflicted the land. For instance, the rinderpest outbreak, which killed thousands of cattle in 1895–96, and swarms of locusts that devoured crops were attributed to the white settlers who did not understand the ritualised Shona land ecology and in the process had violated the land. The folk song '*Mapfupa achamuka*' (Bones shall rise) is an articulation and celebration of this myth:

L: *Mapfupa achamuka uyai titambe ngoma yababa*	The bones will rise; come let us dance to our father's tune
R: *Uya titambe*	Come let us dance
L: *Nehanda wakafa uyai titambe ngoma yababa*	Nehanda died; come let us dance to our father's tune

This myth introduces another dimension, that of *ngozi*, the avenging spirit, which also contributes to the conceptualisation of Zimbabwe's land struggles. In Shona religious belief, *kumuka kweakafa* – the rising of a dead person – is not a positive thing. Rather, it is synonymous with a deceased person's aggrieved spirit coming back to haunt the living in a relentless quest for justice for wrongs done to the deceased person when he or she was alive. This means that the spirits of Nehanda and Kaguvi, and all the Shona people executed during the First Chimurenga for fighting against the colonisation of their land, are aggrieved spirits, *ngozis*, coming back to haunt white settlers and to seek redress for their lost land.

Interpreted from the perspective of land mythology, the three land wars, or Chimurengas, have a strong *ngozi* motif. The wronged Shona spirits were avenging white injustice over land. From this analysis emerges another key aspect of the Shona land mythology: how the land belongs to the black people. The land is said to belong to black people, and not aliens – particularly not the white man. This notion is expressed in many *chimurenga* songs, including the Born Free Crew's '*Ndatadza kukanganwa*' (I have failed to forget), the Mbare Chimurenga Choir's '*Muri musoja*' (You are a soldier) and Cde Chinx's '*Maruza imi III*'. In '*Maruza imi III*', the phrase *nyika yavatema* (the land of the blacks) is repeated four times for emphasis and in the Born Free Crew's song it appears six times, together with the closely related expression *simba kuvatenga* (power to the blacks) and *nyika yava yedu* (the land is now ours) – which all underscore the sovereignty aspect of Shona land, previously discussed.

During the Zimbabwean land invasions, songs were sung stressing this black identity of the land to challenge and force white farmers off the land. One of the songs, '*Vanhu vatema varidzi venyika*' (Black people are the owners of the land), belabours this idea in its title. In the *tora gidi uzvitonge* myth, it is said that to reclaim their land, Nehanda instructed her children to take up the same guns that the Europeans had used to acquire the land. This myth is said to originate from just before Nehanda's execution and idea of the land as sovereignty is enshrined in the myth. In 1973, speaking through a medium, the spirit of Nehanda is said to have instructed in categorical terms that 'upon gaining independence land had to be taken from the white settlers, redistributed and administered according to the precolonial philosophy of territorial management' (Sadomba 2011: 123). Many popular songs incorporate this myth and several have the word 'gun' in their titles – '*tora gidi*' ('take the gun') or merely '*gidi*' ('gun').[16] One such song that narrates the myth is the ZANLA Choir's Chimurenga wartime song '*Mbuya Nehanda kufa vachitaura shuwa*' ('Grandmother Nehanda died telling the truth'):[17]

L: *Mbuya Nehanda kufa vachitaura shuwa*	Mbuya Nehanda died telling the truth
L + R: *Kuti zvino ndosiye nyika*	That now I leave this land
Shoko rimwe ravakatiudza tora gidi uzvitonge	One message she told us, take the gun and liberate yourself
L: *Wasara kuhondo*	You are left behind in joining the war
L + R: *Vakamhanya-mhanya nemasango*	They ran throughout the forests
Vakatora andieya kuti ruzhinji ruzvitonge	They took the anti-aircraft weapons so that the masses can rule themselves

The *tora gidi uzvitonge* myth is clearly a nationalist construction because in the song it is also attributed to slain nationalists, like ZANU-PF National Chairman Herbert Chitepo, who was killed in 1975 in Lusaka, Zambia. And Sadomba argues that the death of Chitepo (and

Mozambique's independence in June of the same year) had 'a mobilising effect on Zimbabwe's liberation war', as it 'triggered a mass exodus of mostly young pupils and students to Mozambique to join the war' (Sadomba 2011: 20). The Born Free Crew's *'Chishuwo chamagamba'* (The wish of the fallen heroes) reconstructs the desire to take up arms, as exhorted by Nehanda and the slain freedom fighters:

L: *Ndochaiva chishuvo chaNehanda*	That was Nehanda's wish
R: *Tora gidi*	Take a gun
L: *Ndochaiva chishuwo chamagamba*	That was the wish of the heroes and heroines
Mombe nevhu zvose vamupamba	He has been deprived of both cattle and land
Akanzwa izwi raNehanda richiti:	He heard the voice of Nehanda saying:
Tora gidi uzvitonge, kurwira	'Take the gun and rule yourself, to fight
ivhu renhaka yako	for your land, your heritage
Tora gidi uzvitonge Zimbabwe	Take your gun and rule Zimbabwe
Zimbabwe nyika yedu sevatema'	Zimbabwe our country as blacks'

Notice how in this song Nehanda's instruction is presented as a voice projected to every Shona person whose cattle and land have been taken, persuading them *kurwira ivhu renhaka yako* – 'to fight for your land, your heritage'. This voice evokes the voice of Mwari in the shrines of the Matopos Hills – a voice that did not speak through a human medium but could be heard in the trees, caves and rocks (see Daneel 1970 and Ranger 1999). Again note how the central motifs of Shona land mythology are embodied in the song – ancestors, land as *'nhaka'* (inherited wealth), sovereignty and the black identity of land. The *tora gidi uzvitonge* and the *mapfupa angu achamuka* (discussed earlier) are therefore coterminous myths: they overlap and heeding the first leads to the second. By believing and accepting the first, a person is transformed into 'rising bones', i.e. he will be a fighter for the land, as the Born Free Crew's song *'Ndatadza kukanganwa'* (I cannot forget) expresses:

L: *Asi shungu dzaNehanda dzazadziswa*	But Nehanda's strong wish has been fulfilled
Mapfupa ake akamuka muzimbaremabwe	Her bones have risen in the house of stones

These were talismanic myths because, as pointed out earlier, thousands of young men and women left school to join the struggle, believing that they were Nehanda's 'bones', and by implication the land that had risen. In ZANLA's anthem *'Mwoyo wangu watsidza kufira Zimbabwe'* (My heart has vowed to die for Zimbabwe), another interesting dimension of the two myths is communicated in the line *'Kudzimara pfumo rangu ramutsa Zimbabwe'* (until my spear has resurrected Zimbabwe). This implies that colonisation and the alienation of land led to the 'death' of the land. In the context of the Second Chimurenga, the *pfumo* (spear), used in this song as a metaphor for the modern gun, is said to restore life to the dead land by resurrecting it (*kumutsa*). The resurrection connotation in the *mapfupa angu achamuka* myth becomes clear, while the *pfumo* represents the *tora gidi uzvitonge* myth. The way these myths are anchored in religion and their impact on the war also explains why Shona spirit mediums, including that of Nehanda, were believed to support the Second Chimurenga, sometimes against traditional chiefs who had become the colonial government's civil servants. Spirit mediums knew that without land their status and respect would never be restored.

Together, the myths have given rise to the construction of another land myth – *Zimbabwe ndeye ropa* (Zimbabwe is [of] blood). For the Shona people to heed the *tora gidi uzvitonge* and become the rising bones entailed sacrificing their lives for the return of lost land. Since the First Chimurenga, blood had been shed in wars over land – the blood of Nehanda and Kaguvi, and all the First Chimurenga fallen heroes and heroines, and the blood of the guerrillas and peasants who fought in the Second Chimurenga. Like the *mapfupa angu achamuka* and the *tora gidi uzvitonge* myths, the *Zimbabwe ndeye ropa* myth is a folkloric construction appropriated to serve the nationalist agenda of an armed struggle to free the land. The folk song '*Zimbabwe ndeyeropa*' (Zimbabwe is [of] blood) immortalises this myth:

L: *Ndeyeropa ndeyeropa ndey-eropa ramadzibaba*	It is of the blood, it is of the blood, it is of the blood of the fathers
R: *Zimbabwe yedu ndeyeropa*	Our Zimbabwe is of blood

A great deal of pro-ZANU-PF songs composed to promote its fast-track land-reform programme justify state land seizure by invoking this myth. The Hatcliffe Chimurenga Choir song '*Zimbabwe yakauya neropa*' (Zimbabwe came through blood[shed]) is a good example:

L: *Hona Zimbabwe, Zimbabwe, Zimbabwe*	See Zimbabwe, Zimbabwe, Zimbabwe
R: *Zimbabwe, Zimbabwe, Zimbabwe yakauya neropa*	Zimbabwe, Zimbabwe, Zimbabwe came through blood
L: *Hona paChimoio paNyadzoia zvinorwadza*	See at Chimoio, at Nyadzoia, it is painful

ZANLA's military bases at Nyadzoia (Mozambique) and Chimoio were attacked by Rhodesian forces in August 1976 and November 1977. The raids, which killed thousands of guerrillas and refugees, are mentioned in the song not only to raise sympathy with ZANU-PF's land agenda, but also to link blood with land. In the Mbare Chimurenga Choir song '*Muri musoja*' (You are a soldier), the loss of blood at Chimoio is described as *paChimoio pane dhamhu reropa revana* (at Chimoio there is a dam [full] of the blood of children). Linking the Chimoio blood with the *mapfupa achamuka* myth, Agrippah Mutambara, a former guerrilla who survived the attack, tells why the struggle went on despite ZANLA's devastating loss after the Chimoio attack:

A comrade and comradeship is the resilient spirit that resides in the body ... The enemy, no matter how strong, can destroy the body but not, and never, the spirit. It is precisely for this reason that Mbuya Nehanda prophesied that her 'bones' would rise to continue the struggle. 'Bones' was a prophetic reference to the undying revolutionary spirit that would find other human forms to reside in and prosecute the struggle until final victory. (Mutambara 2008: 87)

The blood-is-land or land-is-blood philosophy is the central theme in ZANLA's previously cited anthem, in which a guerrilla articulates his or her resolve to die to liberate the land:

Mwoyo wangu watsidza kufira Zimbabwe	My heart has vowed to die for Zimbabwe
Mumakomo nemunzizi ndichararamo	In the mountains and rivers I will sleep
Kudzimara pfumo rangu ramutsa Zimbabwe	Until my spear has resurrected Zimbabwe
Rufu rwangu ruchava rweZimbabwe	My death shall belong to Zimbabwe (Sadomba 2011: 139)[18]

Another song, '*Ndinofunga nezveropa*' (I think about blood [that was shed]), makes the same point more explicitly:

Ndinofunga nezveropa rakadeuka	I think about the blood that was spilt
Rakadeuka kusunungura masi yemuZimbabwe	That was spilt to liberate Zimbabwe's masses
Ropa iri rakakosha zvikuru	This blood is very important (Sadomba 2011: 139)

Although land reform was carried out two decades after independence, the land-is-blood myth is invoked to link the land-reform programme with the First and Second Chimurengas, hence the statist reference to this programme as the Third Chimurenga.

Shona mythology and land reform in the postcolonial period

During the liberation war, peasants, guerrillas and nationalist leaders seemed to have been united by the Shona land mythology. However, independence exposed the fallacy behind nationalist leaders' wartime promises of land. Tied by the Lancaster House constitution of 1979, which outlawed land reform within the first ten years of Zimbabwe's independence, save for government land acquisition, guided by the 'willing buyer, willing seller' doctrine, the new government's land policy was at odds with the popular peasant imagination of free, unrestricted occupation of land. The (uneducated) peasants had literally believed in the nationalists' promise of repossessing the white-owned land and redistributing it to the peasants – a promise on which guerrilla politicisation of the peasants during the war had been built. In fact, as myth-making went, peasants were to live freely on any land of their choice and resuscitate the idyllic *pasichigare* life. They had been made to believe that independence would enable them *kudzokera chinyakare* (to return to the ritually regulated traditional life of the pre-European era. They had been told that after the war they would no longer 'live like this in the mountains. You must go and live in the valleys on the white farms' (Kriger 1992: 229).

Thomas Mapfumo's 1980 hit, '*Chiruzevha chauya*' ([Our] traditional life has returned) poignantly captured peasant land expectations and the anticipated traditional life that they believed land repossession would bring. Norma J. Kriger (1992: 229) rightly points out that many peasants 'had understood guerrilla promises of "free living" to mean that they could select whatever land they wanted, and farm free of any [official] rules and regulations'. Albeit naively, many peasants went to fulfil this promise, convinced that, as they had been told during the war, they were going to repossess the land of their ancestors. In the early 1980s they occupied many white-owned farms, particularly those abandoned by white farmers during the war. However, to their shock, they were forcibly evicted as armed police and soldiers descended on them, destroying their shelters and driving them out of the farms they had occupied. They had no choice but to return confused and despondent.

Meanwhile, the new independent government told the people that if they wanted land, they should join the resettlement schemes it had introduced in the 1980s. Generally, peasants resented the new government's land policies. They felt that resettlement land had no security of tenure and they could be removed from the land 'at the whim of a government official' (Kriger 1992: 229). Clearly, the black government's land policies were not in harmony with the people's anticipation of free land repossession and unregulated land use. Peasants were not in favour of government's involvement in the way they dealt with land. They felt that they had greatly suffered in the colonial period, during which they had been forced to pay taxes, implement soil-conservation measures and destock. So, many people who accepted the government's resettlement schemes did so because they offered some form of rehabilitation – they had nowhere else to go, having been displaced by the war.

A political and economic crisis started to emerge in the late 1990s as the demand for land escalated and the economic performance of the country greatly slowed down under the International Monetary Fund and World Bank's economic structural adjustment programme. This forced the ZANU-PF government, now in great fear of losing political power to the rising opposition party, the Movement for Democratic Change, to shift its land policies and align them with the people who had closely worked with spirit mediums during the war – the war veterans and guerrilla peasants. There can therefore be little or no debate over the argument that the 2000 land invasions are a triumph of the popular Shona land mythology that the peasants so fervently continued to believe in, irrespective of the nationalist leaders' inconsistent land policies.

The peasants' yearning for the freedom to occupy land and enjoy 'free living' was somewhat achieved in 2000. Their unrestricted occupation of white-owned farms took the form of what is known as *jambanja* – a Shona term that means a sort of violent anarchy. The peasants were allowed to invade white commercial farms first in June 1998 and then on a large scale from 2000. These actions resulted in the controversial land reform that stands today. This time, the land myths of the liberation, which had united the nationalist leaders, peasants and guerrillas, were officially backed by the authorities, and neither the police nor the army were called upon to evict the peasants and war veterans occupying white commercial farms all over the country.

Mugabe supported the peasants' and former guerrillas' farm invasions, describing them as 'occupations', and not 'invasions'. He argued that Africans cannot 'invade' but only 'occupy' the land that had always been theirs – property their ancestors had bequeathed to them. The farm invasions were quickly dubbed a fast-track land-reform programme and politically christened as the Third Chimurenga. The use of the term 'Chimurenga' in reference to the land reform meant that the Shona land mythology had been officially accepted as the framework and basis for mobilising Zimbabweans to support the land seizures. The powerful influence of the mythology is seen in the fact that, although the land reform was carried out two decades after independence, the mythology still greatly evoked people's imagination about land, leading to the countrywide land invasions.

As stated earlier, popular songs were among the most effective ways of transmitting through the media and other communication channels the emotive Shona mythological land beliefs – *mwana wevhu* (child of the soil); *mapfupa angu achamuka* (my bones will rise); *tora gidi uzvitonge* (take the gun and liberate yourself); *Zimbabwe ndeyeropa* (the land is blood); *ivhu inhaka yevatema* (land is the black people's heritage). The Mbare Chimurenga Choir song '*Hatibve muno*' (We will not vacate [this land]); Cde Chinx's '*Maruza imi III*' (You have lost for the third time); the Hatcliffe Chimurenga Choir's '*Zimbabwe yakauya neropa*' ('Zimbabwe came through [the loss of much] blood'); Tafara-Mabvuku Chimurenga Choir's '*Negidi*' (By the gun), and countless other songs besides, were composed to express these Shona land myths.

Despite the initial *jambanja*-style land invasions, which, according to Scoones *et al.* (2010: 190) 'has come to define the land reform in Zimbabwe', the government has attempted to introduce a sense of order in the invaded farms, subdividing them into plots for peasant resettlement. The allocation of land falls broadly into two types of schemes, the A1 and A2 models, the former being assigned for small plots and the latter for large-scale commercial farming. By 2008, 145 775 families had been allocated land under the A1 model and 16 386 for the A2 pattern (Scoones *et al.* 2010: 7). To ensure that the new land owners adhere to cultural practices relating to land use, their properties have been put under the jurisdiction of traditional chiefs, who enforce, for example, the observance of the *chisi* day and outlaw the felling of trees. However, during the *jambanja* period, which continued up to about 2008, war veterans and peasants wantonly destroyed the environment. While preparing land for farming, they cut down trees and burnt grass, as they considered themselves to have been in the vanguard of farm invasions. In desperate need of political support in the 2002 presidential elections, the 2005 parliamentary elections, and the 2008 and 2013 harmonised elections, Mugabe's government danced to the whims of the peasants and war veterans, and left them to do as they pleased.

However, in the final analysis it is clear that the popular land imagination drawn from Shona mythology has greatly shaped Zimbabwe's recent land reform. Although a return to the traditional life of pre-European times was not possible, the repossession of land has been possible. There appears to have been a compromise between traditional Shona and modern attitudes towards land management. In resettled areas, besides the continuing role of traditional chiefs in dealing with religious and cultural issues related to land, the new farmers are now market-oriented. They grow crops such as tobacco, wheat, vegetables, soya beans and maize, and venture into cattle ranching, poultry, bee-keeping, etc., using modern methods of farming guided by the Ministry of Lands and Agriculture.

As illustrated through the study of popular songs, Shona is by and large a land-based nature-culture. There is an intricate and intimate relationship between the Shona people and the land, a relationship that is regulated by a system of beliefs that constitutes what I have termed a 'Shona land mythology'. This mythology is the most important pillar of Shona religion.

Although constructed and expressed through many modes of expression, because of their mobilising and unifying effect, popular songs have been the most appropriated medium for reconstructing, communicating and popularising Shona land mythology. The *mwana wevhu* myth is at the centre of this mythology, as it spells out who owns the land, and how it should be managed and bequeathed. It conceptualises land as an embodiment of the ancestors and land as belonging to the ancestors' living descendants, who are called *vana vevhu*. Other key tenets of the mythology, formulated especially during the colonial period – which include the *mapfupa angu achamuka* and the *tora gidi uzvitonge* myths; *chimurenga* as land wars; land as *ropa* (blood) and land as *nhaka yevatema* (black person's heritage) – are all intertextualised in Shona nationalist songs. The total dependence of Shona cultural life on land meant that the European colonisation of Zimbabwe precipitated not only the death of the land, but also the land-centred culture that sprang from it. The religious beliefs and taboos regarding the ecological management of land were shattered, in the process severing the peaceful bond between land and people.

I have argued that the Chimurenga land wars of Zimbabwean nationalism and the 2000 land invasions of white-owned farms were an attempt to restore the historical land–human relationship of precolonial Shona society. Clearly, it is difficult to imagine how the nationalist agenda could have found grass-roots support and, above all, united the Shona people from different regions and other Zimbabwean ethnic groups in the absence of the land mythology. Historically and today, Shona land mythology has been one of ZANU-PF's most influential sources of legitimisation and hegemony.

References

Bourdillon, Michael F. C. 'The cults of Dzivaguru and Karuva amongst the northeastern Shona peoples', in Matthew J. Schofeleers (ed.), *Guardians of the Land: Essays on Central African Territorial Cults*. Gweru: Mambo Press, 1979.

Bourdillon, Michael F. C. *The Shona Peoples: An Ethnography of the Contemporary Shona, with Specific Reference to Their Religion*. Gweru: Mambo Press, 1987.

Bremmer, Jan. 'What is a Greek myth?', in Jan Bremmer (ed.), *Interpretations of Greek Mythology*. London: Routledge, 1987.

Csapo, Eric. *Theories of Mythology*. London: Blackwell, 2005.

Daneel, Marthinus L. *The God of the Matopos*. The Hague: Mouton & Co, 1970.

Hirsch, E. D. Jr, Kett, Joseph F. and Trefil, James. *The Dictionary of Cultural Literacy*. Boston: Houghton Mifflin, 1988.

Hodza, Aaron C. and Fortune, George. *Shona Praise Poetry*. Oxford: Clarendon Press, 1979.

Hubacek, Klaus and Van den Bergh, Jeroen C. J. M. *The Role of Land in Economic Theory*. Interim report IR-02-037. International Institute for Applied Systems Analysis, 2002: 1–54, www.iiasa.ac.at.

Jackson, Joanne B and Steiner, Frederick R. 'Human ecology for land-use planning'. *Urban Ecology* 9 (1985): 177–194.
Kirk, G. S. *The Nature of Greek Myths*. Harmondsworth: Penguin, 1974.
Kriger, Norma J. *Zimbabwe's Guerrilla War: Peasant Voices*. Cambridge: Cambridge University Press, 1992.
Lan, David. *Guns and Rains: Guerrillas and Spirit-Mediums in Zimbabwe*. London: James Currey, 1985.
Leach, Edmund R. *Political Systems of Highland Burma: A Study of Kachin Social Structure*. London: Athlone Press, 1954.
Musiyiwa, Mickias. 'Gender, ritual and politics in Shona brother-sister narratives'. *Sonkofa: A Journal of African Children's and Young Adult Literature* 10 (2011): 16–23.
Mutambara, Agrippah. *Chimoio Attack*. Harare: Department of Information and Publicity, 2008.
Ong, Walter J. *Orality and Literacy: The Technologising of the Word*. London: Routledge, 1982.
Pfukwa, Charles. 'Black September *et al*: Chimurenga songs as historical narratives in the Zimbabwean Liberation War.' *MUZIKI: Journal of Music Research in Africa* 5, 1 (2008): 30–61.
Pongweni, Alec J. C. *Songs that Won the Liberation War*. Harare: College Press, 1982.
Posselt, F. W. T. *Fables of the Veld*, London: Oxford University Press, 1929.
Ranger, Terrence O. *Revolt in Southern Rhodesia, 1896–97: A Study in African Resistance*. London: Heinemann, 1967.
Ranger, Terrence O. *Peasant Consciousness and Guerrilla War in Zimbabwe: A Comparative Study*. London: James Currey, 1985.
Ranger, Terrence O. *Voices from the Rocks: Nature, Culture and History in the Matopos Hills of Zimbabwe*. Harare: Baobab, 1999.
Rappaport, R. A. 'Regulation of environmental relations among a New Guinea people', in A. P. Vadya (ed.), *Environment and Cultural Behavior*. New York: The Natural History Press, 1969.
Sadomba, Zvakanyorwa W. *War Veterans in Zimbabwe's Revolution: Challenging Neo-colonialism and Settler and International Capital*. London: James Currey, 2011.
Schofeleers, Matthew J. 'Introduction', in Matthew J. Schofeleers (ed.), *Guardians of the Land: Essays on Central African Territorial Cults*. Gweru: Mambo Press, 1978.
Scoones, Ian, Marongwe, Nelson, Mavedzenge, Blasio et al. *Zimbabwe's Land Reform: Myths and Realities*. London: James Currey, 2010.
Taringa, Nisbert. 'How environmental is African traditional religion?' *Exchange* 35, 2 (2006): 191–214.

Discography

Born Free Crew. 'Chishuwo chamagamba.' *Get Connected*. Gramma Records, 2010.
Born Free Crew. '*Ndatadza kukanganwa.*' *Get Connected*. Gramma Records, 2010.
Chimbetu, Simon. '*Zimbabwe iyoyi*'. *Lullaby*. Gramma Records, 1998.
Chinx, Cde. '*Maruza imi III.*' *Hondo Yeminda Volume 2*. Shed Studios, 2001.
Chinx, Cde '*Tinotenda midzimu mukuru.*' *Hondo Yeminda Volume 2*. Shed Studios, 2001.
Hatcliffe Chimurenga Choir. '*Zimbabwe yakauya neropa.*' *Zimbabwe Yakauya Neropa*. Metro Studios, 2011.
Mapfumo, Thomas. '*Chiruzevha chauya.*' *Greatest Hits*. Gramma Records, 1992.
Mbare Chimurenga Choir. '*Hatibve muno.*' *Simukai Tiverengane*. Gramma Records, 2011.
Tafara-Mabvuku Chimurenga Choir. '*Negidi.*' *Baba Tinotenda*. Gramma Records,

Chapter 3

THE ENVIRONMENT AS SIGNIFICANT OTHER: THE GREEN NATURE OF SHONA INDIGENOUS RELIGION

JACOB MAPARA

Renhasi rapfuura, remangwana rinozihwa naNyadenga.
(Today has passed, but tomorrow's events are known only by the Heavenly One.)

The Shona expression above is a classic example of how religion has always played a central role in Africa's existence – even when people go to sleep, they talk to their Creator. Every occurrence, no matter how small, has a religious ritual or ceremony attached to it. This expression indicates the depth of African religiosity. Although people may not recite these words as a prayer, they are nevertheless an admission that they leave everything in the hands of their Creator. The statement '*Renhasi rapfuura ...*' captures the belief that the Creator (in Shona, Musiki or Musikavanhu) takes care of each of their living days. These words, even though uttered in an environment that, in the sense of Western Christianity some time ago may not have been considered as religious by most denominations, go a long way to underscoring the reality about Africans – that they are a religious people.

Since early colonial perceptions about Africa as backward and savage, the world has moved on and has embraced the continent. As a result of growing religious dialogue and respect for other people's religious beliefs and practices, hegemonic European cultural practices are on the wane. Most people in Europe and the Americas have come to appreciate that African cultures do not need to be taught to respect nature from Europe.

This chapter examines what Shona indigenous religion says about nature and why it qualifies as a 'green religion'. I argue that it is a religion based on practice, as opposed to a green religion based on preaching.

The nature of African indigenous religions

African indigenous religions are deliberately given this nomenclature because they are religions that are largely indigenous to Africa and are founded on African soil, although some have been exported to the diaspora through the slave trade. These religions are handed down from one generation to another; they are also part and parcel of African life. They are an amalgamation of religions that pre-date Christianity and Islam. Therefore, they entail religious practices that are founded on millennia of accumulated wisdom and experiences, and act as guides for good moral behaviour and ethical environmental practices – all done for the common good.

It is essential to point out that the word 'indigenous' is used in the term 'African indigenous religion' because it refers to

> a religion and culture that [are] based on the life of the Africans. This pattern of life has been handed on from their forefathers from generation to generation. Its mode of worship, articles of faith, materials used for worship in temples, shrines and holy places are all from the African local environment. (Shishima: 50)

Even though the title of Shishima's work contains the term 'traditional religion', this quotation is still an apt definition of the nature of African indigenous religions, and the word 'traditional' can be substituted for 'indigenous'.

African indigenous religions are also adaptive. Although Shishima (50) claims that the tools used to practise indigenous religion came from Africa, many African indigenous religions now incorporate Western items, such as the blue-and-white or black-and-white cloaks called *machira emidzimu* (cloths for the ancestral spirits), which are used by the Shona. This means that African indigenous religions are mutable, dispelling the notion that they are stuck in the past.

African indigenous religions filter through to all facets of life – political, economic, social and educational. They are not religions to which one is converted, but rather into which one is born (Mbiti 1990: 3). The principles and practices of African indigenous religions are learnt through practical examples and passed down from one generation to another. It is also important to note that most insights into African indigenous religions are learnt through artistic expressions, such as myths, folk tales, proverbs and other creative forms.

The central principle of African indigenous religions is the importance of all life forms. This is why these religions can be considered biocentric – in other words, their doctrines include the necessity to preserve life. Although some African indigenous religions practised human sacrifice, most of them did not. (There is, however, a literary example of a human sacrifice in Chinua Achebe's *Things Fall Apart*, when Okonkwo sacrifices Ikemefuna.) There was also animal sacrifice for ritual purposes and, even today, some people still practise this. Although the sanctity of life is highly prized, there are instances of religions where life can be destroyed. This only happens, however, when it is necessary for the greater good – to prevent starvation or when the destruction of one life will lead to the preservation of many more. The Shona believe that it is better for one person to die than for the whole family or clan to die. This is never undertaken for the purpose of bloody sport or trophy collecting. In this respect, African indigenous religions can be called green religions.

The Shona people and their languages

The term 'Shona' is the name given collectively to a group who speak related dialects of the southern Bantoid languages, who are found in eastern Botswana, central and eastern Zimbabwe, the Manica and Sofala provinces of Mozambique, and southern Zambia. The related dialects that they speak are Kalanga (spoken in western Zimbabwe and eastern Botswana, which has for a long time been considered a separate language from Shona); Manyika (spoken in Zimbabwe and Mozambique); Teve (treated as a separate language in Mozambique, but as a sub-dialect of Manyika in Zimbabwe); Ndau (a dialect in Zimbabwe but a separate language in Mozambique); Korekore; and Zezuru. Barwe and Hwesa, which to the untrained ear sound very much like Budya, a variation of Korekore, are also considered Shona, although Doke, in his *Report on the Unification of the Shona Dialects* (1930), did not accept them as such.

The term 'Shona' as a reference to this group is problematic because it has only existed officially since 1931 after linguist Clement Doke's development of a unified writing system for related dialects spoken in what was then known as Mashonaland. Before Doke's 1931 report, Karanga had been used by some writers as a collective term since the days when the Shona-speaking people were in contact with the Portuguese. The last such usage was probably in Francisque Marconnes's elaborate book titled *A Grammar of Central Karanga: The Language of Old Monomotapa as at Present Spoken in Central Mashonaland, Southern Rhodesia* (1931). Doke formally recommended the official use of the collective term 'Shona' for the clusters of sub-dialects that he had identified in his comprehensive survey, and had grouped under the terms Zezuru, Karanga, Korekore, Manyika and Ndau (Chimhundu 2005: 29).

Therefore, the term 'Shona' is a linguistic coinage that refers to a grouping of people who speak related language variations that are highly mutually intelligible. The term was accepted by the colonial Rhodesian government, so, in a way, it is a political construct because outsiders who wielded political power imposed the name on this grouping of related dialects. It is important to note that the term 'Shona' was never used by the speakers of these south central Bantu languages to describe themselves before 1931. The term '*amaTshona*' (those who disappear) had been used, however, by the Ndebele under Mzilikazi, king of Matabeleland, to refer to the people who are today called Shona because they disappeared into caves and mountains. Hence, the name 'Shona' is not a self-description, but was ascribed by the Ndebele to a grouping of people, and was later linguistically consolidated by the colonial power. The Ndebele had political and military power in what is today western Zimbabwe. Mudenge (1988) believes the people now called Shona arrived in Zimbabwe during the late Iron Age from the Shaba region (in what is now the Democratic Republic of the Congo), or from north of the Zambezi or from the Great Lakes region of East Africa. This claim is also advanced by David Beach (1984) and Aenias Chigwedere (1980). Mudenge (1988: 21) remarks: '… it would appear that the term *Karanga* is also the historic name of most of the people known today as the Shona in Zimbabwe'.

In addition to language, two other main features are common to the Shona. The first is their use of totems, especially of living animals, whether land or aquatic, and the second is a common indigenous religion. They believe in ancestral spirits (*midzimu*), who are intermediaries between themselves and the Creator, Mwari, also known as Nyadenga (the Heavenly One). Nyadenga is also an ancestral spirit and the arch-ancestor, hence the name given to Nyadenga, Mudzimu Mukuru (the chief ancestor). To the Shona, Nyadenga is too remote, so their day-to-day activities are governed and directed by their ancestral spirits.

The Shona also believe there are other spirits, which can be spiteful and malicious, called *mashavi* (alien spirits). The *mashavi* are the spirits of deceased non-relatives and other animate beings that are not necessarily human. The *midzimu* and *mashavi* give guidance on how humans are to live with one another and the environment. *Midzimu* and *mashavi* also advise people on how they are supposed to derive benefit from nature and warn of the consequences of non-compliance with their guidance. The role of the *midzimu* and *mashavi* therefore underscores the fact that Shona indigenous religion can be called a green religion. Shona culture is a political, social and religious reality, and the use of common religious practices, based on *midzimu* and *mashavi*, corroborates this reality.

What is a green religion?
The term 'green religion' is difficult to define. It has close affinities with natural religions and so-called dark green religions.[1] Bron Taylor, in *A Green Future for Religion?*, suggests that 'nature religion' is a term

that is used as a common umbrella expression to refer to religious perceptions and practices characterised by a great reverence or respect for nature, and which consider the destruction of nature as a desecrating act (Taylor 2004: 995). Taylor also notes that adherents of natural religions often describe feelings of belonging and connection to the earth. They perceive themselves as bound to and dependent on the earth's living systems.

Taylor (2004) also states that a green religion is one that sees positive interaction with nature as a religious obligation (as opposed to an aesthetic or extrinsic one). Dark green religion, on the other hand, is the acknowledgement that nature is sacred and has intrinsic worth. Subsequently, nature should be revered and regarded as holy. The terms 'greening of religion' and 'religious environmentalism' have also been used to describe green religion.

Gary Stearman (in *Green Religion*) discusses the possible origins of green religion. Commenting on the rise of the green-religion movement in the US, he states:

> We've watched the recent philosophical and religious greening of America with amazement, as it condemns the release of chemical by-products of various kinds. In particular, it reviles our carbon-based economy, based as it is on the use of coal and natural gas. (Stearman 2012)

Stearman (2012) observes that some people view green religion as a belief that has arisen as a result of global warming. Stearman does not see a difference between nature religion and green religion. Quoting Romans 1:25 ('Who changed the truth of God into a lie, and worshipped and served the creature more than the Creator, who is blessed forever'), Stearman underlines his point that taking good care of the environment is as good as worshipping it.

Further insight into the possible origins of green religion is given by Mark Stoll (2001: 412), who quotes Murray Bookchin's keynote address in 1987 to the second National Green Gathering. Here Stoll unleashed an attack on two influential groups of environmental radicals, Earth First!

and the Deep Ecologists. Stoll argues in later publications that deep ecology was a product of the influence of Eastern spiritual cults combined with Disneyland- and Hollywood-style fantasies, and that the proponents of Deep Ecology and the Earth First! were mystifying nature. He views these groups as anti-humanity – in other words, reducing humanity to the level of other animal species. To Bookchin, green religion is nothing more than an attempt to give nature the status of a deity.

Peter Illyn (2011: 47) argues that, according to Taylor's definition, dark green religion 'considers nature to be sacred, imbued with intrinsic value, and worthy of reverent care'. Illyn states that, according to this definition, Taylor practises dark green religion. Although Illyn does not claim to be a practitioner of green religion, he 'propose[s] that dark green Christianity is historically relevant, biblical and theologically appropriate, and increasingly urgent in today's global ecological degradation' (Illyn 2011: 47–48). Even though he professes to be a Christian, Illyn, in fact, is a green-religion practitioner. This is evident because his religion is a response to problems like global warming and natural disasters (e.g. unprecedented floods and heavy snowfalls), which traditional Christian denominations have not been interested in. In fact, Illyn is the founder of a Christian environmental organisation, Restoring Eden (Illyn 2011: 48).

In light of what Taylor, Stearman and Illyn observe about religion, nature and the environment, it is apparent that what they refer to as green religion is an attempt by sections of the Christian community to be pro-nature, and to help raise awareness of and minimise the effects of global warming. Taylor (2004: 992–1000; 2008: 90–100) goes further and lumps other world religions into the group of green religions. Although his attempt is plausible, the current writer is of the view that the term 'green religion' should be used only with reference to religious movements that have had a recent reawakening, in that they have not always embraced humanity's stewardship over the earth. Only after realising the dangers of global warming have such movements chosen to abandon, or in some instances moderate, their greed, which derives from the misconception that humanity is to have dominion over everything on earth.

The preceding paragraph attaches a negative connotation to the concept of green religion. This concept emerges through the discussion of recent interpretations of the Bible, which are seen to be reactive to a situation that earlier interpretations created. This is unfortunate because the term 'green religion' is positively conceived. For example, Shona indigenous religion is a green religion, since the question of changing interpretations of a text does not arise. Furthermore, although the concept of green religion may be a recent one, the phenomenon goes back several millennia in the case of African indigenous religions, as the practices and rituals associated with African indigenous religions have always promoted a healthy relationship between people and nature.

It is important to point out here that Shona indigenous-religious practices make it difficult to differentiate them from animism, whereby believers attribute a living soul to plants, inanimate objects and natural phenomena. Animism entails the belief in a supernatural power that is considered to organise and animate the material universe. In a way, the green nature of Shona indigenous religion is anchored in animism.

What qualifies Shona indigenous religion as a green religion is discussed in the following section. In this religion, inanimate objects and animate life forms assume a religious significance because they are perceived as making manifest the will and pronunciations of God. Since the environment and animals are seen as an expression of the Supreme Being, the religion may be described as a green religion.

The green nature of Shona indigenous religion

Shona indigenous religion is anchored in a belief in ancestral spirits, *mashavi* and other religious figures, such as mermaids and mermen. These spirits are associated with certain regions and sites, like trees, groves, wetlands and pools. Fig trees and groves that have fig trees are considered sacred because they are places of worship. Consequently, the fig tree is not supposed to be cut down. Local spirit mediums must be consulted before certain wetlands may be cultivated. People are not supposed to swim or bathe in pools believed to be the abode of merfolk. It is apparent that these religious practices were meant to sustain life for the benefit of both humanity and fauna. The same is true of wetlands. If these are disturbed, water shortages and flooding will ensue, it is believed, as wetlands act as sponges during periods of heavy rainfall. Such practices ensured that humanity was safe from nature, which at times can be ruthless.

These beliefs used elements of folk wisdom, such as taboos, in their execution. Gelfand, in *Growing Up in Shona Society* (1979), describes taboos as 'avoidance' rules. Gelfand groups these rules into six categories – living in the correct way; successful pregnancy; avoiding danger; good behaviour; healthy living; and religious teachings. All taboos are influenced by religion and the consequence of disobeying them is punishment by ancestral spirits. The vast numbers of Shona taboos are all linked to how people should interact with the environment and what will happen if they do not.

Totem animals are an important element of Shona taboos. People are not allowed to eat the flesh of their totem animal. If they do, it is believed that they will lose their teeth. So, in the past, instead of killing the totem animal, hunters would treat the animal as their kin. Fellow hunters would also avoid killing the animal as a sign of sympathy.

Similarly, there are taboos that relate to the conservation of forests that focus on rules concerning debarking trees. The consequence of violating the taboo of debarking the whole tree was that one would make the ancestral spirits angry. Likewise, violating the taboo of removing the remaining bark of a tree that has been debarked on one side meant that one could expect to skin the back of the mother of the one who would have removed the bark in the first place. This was seen as a cruel and unacceptable act. These taboos existed so that trees would not die as result of having the bark removed. The reference to the potential anger of the ancestral spirits that is said to result from the violation of such taboos testifies to the reality that Shona indigenous religion is a green religion, regardless of whether the term 'green religion' is a recent development or not.

For traditional herbal-medicine practitioners, it was taboo to dig out the roots all around a plant. Rather, they were required to dig on the eastern or western side of the tree or plant. This ensured that it would not die as a result of having had all its roots pulled out. The importance of ancestral spirits in such conservation practices is captured by Anthony Cunningham (1993) in his work on African medicinal plants.

He refers to the use of the *warburgia salutaris*, or pepper bark tree, known in Shona as *muranga*. This species has many uses as a treatment for malaria, colds, chest pains, coughs, diarrhoea, muscle pains, stomach aches and general body pains. As Cunningham notes, religious observances seek to limit the overexploitation of *muranga*: 'In Zimbabwe, clearance has to be obtained from ancestral spirits before entering certain forests where *warburgia salutaris* occurs' (Cunningham 1993: 7). Although Cunningham focuses on the exploitation of herbal and medicinal plants in Africa, the reference to the ancestral spirits is an indication that Shona indigenous religion is a green religion because it is largely interested in preserving the natural environment as a benefit for humankind.

In African indigenous religions, as already observed, trees should be conserved and not felled ruthlessly. For example, to procure firewood, people are encouraged to select timber that is dry and has fallen. According to Anthony Githito (2009: 67), in the sacred Mijikenda coastal forest of Kenya, cutting down trees was banned except for cutting deadwood, a procedure where there are some variations between the local sects. For instance, there were some sacred forests that allowed women to collect dry wood from the forest floor, but not in extremely sacred sites, such as the central clearing. These practices in the Mijikenda forests are also true of some Shona groups today. In most of rural Zimbabwe, people may not cut trees for firewood, but only collect wood that has fallen. Furthermore, there are some forests, like those around Mount Nyangani, in the Nyanga district of Manicaland Province, where the Department of National Parks and Wildlife, as well as local traditional leaders, prohibit fires. This rule is vital for contemporary conservation efforts. In the early years of the Fast Track Land Reform Programme, from 2000 to about 2003, a lot of trees were felled. This may be because there were no traditional leadership structures on the former white commercial farms or because people wanted to clear land for crops. Irrespective, a lot of trees were destroyed unnecessarily (although cutting down trees is not forbidden when there is a valid reason for doing so). Something similar happened with resettled peasants during the land-reform programme on the A1 farms (small-scale farming units of about 37 hectares), which had to be cleared for farming. Often this was just a pretext for the unjustifiable felling of trees for firewood, and land was cleared where there was no subsequent planting of crops. Tobacco farmers continue to fell trees today for firewood to cure tobacco. Areas resettled as A1 farms have been incorporated under existing traditional chiefdoms, and both modern and traditional approaches to environmental management are now enforced by the chiefs.

Besides their environmental role, taboos also have a function in regulating the relationships of people with animals. This idea is aptly illustrated by the tale of Susan Guta of Nyanga. In an informal interview on 29 November 2013, Guta related the story of a person who had endured destructive baboon raids on his farm. He set traps for the baboons. He managed to capture one, which he took home and shaved its head, subsequently releasing it back into the forests. The other baboons are said to have run away, scared, from this clean-shaven baboon. The baboon kept running after the others and ultimately died of exhaustion. It is said that after the animal's death, the owner woke one day to find his crops destroyed by hundreds of baboons. The local people said that the baboons had descended on the farm to collectively avenge the death of their companion. Whether this actually happened or not is irrelevant. The moral of the story is that people should avoid being unnecessarily cruel to animals even if they have been frustrated by them.

Guta explained that, in her area, baboons are treated with respect and given the honorific name Samasango. In this name, the Shona prefix *sa-* needs to be explained for context. *Sa-* has a dual function. Firstly, it is a form of respect. (In English, Samasango would roughly translate as something along the lines of 'Mr Forest'.) The second meaning of *sa-* denotes ownership, which in this context signifies 'Owner of the Forest'. This honorific Shona name is used for baboons in the belief that it shows due respect to the animals, and otherwise, using their standard Shona name might anger them and cause them to wreak havoc on the farmland.

In the same way that observing taboos helped ensure the conservation of baboon populations, taboos were also observed during hunting, which in precolonial Zimbabwe was an important part of economic life.

Skilled hunters and fishermen were believed to have hunting and fishing spirits as guides. Before embarking on a hunting or fishing expedition, they informed their ancestral spirits and *mashavi* of their intended mission. They prayed for protection, for an abundance of quarry to give them a good supply of meat and the ability to kill as many animals as they could. There were taboos that had to be followed to guarantee the success of hunting expeditions. For example, it was taboo to kill female animals, especially those that were heavily pregnant, and if a female prey was caught the animal was supposed to be set free. It was said that killing a female animal would anger the ancestral spirits and the hunter would fail to take animals in future hunts, and would consequently lack meat and clothing. In reality, if females were killed it would affect the reproductive capacity of the herd and diminish the supply of animals needed to sustain the community. Digging pit traps was a common practice, however, that sometimes led to the capture of female animals. If the trapped females had broken legs, they could not be set free and it was then permissible to kill them. Nonetheless, the use of pit traps was strongly discouraged, as they caused injury and, at times, death of people as well as livestock. In Mutasa, in what is today Manicaland Province in eastern Zimbabwe, hunting expeditions were organised by the king (Duri and Mapara 2007). No one hunted outside the hunting season, although people were permitted to catch small animals, like rabbits and dassies. This rule had its basis in religion, but ostensibly ensured a sustainable supply of meat.

Another activity regulated by taboos is one that still helps supplement the diets of many families today, namely fishing. In the past, overfishing was a punishable offence that could result in the transgressor being expelled from his community. It was taboo to use poisons to catch fish because poisons would kill fingerlings and leave the fish spawn vulnerable. Poisons were not permissible because they polluted the water and killed other aquatic creatures, such as frogs and crabs.

It was also taboo to kill creatures that one had no use for. It was believed, for example, that one should not kill frogs. This idea is encapsulated in the Shona expression '*unouraya datya, unoridya here?*' (You kill frogs! Do you intend to eat them?). This expression is an admonition against senseless, uncalled-for killings of life forms that provide no utility. Another reason given was that killing frogs would cause water bodies to run dry. The reality is that dead frogs pollute water, another reason why it was believed they should not be killed.

Preserving human life, as well as the life of animals and the environment, is also important to the Shona. There is a health-related taboo that concerns fetching water from rivers after the first rains of the season. In most areas the chief gives the go-ahead for people to start fetching water after the first rains. Chiefs deter people from drinking the water immediately because, in a rural environment where most people use the bush system to relieve themselves, excreted human waste will have to be cleared by the first rains. The carcasses of animals that may have died in winter would also have to be cleared from rivers and streams. The very first rains of the season help alleviate these human health hazards, so the taboo safeguards lives.

Human burial grounds are held in awe by the Shona, who believe that these places are not supposed to be burnt or have trees cut down in them. The trees are believed to provide shade for the spirits of the deceased who have been laid to rest there. It is said that if trees are cut from such places, people in the area will face challenges they may find difficult to overcome. Setting the burial places of the elite alight is believed to cause droughts because royal burial places are also places of worship, where people go to pray for rains. Although these practices highlight the link between the living and the dead, what is important is that they also promote environmental conservation.

The next section discusses how Shona practices provide a good example of why African indigenous religions should be classified as pro-life religions.

African indigenous religions as pro-life religions

Although it may seem contentious to describe African indigenous religions as pro-life religions, as some entail sacrifices, especially of animals, for ritual purposes, the point is that most of these religions value all living beings. As with other religions, their pro-life approach has helped to protect and maintain biodiversity. Given contemporary thinking and debates, it is clear that African indigenous religions qualify for the label 'green religions'.

African indigenous religions have stewardship of the environment at their core and incorporate all flora and fauna into this. Unlike Western Christianity, which has only recently begun to appreciate that humanity is part of nature, African indigenous religions have always had at their centre the interdependency of all life forms (Stearman 2012). Furthermore, this shift has been a recent one in the Western world, despite warnings by, for example, Rachel Carson, who declared:

> The 'control of nature' is a phrase conceived in arrogance, born of the Neanderthal age of biology and philosophy, when it was supposed that nature exists for the convenience of man. The concepts and practices of applied entomology for the most part date from that Stone Age of science. It is our alarming misfortune that so primitive a science has armed itself with the most modern and terrible weapons, and that in turning them against the insects it has also turned them against the earth. (Carson 1960: 262–263)

The reference to entomology to Carson may appear insignificant, but to the Shona, all creatures and the bio-physical world are intricately intertwined. It is this interweaving that the Western world and its version of Christianity elided in their system as they tried to define nature. The consequences were paradoxical, in that while some saw nature as part of the heritage that God bequeathed to humanity and had to be used wisely and protected, some saw it as a resource that had to be exploited without care and concern for future generations. In fact, the situation has worsened since Carson's time. The worsened state is realised by the fact that the world has now experienced higher levels of pollution, which has led to the problem of global warming. The transformations in environmental thinking taking place in Western Christianity are reactionary, and not proactive. Most African indigenous religions, on the other hand, do not perceive nature and other life forms as deities but as creations of one Supreme Being, whom they call by different names depending on the language group, and who has delegated the stewardship of the world to ancestral spirits. Although Western Christianity has tended to view nature as there for the benefit of humanity, some scholars, like Haught, see nature as an epiphany of

God through the revelation of the earth and see the world and creation as God's handiwork (Haught 1993: 272).

In African indigenous religions, natural features, such as mountains and sacred trees and forests, are perceived as manifestations of the Creator, so their preservation is not an indication that Africans worship nature. Rather, believers and followers express their awe for the Creator of all things, living and non-living, found on earth. To give an analogy of this relationship, if a person does not look after a house that was bought for him by a close relative it is a sign of disrespect for the person who bought the present. Similarly, caring for the gift is an indication of appreciation, not worship. That is how the African sees his or her relationship with God – nature has to be protected as a sign of appreciation of the Creator, but not because the African worships nature. This deep appreciation of the environment is what qualifies African indigenous religions as green religions.

African indigenous religion among the Shona includes relying on ancestral spirits who are believed to relay people's requests and aspirations to God. This is a replication of how the Shona communicate on important family matters. In traditional Shona marriage, for example, a man needs an intermediary to provide a bridge to the bride's parents and other relatives. On the bride's side, her father's sister acts as the intermediary and answers questions on behalf of the bride. And, in a similar way in terms of Shona religious belief, no one approaches God directly.

African indigenous religions can also be called 'green religions' because they are based on practices involving the preservation of the natural environment. Although they are faith-based religions, the propagation of faith is more in practice than preaching, unlike other religions, such as Christianity and Islam. Practitioners' beliefs are not a response to environmental disasters, as is the case with green Christianity, but are part of their everyday practice. Natural disasters are interpreted as manifestations of something that has gone wrong in the relationship between the ancestral spirits, the Creator and humanity. The practitioners of indigenous religions do not interpret natural disasters as the result of humankind's impact on the environment – as the green movement does. They are, however practised in efforts to minimise or avoid environmental degradation because they have to live in harmony with nature, as nature is what nurtures them.

So far, this chapter has focused on the relationship between human beings and nature, especially other living organisms. This section focuses on how in African traditional life, the existence of human beings is also held sacred. In this context, the term 'pro-life' applies to traditional social activities intended to promote all forms of life, including those of humans, in the same way that the term is used in relation to people's sensitivity to the environment. In African indigenous religions, the connection between environmental conservation and religious practice is not debatable: the two are interwoven. This intertwining is summed up by Gumo *et al.* (2013: 525), who observe:

> African philosophy on resource utilization and environmental protection is spiritually-based. Major conservation efforts and the control of resources are influenced by this spirituality. Religious beliefs and taboo systems are at the centre of life as a whole. The African spiritual worldviews create respect for nature, reverence for hills, forests, animals, and rivers.

The importance of these words can be seen in the context of human reproduction. One of the key tenets supporting the pro-life nature of African indigenous religions is reflected in the importance placed on marriage and the act of procreation. In African indigenous religions, marriage is perceived as a unity between not only the two individuals, but also between the ancestral spirits of both their families. This explains why, in Shona traditional culture, when a man dies his wife is inherited by his young brother, cousin or nephew to ensure continuity of the family line.

The pro-life element among the Shona is also realised through traditional courtship acts known as *kuganha* or *chimhurira*. There is a traditional system that has supported Shona courtship practices based on the belief that, in some cases, the ancestral spirits are uniting or bringing together a young woman and her suitor.

Some religious customs have become embedded in certain cultural practices. Marriage, for example is perceived as more than just a social institution. It is also religious, and this religious side is realised when a married person dies. In an effort to avoid drawing the anger of the deceased, arrangements are made for the deceased's family to multiply posthumously. This is reflected among the Shona in another pro-life aspect reflected in the Shona traditions of *chimutsamapfihwa* (raising the hearth stones) and *chimutsamusha* (raising the home). The two are closely interwoven. The first was meant to continue the genealogical line of an elder sister or paternal aunt who has died. The deceased woman would be 'replaced' through marriage to the widower by a young sister or her brother's daughter. The second is when a woman fails to have children and a kinswoman of hers is brought in to have children on her behalf. Through these traditions, the clear intention is that not only should life be protected, but it should also be propagated.

In Africa most forms of life have to be protected and propagated. There is therefore also the need to realise that to control population growth in Africa is perceived as tampering with the plans of the Creator. This perception is evident in some Zimbabwean religious sects, like the Johane Marange Apostolic Church, which have embraced the Christian religion but retained certain practices, such as polygamy, which is central to African indigenous religions. The belief is that people are not equally capable of bearing children, so those who can should have as many children as they can. Another noteworthy issue is that before the advent of modern medicine, the infant mortality rate was very high – and still is in some areas owing to factors such as civil wars, poor provision of basic services and poor governance. According to some, therefore, there is no need to control population growth.

The issue of polygamy, or polygyny, as it is also known, has created polarisation between those who support it and those who oppose it – the latter being generally from outside Africa or from African urban areas. It has been noted in research that in the case of Africa, polygamy is acceptable for cultural and religious reasons influenced by adaptive functions of which climate is one (Barber 103). Some perceive polygamy as contributing significantly to the destruction of the environment by human beings, who are also considered as parasites. Among certain communities in Africa, including some Zimbabweans, a viewpoint exists that there is a need to ensure continuity of the family line or clan, and in a continent that is ravaged by conflict, misgovernance and health challenges, polygamy is seen by some as the only means to ensure that continuity. In this context, through the use of taboos, as discussed, people in Africa are traditionally taught to harvest from nature only what they need, so the parasitic tendencies that are a malaise to some in the global North are not therefore a concern in Africa. The problems wherever they occur, like those related to logging, are by outsiders who come and exploit Africa's forest resources. The problems of environmental destruction thus are not caused by increased procreation as a result of polygamy. They are caused by a lack of respect for nature.

Another factor that underscores the pro-life nature of African indigenous religion is the fact that, traditionally, abortion was taboo. Among the Shona, traditionally, anyone who wilfully terminates a pregnancy is called murderer or a witch. Labels like these indicate how much the Shona value life. Those wishing to terminate a pregnancy would be traditionally warned that they would not be able to conceive again. This warning reflects the concern that some people only manage to have one child in their lifetime. It is therefore clear that, for the Shona, human life is not seen as an environmental parasite but something to be celebrated.

With developments in modern technology, and improved medicine and healthcare, populations are getting larger and living longer than ever before, especially in the global South. It is hoped that African indigenous religions will respond to this transformation in the material environment and put more emphasis on the conservation of nature and population control.

This chapter has argued that African indigenous religions, also called African traditional religions in other circles, can be called green religions, not because the practitioners and believers worship nature but because the preservation and use of natural goods in a sustainable manner are at their core.

The major tenets of these religions are practices known as taboos, which set out rules that have to be adhered to if one is not to upset the ancestral and alien spirits, believed to provide guidance to the living. The observance of taboos has also gone a long way in promoting biodiversity in communities where these practices occur.

Another aspect discussed in this chapter is that people embrace their role as stewards of the environment through their cultural custodians, who penalise those who have gone astray. These practices have been passed down from generation to generation and this helped ensure their continued survival – especially in rural communities. Some, however, have been affected by the Christian faith and urban encroachment.

References

Achebe, C. *Things Fall Apart*. London: Heinemann Educational Books, 1958.

Barber, N. 'Explaining cross-national differences in polygyny intensity resource-defense, sex ratio, and infectious diseases.' *Cross-Cultural Research* 42, 2, (May 2008): 103–117.

Beach, D. N. *Zimbabwe before 1900*. Gweru: Mambo Press, 1984.

Carson, R. *Silent Spring*. Boston: Houghton Mifflin, 1960.

Chigwedere, A. S. *From Mutapa to Rhodes*. Salisbury: ZPH Publishers, 1980.

Chimhundu, H. 'Doke and the development of standard Shona', in C. M. Doke, *Report on The Unification of The Shona Dialects* (photographic reprint). Harare and Oslo: ALLEX Project, African Languages Research Institute and Department of Scandinavian Studies and General Literature, 2005.

Cunningham, A. B. 'African medicinal plants: Setting priorities at the interface between conservation and primary health care.' People and Plants Working Paper. Paris: UNESCO, March 1993.

Duri, F. and Mapara, J. 'Environmental awareness and management in pre-colonial Zimbabwe.' *Zimbabwe Journal of Geographical Research* 1, 2 (2007): 98–111.

Gelfand, M. *Growing up in Shona Society*. Gwelo: Mambo Press, 1979.

Githito, A. N. 'The sacred Mijikenda Kaya forests of coastal Kenya: Traditional conservation and management practices', in T. Joffroy (ed.), *Traditional Conservation Practices in Africa*. ICCROM Conservation Studies 2 UNESCO, 2009.

Gumo, S., Gisege, S. O., Raballah, E. and Ouma, C. 'Communicating African spirituality through ecology: Challenges and prospects for the 21st century.' *Religions* 3 (2012).

Haught, J. F. *Christianity and Ecology: The Promise of Nature*. New Jersey: Paulist Press, (1993): 270–285.

Illyn, P. 'Belly-button Christianity: Tribal Christians speak to today's church: An interaction with "dark green religion."' *Sacred Tribes Journal* 6, 1 (2011): 47–65.

Marconnes, F. *A Grammar of Central Karanga: The Language of Old Monomotapa as at Present Spoken in Central Mashonaland, Southern Rhodesia*. Johannesburg: Witwatersrand University Press, 1931.

Mbiti, J. *African Religions and Philosophy*. London: Heinemann Educational Books. 1990.

Mudenge, S. I. G. *A Political History of Munhumutapa c 1400–1902*. Harare: African Publishing Group, 1988.

Shishima, D. S. 'African traditional religion and culture', course guide CTH 491. Abuja: National Open University of Nigeria, http://www.nou.edu.ng/NOUN_OCL/pdf/SASS/CTH%20491%20AFRICAN%20TRADITIONAL%20RELIGION%20CULTURE.pdf.

Stearman, G. *Green Religion*, 2012, http://www.prophecyinthenews.com/green-religion.

Stoll, M. 'Green versus green: Religions, ethics, and the Bookchin-Foreman dispute.' *Environmental History* 6, 3 (July 2001): 412–427.

Taylor, B. A. 'Green future for religion?' *Futures Journal* 36 (2004): 991–1008.

Taylor, B. A. 'From the ground up: Dark green religion and the environmental future', in D. K. Swearer (ed.), *Ecology and the Environment: Perspectives from the Humanities*. Centre for the Study of World Religions/Harvard University Press, 2008.

Taylor, B. A. *Dark Green Religion: Nature Spirituality and the Planetary Future*. Berkeley, Los Angeles and London: University of California Press, 2010.

Chapter 4

ANIMAL ORAL PRAISE POETRY AND THE SAMBURU DESIRE TO SURVIVE

James Maina Wachira

Praise poetry is mainly associated with celebrating the achievements of great men. In the case of the Samburu[1] of Kenya, there is a tradition, however, of praise poetry that praises non-human animals – both the domestic livestock that they raise, as well as undomesticated animals found in their environment. This study considers the Samburu praise poems recited to undomesticated animals. The poetry, as I shall show in this chapter, is one of the means that the community employs to safeguard its survival. The Samburu's poetry quite literally ensures their continued existence by stressing the connections between human and animal life, and the environment.

To analyse how the poetry fosters the continued life of the Samburu ethnic identity, this chapter outlines the context in which the poetry is produced and provides some theoretical appraisals of the texts. The chapter then analyses three animal praise poems, each sung by different groups in the Samburu community. These poems illustrate how the community uses poetry to articulate its desire to survive. The Samburu community's desire to survive counters the temptation to view traditional cultures as static and unchanging. Through the community's orature in general, and the animal oral praise poems in particular, this chapter shows the shifts in the community's efforts to safeguard its existence.

Studies on the Samburu oral tradition have helped scholars piece together facts about the pastoral and nomadic aspects of the Samburu's way of life (Osaaji 2009: 21; Waruinge 1986: 21; Wasamba 2009: 146). Waruinge (1986: 21) observes that the Samburu community is a distinct entity, even though it is related ethnically and linguistically to the Maasai. From the oral sources, she notes that the Samburu derive their name from the Laikipiak Maasai owing to a leather bag that Samburu women carried. The word "bag", *samburie*, is the source of the name Samburu. Before adopting this name, the Samburu referred to themselves as Loiborkineji, meaning the people of the white goats (Waruinge 1986: 21).

The change of name points to a change the community embraced at some point in its history. And other examples from its past are evidence of the community's effort to adapt to new experiences in the course of its existence. The catastrophes that the community has faced include the colonial attempts to destock it, the smallpox epidemic in the second half of the 1880s and droughts that resulted in loss of livestock.

These experiences help explain why the community has learnt to deal with its challenges in innovative ways (Waruinge 1986: 21–22, 24). For example, field findings indicate how a segment of its population adopted an alternative economic activity. A section of the Samburu who were unable to restock turned to hunting and gathering. And in the 1970s, the Samburu embraced camel keeping. The Samburu had learnt from a neighbouring ethnic group, the Rendille, that camels were more capable of resisting drought than other livestock. Hence, the praises the community performs to camels, for instance, represent their efforts to address the challenges of perennial drought.

Besides representing the Samburu's readiness to accommodate innovative means to assure their survival, their poetry also serves as a vehicle for the community to vocalise certain tensions it has to contend with. An example of a tension that is negotiated through the poetry is the notion that the various social groups in the community, despite their differences, all identify themselves as Samburu. This idea of differences within the collective is emphasised by the fact that certain praise poems may be sung only by particular groups in certain contexts. For example, there is a distinction made between the descendants of the Samburu who managed to restock and those who turned to hunting and gathering. The latter are defined by the term 'Dorobo'. The word *'dorobo'* in Samburu means 'one who has nothing' or 'one who relies on gathering and hunting'. At some point in the history of the Samburu, the term denoted the poor among the community. Thus, the term came to apply to the descendants of the Samburu community who opted for an alternative economic activity after having lost their livestock. This distinction between the groups is observed in their poetry. For example, only the Dorobo Morans, or initiates, are allowed to praise rhinos. (The Moran" age group is discussed in more detail later when the hunting song to the rhino is discussed.)

By the time that this fieldwork was carried out among the Samburu, the Dorobo respondents had acquired some livestock but they still identified themselves as Dorobo. The distinction is more than just a name – it encourages both groups to explore different means that allow the collective survival of the Samburu. The Dorobo, for example, are recognised for their skills in gathering honey, which they sell to the group among the Samburu who take pride in raising livestock. The Dorobo, in turn, purchase livestock from the groups that raise animals. Honey has many uses among the Samburu. It is used as food, for rituals and as a preservative. The Dorobo are also experts in hunting. For these skills, they earn the respect of, and are able to negotiate recognition from the group that raises livestock. Somehow, in the process of safeguarding this distinction, both groups contribute to the survival of the Samburu as a whole. This accounts for the community's keenness to specify the praise poems that the Dorobo compose and perform. The praise poetry entails the idea that being Samburu means having an identity that is flexible and changing, and that there needs to be a shared conception of what it means to be Samburu. Animal praises are part of what identifies different groups in the Samburu, but also of the Samburu as a whole.

In their praise poetry the Samburu make distinctions not only according to livestock ownership. There are also other aspects that impinge on how they perform praise poetry. For instance, the poetry that Samburu women use to praise a ewe differs from the poetry they use for a female goat. The differences are apparent in diction and pitch. There are also distinctions in the poetry they perform while milking a cow or a camel. Every praise poem has a specific performer and occasion, and rules that govern its performance. The praises performed to animals are one dimension of a network of poems – some of which are sung by old men, some by young men, and so on, and this whole matrix binds together humans, animals and the environment. These elements are part of a greater whole – the Samburu cosmos, as it were, and the community zealously protects this cosmos, indefatigably working to ensure its survival.

Conservation efforts are exemplified in the Samburu's praises for such animals as ostriches, rhinos and elephants. This chapter foregrounds the Dorobo praise poems to rhinos, young boys' praises to ostriches and the Talas clan's praises to elephants. These animals play a role in nature conservation and the survival of all who form part of the Samburu 'cosmos'.

Some fascinating issues that arose in the course of my research into the Samburu were the question of why the members of this community sing praise poems to animals. Of what significance are these poems? What do they say about their understanding of the world in which they live? This chapter attempts to describe and discuss the role of this poetry in shaping the Samburu cosmos. The discussion is in line with Asante Darkwa's (1986a: 134) observation that the praise poetry is an embodiment of how the Samburu make sense of their livestock, wild animals and birds, God, people, trees, grass, beliefs, wives, girlfriends and husbands, as well as serving to communicate their feelings of love, hate, misery, fear and bravery.

This chapter extends the 1994 research by Peter Amuka on oral literature and the constituents of knowledge. From Amuka's position that oral literature serves epistemological ends, this chapter builds an argument on how the community's regard for some animals as the target audience of praise allows us the space to critically analyse not only the reasons governing such perceptions, but also the discourses that emerge when a particular member of the community performs an oral praise to an animal.

The research drawn upon in this chapter goes beyond acknowledging the mere existence of animal praise poetry. It also goes further than Darkwa's affirmation that there are '... songs in praise of cows. Praises for the cattle are sung by the Moran and uncircumcised boys, who make mention of the colours, abundant milk, and good grade beef, durable hides and services provided by cows, bulls ...' (Darkwa 1986b: 133–134). Apart from affirming that the community sings praises to animals, Darkwa (1986b) does not give a single example of such a poem and does not analyse the significance of these poems. In this chapter, the aim is also to go beyond the thinking that praise poetry is restricted to domestic animals. For this reason, three praise poems to undomesticated animals are analysed in the chapter to illustrate how the Samburu use the poems to embody their desire to survive.

The analysis of animal praise poetry in this chapter also challenges a number of assumptions that exist in the study of oral cultures in general. In a chapter on panegyrics, Ruth Finnegan (1970) makes some observations about praise poetry in Africa. Drawing on examples of praise poetry from various parts of the continent, she describes the formal features of praise poetry and presents some directions for further exploration of the genre. She acknowledges that '... in Eastern and Southern Africa, cattle form a popular subject in praise poetry' (Finnegan 1970: 12). The acknowledgment of the existence of animal praises is significant, but Finnegan's study is silent on the audience of the poetry. In this chapter, I have interrogated the place of animals in the actualisation of this poetry. For the poet/performer, animals are the target audience of the poems. For Isidore Okpewho, another scholar of African oral traditions, the full impact of oral performance integrates both the oral poet and the audience. In the introduction to *The Heritage of African Poetry*, Okpewho (1985) claims that 'oral poetry achieves its forcefulness not only at the hands of the performer himself. Part of this forcefulness comes from the participation of various persons present at the scene of performance in the creative act taking place' (Okpewho 1985: 8). Clearly, Okpewho operates within a frame that encompasses only human subjects, and not animals as participants in the oral performance, as Samburu praise poetry makes evident.

Another erroneous notion that is brought to light by animal praises is the question of the impact of audience response on the oral poet. In the chapter on oral poetry in Okumba Miruka's *Encounter with Oral Literature* (Miruka 1994), the author suggests that the audience plays a major role in the performance of an oral poem. He states that the audience's role can either motivate or demoralise a performer. This observation invites an exploration of the nature of audience motivation in the performance of the praises the Samburu sing to animals. For instance, as mentioned, women perform praises to cows during milking to stimulate them to produce more milk and to make them remain calm during the process. So, the desire for a cow to remain calm is the motivator for the performance of praise to a cow during milking. In another scenario, if a goat will not suckle her kid, a woman sings a praise to her until she suckles. Once the animal complies, it would appear there is no motivation to continue performing to the animal. However, among the Samburu the performer continues to sing to the animal, even though the motivation no longer exists. Therefore, based on the research into animal praises, Miruka's idea about the nature of the audience's motivation in a performance needs re-evaluation.

Locating the Samburu

The Samburu speak KiSamburu, which is part of the Maa cluster of the eastern branch of Nilotic languages. The Samburu inhabit, but are not limited to, Samburu County, Kenya. The region lies within the arid and semi-arid lands, whose degree of aridity ranges between 85 and 100 per cent. The rainfall pattern of the area is erratic, unreliable and unevenly distributed.

The harshness of the environment in which the Samburu find themselves has encouraged a cultural response whereby survival is paramount. While rainfall and water-distribution patterns influence the grazing practices of the Samburu, they also prompt the community to devise strategies for representing and perpetuating their knowledge of how they garner the means to allow them to survive in this environment. The Earthwatch Institute notes in its 2010 report, *Samburu Communities and Wildlife: Expedition Briefing*, that the Samburu cope with their environmental context by migrating with their herds to wetter areas where more grazing is available for their animals. The report indicates that the region has low vegetation because the sandy and clay soils in the area are fragile and unstable. The environment is also notorious for frequent and persistent droughts, which often last for several months and sometimes even years.

In Samburu County, the nomadic Samburu pastoralists, their livestock and 'wild' animals live in proximity. I use the term 'wild' with caution because, among the Samburu, the concept of animals that are wild, in the sense of undomesticated and having no relationship with human beings, is lacking. The community believes that there was a time when humans and animals interacted closely but that these intimate relations were disrupted by the bad behaviour of human beings. In Samburu lore, this separation occurred when a woman kept sending an elephant back into the forest to replace the large logs he had brought with smaller ones. The elephant, dismayed at the woman's ingratitude, wandered off to keep his own company and the other animals followed suit, fearing similar treatment at the hands of human beings.

As far as domesticated animals are concerned, the community believes that some animals – like cows, for example – are a gift from God. Ideas about domestication are vague, but they seem to be linked more with the community's association with other human communities than with animals. There are stories of inter-community interaction in relation to the keeping of goats, donkeys and camels. Some of the animals that are found in Samburu County play a role in the survival of the community. The roles these animals play find expression in the poetry the community composes. The poems describe and engage the animals, and highlight the significance of the plants on which the community relies. The poetry explicitly acknowledges the roles of the animals and plants in ensuring human survival. The community's ingenuity in preserving and disseminating this knowledge of animals and plants is what allows it to endure. This chapter therefore treats the poetry as an aesthetic expression in which the Samburu vocalise, firstly, their awareness of the specific animals and plants that inhabit their environment, and, secondly, the need to conserve the environment. The poetry thus articulates the Samburu's desire to survive.

Some notes on the collection of the Samburu poetic texts

To collect the poetic texts of the Samburu, I relied on the fieldwork approaches of Dan Ben Amos (1975) and Johannes Fabian (1990). In 'Folklore in African society', Amos underscores the centrality of sensitivity to the context within which:

> ... forms of folklore, as speakers delineate and recognize them, have cultural symbolic meanings. Texts framed into genres and performed in socially defined communicative situations acquire significance beyond the literal meanings of their constituent words. The defining features of forms and genres are hence capable of communicating in society the symbolic meanings of a category of expressions, or of a single subject. (Amos 1975: 165)

According to this, it is clearly necessary therefore to 'read' these poetic texts in a wider context as a form of folklore to uncover the symbolic meanings in the oral praise poems.

According to Fabian (1990), the broader significance of such oral genres may be determined through the performance of the genres. Furthermore, the texts themselves contain clues that direct enquiry about their significance. In addition to my fieldwork, which allowed the texts to be collected, further fieldwork was imperative to generate additional texts in the form of what Fabian (1990: 6) terms 'narratives about the community' and narratives about the significance of the genre within the community. Performance is central to both these endeavours, in the sense that only through the embedded 'performance' of the researcher, which Fabian (1990: 6) terms 'performative ethnography', can an encompassing cultural knowledge of the community be acquired. In addition, it is only through the performance of the poetic texts that their wider role and importance may be determined. In this regard, Fabian suggests that the members of a community have an embodied knowledge of their practices, which may not be articulated in the context of a specific communicative event. Fabian expresses this dimension of 'performative ethnography' as follows:

> Members of all societies have ... certain kinds of knowledge and skills, which they can convey directly or indirectly ... What has

not been given sufficient consideration is that about large areas and important aspects of culture no one, not even the native, has information that can simply be called up and expressed in discursive statements. This sort of knowledge can be ... made present only through action, enactment, or performance. (Fabian 1990: 6)

The performance of the praise poems about animals at Wamba, in Samburu County, informed my understanding of the Samburu effort to survive.

The poems

This section of the chapter presents transcriptions of three praise poems, each performed to a different animal: the 'Lebarta', which is the song of the boys to the ostrich; the Talas song to elephants; and the song of the Dorobo for the rhino. For each praise poem, I shall contextualise the performance of the poem, clarify who generally sings these poems and analyse the content.

Lebarta – song of the boys to the ostrich
Aa ooyiayooia sidai elopir oorok
Mikitara lngatunyo
Ooyiayooia abayie maiteki
Sidai elopir oorok
Mikitara lngatunyo
Oolale-olaleoyia-ooyiohoo-ololale
Sidai-iai naitore nkuo
Near sipen engatuny
Oyia-oolale
Sidai-iai elopir oorok
Mikitara lngatunyo
Oolale-olaleoyia iyioyiohoo oolale

Aa ooyiayooia black-feathered ostrich
May a lioness kill you
Ooyiayooia I left unexpectedly
Oolale-olaleoyia-ooyiohoo-ololale

> Black-feathered ostrich
> May a lioness kill you
> Oolale-olaleoyia-ooyiohoo-ololale
> My dear ostrich that watches over its chicks
> And kills cubs
> Oyia-oolale
> Black-feathered ostrich
> May a lioness kill you
> Oolale-olaleoyia iyioyiohoo oolale

The 'Lebarta' is a kind of praise poem, which, although addressed to a male ostrich, is in fact a prayer uttered by a male initiate to a lioness. Through the poem, the initiate prays that the lioness will kill the ostrich, so that the initiate may obtain the ostrich's black feathers. During the circumcision season for boys, candidates are required to be attired in the black feathers of the male ostrich. It is necessary for the lioness to kill the ostrich because the Samburu do not allow the eating of ostrich meat or the killing of ostriches. A paradox therefore presents itself: the boy is required to be dressed in black ostrich feathers, the insignia of the initiate, but is simultaneously forbidden from killing the bird. Curiously, this paradox is the basis of understanding how the Samburu rely on the environment as a 'resource' for products it needs, while at the same time they participate in conserving the environment that sustains the community.

Killing male ostriches for their feathers does not occur every time a circumcision is carried out. The feathers are preserved, so that they can be used by several generations of initiates, a way of conserving the precious resource. If the number of initiates exceeds the number of feathers available, sharing of feathers is not permitted and initiates then have to search for feathers. Nevertheless, killing an ostrich is strictly forbidden. Ostrich feathers are used rather than the hide of some other animal because, in an environment that has scarce resources, animal life is easily depleted.

The fact that a lioness and an ostrich should be mentioned in the same poem roused my curiosity to enquire further into the ecological context of the performance of this praise poem. The poem is chanted in areas where the initiates know they are likely to find ostriches and lionesses together. I discovered that the Samburu believe that lionesses can understand human language. They also believe that, on hearing the prayer, the lioness will obey the imprecations of the initiate and kill the ostrich. Members of the community explained that once a lioness has killed an ostrich, it eats its share of the meat and leaves the rest for scavenging animals. Since the Samburu who raise livestock do not eat game, the carcass is left unused, except for the feathers, which they collect.

The wording of the praise poem, 'My dear ostrich that watches over its chicks/ And kills cubs', also reveals an understanding of animal behaviour. According to the community, a lioness that is nursing cubs is more likely to kill an animal that is a threat to the survival of its cubs. The initiates take advantage of this practical knowledge when searching for their feathers. They will identify the lair of a nursing lioness where ostriches have been seen in the vicinity. The initiates then chant the praise poem as they move towards a male ostrich in the direction of the lair where there are cubs, in the hope that, threatened by the advancing ostrich, the lioness will pounce on it and kill it. The lines of the poem also reveal an intimate knowledge of ostrich behaviour. In the same way that lionesses are highly protective of their cubs, ostriches are also protective of their chicks, which are preyed upon by lion cubs. Ostriches therefore sometimes kill the cubs. The Samburu believe that, on hearing the poem, ostriches go into hiding, which makes it all the more vital for the lions to hunt them down.

The Talas songs for elephants

There are two Samburu groups who sing to elephants – the Talas and the Dorobo. The Talas clan are herders; the Dorobo are hunter-gatherers. Among the Samburu, livestock keeping is associated with prestige, since livestock keepers are self-reliant. Mzee John Lodikir, an elderly Dorobo from Golgotim village, in Wamba, who was an important informant in my research, explained that the Dorobo turned to hunting and gathering as an expression of the group's desire to earn dignity from the Samburu, who were livestock owners. Over time, the Dorobo acquired extensive hunting and gathering skills. They hunted elephants and rhinos, among others. Their hunting techniques are beyond the scope of this chapter. They also gathered honey, and fruits that grow in the forest. While hunting, the Dorobo recite praise poetry, but it was impossible for a number of reasons to obtain a recording or transcript of all their praise poems. So here I discuss the Talas song for elephants, and in the next section the Dorobo hunting song for rhinos will be analysed.

Elephants are quite numerous throughout Samburu County, so members of the Talas community perform praise poems to elephants to warn against possible human–animal conflict. The Talas argue that elephants are their brothers and sisters. They claim the ability to communicate with elephants. They perform poems in the presence of one elephant, several elephants or in the absence of elephants. Even if there are no elephants present, they believe that the power of the praise poem will reach a desired elephant or herd. In most cases, through this poem, they plead with elephants to spare either people or the trees and shrubs that grow in the county. Singing a poem to elephants to restrain them from destroying the vegetation is a privilege of the Talas. Only men and women from this clan are allowed to perform it, and they recite the poem when the community is in need of their service.

In a few simple lines the poem portrays a network of human, animal and environmental relationships. It identifies the plants that support the existence of the Samburu and their livestock. It also celebrates the elements by rejoicing at the arrival of the rainy season, which is considered from the perspective of both humans and animals. The lines of the poem chastise elephants for what is seen as their environmentally destructive behaviour. Finally, the poem delivers social criticism by comparing the conduct of elephants with that of wealthy members of the community who have grown powerful.

Talas song to elephants
Ooyioe aeoyia kejo lparakuo kirisio mikirisio ooyioe aeoyia
Olodarulai mijo nkoperia narumu ooyioe aeoyia
Sapuki moduo near ltepes leai aeyia
Olodarulai ooyioe mijo nkopelia narumu ooyioe aeoyia
Kejo lparakuo ooyioe
Mikirisio kirisio ooyioe aeoyia
Kore tenesha ooyioe near ltepes leai ooyioe aeoyia.

Ooyioe aeoyia you say we are equal and we are not
Olodarulai, do not say *nkoperia* is what is carried by floods aeoyia
The big-dunged elephant that breaks down acacia trees of God ooyioe aeoyia
Olodarulai ooyioe do not say *nkoperia* is what is carried by floods ooyioe aeoyia
The wealthy (in livestock) say ooyioe we are not equal while we are equal ooyioe aeoyia
While we are equal ooyioe aeoyia
When it rains ooyioe it destroys acacia trees of God ooyioe aeoyia.

The praise poem refers to plants that the Samburu find useful and warns against dismissing certain plants as useless. The acacia tree is highly valued among the Samburu for its various uses. The leaves are used as fodder for animals and the tree produces pods, which provide sustenance for humans and animals at times of drought. Acacia bark is used by members of the community to strap together their goods when migrating. According to Mzee Leadekai, a respected elder in Ngilai, who acted as my host and who at the time worked as a warden for the Kenya Wildlife Service, the thorns of the acacia tree are used as a kind of surgical instrument for piercing the ears of Samburu women. The acacia tree also provides the best charcoal and firewood, and this is used for roasting meat at important rituals.

As the acacia is so valuable to the community, a sense of greed for this tree is admonished in the poem by reminding listeners and singers that, ultimately, all acacia trees belong to God. But the poem also makes mention of plants that many Samburu regard as useless. There is a reference to a kind of grass, *nkoperia*, that grows along the banks of gullies. During the rainy season, this grass is often swept away by floods. The poem implicitly compares the elephant and the destructive flood with humans, who may destroy vegetation for which they have no immediate use. The praise poem reminds members of the Samburu community that all cover vegetation is valuable to their existence in the arid county and that their livestock feed on all vegetation.

This warning in artistic form is captured in the cautionary tone that runs through the entire poem. The admonition against the destruction of acacia is derived from the community's knowledge of acacia and elephants. One element of this knowledge is contained in the lines, 'The big-dunged elephant that breaks down acacia trees of God/ ooyioe aeoyia/ Olodarulai ooyioe do not say *nkoperia* is what is carried by/ floods ooyioe aeoyia'. Through onomatopoeia, these lines capture the trumpeting of the elephants, which is interpreted as the animal's way of celebrating the coming of the rains. (Elephants trumpet mainly in the rainy season.)

The lines also mention elephant dung. Elephant faeces are remarkable to the Samburu because of their sheer size – larger than the faeces of any other animal they know. But the words also point to another fact. According to members of the community, elephant dung contains 'unbroken' acacia thorns and specks of splintered acacia wood, the indigestible remains of the elephant's consumption of acacia, which they eat for its leaves. The Samburu view the elephant as capable of destroying all acacia trees. This sense of the animal's total destructive power is underscored by the fact that the acacia thorns pass through the digestive tract of the elephant without causing physical harm. This evidence of the might of the elephant persuades the community to sing to them, imploring them to spare the environment to which the Samburu (and the elephants) owe their existence. Furthermore, the acacia trees produce their pods in the rainy season. These pods are dried and stored for consumption by humans and animals in times of scarcity, highlighting another reason why the acacia is indispensable, and why the poems must be sung to the elephants in a plea to limit their consumption and spare the acacia trees.

But the poem appeals to the elephants in another way, also linked to their massive size and movement. The poem observes that at times in the rainy season Samburu County experiences flooding, which carries away some plants and trees, like the acacia. The elephants are regarded ambivalently. Like the flood, which brings rain, but also causes damage, the elephants sometimes destroy the acacia trees, so they are likened to the flood. Embedded in the poem is the notion that the survival of the acacia spells the survival of the Samburu. Nevertheless, the community does not call for the elephants to be killed. Instead, it calls upon the talent of a section of its members to sing poems of praise to the elephants, persuading them to be restrained. In this way, an attempt is made to resolve human–animal conflict and as a result the community guarantees its existence.

The poem also delivers a subtle form of social warning. There is a critical, cautionary tone in the poem that urges the community to reflect on itself and its relationship with animals and plants. When elephants move from one location to another, they tend to break and uproot trees, much like floods that destroy everything in their course. But the elephants are also indirectly compared with members of the community who have metaphorically grown big through the wealth represented by their livestock. The wealth of these individuals is represented by the image of 'the big-dunged elephant', which destroys acacia trees and other plants. The poem implicitly warns against dismissing anything on its appearance. Just as no plants are useless, even though they may appear to be so, likewise, no animals or human beings are useless. The lines of the poem resonate with the idea of how it is important to preserve all life through the conservation of the environment of the Samburu.

The Dorobo song for the rhino

This poem is sung by Dorobo Morans and relates most of what the Dorobo know about the rhino. Moranhood is a highly revered institution, which ceases only when the elders allow a given number of Morans to be married to create room for the admission of a new set of Morans.[2] According to Mzee Lodikir and Mzee Solomon Lenaipa, chief of Ngilai location, the Dorobo staple diet consists of game, honey and fruit. However, rhino, elephant and buffalo are hunted only when fruits are not in season. The meat of large animals is preserved in honey for consumption during times of drought. The Dorobo therefore preserve meat and supplement it with a diet of fruit and honey to ensure they do not deplete the animal life of the area.

Song of the Dorobo for the rhino
Ee ninye neyieyio,
Eepae neiyia nkutuk nalaria
Kore ake paye elo ayiaya neisarashie

Ooyie pae nemelau netii ninye laria
Aa-haa-haa lmurani
Tenieru nkweny
Oo-hoo mati nkang
Ltolut ooyie pae neti ltam nkoriong
Nimikinshilari iyie lmurani Loolkunet
Oo-hoo-marti aai naliki yioo
Hoo lmurani loolkunet
Ooyioo-hoo loshuku nkawuo
Kulutoo siat kimbartu laingoni lemony
Oohoo-oyiepae, nairoshi esupuko
Ohoo-oo-oyiepae nadokutuk epapa
Karujaki ntunatun tanaku etepero
Oohoo-ooyiepae nairoshi epapa
Keirukrukore laria nelo
Nemeliki netii tankaraki laria

Yes! She is the one of my father,
Oo yes, whose mouth looks like that of oxpecker,
Wherever she goes to search for a little food
Oo yes! She never fails the oxpecker
Aa-haa-haa warrior
When birds sing in their nests
Oo-hoo when I am not at home
Oo yes! And the bags are on the back
And I, the warrior of Loolkunet, cannot fear it
Oo-hoo it is the rough terrain that shows us
Hoo warrior of Loolkunet
Ooyioo-hoo we carry along bows and arrows
As we crawl under the grass trying to spot where the rhino bull is
Oo yes! The heavy one of the forest
Oo yes! The red-mouthed of my father
I target it when it has slept
Oo-yes! The heavy one of the forest
Ever accompanied by an oxpecker
You never fail to recognise it because of an oxpecker.

This praise poem, sung during rhino hunts, reveals much about the Dorobo's relationship with and knowledge of the rhino. The physical features of the rhino are emphasised by the description the 'heavy one of the forest'. The performer presents detailed knowledge gleaned from being close to the animal in the observation that its mouth is red – like the beak of the oxpecker, the rhino's symbiotic partner. The poem reveals that the presence of a rhino may be deduced from the presence of oxpeckers, which are often found where rhinos graze because the birds feed on ticks found on rhinos' backs and on insects disturbed by their movement. Hence, the sight of an oxpecker or the sound of its chirping help direct the hunter to his prey. The oxpecker is indispensable to a successful rhino hunt.

The praise poem indicates the time of the hunt, which usually begins in the early morning, when the birds start to sing: 'When birds sing in their nests/ Oo-hoo when I am not at home/ Oo yes! And the bags are on the back'. The poem also records the travails of rhino hunting, which takes place away from the security of home. Hunters need to be careful to survive the challenges of the rough terrain and the lack of hiding places. The equipment used for the hunt is also identified: 'We carry along bows and arrows.' The difficulties and dangers of rhino hunting are also specified in the lines 'As we crawl under the grass trying to spot where the rhino bull is/ I target it when it has slept.' The hunters have to be vigilant and crawl and camouflage themselves. It is also evident that the hunt calls for bravery: 'And I, the warrior of Loolkunet, cannot fear it.'

The poem as a whole captures the many challenges faced by the community and its determination to overcome them.

Oral praise poems and conservation

As mentioned, the Samburu employ praise poetry to preserve knowledge and information about the environment, and record the manner in which the community benefits from that knowledge. The social performance of the poetry implies that it is part of the community's system of knowledge. The poetry can therefore be regarded as a form of discourse that provides an index of social practices of the Samburu. The language of the poetry embodies the experiences of the Samburu from their own perspective.

If one considers the practices surrounding the singing of the young men's poem for the ostrich, the following conclusions may be drawn. The initiates are faced with the daunting task of obtaining the feathers of an ostrich without being permitted to kill ostriches. To satisfy that requirement while fulfilling the transition to the next stage in their life journey, the initiates employ a strategy that encompasses the values they need to cultivate in their development into men. The initiates need to be tactful and resourceful in getting a lioness to kill the ostrich. Tact and ingenuity are qualities that the community values and wishes to perpetuate. Furthermore, the search for feathers is a marker of the initiate's preparedness to join the institution of Moranhood. The qualities of discipline, patience and control are considered virtuous for the Moran. These qualities are all tested in this rite of passage. The Moran cannot impetuously kill the ostrich. Instead, he has to exercise patience and persuasiveness to get the lioness to make the kill. The poem also emphasises the power of prayer in conservation. Belief in the power of prayer is so strong among the Samburu that they believe their imprecations can make the lion kill the ostrich. Importantly, the feathers are not used only once – they are preserved for generations. Therefore, through the practice of performance and the taboos associated with them, the population of ostriches is preserved in Samburu County.

The need to conserve the environment is also displayed when the members of the Talas clan plead in their poem to the elephant to spare vegetation, in particular the acacia. As discussed above, acacia trees are vital to the life of the Samburu and the animals in their environment. The dedicated section of the community charged with communicating with the elephants sing to them, beseeching them to spare the environment for the sake of their mutual survival.

The striking feature of the Dorobo poem to the rhino is that it reveals the ritual hunters' intimate knowledge of the life of animals. The two groups make use of special talents. For instance, the Dorobo are revered for their hunting skills. They know which animals to hunt and which to avoid. They do not hunt a pregnant animal or sick animal, or one that is lactating. Once they make a kill, they preserve the meat and ensure that it is shared by as many members of the community as possible.

Through their poetry, the Samburu impart to the younger members of the community the need to conserve their environment. This way, the community nurtures the desire to survive. The community knows that its survival is also dependent on the survival of the flora and fauna in the environment.

Every performance of the praise poems is an opportunity to disseminate knowledge about the Samburu's determination to survive. The poems are therefore part of an instruction process: the performers are the instructors and other members of the community are the learners. In this community, special regard is given to those with particular talents. For instance, the Talas clan is credited for having a special talent that stops elephants from destroying plants, and the community harnesses such talents to help ensure its collective survival.

The community recognises that all flora and fauna are a necessary part of the environment. This is evident in the way in which the Samburu refer to animals. I do not recall the community ever applying the adjective 'wild' in reference to any of the animals in their environment. In their culture, the Samburu use various terms to distinguish categories of animals, but 'wild' is not one of them. There are words that signify livestock and other animals that they raise, such as dogs and chickens, and words that designate herbivores and carnivorous animals. But there is no word for wild animal. This is because, for the Samburu, all animals are creatures whose cooperation they need. The community underlines its knowledge of its habitat and what the environment provides for its survival.

The Samburu's concern for their ongoing existence makes sense when one considers the challenges posed by the way they are increasingly incorporated into the modern Kenyan nation and drawn into global networks of exchange. For instance, the Samburu are found in more than one county. These administrative units have defined boundaries and administration headquarters. Each headquarters requires administrative infrastructure, which involves cutting down trees and confining undomesticated animals in national reserves and conservancies, in what were once wilderness areas. This process is interfering with the traditional lifestyle of the Samburu, with the result that the community is gradually losing aspects of its traditional culture.

Artificial boundaries are created between them and the animals, so the community is forced to accept new forms of relationships with undomesticated animals and they become indoctrinated to view them as wild. The animals that their culture has been conserving are now turned into national resources.

Creating national reserves and conservancies, and the exclusive hotels that are built inside them, largely serves the economic interest of the state, and not the Samburu community. Such places have become out of bounds and the community cannot carry on with its traditional life there. As a result, the Samburu knowledge of the flora and fauna may fail to be passed on to future generations. Despite this, however, the community still finds reason to emphasise to the initiation candidates – irrespective of whether they are at school or have converted to new religions – the need to conserve ostriches. The young initiates have to participate in the performance of Lebarta. In the process, they learn to appreciate not only the beauty of their natural environment, but also its resources. This way, the Samburu continue to pass on the need to conserve resources for the sustainability of the community.

References

Amos, Dan Ben. 'Folklore in African society.' *Research in African Literatures* 6, 2 (1975): 165–198.

Amuka, Peter Sumba Okayo. 'On oral literature and the constituents of knowledge', in Jane Nandwa, Okoth Okombo, Wanjiku Mukabi Kabira and Austin Bukenya (eds), *Understanding Oral Literature*. Nairobi: University of Nairobi Press, 1994: 4–15.

Darkwa, Asante. 'Music and dance.' Samburu District: Socio-cultural profile. Nairobi: Government of Kenya, Ministry of Planning and National Development, and the University of Nairobi, Institute of African Studies, 1986a: 133–139.

Darkwa, Asante. 'Recreation.' Samburu District: Socio-cultural profile (eds) Gideon Were and Joseph W. Ssennyonga. Government of Kenya, Ministry of Planning and National Development, and the University of Nairobi, Institute of African Studies, 1986b: 140–144.

Earthwatch Institute, *Samburu Communities and Wildlife: Expedition Briefing 2010*, http://earthwatch.org/briefings/samburu_briefing.pdf, 2010.

Fabian, Johannes. *Power and Performance: Ethnographic Explorations through Proverbial Wisdom and Theater in Shaba, Zaire*. Wisconsin: University of Wisconsin Press, 1990.

Finnegan, Ruth. 'Panegyric', in Ruth Finnegan, *Oral Literature in Africa*. Ibadan: Oxford University Press, 1970.

Miruka, Okumba. *Encounter with Oral Literature*. Nairobi: East African Educational Publishers, 1994.

Okpewho, Isidore. *The Heritage of African Poetry: An Anthology of Oral and Written Poetry*. London: Longman, 1985.

Osaaji, Mumia G. 'Subversion of patriachal ideology: A case study of Magdalene, a woman oral narrative performer from the Samburu of Kenya.' *Research in African Literatures* 40, 1 (2009): 19–26.

'The heritage of African poetry: Introduction,' in Isidore Okpewho (ed.), *The Heritage of African Poetry: An Anthology of Oral and Written Poetry*. Longman, 1985: 3–33.

Waruinge, Marjory. 'History.' Samburu District: Socio-Cultural Profile. Nairobi: Government of Kenya, Ministry of Planning and National Development, and the University of Nairobi, Institute of African Studies, 1986.

Wasamba, Peter. 'The concept of heroism in Samburu Moran ethos.' *Journal of African Cultural Studies* 21, 2 (December 2009): 145–158.

Chapter 5

THE PARADOXES OF VOLUNTOURISM: STRATEGIC VISUAL TROPES OF THE NATURAL ON SOUTH AFRICAN VOLUNTOURISM WEBSITES

REINIER J. M. VRIEND

The world of voluntourism is a peculiar one. To present how the concept of the natural is used in the promotion of voluntourism, and to discuss the paradoxes and dilemmas of this usage, I shall introduce voluntourism's global dynamic by means of a parable.

Imagine you are John. John lives in a hypothetical neighbourhood made up of well-built, attractive houses. In this suburb, all is well and everyone seems happy with his or her home. But the edge of happiness is visible. On the border of the neighbourhood is a wall. John is able to look over the wall and make out the contours of life on the other side. It seems that people are building houses, but the view is somewhat obscured. From his secure and comfortable house, John starts getting the feeling that the people on the other side of the wall might need some help constructing their homes. But the wall itself also draws John's attention. The wall is mesmerising, as it is covered with notices and posters and advertisements and billboards. John gets the feeling that he ought to go over to help the people on the other side to build their houses. It is not clear whether his feelings spring from within himself or whether he has been led by the captivating notices on the wall. Whatever the case, John decides that he will go to the other side of the wall to offer his assistance.

Quite unexpectedly, John gets stopped at the wall by a man who looks well meaning. He warns John about some of the difficulties and dangers for someone like John on the other side, and explains that he can help John achieve his aims. Even though John could quite easily have gone through the gate to the other side of the wall of his own accord, he now is overtaken by caution and listens to the man. In the communication that develops, it turns out that to provide his help, the man at the gate demands that John pay him. The man explains that if John wants to help these people, then the best way would be to give them building materials. These would have to be delivered. John will probably also want to help in the construction of the homes. And, while that is happening, John would have to have access to amenities and would need to be served meals, would he not? The total cost for all the services the man offers to render is quite steep. But since John has already volunteered his services, he feels guilty about pulling out now – it would make him look small and unworthy. Also, when he enquires, he discovers that the men at all the other gates are charging pretty much the same price. So, in the end, John decides to pay up.

The story has two possible outcomes. In the best-case scenario, with a lot of luck, John will see that the ramshackle houses on the other side begin, with his help, to look much better. And he has discovered that he is getting along well with the local people and can get by without support. He has also noticed that, recently, the man at the gate has begun to arrive in a smart new car. If John is less lucky, however, he will see that, despite his well-intentioned efforts, the homes on the other side remain as run down as when he first got there. Perhaps this is because the building materials John paid for never arrived, or perhaps because he is simply not cut out for the manual labour that the work entails. What is more troubling, however, is that the people on the other side did not even feign appreciation. In fact, they were openly hostile and destroyed whatever John tried to build.

The problems John faces in this scenario may to a large degree be the consequence of the nature of the gatekeeping, whereby a small number of so-called experts regulate and dictate access to certain wares. But in the real world of voluntourism, the merchandise to which access is regulated is not goods or trade data, or even journalistic news. What is on offer, in this case, is the *act of doing good*. And this adds a specifically ethical and moral dimension to the consumerist dynamic.

This parable helps to explain a situation that is prevalent in voluntourism. John is the voluntourist; the gatekeepers are the institutions and companies that both accentuate and bridge the divide between those who care to help and those who are presented as needy. The World Wide Web plays a significant role in the gatekeeping activity. Usually, in the voluntourism context, someone is intent on helping out somewhere else a great distance away and finds that the web is the easiest way to bridge his knowledge gap. The web has myriads of websites that offer voluntourism experiences, usually on a for-profit basis. And because of the money consideration, the voluntourism activity itself becomes morally devalued.

Cases abound of unhappy voluntourists and voluntoured (the communities visited by voluntourists). Voluntourism, or voluntary work that volunteers pay to do away from home, has been on the rise in the last few decades, and South Africa is a major destination. Thousands of volunteers, usually originating from Europe and North America, decide to spend their time and money on helping others. But because a large part of the voluntourism industry is dominated by for-profit businesses, a marked clash of interests lies at the core of this global phenomenon.

In this chapter, I will develop the argument that the use of the natural as a ubiquitous theme in voluntourism's online advertising reflects the core paradoxes of the voluntourism phenomenon. Because of the monetary compensation involved, the political economics of voluntourism are controversial, and several historical imbalances that have their origins in colonialism are invoked in the practice, which makes it a key area to locate an inquiry into the role of South Africa, generally, in a globalising world.

The overwhelming presence of nature in advertising in general has been considered at length by Anders Hansen (2010). He states that advertising 'effortlessly and seamlessly draws on culturally deep-seated, ontological and taken-for-granted meanings of nature and the natural, and reworks these in ways which promote consumption, particular world views and particular identities' (Hansen 2010: 135). However, the relationship between nature and advertising has not yet been examined in the context of the online marketing of voluntourism. Since the problematic relationship between the global North[1] and southern Africa is central to voluntourism, how the theme of 'the natural' is shaped by this relationship in the advertising of this tourism niche provides fertile ground for critical exploration.

I shall set out to analyse the role that the natural world plays in online advertising of voluntourism in southern Africa,[2] considering how the visual appeal of the natural is often mobilised. In a research sample of over 100 voluntourism websites, 25 per cent of the websites' photographic material featured wild animals and 20 per cent featured recognisable nature landscapes. These are significant proportions. Yet the fact that images of the natural world should occur at all is surprising, given that most of the volunteer programmes are urban-based and often deal with humanitarian issues. If this is the case, then why is the African landscape such an important feature in online voluntourism advertising? In addressing this, my analysis includes explanations from several relevant academic fields – tourism studies, art history, postcolonial studies and development theory. The analysis will lead me to the conclusion that voluntourism's online advertising shows a true balancing act. On the one hand, voluntourism is forced to adopt the tourism industry's commercial standards of advertising photography; on the other hand, voluntourism sites strategically appropriate non-commercial discourses in an attempt to appeal to their critical demographic of customers. But before I can discuss the heart of this dilemma, I shall first introduce the concepts used in this chapter.

Let us start with the term 'voluntourism'. Although there are various definitions in current use, I describe voluntourism as travelling to a place away from one's home to do unpaid work, while paying a fee to do this. I choose to focus on paying volunteers because it is the idea of paying to be allowed to help that causes several intrinsic dilemmas. One of these dilemmas is the dominance of for-profit businesses running altruistic programmes. Another is that, because voluntourists pay, it can be an incentive for organisations to take on unnecessary labour simply for the capital that is brought in. This, in turn, allows voluntourism to become a volunteer-centred endeavour, instead of being based on the needs of the receiving communities. The full extent of these implications will become clearer as this chapter develops. However, I shall first describe how the image of nature is used strategically in the recruitment of voluntourists.

What is nature? Cultural theorist Raymond Williams (1983) is widely quoted for describing 'nature' as 'perhaps the most complex word in the language' (Williams 1983: 219). The word has come to denote so many historically and geographically specific meanings that I shall take a pragmatic approach in offering a genealogy of the different meanings of the word 'nature'. I shall first use the term to describe the representation of flora, fauna and ecological landmarks in online voluntourism advertising. We shall see that because my analysis depends on the way in which the natural is used in advertising, there will be further analysis of the ramifications of the term when it is theoretically necessary in the context of a particular discussion. This way, I draw from a wide range of specialised discourses to understand the ambivalent term 'nature'.

The object of this study concerns the visual material found in websites selling voluntourism. The visual analysis is based on a data set of over 1 000 advertisement photographs, gathered from over 100 websites offering voluntourism packages in southern Africa. These images are complemented with findings drawn from textual analysis of websites. But this primary source material is merely a starting point for the analysis. The material needs at least two more levels of context to become meaningfully addressed. For one, there is the website in which the photographic material is embedded, which is made up of other textual elements and the electronic embedding that characterises the medium. Secondly, there are wider sociocultural contexts from which representations derive (part of) their meaning. In this case, I focus on advertising, tourism, altruism, colonial history, art history and development. How these sociocultural contexts relate to the visual material is key in understanding the role that is ascribed to nature in these visual narratives. Next I shall address how these contexts are made accessible.

I have combined methodologies, so that a visual analysis of the material is complemented by a critical reading framed by theory drawn from the relevant fields mentioned above. The two methods are not presented serially, but rather the subject matter is addressed thematically. In its interplay, this approach may be termed hermeneutic. Hans-Georg Gadamer (1989) described human understanding as a process whereby a text becomes meaningful in its historical context. The text is understood as part of the 'hermeneutic circle', where the parts inform the whole, and the whole is derived from the different parts. Historical and geographic specificities are part of this circle that enables understanding. Voluntourism photography draws meaning from many historical and geographic contexts that need to be considered. Here we also enter into the discussion of what photographs might mean, which itself has a rich history. In this context, I draw on the idea of signification explicated by Stuart Hall, whose approach forms an important part of cultural studies. Hall's cultural studies takes a markedly post-structuralist approach to meaning and always brings an extra level of critique to the production and consumption of representation. Around the question of power, cultural studies seek to find how certain meanings are given weight, selected and prioritised, but also how other minority meanings may find alternative audiences (Hall 1997). This nuance will prove invaluable in my argument when it comes to explaining the paradoxes encountered in voluntourism.

Branding, representation and audience

I shall start by introducing voluntourism advertising from a tourism-studies perspective. The claim that the decision of travellers to visit a location is based on their perception of the place, rather than its geographic reality, will not raise eyebrows in tourism-studies circles. Robert Britton (1979) shows that studies on the importance of how a location is represented have been common since the 1970s. This led to an academic field that focuses on the means and practices of marketing and branding in tourism. If one pays attention to the current practice of visual advertising common in tourism in southern Africa, the prominent and often clichéd featuring of nature cannot be missed. Tourism is usually for the happy few, and voluntourism is no exception to this rule. The focus of this chapter is a type of tourism that is initiated by the tourism industry and that caters for a reasonably well-to-do clientele. Voluntourism might have started off as a non-profit sector, but currently much of the activity is carried out by for-profit businesses. It is mainly the middle class in the global North who are the clients in this form of tourism and their capacity to travel alone means they are wealthy compared with the voluntoured communities. Therefore, voluntourism is well entrenched in the commercial structures of the tourism industry.

With the rise of marketing and advertising in general through the 20th century, tourism marketing has evolved to the point where it is a central, ubiquitous part of tourism. The rise of the World Wide Web has spurred on this development. Noel Salazar (2009: 50) describes this phenomenon as 'tourismification'. He states that communities come to see themselves as destinations: 'Tourismification is a universal phenomenon and an integral element of globalisation. Global tourismification rapidly interlinks and intensifies the circulation of people, capital, images and commodities' (Salazar 2009: 50). Very few countries, cities or wildlife parks have not drawn up tourism policy documents that indicate 'strategic plans', 'core segments' and 'unique selling points', and these are matched with publicity campaigns, including websites. This has consequences for local communities, who 'often have little (economic) choice but to accept and to adapt to the tourismified identities and cultural views that are created for them' (Salazar 2009: 50). It could be claimed that this process of tourismification is aided by tourism studies. As an academic field, tourism studies is often based on social-science methodology and is closely connected with actors in the tourism business, explaining the technical and calculated way in which tourism branding takes place. In all of these developments, nature is given centre stage in the representation of southern Africa.

Branding usually appeals to uniqueness. Hence, the prominent features of a particular area are mentioned and represented in tourism branding so that they are appealing. Because of the undeniable existence of poverty on a large scale, Britton mentions that this appeal to uniqueness presents a dilemma for what he calls 'third world countries' (Britton 1979: 320). He claims such countries need to resort to 'shiny illustrations and flattering text to overcompensate for the poverty immediately evident in destination places' (Britton 1979: 320). Because the characteristics for which 'third world countries' are known are often negatively perceived in the global North – for example, widespread poverty and sparse infrastructure – the tourism industries in these countries have the choice either to ignore their social realities or to use them constructively. The use of images of nature is a strategy that accedes to the industry's 'conservatism of metropolitan tourism interests ... and the strong dependence of many states [on tourism]' (Britton 1979: 326). Imagery of flora and fauna therefore draws attention away from social problems and focuses it on the opposite: it makes the absence of infrastructure an attractive selling point.

An example of branding that does this can be found in the official website of South African Tourism, the 'agency responsible for marketing South Africa as a destination internationally and domestically' (South Africa.net 2014). In South Africa's official image of itself as a tourist destination, the category of nature becomes an important tool. On the website, there is a striking absence of reference to socio-economic problems in South Africa. The home page is set against the backdrop of Table Mountain at dusk. The text mentions culture, arts, people, nature and wildlife – the last category is especially relevant to this research. The website prominently features nature and wildlife. Listed as number 2 and number 8 on the list of reasons to visit South Africa, respectively, nature and wildlife have clearly been identified as appealing. Reading nature and wildlife against the reference to South Africa as 'cheap' (a constructive use of 'poverty'), one might infer that nature here serves as a way to draw attention to only one part of South Africa's reality, as opposed to that which is kept out of view.

Nature and the natural are by no means uncommon elements in advertising. Hansen's study shows that raised public awareness of the environment during the 1970s, 1980s and 1990s has made nature a welcome subject in advertising. This change in awareness sprang from the environmentalist movement. In environmental advertising, references to nature usually show a brand or company as 'environmentally friendly' or as 'nature's caretaker' (Hansen 2010: 141–144). I have referred to Raymond Williams's observation about the complexity and cultural specificity of the term 'nature', which translates into a need for location-specific meaning when nature is described. However, surprisingly, Hansen notices no great difference in the use of nature in advertising between East and West, pointing out that 'traditional – and well-documented – differences in views of nature may be subsumed under the homogenizing influence of globalization' (Hansen 2010: 157). The image of nature in advertising is canonised to mean 'green'. But this use of nature in advertising presents a number of paradoxes. Much of the caretaker imagery and discourse may be valuable for tourism in general, but they are belied by the negative environmental impact associated with air travel and concreted seaside destinations, as two examples.

The nature's caretaker image seems to fit voluntourism even less, because many of the core activities of voluntourism are located in the humanitarian sector. The use of nature for advertising these activities is therefore not straightforward. Some of the paradoxes have their roots in how voluntourism sets itself apart from regular tourism. From interviews I conducted with voluntourists, it became clear that they often do not see themselves as tourists. They make this distinction based on their 'usefulness'. Much more than Dean MacCannell's (1976) tourist prototype of the Westerner as an onlooker in search of the authentic behaviour the tourist prototype has come to lack, the voluntourist is primarily an 'interventionist tourist', not just meddling and shaping her/his surroundings unconsciously, but actively propagating change.

To return to the question of nature, Hansen identifies certain discourses around the use of the natural in advertising. Especially apt for voluntourism websites are those that describe nature 'as intrinsically good [... and] a guarantor of genuineness and authenticity' (Hansen 2010: 144). The claim to be 'intrinsically good' and 'authentic' is a common discourse found on voluntourism websites. Words like 'experience', 'help', 'opportunities' and 'provide' signal a claim to offer an alternative form of tourism, one that is less connected to the idea of mass consumption, and more with the idea of the inherent goodness and authenticity of nature. The trope of nature can therefore at one and the same time connote an alternative appeal to mass tourism, but fit in simultaneously with standard tourism industry-wide advertising strategies. Here we witness another voluntourism paradox. On the one hand, poverty is one of the main reasons behind the need for voluntourism but, on the other hand, depicting this poverty would clash with the image that the regular tourism industry uses to brand a country like South Africa. The dilemma that flows from this is how to imagine voluntourism acceptably, and the voluntourism industry opts for the use of an image that has already proven its worth as signifying Africa, namely the African as natural. An industry-wide standard of visual possibilities can therefore be found in a niche where one might not expect this.

Salazar's idea of tourismification seems paramount to this imagery. On the face of things, the inclusion of the natural in voluntourism advertising might seem out of place, but when seen in the light of country branding and the tight-knit propaganda machine of South African Tourism, it might be that voluntourism agencies feel the need to keep in step with the dominant destination discourse for economic reasons. To benefit from the exposure that South Africa's tourism industry generates, concessions to the industry's norm seem necessary when advertising voluntourism. One is therefore confronted with a situation where nature and wildlife tropes are over-represented in South African tourism advertising. The imagery of wild animals in an identifiable type of landscape operates as a gratuitous (because it is unrelated) signifier of voluntourism. The voluntourism reality is intrinsically less rural and more based around human need than is shown in its advertising imagery.

But conformity to the standard form of advertising that is common in the tourism industry cannot entirely explain the popularity of nature imagery. Another explanation presents itself when we consider the relationship between the geographic regions where the voluntourists and voluntoured originate. Here we find that in the history of representing Africa to the global North, nature has a long and rich past.

Misrepresentations of Africa to a Western audience are numerous and obstinate, and the natural has a central place in the constructed narratives. These historical nature narratives are founded on, and aided by, ongoing power imbalances. They are both symbolic and political. To contextualise these narratives of the natural, I will first introduce how the process of representation and signification of nature can be understood. Signification is a prickly issue because the structuralist idea that one picture contains one definite meaning has lost currency. Meanings are actually derived from the audiences' frames of reference. But these frames of reference are not just individual: sociocultural values in specific historical contexts privilege certain meanings over others. So, when people attribute to nature the meaning 'intrinsically good', for example, that meaning, even though it is drawn from photographic material, is by no means absolute or univocal. Although we see a tree, we seldom see just that. A tree can mean the actual plant but it can also symbolise an appreciation and respect for the planet's resources. These meanings are drawn from audiences' frames of reference, and these frames need closer examination. Therefore we are forced to recognise that the audience is an important factor in establishing meaning.

To understand how nature takes shape in voluntourism advertising, it is important to give attention to the context of its reception. Research shows that 90 per cent of voluntourism worldwide takes place in Africa, Latin America and Asia, and that the majority of voluntourists are not from these continents (Tourism Research and Management 2008). Most advertising for voluntourism in southern Africa is aimed at the global North, a claim that is corroborated by comparing the geotags of the websites offering voluntourism online with the physical locations of their offices. Even when organisations are based on the African continent, their websites are often hosted in Europe or North America. This suggests that the advertising functions transculturally as a depiction of Africa for and/or by the global North. When discussing the use of photography in the context of voluntourism, the importance of power in the equation is clear. The purchasable goods on offer are African, the client is typically from the global North and the seller is usually from a much more privileged position than those receiving 'help'. In this context, nature and wildlife seem prevalent as gratuitous signifiers for African reality. But this trend is not new. In the historical relationship between the southern African region and the global North, nature has always held centre stage.

The image of nature carries a lot of historical weight in the context of southern Africa. In Africa's history of ruthless colonisation by several European powers, the image of the natural has served in many instances to support Western suppression of local people and intervention in their politics. And the phenomenon of voluntourism is historical in many other ways too. The central premises of Western guilt and the moral superiority inherent in the idea of charity can be traced to the history of southern African colonisation. By identifying and essentialising Africa as one with nature through its modes of representation, Western appreciation of local culture and society was rendered increasingly impossible. The image, as we see it today on voluntourism websites, is indebted to this visual tradition, which cannot be disconnected from the imbalanced political realities of both the colonial past and the current global postcolonial power constellations. In this light, the visual representations of contemporary voluntourism advertising, aimed at a Western audience and representing the global South, can be seen as an extension of the means of representation that have developed through the history of contact between the global North and southern Africa. Although the context has changed, exoticising 'the other' is still an inherent feature in the use of the natural when portraying southern Africa. Voluntourism acts on many fronts as a current-day incarnation of Western intervention, and its advertising imagery perpetuates this.

As Hall (1992) has shown, the representation of the racial 'other' has a long history founded on the uneven power balance between Europe and the nations that were colonised from the 15th century onwards. Hall shows that by defining the non-European, the identity of the European is assumed as the naturally superior norm ('the West and the rest'). The concept of the West thus became 'both the organizing factor in a system of global power relations *and* the organizing concept or term in a whole way of thinking and speaking' (Hall 1992: 187).

Hall bases this argument on Edward Said's *Orientalism* (1978) but includes Africa in the model. The production of knowledge that the colonising powers systematically undertook was moulded in such a way as to assert symbolic power. Among the first elements of this knowledge were works of art that categorised and described local people, and flora and fauna. Although not always intended for such purposes, this art often functioned in a political way.

I briefly touched on the way that sociocultural norms privilege certain meanings over others. In defining a phenomenon, a binary opposition is bound to be constructed, and power defines which of the two is superior. During the era of colonisation, this mechanism led the West to (mis)understand the difference of 'the rest' as a sign of their inferiority, deeming everything notably 'African' as inferior to its European counterpart. Paul Landau (2002) argues that, counter to expectation, this narrow understanding of Africa has held firm in a time of subsequent decolonisation: 'Despite the forward march of scholarship on Africa from the 1930s on, the Western public today is by and large left with decontextualized vision-bites of the continent and its peoples' (Landau 2002: 5). In this context, 'nature' – as opposed to the culture of the West – became a term negatively associated with the uncivilised and wild. Even though some of these characterisations have also been described as positive traits (e.g. the African close to nature, the sexually desirable female, etc.), they derive their meaning from stereotyping: reducing a group of people to several simple characteristics and robbing them of individuality (Hall 1992: 215–216).

It is hardly surprising that, although direct colonial power has waned, previously existing thought structures and value systems have prevailed in the postcolonial era. And the binary-opposed imagery drawn from Western stereotypes is very common in advertising. The promotional website of South African Tourism, mentioned above, serves as an example: South Africa markets itself for tourist consumption as 'cheap' and 'wild'. Although the online advertising does not categorically state it, by implication it is suggested that the global North is not wild and not affordable.

In the remaining part of this chapter I investigate three different ways in which nature is used in a binary structure of meaning in online voluntourism advertising. The three examples can be seen as case studies. I draw on different theories to position these visual discourses.

Three case studies explained

Often, the natural is used as a contrasting background to the central image. As discussed above, visual material used online to advertise voluntourism shows a strong connection with styles of historical imagery. In terms of this history of visual discourse, the natural is presented as an inferior element when positioned against its counter-images that are drawn from a Western context. But since this reading is also the most obvious, I shall limit myself here. In this case, the natural receives its meaning from what southern Africa lacks. Empty landscapes are inviting to the Western voluntourist, echoing the *terra nullius* myth of a God-given empty land, a myth that recurs in colonial landscape painting. If Africans are featured, they are naturalised with the surroundings, sporting either traditional dress or the renowned 'khakis' to suggest their nativeness. This resonates with Njabulo Ndebele's observations on how African culture is presented as part of nature in safari tourism, therefore limiting the role an African tourist can play:

> [Black South Africans] experience the most damning ambiguities. They see the faceless black workers and instinctively see a reflection of themselves ... They experience cultural domination in a most intimate way. Especially when they go game viewing. It is difficult not to feel that, in the total scheme of things, perhaps they should be out there with the animals, being viewed. (Ndebele 1999: 3)

Here Ndebele is mainly referring to the racial dimensions of post-apartheid tourism. Voluntourism advertising, however, reveals a mechanism that goes beyond black or white to distinguish African from non-African. In the advertising imagery, urban leisurewear often sets the voluntourists apart from the African – whether black or white. The voluntourist is usually in the centre of the photograph, often shot from a low angle.

The character of the voluntourist within the natural narrative is similarly powerful. An air of expertise in relation to the flora and fauna is suggested. Voluntourists are positioned as people able to address a situation that requires a solution, whether it is ecological or human. From this reading, it becomes clear that nature is used as a way to perpetuate a historical misconception about the relationship between the global North and South. However, rather than being fuelled by neocolonial ill will, this perpetuation of the natural as inferior seems to persist despite the idealistic motivations referred to by the interviewees involved in voluntourism. Here we see another paradox bound up with voluntourism's moral position in general: good intentions might result in undesired outcomes. The use of nature imagery perpetuates a narrative that the voluntourism industry itself is so eager to change.

The second trope of the natural in my study is that of African nature, as opposed to African urbanity. This trope might seem to ascribe greater value to African reality than the previous discourse – but this is just on the surface. This division is also built on a devaluative mechanism whereby unspoilt nature is privileged over the complex fabric of current-day South African society. A romantic nostalgia is conjured to function as an appealing counter-image to a society fraught with numerous challenges. South African society is undeniably marked with numerous social issues. Some of these are worldwide problems, like poverty and unemployment, whereas others have a reputation for being more typical of South Africa – the high HIV infection rate being the most prominent of them (Whelehan 2009). Many of the voluntourism projects in southern Africa focus their efforts on these social issues: feeding programmes in schools, medical assistance, orphanage relief, teaching, children's sports and leisure, and so on. Voluntourism therefore seems dependent on, and springs from, the social circumstances in South Africa. These are tied to the current (post-)industrial nature of South Africa's economy in a globalising world. But instead of using this coeval reality to appeal to volunteers, in other words by showing the perceived needs that require volunteer action, the African is portrayed as 'natural' rather than urban, occupying the same globalised world inhabited by the voluntourist, but without the voluntourist's relative position of power.

In this binary opposition of urban versus rural, the power balance has flipped and nature is favoured over urbanity. On the face of it, this might suggest a positive reversal of the culture-nature binary, with nature superseding the culture and civilisation associated with the global North. However, something more is at play here. In this context, the binary opposition is not between the global North's conception of urbanity and African nature, but between African urbanity and African nature. Once again, the power balance is in favour of displaying the African as naturally natural. This way, attention is drawn away from South Africa as a functioning 21st-century society and is drawn to an Africa stuck in a wild and untamed condition. Whereas destinations like New York or Amsterdam are always framed through their urbanity, here the absence of reference to the urban is an implicit affirmation of the notion that South Africa is in some horrible condition. No need to mention the needy – the implication is along the lines of, 'If we show enough animals and wild nature they surely will start to worry about the state of our cities.' It seems that need requires a sugar coating when advertising voluntourism – and here the sticky ingredient is sweet nature.

So, although many of the volunteer programmes focus on complex urban issues that emanate from the problems of globalised (post-)industrial society, the visual representations used on voluntourism websites largely favour the rural over the urban and the natural over the industrial. Hansen (2010) notes that this use of nature in advertising contains an idyllic reference to the past. That past similarly operates to essentialise the African in imagery where 'need' is framed as something originating from Africa naturally 'back in time'. This blurs how that need exists in a coeval society that is *currently* unfavoured. It was not only unfavoured by history, but it is also unfavoured by contemporary socio-economic systems in a globalised market economy. And, unfortunately, this discourse of nature is not limited to advertising: travel writing and films are examples that show similar patterns in their use of subject material. Nature, as inherently African, triumphs over spoilt and corrupted urbanity.

The third trope of nature to be discussed here is the way in which nature is used to downplay classic white-guilt narratives. The postcolonial relationship between the global North and South bears the traces of the history of colonisation and the extent to which yesteryear's actions can be held responsible for current socio-economic circumstances and worldwide imbalances. It seems that current trends in criticism on classic development models, while trying to outline the best ways to integrate formerly colonised societies into the global order on an equal footing, also downplay the responsibility of the global North. Whereas early development theory either proposed a strong state or assumed betterment through the market, post-development theory criticises the (basis of) traditional development's interference in target countries. The argument that development is not effective can spread the idea that, consequently, help should not be attempted at all.

But let's take a few steps back. Where does the unexpected connection between guilt narratives and depictions of nature come from? The answer to this question lies at the core of the advertising phenomenon: the voluntourist himself or herself.

Because voluntourists do not usually see themselves as tourists, a closer look at their profile as consumers of advertising will help explain the link between nature and guilt. Consider the profile of the typical voluntourist. Voluntourists are usually young, and given that they come from the global North, they are assumed to be a media-savvy target audience. And because they are voluntourists, we can attribute to them a certain amount of idealism or adherence to the idea of social justice. Given the saturation of global Northern media with calls for help that are phrased as originating from the African continent in the last three decades, a generation has grown into their late teens and 20s with a media memory filled with visual clichés depicting a poor and desperate Africa. It might be that for this age group, the humanitarian images of hungry Africans, who traditionally accompany these calls for aid, are not as appealing as they might have been for an older demographic. The voluntourist may therefore be aware of the fabricated demarcation of global North and South. We can recognise a discomfort among this group with the regular imagery of human need. Two readings from tourism studies help explain this argument.

John Urry's (1990) theory of the 'tourist gaze' and Alex Gillespie's (2006) alternative reading of this phenomenon help us imagine how a younger generation might feel more self-conscious about their role as agents of charity. Urry draws from Sigmund Freud and Jacques Lacan when he defines the experience of tourists as a 'difference' between themselves and the situation they encounter:

> There is no single gaze as such. It varies by society, by social group and by historical period. Such gazes are constructed through difference ... the gaze in any historical period is constructed in relationship to its opposite, to non-tourist forms of social experience and consciousness. What makes a particular tourist 'gaze' depends on what it is contrasted with – in other words, what the forms of the non-tourist experience happen to be. (Urry 1990: 1–2)

So, where the tourist at a seaside resort, for example, is defined by how his gaze is met with the welcoming manner of the resort hotel, the voluntourist is defined not just by what he sees, but also by how he sees it. The voluntourists' gaze, we can reason, describes a unique way of seeing the same African subject (i.e. the voluntoured) that populated the advertising of their parents' generation. Because the voluntourists' gaze differs from that of other groups, reflective voluntourists will be likely to interpret typical photographs in a different light. So, for example, what might induce compassion in a person of one generation might upset the next generation. For one generation, images of human suffering may have engendered a feeling of compassion, whereas the next generation might be appalled by the same images, as they recognise a marketing strategy as a reason for their use.

To better understand the historical position of the voluntourist, I suggest that it is necessary to take into account the progress of development theory since World War II. As the history of charity and voluntourism has changed over the decades, from mission work and the Peace Corps to mainstream commercial voluntourism, similar changes have also occurred in development theory. Criticism of development aid has recently made a big impact in the international aid community. The works of William Easterly (2006) and Dambisa Moyo (2009) exemplify a way of thinking that has dared to criticise development in itself, and this approach has gained momentum in the last two decades. John Rapley's (2007) short history of development theory shows that since development was adopted after World War II, the main discussion in development theory was between left- and right-wing theorists about whether the state or the market should supply the support needed to elevate the decolonised states. However, during the 1990s, post-development theory came to criticise the idea of development in general. Although this sea change can arguably be held responsible for a diminished adherence to the idea of development by certain states in the global North, development aid itself has not simply stopped – but the climate in which its policy is drawn up has been affected. There is more room today for evaluative discussion about the goal of development aid and its implementation. As Rapley (2007: 5) explains, 'As is often the case with new currents of thought, postdevelopment thought has been more heard than implemented [leading to] widening agreement that "better" rather than more or less, is what matters.'

Post-development thought – or the idea that development aid needs to be self-critical and reflective – might therefore be an appropriate way to describe the thinking of this media-savvy group of voluntourists. This group has arguably accepted the need to move beyond the simplified narrative that Africa can 'develop' only with the help of the West. But they still feel a sense of obligation to make an impact on a small scale. A similar feeling is evident in recent media coverage of voluntourism: critical press reports about the opaque economic structures of voluntourism companies and psychological attachment problems caused by large-scale orphanage tourism make voluntourists sceptical of their own role in alleviating the challenges.

We can apply Gillespie's reversal of Urry's tourist gaze to prove a point. The perspective of the post-development enthusiast can be likened to that of the media-savvy voluntourist. Both exhibit the discomfort that Gillespie recognises tourists feel when meeting the 'reverse gaze' of the photographed local. Gillespie (2006: 344) inverts the all-powerful position that Urry awarded to the photographer:

> It is not only the photographee who is influenced by the interaction, so too is the photographer. The ... dynamic and situated

emergence not only of the photographee self, but also of the tourist photographer self, is evident. The photographee can gaze on the tourist photographer, and this 'reverse gaze' can play an important role in constituting the emerging self of the tourist photographer.

Inverting the principle of Urry's tourist gaze, the reverse gaze brings forward a reflective quality that forces voluntourists to evaluate how they will be seen by the voluntoured. Gillespie (2006: 347) describes this as follows:

> The photographee, by a prolonged stare, a questioning look, or even just a raised eyebrow, can momentarily reverse the relationship between photographer and photographee. In a glance the photographee can ... capture and objectify the tourist photographer as a particular type of tourist. That is to say, the reverse gaze, in its various forms, can mediate the emerging tourist self.

As Gillespie describes the need for tourists to reflect on their identity as tourists by meeting locals, voluntourists are similarly forced to consider their purpose in the light of their contact with the voluntoured. At the same time, the voluntoured are presented as the sole justification for the presence of the voluntourists and as the source of their existential confusion regarding the voluntourists' usefulness. Being the product of a culture that has embraced scrutiny of the global North's intervention in the global South, the voluntourist is therefore forced to come to terms with the uncomfortable image of the intervening self that might very well be creating the problems it thought to eradicate.

Interviews with voluntourism professionals and voluntourists make it clear that both groups constantly reflect on and criticise the effectiveness of their interventions. For the voluntourist group, images of the natural might offer a medium of escape from the enquiring eye of peers and others – which might hamper their sense of self as doing good. With the camera focused on the flora and fauna, therefore, the tourist will not be reminded of how his presence might actually be detrimental to the people he or she is supposed to be helping. So, we are once again faced with a paradox: although criticism of voluntourism takes into account its human disadvantages, the environmental disadvantages that are bound up with mass tourism remain entirely unquestioned and out of sight.

Voluntourism advertising seems to follow trends in tourism advertising in its abundant use of imagery of the natural world. However, simple adherence to an industry standard does not explain all the intricacies at play in this industry. The way imagery of the natural is used touches upon the paradoxes central to voluntourism, which needs to be seen in its historical context as a typical postcolonial phenomenon. The way voluntourism is advertised presents southern Africa to an audience from the global North through meanings based on binary opposition. This discourse is rife with historical colonial references and creates a sense that southern Africa is dependent on the West. Depicting nature as part of South African reality, for example, seems to be a way to position African 'need' as 'natural'. The naturally needy are then binarily opposed to an able and expert voluntourist intervention. This discourse is most blatantly based on a mainstream tourism imagination of southern Africa and seems to be dominant in voluntourism through its structural strategic alignment with the institutions of the tourism industry.

The second discourse of nature identified in voluntourism advertising positions nature as a deflection from the social issues that South Africa faces as a (post-) industrial urban society. Voluntourism is largely based on urban needs and programmes to address these needs. However, imagery of nature is used to lure voluntourists to South Africa to help on these programmes. And, paradoxically, it is nature that bears the brunt of mass tourism's detrimental side effects. The tourism industry therefore finds a way to keep its advertising strategy positive by naturalising South Africa's problems and obfuscating the argument that the global market economy can be identified as a possible source for these same problems. African nature is opposed to African urbanity, and photographic reference to the latter is wisely avoided.

The third reading of nature identifies a non-interventionist trend, whereby imagery of nature might appeal to voluntourists belonging to a self-critical and media-savvy generation. On the one hand, this group is saturated with strategic images of suffering and, on the other hand, likes to downplay its own impact on the location and culture it visits. For these voluntourists, who are uncomfortable with traditional images and narratives depicting need and aid, the presence of the natural can help to offer a seemingly more neutral intervention.

It can be seen therefore that nature in voluntourism advertising serves different purposes and can signify opposite meanings. However, the dominant discourse appears to support the paradox of voluntourism, namely that although the industry is based on a need, showing this specific need in its marketing imagery seems to be off limits. Instead, nature is used for various reasons – because it appeals to those who see themselves as expert interventionists, or because it allows a way to avoid the discussion of South Africa as a coeval society with current-day problems, or because it allows for a group of increasingly self-critical volunteers to downplay the interference their holidays cause in the lives of the voluntoured. These findings indicate that discussions mobilising the natural are always loaded, and often in unexpected ways. They need careful and contextualised readings before any meaning can be attributed to them. It is unwise to make any general claims about the use of visual tropes of nature in broader society based on the above reading, but what the reading does show is that in the context of voluntourism, visual tropes of nature can be used in advertising to functionally deflect attention away from the underlying economic, social and cultural questions that are central to the dynamics of voluntourism.

References

Britton, Robert. 'The image of the Third World in tourism marketing'. *Annals of Tourism Research* 6, 3 (1979): 318–329.

Easterly, William. *The White Man's Burden: Why the West's Efforts to Aid the Rest Have Done So Much Ill and So Little Good*. Oxford: Oxford University Press, 2006.

Gadamer, Hans. *Truth and Method* (2nd ed.), translated by J. Weinsheimer and D. Marshall. New York: Continuum, 1989.

Gillespie, Alex. 'Tourist photography and the reverse gaze'. *Ethos* 34, 3 (2006): 343–366.

Hall, Stuart. 'The West and the rest', in S. Hall and B. Gieben (eds), *Formations of Modernity*. Cambridge: Polity Press, 1992.

Hall, Stuart. *Representation: Cultural Representations And Signifying Practices*. London: Sage, 1997.

Hansen, Anders. 'Selling "nature/the natural": Advertising, nature, national identity, nostalgia and the environmental image', in Anders Hansen, *Environment, Media and Communication*. London: Routledge, 2010.

Landau, Paul. 'Introduction: An amazing distance', in Paul Landau and Deborah Kaspin (eds), *Images and Empires: Visuality in Colonial and Postcolonial Africa*. Berkeley: University of California Press, 2002.

MacCannell, Dean. *The Tourist: A New Theory of the Leisure Class*. New York: Schocken, 1976.

Moyo, Dambisa. *Dead Aid: Why Aid is Not Working and How there is Another Way for Africa*. London: Allen Lane, 2009.

Ndebele, Njabulo. 'Game lodges and leisure colonialists', in Njabulo Ndebele, *Fine Lines From the Box: Further Thoughts About Our Country*. Cape Town: Umuzi, 1999.

Rapley, John. *Understanding Development: Theory and Practice in the Third World* (3rd ed.). Boulder: Lynn Rienner Publishers, 2007.

Said, Edward. *Orientalism*. London: Routledge, 1978.

Salazar, Noel. 'Imaged or imagined? Cultural representations and the "tourismification" of peoples and places.' *Cahiers D'études Africaines* 193, 194 (2009): 49–71.

South Africa.net. 'About South African Tourism, Who We Are', 2014, http://www.southafrica.net/media/en/page/static/general-copy-media-and-stakeholder-who-we-are, accessed 27 February 2014.

Steger, Manfred. *Globalization: A Very Short Introduction*. Oxford: Oxford University Press, 2009.

Tourism Research and Management. *Volunteer Tourism: A Global Analysis*. Barcelona: Tourism Research and Management, 2008.

Urry, John. *The Tourist Gaze: Leisure and Travel in Contemporary Societies*. London: Sage, 1990.

Whelehan, Patricia. *The Anthropology of Aids: A Global Perspective*. Gainesville: University Press of Florida, 2009.

Williams, Raymond. *Keywords: A Vocabulary of Culture and Society* (revised ed.). New York: Fontana, 1983.

Chapter 6

TOWARDS AN ECOCRITICISM IN AFRICA: LITERARY AESTHETICS IN AFRICAN ENVIRONMENTAL LITERATURE

CHENGYI CORAL WU

What is African environmental literature? What environmental issues are revealed in African literature? How do African authors represent African environments? Chinua Achebe's (1959) *Things Fall Apart*, a classic of African literature, for example, has been read and studied as an African postcolonial novel that aims to reconstruct precolonial African cultural identity in general and traditional Igbo cultural identity in particular. However, this novel can also be read as an environmental novel. In '*Things Fall Apart* fifty years after: An ecocritical reading', Nchoujie Augustine (2009) foregrounds Achebe's environmental consciousness by examining 'the ecological component' (Augustine 2009: 107) that Achebe integrates into his writing, such as the imageries of the African forest, especially the forest's influence on the sustainability of the Igbo community, as well as its correlation with Igbo customs. Elizabeth M. DeLoughrey and George B. Handley, in their introduction to *Postcolonial Ecologies: Literatures of the Environment* (2011), argue that the 'narrative shift' (DeLoughrey and Handley 2011: 7) of

Achebe's novel from an oral, Igbo-centred narrative (as revealed in the first two parts of the novel) to a written, colonial-dominated narrative (as revealed by the district commissioner's book, *The Pacification of the Primitive Tribes of Lower Niger* in the last part of the novel) suggests the author's critique of the environmental transformation in Igboland caused by European colonisation.

As DeLoughrey and Handley (2011: 6) state, 'Chinua Achebe emphasized the radical ontological shift in understanding place that occurred through the process of European colonialism and Christian missionisation in his 1958 novel *Things Fall Apart*.' In my essay 'From cultural hybridization to ecological degradation: The forest in Chinua Achebe's *Things Fall Apart* and Ben Okri's *The Famished Road*', I argue that Achebe represents the indigenous Igbo relationship with the land and the earth goddess (Ani) – a relationship between ancestral spirits, gods, use of the land, harvest and community sustainability – in order to critique how the advent of British colonialism undermines that relationship. These recent environmental readings of Achebe's novel remind us that to understand environmental issues in the context of the Igbo society represented by Achebe, we need to understand not only the physical environment of Igboland, but also the Igbo people's relationship with it through spiritual and social practices. Achebe's novel therefore represents traditional Igbo cultural life as intertwined with environmental concerns that are also necessarily social. Therefore, the novel's critique of European colonialism is not only from an overtly political or cultural perspective, but also from an indigenous environmentalism attached to politics and culture.

An emphasis on the environmental perspective of Achebe's novel reminds us that the challenge of locating environmental issues in African literature lies in the fact that they may not look like environmental issues, as addressed or represented in Anglo-American environmental literature. In the case of Achebe's novel, the environment refers to the Igbo land as a *whole* – composed of the inhabitants, the gods and ancestral spirits they worship, the village compounds, as well as the forests surrounding the community. The indigenous Igbo environmentalism, as represented by Achebe, is based on the Igbo people's attachment to the land their ancestors had settled for centuries – an attachment they passed on to their descendants.¹ As made apparent by Achebe, 'environment' is not a universal concept, as Anglo-American environmental literature often tends to assume and endorse, and therefore ecocriticism cannot be founded on universal principles. In *Caribbean Literature and the Environment: Between Nature and Culture* (2005), DeLoughrey, Gosson and Handley are pioneer critics who bring ecocriticism to postcolonial literature, especially Caribbean literature. They point out the problem of universalism recurrent in Anglo-American nature writing, a literary genre from which ecocriticism originally developed and to which it is intrinsically connected. To be more specific, DeLoughrey, Gosson and Handley point out the inadequacy of American nature writing with regard to its understanding and explanation of the causes of human alienation from nature:

> Unlike the masculine Anglo-American insistence that alienation from nature is caused by excessive mobility and transience, here [in the context of the Caribbean] we see that there are various causes for alienation from nature that differ according to the historical conditions of people in the wake of the violence of Western expansion. (DeLoughrey, Gosson and Handley 2005: 5)

Although Anglo-American nature writing targets the impact of modernity, especially that of industrialism, capitalism and technology, on colonial societies' home environments, it pays less attention to the fact that both modernity and industrialism go hand in hand with European colonial expansions into non-European regions, and that colonialism has led to environmental degradation in these places. In addition, modernity, followed by capitalism and industrialism, is not a universal development in human cultures (as many Anglo-American writers tend to assume). Instead, it was introduced to or imposed on non-European lands and cultures. For example, although British Romantic writing criticises the impact of industrialism and the enclosure system on British rural lands, it might ignore the dispossession of non-Europeans and the exploitation of their lands caused by British colonisation. Likewise, although American nature writers like John Muir in the late 19th century and Edward Abbey in the mid 20th century appreciate American wilderness and argue for its protection in their writings, they tend to ignore the fact that the American wilderness cannot exist without the removal and dispossession of Native Americans from their homeland. As I will show in detail later in this chapter, common themes recurrent in Anglo-American environmental literature (or Anglo-American nature writing, more specifically), such as the concept of nature as pristine and critiques of industrial modernity, to a large extent overlap with the theoretical and methodological paradigms that dominate Anglo-American ecocriticism. Anglo-American nature writing also provides inspirations for the contemporary wilderness conservationism dictated by Anglo-American ecocriticism.

If Anglo-American environmental literature focuses largely on criticising the impact of modernity, industrialism and technology on pristine natural environments, and emphasises the importance of wilderness conservation, then to define African environmental literature we need to determine the following issues. What does 'environment' mean in an African context? What shapes an African environmental consciousness? To avoid generalisations, what does 'environment' mean to a specific African ethnic group? For example, to what extent would a Kikuyu concept of environment be similar to or different from an Igbo concept of environment? In addition, what are the causes of environmental crisis and ecological degradation in Africa? How do African literary writers approach environmental issues in their literary productions? And what role does African literature play in expressing environmental issues?

Even though, at first glance, Achebe's novel is not really about environmental degradation, it is arguable that the novel's criticism of European colonialism and Christian missionisation presciently points towards future African environmental crises in the postcolonial era, such as those with which Ben Okri's *The Famished Road* (1991) engages.

Environmental criticism in African literary studies before the 1990s

African environmental literature and criticism can be traced back to the 1960s, pre-dating ecocriticism as a specifically environment-oriented literary approach that began to prosper in Anglo-American literary studies in the last decade of the 20th century. That being said, a common assumption among ecocritics that ecocriticism is not popular in and not widely applied to African literature needs to be re-examined. Without exploring the roots of African environmental literature and criticism, non-Africanist scholars may be inclined to treat ecocriticism in Africa more or less as an extension of globalised Anglo-American ecocriticism, as if the former has to participate in global environmental issues under the guidance of the latter.

Emphasising the development of environmental criticism in African literary studies before the 1990s enables us to recognise the limits of the methodologies, the values and the assumptions that Anglo-American ecocriticism tends to dictate while interpreting environmental literature. In brief, the assumptions made by Anglo-American ecocriticism include a number of ideas. First, ecocriticism tends to recapitulate ideas and values rather than provide critical perspectives in reading environmental literature. In 'Blues in the green: Ecocriticism under critique', Michael Cohen (2004: 11) calls US ecocriticism a 'praise-song school' that tends to celebrate assumptions made by traditional American natural writing rather than question those assumptions.

Second, ecocriticism tends to endorse the concept that nature is pristine, pure and somewhere 'out there' (similar to the field's reinforcement of the idea that ecology is an organic, unified whole).[2] As Timothy Morton, in *Ecology without Nature: Rethinking Environmental Aesthetics* (2007: 13), states, ecocriticism, as practised in American literary academia, 'is too enmeshed in the ideology that churns out stereotypical ideas of nature to be of any use'.

Third, ecocriticism's critique of modernity and its attendant impact on the environment assumes that modernity is a universal human condition. This assumption was challenged by DeLoughrey, Gosson and Handley (2005) in their introduction to *Caribbean Literature and the Environment*. For them, human alienation from nature is not a universal human condition, but rather depends on geographical and historical differences. Last but not least, ecocriticism's emphasis on the local has been criticised as an approach that ignores global environmental issues. Ursula K. Heise, in *Sense of Place and Sense of Planet: The Environmental Imagination of the Global* (2008), questions American environmentalism's endorsement of localism without taking globalisation into consideration. Most of these assumptions, as I will show later, are not applicable to African literature.

My aim in developing ecocriticism in the context of African literature is not to explore the extent to which African literature might respond to the popularity of international ecocriticism and global environmental issues, or the extent to which African literature can be approached by ecocriticism, as defined and practised in Anglo-American literary studies. William Slaymaker, in his essay 'Ecoing the other(s): The call of global green and black African responses' (2001), emphasises the potentiality and need to 'spread' ecocriticism to African literary studies:

> The 1990s was *the* decade of rapid and global environmentalist literary growth, and anthologies, literary histories, and the like are notoriously behind the times. Bibliographies of black African literature that appear in the first decade of the twenty-first century will likely reflect a significant growth of interest in ecocriticism and environmental literature. The low visibility of ecolit and ecocrit in recent black African writing is temporary. The green revolution will spread to and through communities of readers and writers of African literature, 'ecoing' the booming interest in other parts of the literary world. (Slaymaker 2001: 139)

Six years after the publication of that essay, Slaymaker (2007), in 'Natural connections; unnatural identities: Ecocriticism in the black Atlantic', conveys a similar idea that ecocriticism is not highly developed in African literary studies, though he believes that African literature is potentially rich in environmentalist discussions: 'To date, there are few African ecocritics and creative writers of environmental literature but the number is growing' (Slaymaker 2007: 129). His later essay pays more attention to the current dearth of African 'ecophilosophy' and 'afroecophilosophers', both of which, for Slaymaker, are crucial for the development of an Africa-focused ecocriticism:

> While ecological studies of West African and Ghanaian environmental problems are relatively easy to uncover, ecophilosophy

and afroecophilosophers are rare to find. They are not endangered because their genesis has yet to evolve fully. Their speciation is in process. African philosophers have yet to specialize in environmental philosophy. (Slaymaker, 2007: 134)

I agree with Slaymaker regarding recognising the inadequacy of ecocritical work on African literature. However, we need to be cautious about this urgent call for the development of an Africa-focused ecocriticism if it is based on the assumption that since ecocriticism is not widely applied to African literature, it is necessary to 'spread' ecocriticism to African literary studies. Instead, Byron Caminero-Santangelo (2011: 150), in his essay 'Shifting the center: A tradition of environmental literary discourse from Africa' (published in *Environmental Criticism for the Twenty-First Century*), emphasises the need to bring the perspectives of 'the environmentalism of the poor'. These perspectives are revealed by environmental writing, activism and other forms of environmentalist traditions in Africa to broaden ecocritical work on African literature. As Caminero-Santangelo states:

> Such a project also contributes to the larger, ongoing effort to widen the scope of ecocriticism not only through the diversification of ecocritical canons but also through the use of critical frameworks informed by environmentalism developed by activists working within marginalized communities in the West and majorities in the Global South – activists like Maathai. (Caminero-Santangelo 2011: 149)

Following Caminero-Santangelo's strategy, I aim to show that African literature had already responded to environmental issues before the 1990s, even though these issues were addressed more on a local than global level. I also show that African literary criticism had already developed environmental perspectives – ones that do not originate in ecocriticism as practised in American academia. I also argue that African environmental philosophy – or 'afroecophilosophy', to use Slaymaker's term – though not theorised or systematised in the same way that might occur in the discipline of philosophy in Western academia, can be found not only in precolonial African oral traditions (as Slaymaker suggests in his essay), but also in contemporary postcolonial African literature.

One example of environmental criticism in early African literary studies is seen in Ojung Ayuk's 1982 essay 'Environmental decadence: A theme in post-independence African fiction'. In this essay, Ayuk focuses on issues of 'environmental decadence' represented by African fiction published in the 1970s:

> Decadence is a process or a period of decline or deterioration, as in, say, literature or morals. In the present essay, the word *decadence* is used to denote the subject or theme in recent African fiction, that is as reflected in an author's preoccupation with the decline in the physical environment from a state of normality or excellence. This decadence entails the destruction of the splendid landscape that characterizes much of the African physical environment and the well-structured and peaceful way in which most Africans have traditionally lived their lives, as well as the installation of the devastation and the degenerate atmosphere that are manifest features of most colonial towns and urban centers inherited by the new nations upon decolonization. (Ayuk 1982: 142)

Ayuk's essay presents an example of African environmental literary criticism outside of the context of ecocriticism, as developed in Anglo-American literary studies in the 1990s. However, I don't mean to argue that Ayuk's environmental reading of African fiction in the 1970s that portrays the degradation of African urban environments is the root of all African ecocriticism, for there are other essays written before Ayuk's that bring other environmental perspectives to African literature. For example, Jacques L. Bede's (1975) 'African town environment in contemporary literature' provides a survey of African novelists' representations of the urban environment (especially in South Africa and Nigeria) that critique the city's corrupt and destructive influences on its dwellers:

> In fact, they [African authors] all have shown that, by uprooting people, destroying ancestral organization and sanction, on

the one hand, inducing into people's hearts an immoderate love of money and futile things, although they are unable to achieve their aims, the City is profoundly immoral and destructive. (Bede 1975: 31).

In learning that African environmental literature and criticism already existed before the 1990s, we might see that it is not Africanist scholars and African literary authors who have remained indifferent or lukewarm to environmental issues and criticism, but rather that Anglo-American ecocriticism has developed so narrowly that it has ignored ecocriticism that developed outside of Anglo-American contexts.

Cheryll Glotfelty and Harold Fromm, in their anthology, *The Ecocriticism Reader* (1996: xv), point out the inadequacy of Anglo-American literary criticism, calling for its response to 'the global Environmental Crisis'. While ecocriticism made its official debut with the publication of *The Ecocriticism Reader*, Gerald Moore, in his essay 'Literature and environment in East Africa' (1966), predicted a potential environmental direction for African literary studies 30 years before *The Ecocriticism Reader* was published, calling for an African literary response to African environmental degradation in the post-independence era. Citing George Lamming's idea of 'nationalism as a feeling of total harmony with the presence of a native place' (Moore 1966: 115), Moore explores African environmental sensibility/consciousness based on the postcolonial development of nationalism:

> Nationalism is not only frenzy and struggle with all its necessary demand for the destruction of those forces which condemn you to the status we call colonial ... It is the private feeling you experience of possessing and being possessed by the whole landscape of the place where you were born, the freedom which helps you to recognize the rhythm of the winds, the silence and aroma of the night, rocks, water, pebble, and branch, animal and bird noise, the temper of the sea and the mornings arousing nature everywhere to the silent and scared communion between you and the roots you have made. (Lamming, in Moore 1966: 115)

For Moore, the future of East African literature lay in the focus on a nationalism through which an indigenous African attachment to the environment could be expressed: 'And my first question is this: will East Africa be able to jump right over the exile phase and get straight down to the task of realizing its own sense of place, in the manner indicated by Lamming?' (Moore 1966: 116). If – as early as 1966 – Moore argued that nationalism, as developed in post-independent East African literature, aims to express not only African political and cultural rebellion against colonial legacies, but also an African environmental attachment or sensibility to land, then why does ecocriticism, in the present day, need to expand or 'spread' to African literary studies? Likewise, if environmental perspectives have already been part of African literary studies for some time, as shown by Ayuk and Bede's essays, then why has African literary criticism been seen as indifferent to environmental issues?

More examples of early environmental criticism developed in African literary studies can be found in the 1998 special issue of *Bridges: An African Journal of English Studies*. This issue focuses on 'Literature and the Environment' – particularly 'the way the Environment appears in discourses, especially *literary* discourses' (*Bridges: An African Journal of English Studies* 1998: i, emphasis in original). Essays included in this special issue focus on 'environmental issues' portrayed in Anglo-American literature and African literature.[3] What makes this issue surprising and interesting is that, although it was published after Glotfelty and Fromm's *The Ecocriticism Reader*, none of the African essays included in this issue refers specifically to the literary approach 'ecocriticism,' as newly developed in Anglo-American literary criticism. This suggests the existence of some particular environmental perspectives in African contexts that are outside the scope of Anglo-American ecocriticism.

By recognising and foregrounding early African environmental criticism, we as ecocritics might avoid making misleading assumptions and conclusions, such as the idea that environmental criticism is not popular in African literary studies, as if Africanist scholars and/or African writers are not interested in environmental issues in Africa. In his 2001 essay, Slaymaker provides an explanation for his assumption that 'the

African echo of global green approaches to literature and literary criticism has been faint' (Slaymaker 2001: 132). According to him, one possible reason for this lack of ecological readings of African literature is that African scholars are suspicious of ecocriticism. Slaymaker uses the neologism 'ecohesitation' to describe this phenomenon, because the field originally developed and prospered in Western metropolitan centres, so to apply ecocriticism to African literature is to subsume African literature into Western environmental values:

> For some black African critics, ecolit and ecocrit are another attempt to 'whiteout' black Africa by coloring it green. To some African critics and writers, who directly practiced in the liberation of their nation-states from colonialism, what ecocritics offer is not another theory of liberation like Marxism. Rather it appears as one more hegemonic discourse from the metropolitan West. ...
>
> This ecohesitation has been conditioned in part by black African suspicion of the green discourses emanating from metropolitan Western centers ... And the suspicion that environmentalism in all its various shades of green (including red greens) is a white thing is borne out by the explosive growth of research and participation in it by white scholars in and outside Africa. (Slaymaker 2001: 132–133)

Slaymaker's assumption that African scholars are sceptical about ecocriticism as one of the dominant Western discourses corresponds to some literary critics' critique of ecocriticism. According to environmental-justice critics and postcolonial ecocritics, ecocriticism has come under fire as a perspective that privileges white middle-class-male values of environmentalism, and ignores class, racial and gender difference, and the colonial/neocolonial violence perpetrated on colonial/postcolonial environments.[4] To expand on Slaymaker's assumption about an African 'eco-hesitation', I would suggest that what African scholars are sceptical about with regard to ecocriticism is not ecocriticism itself as an environment-oriented approach, but rather the methodologies or values and assumptions that Anglo-American ecocriticism tends to endorse and treat as universal. The two examples of early African environmental literary criticisms I cite above – Moore's correlating the development of African nationalism with African expressions of indigenous attachment to the land and Ayuk's critique of degeneration of African urban environments – show how environmental perspectives developed well before ecocriticism became popular in the West.

Instead of calling for African responses to ecocriticism or global environmental issues, what seems to be more important is to focus on how African literature expresses different ideas and highlights different environmental issues from Anglo-American literature, and how African literary criticism approaches environmental issues differently from the way Anglo-American ecocriticism does. In the introduction to *Postcolonial Green: Environmental Politics and World Narratives* (2010), Bonnie Roos and Alex Hunt, point out that although in the age of globalisation environmental issues are global issues, Western powers still play the dominant role in deciding on global environmental policies and take a patronising attitude towards environmental issues in non-Western countries: 'While much has changed, much seems familiar: Western powers come to the economic, humanitarian, and occasionally military "rescue" of "developing" nations as predominantly "white" civilization rides to the rescue of those needy "others"' (Roos and Hunt 2010: 2). Instead of finding universal environmental issues among the postcolonial worlds, Roos and Hunt emphasise the importance of paying attention to a variety of issues or problems related to postcolonial environments:

> As we see it, postcolonial green scholarship must define itself not as a narrow theoretical discourse but as a relatively inclusive methodological framework that is responsive to ongoing political and ecological problems and to diverse kinds of texts ... Our goal is not to suggest a universalizing approach through some magical half-way, in-between 'common ground,' but rather to grapple with the issues that each of the various writers presented here offers us. (Roos and Hunt 2010: 9)

Like Roos and Hunt, both of whom critique the hegemony of Western environmentalism, DeLoughrey and Handley (2011: 9) also foreground the limits of ecocriticism's seemingly theoretical and methodological universalisms:

> In fact, adopting one genealogy of ecocriticism as the normative one that is blind to race, class, gender, and colonial inequities tends to marginalize the long history of precisely this critique articulated by indigenous, ecofeminist, ecosocialist, and environmental justice scholars and activists, who have theorized the relations of power, subjectivity, and place for many decades.

DeLoughrey and Handley (2011: 9) also emphasise rhizomatic trajectories of ecocriticism in their exploration of

> a broader, more complex genealogy for thinking through ecocritical futures, and a turn to a more nuanced discourse about the representation of alterity, a theorization of difference that postcolonialists, ecofeminists, and environmental activists have long considered in terms of our normative representations of nature, human and otherwise.

Building upon DeLoughrey and Handley's project in *Postcolonial Ecologies* (2011), and Roos and Hunt's in *Postcolonial Green* (2010), I aim to develop an ecocritical methodology in an African context, showing how African environmental literature pushes beyond Anglo-American pastoral traditions and wilderness/conservation narratives by emphasising Africa's colonial history, which complicates global environmental issues, as well as emphasising its literary productions that enrich globalised ecocriticism.

Africa-focused ecocriticism: Alternative methodologies

Examining African literature for narrative strategies that turn upon the environment and people's relations to the environment enables us to see how standard histories of and approaches to environmental writing in American and British literature rely on a definition of nature as pristine and untouched, in contrast with the idea of nature as interdependent with human culture, as revealed by African environmental literature.

To be more specific, whereas Anglo-American environmental literature critiques the impact of modernity, industrialism and technology on human society, such as the alienation of humans from nature, and pollution and climate change, African environmental literature critiques the impact of colonialism/neocolonialism and globalisation on African environments, such as the weakening of indigenous inhabitants' attachment to the land[5] and dispossession of the land.[6] Whereas Anglo-American environmental literature tends to endorse concepts of pristine nature (or the Sublime) and wilderness (or wilderness conservation), African environmental literature is concerned more with issues of urban slums and urban environmental degradation brought about by the colonial demands of modernisation.[7] Whereas Anglo-American environmental literature conveys nostalgia about pastoral and agrarian life, African environmental literature highlights the crisis of famine and food shortage caused by the shift from subsistence farming to global, market-oriented farming under globalisation.[8] These contrasts between Anglo-American and African environmental literature remind us that nature and environment are not universal concepts, and that environmentalism in the context of Africa, or 'environmentalism of the poor', to use Ramachandra Guha's term,[9] should not be founded on universal principles.

If, on the one hand, I am arguing for a specifically African approach to and comprehension of the environment and its place in culture, I also want to be clear that this essay does not seek to uncover or recover a pure, essentialist methodology of Africa-focused ecocriticism. Locating and defining the particularity of an Africa-focused ecocriticism and environmental awareness enable us to see alternative methodologies applied to, and more environmental concepts and tropes revealed in, African literature with the larger project of imagining a global ecocriticism. This ecocriticism does not universalise but finds its local echoes in a series of complex, lateral relations across the world. This kind of disaggregated vision of a global theory and praxis for ecocriticism allows us to see convergences and distinctions, and to steer clear of the pitfalls of Euro-Americanism and essentialism.

Michael Lundblad, in his essay 'Malignant and beneficent fictions: Constructing nature in ecocriticism and Achebe's *Arrow of God*' (Lundblad 2001), responds to Slaymaker's 2001 essay, by questioning the validity of Slaymaker's call for African responses to ecocriticism without first listening to African expressions of environmentalist ideas. He states:

> But the terms of this hope are still flowing outward from the metropole, refusing to listen to the message being generated by activists like Ken Saro-Wiwa and writers like Achebe ... But the answer, it seems to me, lies in the broadening of our definition of what counts as 'the environment' and continually questioning whoever claims to be speaking for nature. (Lundblad 2001: 16–17)

Like Lundblad, Caminero-Santangelo (2007), in 'Different shades of green: Ecocriticism and African literature', questions the 'criteria' Slaymaker uses to suggest the potential richness of ecological readings of African literature:

> Yet although Slaymaker claims that ecocriticism is global, the criteria he uses to determine if a piece of writing is properly environmental come from a primarily Anglo-American ecocritical framework, associated with the application of the sciences to literature and with deep ecology, which focuses on attacking 'anthropocentrism.'
> Now, it is true that if one uses these criteria, there has certainly been little environmental writing – literary or critical – from Africa. The problem, however, is precisely that Slaymaker embraces these criteria and the principles underpinning them – principles which represent a potential ecocritical orthodoxy, primarily developed in the West using American and British literature, and which has some serious limitations (at least in the African contexts). (Caminero-Santangelo 2007: 698)

If the concept of 'environment' in Anglo-American literature needs to be challenged, re-examined and revised in the context of African environments, as Lundblad and Caminero-Santangelo attempt to do, then what should ecocriticism do in terms of interpreting African literature? Anthony Vital (2008), in 'Toward an African ecocriticism: Postcolonialism, ecology, and *Life & Times of Michael K*' – the first essay in African literary studies that uses the term 'African ecocriticism' – emphasises the importance of paying attention to 'regional' and 'national' differences, as well as to colonial history in treating environmental issues in an African context. He states:

> Ecocriticism, if it is to pose African questions and find African answers, will need to be rooted in local (regional, national) concern for social life and its natural environment. It will need too, to work from an understanding of the complexity of African pasts, taking into account the variety in African responses to currents of modernity that reached Africa from Europe initially, but that now influence Africa from multiple centers, European, American, and now Asia in the present form of the globalizing economy. (Vital 2008: 88)

While Vital reminds ecocritics of the geographical and historical particularity of African environments, Caminero-Santangelo and Myers (2011), in their anthology, *Environment at the Margins: Literary and Environmental Studies in Africa* – the first collection of essays that aims to create dialogues between African literary studies and African environmental issues – foreground the interdisciplinary nature of developing an Africa-focused ecocriticism. They state:

> The two key questions that we focused on were how African literatures and modes of analysis drawn from literary studies might contribute to ways of reading the environment in the other disciplines and how African literary studies might productively draw from studies of African environments. These questions point to the need for dialogue across disciplines to develop better understandings of different discourses regarding African environments and people's relationships with them. (Caminero-Santangelo and Myers 2011: 2)

The key questions that Caminero-Santangelo and Myers focus on in their book show that to understand and develop ecocriticism in African literary studies, one cannot simply follow already established methodologies in ecocriticism and in African literary studies. Instead, one has to question how these two disciplines must adjust to each other and learn from each other's provenances.

Methodologically, I aim to pursue Caminero-Santangelo and Myers's questions further, exploring the extent to which African environmental literature complicates an Anglo-American notion of the environment and enriches global ecocriticism by creating dialogues between disciplines. Four broad directions can help locate environmental issues that are different from those found in Anglo-American literature. First, African literature conveys indigenous Africans' attachment to the land that the ancestors settled and left to the descendants, in other words, 'kincentric' relationships with, and understanding of, the land and environment. Taku Victor Jong (2010: 793) uses the word 'kincentricity' to describe traditional Cameroonian ecological knowledge – a knowledge that underscores the traditional Cameroonian relationship between humans (especially people in a family), animals and nature. Second, African literature criticises the West's colonisation of Africa, and its impact on African environments and ecologies (in the form of development, modernity and resource exploitation).[10] Third, African literature portrays the impact of war (colonial military invasions and postcolonial political turbulences) and other forms of violence – such as Western biological invasion – against the environment and African ecologies.[11] Last but not least, African literature focuses on neocolonialism, especially on the continued global multinational exploitation of African natural resources and the imposition of Western mainstream environmentalism on postcolonial Africa.[12]

These four directions suggest that ecocriticism in Africa involves interdisciplinary and contextual understandings of African environments. For example, without gaining a rich, complex understanding of indigenous African cultures as historically situated and politically diverse entities, one may not fully grasp the meaning of an indigenous African 'kincentric' attachment to the land. Likewise, one needs postcolonial theory and postcolonial ecocriticism to trace the complex politics of environmental degradation in the African continent.[13] One also needs to have some knowledge of postcolonial environmentalism to understand the complicity between colonial/neocolonial discourses and the development of Western environmentalism, especially its impact on postcolonial environments and its influences on the postcolonial practices of Western environmentalism.[14] The complexity of African environmental issues makes ecocriticism in Africa more than simply a perspective composed of African responses to ecocriticism and global environmental issues.

Towards literary aesthetics in African environmental literature

These four directions that can help locate environmental issues in African literature, as I explain above, may lead to an exclusively content-oriented or justice-oriented criticism of African environmental literature, which focuses on environmental issues, including environmental policies and problems (dispossession, exploitation of natural resources, pollution, population and urbanisation, for example). Yet if an Africa-focused ecocriticism focuses exclusively on environmental justice, it might ignore the role that African literature plays in responding to environmental issues and, in turn, the role of literary aesthetics in political debates. That being said, we should also pay attention to the formal aspects of African environmental literature, such as narrative form and perspective, structure, characterisation, plot, setting, metaphors, figures of language, and more, through which a specific African environment is represented and environmental issues are addressed. Elaborating on how African authors use varied literary devices to represent an African environment of a specific time enables us to recognise African literature's critique of colonialism and neocolonialism, and, more importantly, its reconstruction of an indigenous African environmental consciousness and environmentalism. Graham Huggan and Helen Tiffin, in *Postcolonial Ecocriticism: Literature, Animals, and Environment* (2010: 3), argue for the need to bring both postcolonialism and ecocriticism together as 'a means of challenging continuing imperialistic modes of social and environmental dominance', as exemplified by the continuing development of global capitalism and multinational corporate exploitation of postcolonial countries. In addition to issues of environmental justice/injustice, they also suggest the importance of paying attention to the function of 'representation' and 'imagination' in postcolonial literature:

> What the postcolonial/ecocritical alliance brings out, above all, is the need for a broadly materialist understanding of the changing relationship between people, animals and environment – one that requires attention, in turn, to the cultural politics of representation as well as to those more specific 'processes of mediation ... that can be recuperated for anti-colonial critique' (Cilano and DeLoughrey 2007: 79). This suggests (1) the continuing centrality of imagination and, more specifically, imaginative *literature* to the task of postcolonial ecocriticism and (2) the mediating function of social and environmental *advocacy*, which might turn imaginative literature into a full-fledged form of engaged cultural critique. (Huggan and Tiffin (2010: 12)

In the case of African literature, Huggan and Tiffin's emphasis on the imaginativeness of postcolonial literature reminds us not to reduce the function of African literature simply to political responses to current environmental issues in Africa, but to appreciate the complexity of aesthetics in African environmental literature. Although some Africanist ecocritics might critique colonialism and neocolonialism, to focus solely on that is to define the African experience as always being beholden to colonialism, a perspective that is as limiting as it is ahistorical. Instead, paying attention to African environmental imaginations, as revealed in African literary productions, enables us to recognise indigenous African environmentalisms and avoid misconceptions or oversimplifications that ignore the possibility of resistance or the existence of an agency, or an ethnic and local-based environmentalism.

Heise (2010), in her afterword to Roos and Hunt's *Postcolonial Green* (2010), pushes Huggan and Tiffin's reminder further, arguing that postcolonial ecocriticism should shift from social justice/injustice (content-oriented criticism) to addressing 'questions of aesthetics' or 'questions of literary form' (Heise 2010: 258) in postcolonial literature – questions that explore the relationship between literary representations of environmental issues and social justice. She writes:

> This question of the aesthetic arises with double force. If we believe ... that the aesthetic transformation of the real [environmental issues] has a particular potential for reshaping the individual and collective social imaginary, then the way in which aesthetic forms relate to culture as well as biological structures deserves our particular attention. (Heise 2010: 258)

Heise suggests that the emphasis on issues of justice/injustice in postcolonial ecocriticism is not enough because that would ignore literary particularities (and literary aesthetics) in postcolonial literature with regard to its expression of environmental issues. Like Heise, DeLoughrey and Handley (2011), in *Postcolonial Ecologies*, shift their focus from the postcolonial notion of nature/landscape as history, as emphasised in *Caribbean Literature and the Environment* (DeLoughrey, Gosson and Handley 2005), to a focus on the notion of environmental imagination and representation in postcolonial literature. DeLoughrey and Handley's (2011: 4) emphasis on the postcolonial 'literary imagination' about the land or 'a spatial imagination made possible by the experience of place' corresponds to what Heise reminds us: instead of paying attention mainly to issues of environmental justice/injustice in postcolonial literature, postcolonial ecocritics should also focus on the literary reconstruction and representation of postcolonial environments. Focusing not only on issues or the trope of social justice/injustice in African environmental literature, but on the literary imaginations and varied representations of colonial/postcolonial African environments, enables us to see how, in unique and particular representations of African environments, environmental issues and ideas have already been included in African literature.

The following is a list of environmentalist themes or tropes recurring in African novels, a list that would help us approach African literature from an Africa-centred perspective, both literally (i.e. content-oriented criticism) and literarily (i.e. form/aesthetic-oriented criticism):

1. Indigenous 'kincentric' attachment to the land (oral traditions, dialogues and dialect, communal consciousness)
2. Dispossession of the land (land tax, enclosure, displacement)
3. Agriculture (local, subsistence farming versus global, market-oriented farming)
4. Country and city (tradition versus modernity, nostalgia, 'retreat and return')
5. Colonial/neocolonial biological control (conservationism, hygiene, birth control, population)
6. Extreme weather/climate change (heat, drought, rain), especially its impact on humans (food shortage, famine, disease)
7. Natural resources, such as oil, mines, and forests (exploitation by multinational corporations)
8. Specific African landscapes, such as savannah, desert, bush, mountain, river, and their impacts on human psychology, memory, social practices, customs (representation, Africa-focused environmental aesthetics/imaginations)
9. Urban environments (rapid urbanisation, elite neighborhood versus working-class slum or industrial neighbourhood)
10. Plant, food, animal, disease (native and imported, local colours)
11. Modernity/development (technology, car, railroad) and its impact on human living conditions and psychology
12. Impacts of war (civil war and/or 'white man's war'; resource war)
13. Indigenous knowledges (holistic worldview, religion, local practices/customs) versus Western knowledges (Cartesian dualism, rationalism, technology and science)

Although the environmentalist tropes or themes recurrent in African literature are not limited to the ones listed above, these themes demonstrate that African authors have already addressed environmental issues and incorporated environmental aesthetics into their literary creations. More importantly, while some of the tropes are also popular in Anglo-American environmental literature, looking closely at those tropes in African contexts reminds us that although environmental consciousness may exist in all cultural systems and products, it should not be treated as a universal human condition. Instead, it is historically, socio-economically and geopolitically situated. An Africa-focused ecocriticism should not be treated as part of the expansion of Anglo-American ecocriticism, nor should an environmental or ecocritical reading of African literature be done simply by applying the ideas and theories of Anglo-American ecocriticism because these would ignore the uniqueness of Africans' approaches to their environments. Acknowledging particular environmental perspectives addressed in African literary studies enables us to challenge Western concepts of environment and environmentalism. Whereas Anglo-American ecocriticism tends to universalise the concept of environment, an Africa-focused ecocriticism can remind Anglo-American ecocriticism that environments are historically and culturally situated, and that an African environmentalism revealed in an African literary text does not necessarily emphasise the global environmental crisis or propose top-to-bottom conservationism. Focusing on the literariness and aesthetics of African environmental literature enables us to recognise the historicity and particularity of an indigenous African environmental consciousness.

References

Abani, Chris. *Graceland*. New York: Picador, 2004.

Achebe, Chinua. *Things Fall Apart*. New York: Anchor Books, 1959.

Augustine, Nchoujie. '*Things Fall Apart* fifty years after: An ecological reading', in Joseph Ushie and Denja Abdullahi (eds), *Themes Fall Apart But the Centre Holds: 50 Seasons of Chinua Achebe's Things Fall Apart (1958–2008)*. Lagos: Association of Nigerian Authors, 2009: 106–118.

Ayuk, Ojung. 'Environmental decadence: A theme in post-independence African fiction.' *Africana Journal* 13, 1 (1982): 142–151.

Bede, Jacques L. 'African town environment in contemporary literature.' *Commonwealth: Miscellanies* 1 (1975): 18–32.

Caminero-Santangelo, Byron. 'Different shades of green: Ecocriticism and African literature', in Tejumola Olaniyan and Ato Quayson (eds), *African Literature: An Anthology of Criticism and Theory*. Malden: Blackwell Publishing, 2007: 698–706.

Caminero-Santangelo, Byron. 'Shifting the center: A tradition of environmental literary discourse from Africa', in Stephanie LeMenager, Teresa Shewry and Ken Hiltner (eds), *Environmental Criticism for the Twentieth-First Century*. New York: Routledge, 2011: 148–162.

Caminero-Santangelo, Byron and Myers, Garth (eds). *Environment at the Margins: Literary and Environmental Studies in Africa.* Athens: Ohio University Press, 2011.
Cilano, Cara and DeLoughrey, Elizabeth. 'Against authenticity: Global knowledge and postcolonial ecocriticism.' *ISLE* 14, 1 (2007): 71–87.
Cohen, Michael P. 'Blues in the green: Ecocriticism under critique'. *Environmental History* 9, 1 (2004): 108 pars.
Crosby, Alfred. *Ecological Imperialism: The Biological Expansion of Europe, 900–1900.* Cambridge: Cambridge University Press, 1986.
Curtin, Deane. *Environmental Ethics for a Postcolonial World.* Lanham, MD: Rowman & Littlefield, 2005.
Dieng, Gorgui. 'Environmental issues in Buchi Emecheta's *Naira Power.*' *Bridges: An African Journal of English Studies* 8 (1997–1998): 1–15.
DeLoughrey, Elizabeth, Gosson, Renée K. and Handley, George B. 'Introduction', *Caribbean Literature and the Environment: Between Nature and Culture.* Charlottesville and London: University of Virginia Press, 2005: 1–30.
DeLoughrey, Elizabeth and Handley, George B. 'Toward an aesthetics of the earth', *Postcolonial Ecologies: Literatures of the Environment.* New York: Oxford University Press, 2011: 3–39.
Dossou-Yovo, Noel. 'Village and city environment in Ekwensi's major works.' *Bridges: An African Journal of English Studies* 8 (1997–1998): 18–39.
Ekwensi, Cyprian. *Burning Grass: A Story of the Fulani of Northern Nigeria.* London: Heinemann, 1962.
Evans, Mei. '"Nature" and environmental justice', in Joni Adamson, Mei Mei Evans and Rachel Stein (eds), *The Environmental Justice Reader: Politics, Poetics, & Pedagogy.* Tucson: University of Arizona Press, 2002: 181–193.
Falola, Toyin. *Britain and Nigeria: Exploitation or Development?* London and New Jersey: Zed Books, 1987.
Glotfelty, Cheryll and Fromm, Harold. 'Introduction', in Cheryll Glotfelty and Harold Fromm (eds), *The Ecocriticism Reader: Landmarks in Literary Ecology.* University of Georgia Press, 1996: xv–xxxvii.
Griffiths, Tom and Robin, Libby (eds). *Ecology and Empire: Environmental History of Settler Societies.* Seattle: University of Washington Press, 1997.
Grove, Richard. *Green Imperialism: Colonial Expansion, Tropical Island Edens, and the Origins of Environmentalism, 1600–1860.* Cambridge: Cambridge University Press, 1995.
Guha, Ramachandra. *Environmentalism: A Global History.* New York: Longman, 2000.
Head, Bessie. *When Rain Clouds Gather.* Boston: McDougal Littell, 1968.
Heise, Ursula K. *Sense of Place and Sense of Planet: The Environmental Imagination of the Global.* New York: Oxford University Press, 2008.

Heise, Ursula K. 'Afterword', in Bonnie Roos and Alex Hunt (eds) *Postcolonial Green: Environmental Politics and World Narratives*. Charlottesville and London: University of Virginia Press, 2010: 251–258.
Huggan, Graham. '"Greening" postcolonialism: Ecocritical perspectives.' *MFS* 50, 3 (2004): 701–733.
Huggan, Graham and Tiffin, Helen. *Postcolonial Ecocriticism*. London and New York: Routledge, 2010.
Jong, Taku Victor. 'Landscapes, visual arts, and ecocriticism: A reflection on the scenic apertures of Mount Fako in Cameroon.' *ISLE* 17, 4 (2010): 792–796.
Lundblad, Michael. 'Malignant and beneficent fictions: Constructing nature in ecocriticism and Achebe's *Arrow of God*.' *West Africa Review* 3, 1 (2001): 1–21.
Martinez-Alier, Joan. *The Environmentalism of the Poor: A Study of Ecological Conflicts and Valuation*. Northampton: Edward Elgar, 2002.
Moore, Gerald. 'Literature and environment in East Africa', in Mbiyu Koinange (ed.), *East Africa's Cultural Heritage*. Nairobi: East African Institute of Social and Cultural Affairs, 1966. 115–119.
Morton, Timothy. *Ecology without Nature: Rethinking Environmental Aesthetics*. Cambridge: Harvard University Press, 2007.
N'Diaye, Ibrahima. '*The Interpreters*: A study in urban, social and scatological imagination.' *Bridges: An African Journal of English Studies* 8 (1997–1998): 52–72.
Ngũgĩ, wa Thiong'o. *Petals of Blood*. New York: E. P. Dutton, 1977.
Nixon, Rob. 'Environmentalism and postcolonialism', in Ania Loomba et al. (eds), *Postcolonial Studies and Beyond*. Durham and London: Duke University Press, 2005: 233–251.
Nixon, Rob. *Slow Violence and the Environmentalism of the Poor*. Cambridge, MA: Harvard University Press, 2011.
O'Brien, Susie. '"Back to the World": Reading ecocriticism in a postcolonial context', in Helen Tiffin (ed.), *Environment and Empire*. New York: Rodopi, 2007: 177–199.
Ogot, Grace. *The Promised Land*. Nairobi, Kenya: East African Publishing House, 1966.
Okri, Ben. *The Famished Road*. New York: Anchor Books, 1991.
Ombaka, Christine. 'War and environment in African literature', in Patrick D. Murphy (ed.), *Literature of Nature: An International Sourcebook*. Chicago: Fitzroy-Dearborn, 1998: 327–349.
Pena, Devon G. 'Endangered landscapes and disappearing peoples? Identity, place, and community in ecological politics', in Joni Adamson, Mei Mei Evans and Rachel Stein (eds), *The Environmental Justice Reader: Politics, Poetics, & Pedagogy*. Tucson: University of Arizona Press, 2002: 58–81.

Phillips, Dana. 'Ecocriticism, literary theory, and the truth of ecology.' *New Literary History* 30, 3 (1999): 577–602.

Renner, Michael. 'The anatomy of resource war', *World Watch Paper* (ed.Thomas Prugh). Danvers: World Watch Institute, 2002: 5–91.

Roos, Bonnie and Hunt, Alex. 'Narratives of survival, sustainability and justice', Introduction, in Bonnie Roos and Alex Hunt (eds), *Postcolonial Green: Environmental Politics and World Narratives*. Charlottesville and London: University of Virginia Press, 2010: 1–13.

Saro-Wiwa, Ken. *Genocide in Nigeria: The Ogoni Tragedy*. London: Saros International Publishers, 1992.

Sellassie, Sahle. *The Afersata*. London: Heinemann, 1968.

Slaymaker, William. 'Ecoing the other(s): The call of global green and black African responses.' *PMLA* 116, 1 (2001): 129–144.

Slaymaker, William. 'Natural connections; unnatural identities: Ecocriticism in the black Atlantic.' *Journal of African Literature Association* 1, 2 (2007): 129–139.

Vital, Anthony. 'Toward an African ecocriticism: Postcolonialism, ecology, and *Life & Times of Michael K*.' *Research in African Literatures* 39, 1 (2008): 87–106.

Chapter 7

CRITICAL INTERSECTIONS: ECOCRITICISM, GLOBALISED CITIES AND AFRICAN NARRATIVE, WITH A FOCUS ON K. SELLO DUIKER'S *THIRTEEN CENTS*[1]

ANTHONY VITAL

I begin by stating the obvious: those of us who read and write in universities, who research and publish, live lives shaped by modern cities. Whether we live in large cities, in towns of various sizes – or in landscapes that are truly rural – we exist within transportation, communication and resource-distribution networks that rely on an array of urban institutions and their sustaining technologies (though these networks may vary from region to region in how smoothly they operate). Moreover, we make sense of the world by drawing on cultures that bear the imprint of the thinking that humans have required if they are to negotiate and reproduce modern cities successfully. Just as importantly, the actuality of urban existence, its material processes, in addition to its cultures, have formed the subjectivity from which our thinking, moment by moment, emerges. Cities, in this sense, represent a normal and obvious fact of our lives, no matter how upsetting or disturbing we may find our particular urban places, which we negotiate as we earn a living, build personal relationships and seek what gratifies us.

The question motivating this chapter begins to address this complex actuality for us as disciplined readers of literature alert to global environmental concerns: how do we read in a way that acknowledges simultaneously our modern urban realities and the fact that failure to grasp human life in relation to natural worlds can lead to damaging consequences – for both humans and the life forms they encounter? This question becomes especially urgent in an era in which we, as a species, need both to adapt to – and, if possible, to mitigate – the effects of climate change. The question, so daunting to face, raises such a wide range of issues that this chapter can take only the smallest steps to address it. And, because ecocriticism with an urban focus has yet to develop, I am as much concerned with method as with conclusions.

As this chapter illustrates, I envision an ecocriticism that joins in multidisciplinary conversation about environmental futures, contributing literary studies' special insights into language and its crafting. Such multidisciplinarity is crucial: modern worlds take their form from a wide range of discourses, both specialist and non-specialist, and the quest for a less destructive path into the future will benefit from as much communication among representatives of these discourses as possible. Ecocriticism seems well placed to contribute to this critical reflection by illuminating how human behaviours combine their social dimension with some or other relation to nature. In this context, cities call attention to their central importance. It is now commonplace that for the first time in human history more than half the world's population are and will continue to be city-dwellers. What we know as 'globalisation' rests on a network of cities wrapping the planet, and African cities, with the worlds they anchor, participate in this network in ways both material and cultural. So, I first consider an approach to reading literature from within this larger network – and because space in this volume is limited, I name only briefest pointers to what would need to enter such reading to account for what makes African worlds distinct. The focus on African narratives, I hope, makes up for this imbalance.[2]

Global considerations

In what follows, I make some observations, briefly, to frame such ecocriticism:

1. All cities exist in some or other relation to the current global socio-economic order. As this order rests on pasts influenced first by modern colonial activity emanating from Europe and fuelled by capitalist adventure, and then by modern empire, dependent on a thriving industrial capitalism, again centred in Europe but joined by the US, and, now, is influenced by what Arif Dirlik (2007) terms a 'global modernity', with power centres in both the North and the South, it matters that ecocriticism recalls a city's relation to these processes.[3] It is also important that ecocriticism recalls the histories of anti-colonial, anti-imperial and then postcolonial thought, as it works to understand the many different 'natures' that such pasts have helped to foster. If empire produced colonial conservation practices and its print culture fostered the various kinds of dominative attitude towards nature explored by John Miller (2012) in *Empire and the Animal Body*, it also produced, famously, the forest as resistance site in the Kenyan liberation struggle. In colonised places broadly, such cultural resistance is brought into focus by Elizabeth DeLoughrey and George Handley in their introduction to *Postcolonial Ecologies* (2011).[4]
2. While 'global modernity' brings with it both the invitation and pressure to modernise, cities will be places where the tensions associated with modernising are keenly felt. This is especially so as human migration into cities across regional and national boundaries brings with it both the creative opportunities and the hazards of ethnic mingling, and especially as access to social power and position is seldom, if ever, granted equally across any social divide. The discourses about nature, which different cultural memories under stress produce, will be equally varied and will provide an important context for reading particular texts.
3. This urban life is studied in modernity's diverse academic disciplines, which, together, form one key element in global modernity's reproduction. In both the social and natural sciences, scholars

explore the consequences of urban life and its growth. What matters here is that, fed by these discourses, ecocriticism needs to rest on the understanding that cities have never existed 'outside' of nature, and that city-dwellers draw into cities both nutrients and energy, as well as material for their built environments, sometimes from near at hand, but now, in modern worlds, from extended trading networks of a sometimes planetary scale.[5] The built environment, in turn, exists in a place that has location within a matrix of natural flows and, hence, a city's built environment will play its part, along with any material effluent from city-dwellers, in altering these flows (in other words, it will have an impact on the natural environment). Moreover, in modern worlds, and urban environments especially, what we experience as distinctively local is in actuality an interplay of the local and global, with the dominant global civilisation affecting life chances for all life forms, including humans. Current urban subjectivity, especially among the comfortable, is formed by these material processes, which remain mostly accepted, with perhaps only fragmented understanding. How to integrate the drama of human need and desire into a rich awareness of natural processes is difficult enough in modern worlds. However, the complexity of urban material reality adds massively to the difficulty. Yet developing such awareness matters and, in the context of literary interpretation, ecocriticism could serve this project. Such (re)interpretation would, in the most general view, amount to rethinking the social as the ecosocial. In this way, the processes of urbanism, both natural and social, in all their layered complexity, take central place in the struggle to understand and improve human life.

4. I have suggested elsewhere (Vital 2008: 87–90) that ecocriticism on a postcolonial planet might work best by focusing its analysis on discourse, where discourse is understood in material terms and literary discourse is distinct even as it intersects with other discourses reproducing modern realities (both academic 'specialist' and ordinary 'non-specialist' discourses). While it focuses on language, ecocriticism would stay aware of the social relations affected by modernity's pasts – social relations that mediate relations with what

we call 'nature'. With this historical awareness would come, inevitably, awareness of the colonising activities that have fuelled modernity's development, and the role of cities in these activities, both past and present. If ecocriticism pays attention to how language from the past bears traces of this development, it will not forget how its own discursive activity intersects with the present. Globally, academic culture – together with its discourses – would not be possible without significant capital investment, a capital investment that links academic culture to the global order's networks of production and consumption, and their ecosocial consequences.

5. If the social and natural sciences can give insight into the processes involved in modern urban civilisation's material existence on this planet that humans have been so successful at populating, it is the distinctiveness of literary discourse, with its shaping conventions and its attention to tropes and their interplay, that ecocriticism would highlight. All literature's crafting of language works on multiple levels to involve in its naming of the world the stress-filled dynamism of subjective life, with its expression in moral and sometimes political choice. What needs to be emphasised is that, in the modern world, this subjectivity expressing itself in literature is produced in large part by urban realities – material, social and cultural.[6] An ecocriticism of the sort I envisage here would explore how, via the text, 'city' and 'nature' enter into subjective life. Then it would sharpen its critical focus by drawing on other specialist languages, those of the social and natural scientists. Thereby readers would gain significant critical distance from inherited forms of meaning-making that, however plausible they might appear, may not be adequate to the tasks ahead. In the near and distant future, the impact of urbanised human life on our species and on the planet will need to absorb attention. Ecocriticism might thereby help cultivate a version of the 'scrupulous subjectivity' that Edward Said (2000: 184) writes of in 'Reflections on exile', one that makes more conscious our own participation in the pleasures and costs of modern cities, with an understanding of the past and an alertness to an accompanying sense of responsibility for the future.

6. The strategy I suggest in this chapter involves acknowledging that every literary work, in its singularity, distorts and omits, as well as reveals. Reading would grasp richly what the text explores, illuminating how it ties itself to a moment in social and cultural history, and how it draws from available cultural attitudes and literary conventions. But, also, reading would explore what the text does not give us – as every text has limits and presents a partial perspective. Illuminating what the text is silent about would include noting what the discourses of the natural and social sciences reveal about 'cities-in-nature'. Literary works have their own concerns – which, in the case of narratives, tend to be social – and the stronger the work, the more powerful and plausible those concerns will appear. Yet it is precisely in their power and plausibility that they will work to draw attention from the materiality of ecosocial processes. Without expecting to develop solutions to problems in these processes, such ecocriticism can nonetheless enter into multidisciplinary conversation by illuminating literature's exploration of desire and its frustration, of felt need and its thwarting, as these are experienced in specific social worlds. Illuminating this subjective dimension can add significantly to what the objective sciences provide.

For an ecocriticism within and for Africa, the task would be to think of all that makes African worlds distinct, both in relation to worlds on other continents and within Africa – while also acknowledging points at which Africa participates in global realities.[7] Such ecocriticism would incorporate available natural and social-scientific scholarship reflecting local concerns, while advancing understanding of the formal features of African literary discourse. In this way, it would bring literary texts into conversation with understandings of African cities' ecological placement, their regional social and cultural differences, their multi-ethnic characteristics, their relation to regional rural worlds, their past relation to the specific cruelties and difficulties occurring during an insertion into modernity via European colonisation, and their present uneven relation to the globalised economy.

In relation to this economy, African societies have been creating their own African modernities and, in the cultural sphere, resolving, subjectively, attendant tensions (over, for example, social inequalities, the struggle for good governance, and the reconciling of past values, and present rural and urban values). An African ecocriticism would bring into play awareness of such material, as it sets in creative tension African literary texts and African ecosocial realities.

Reading narrative

In turning to literary texts, I focus on K. Sello Duiker's first novel, *Thirteen Cents* (Duiker 2000), while glancing for comparison purposes at Zakes Mda's *The Heart of Redness* (2000) and Doreen Baingana's collection of interlinked short stories, *Tropical Fish* (2005). Each of these narratives – or, in this last case, sequence of narratives – concludes with a sense of limited personal or local possibility in the face of an uncertain or troubled social future. In all of them, it is nature, and not the narratives' cities and their social workings, that offers the characters a sense of (albeit limited) possibility. And, in all of them, this turning to nature precludes awareness of the complexities of the various kinds of relations that exist between nature and city.

Thirteen Cents stands in fascinating contrast to *The Heart of Redness*, published in the same year. In Mda's novel, the focaliser is university educated and ready to take his place in the urban heart of a new South Africa. Quickly disillusioned by the power dynamics that appear to be driving this urban world, he transfers his intellectual engagement to rural life, one that is still shaped by indigenous cultural understandings. The novel, by its conclusion, suggests the value of reconnecting with such rural, ancestral worlds, and defending them in a flexible, postcolonial spirit of negotiation between cultural inheritance and modernity. In this way, the novel suggests, one can confront a South African future made unpleasant and unpredictable by the workings of big capital.[8]

Duiker's novel, like Mda's, articulates a disillusioned response to post-transition South Africa. It represents the urban world as an unappealing, confusing place, where money is power, and power is bent on excluding those in need. However, Duiker's vision is distinctly harsher. By choosing a 12-year-old street child, Azure, to be his novel's first-person narrator, Duiker envisions Cape Town as a place of constant predation, sometimes violent, sometimes coating its desire to control and consume with a veneer of concern.[9] The narrative explores resulting feelings of uncertainty, mistrust and physical vulnerability in the boy, and how he responds to these. Yet it is his struggle for the self-confidence he will need for survival that drives the narrative to its conclusion. The child's voice also communicates a plausibly limited understanding of the world. This, when combined with his concluding achievement of self-confidence, suggests, as I elaborate below, some of the novel's difficult ethical and political implications, deriving, it would appear, from the novel's sense of its historical moment.

The causes of Azure's lack of self-confidence are many and obvious. He suffers physically and emotionally from those he interacts with and, perhaps more damagingly, he is made continually aware of his status as 'boy' in a world of adults – even as he senses that this is a moment of personal transition – 'almost a man, nearly thirteen years old' (Duiker 2000: 1). Exacerbating this sense of inferiority is his increasing awareness of himself as being quite alone, as needing to rely for survival on a sense of his own power. Although he does enlarge, to a small extent, his understanding of his street world, it is more important that he finds resources within himself to boost his sense of being able to stand independently. He knows that the ambiguity of his appearance (he is of African descent but has blue eyes, so he is not 'black', or 'white' or 'coloured') causes him difficulty on the Cape Town streets, scarred by legacies of racism. He knows too that, as a street child in a city dominated by money and the property it buys, he owns almost nothing material, and needs to hustle to survive, selling his body to men. But he also knows that he needs more than material subsistence. He can negotiate with some of the city's untrustworthy adults; he insists that the adults who want sex give as well as take. But his dealings with the gangsters who rule the streets teach a sharp lesson. Gangsters and paedophiles may take physically from Azure, but the gangsters also exact 'respect', reminding him violently of his powerlessness to bargain, even for subsistence. Owning little, he owns nothing unless he owns himself, which he interprets as carrying within himself a sense of his own capacity for violence. The end of the novel underscores this. As the narrative progresses, his reflective abilities increase, as does his rage: 'destroy, destroy' and 'I am getting stronger' appear as refrains.

Duiker noted the biographical origins of the novel in his friendship with street children (see '"The Last Word": Sello Duiker', in Mzamane [2005]). However, the novel is more than an adult's attempt to relay a child's experience though a coming-of-age narrative.[10] In building the child's narration, Duiker draws on attitudes circulating in his historical moment. What is an impressive imagining of a child's mind also becomes a vehicle for exploring an adult response to post-1994 South Africa, with Azure's moment of personal transition recalling the moment of historical transition. The latter should be empowering but, instead, as this narrative 'of a child' suggests, the moment is one in which, for Duiker, it makes sense to feel as an orphaned and homeless child in the face of history. Rather than seeking to find compensation for disillusionment with the contemporary urban order in rural worlds, as Mda's novel does, the novel stays resolutely engaged with what it senses is a predatory civilisation ruled by untrustworthy adults – gangsters, bankers, false friends and helpers – and shot through with inherited racial animosities. Yet references to Cape Town's natural world do carry a kind of saving significance. From the beginning, the narrative reveals that the boy is aware of a reality beyond the Cape Town in which he seeks to live. Even while referring to some of the daily aggression and predation that Azure needs to negotiate, the first chapter sets out neatly what the narrative will develop as a contrast between a nature that is urbanised (its pigeons, rats and sandwich bread) and a nature intuited as free (the ocean). It is the ocean that gives Azure a sense of healing and cleansing power as he bathes in it, especially after sex work (Duiker 2000: 30).

While the ocean appears mildly beneficial in the narrative's early sections, as Azure experiences more and more oppressive violence, including a gang rape, it becomes associated with violence as well as freedom, with, in other words, a liberating violence. A gang leader may forbid him to bathe in it (Duiker 2000: 73), but the ocean has already come to him (Duiker 2000: 50–55). In an extended episode, while this gang leader holds him captive – and during which he suffers the gang rape – he has his first significant encounter with seagulls.

Locked on a roof, Azure watches with excitement as the gulls, suffering no such restriction, drive off the pigeons he scorns and fears for being informants to gang leaders, enacting a tough masculinity not subject to predation – 'seagulls have pride' (Duiker 2000: 51). Then, in front of one of these representatives of the ocean, a large 'man seagull' (Duiker 2000: 54), Azure performs his own display of dominance by urinating on the gull's excrement, playing out behaviours that are crucial, he feels, for his survival. This small drama enacts attitudes echoed in his refrain, 'I'm getting stronger' (Duiker 2000: 55), attitudes that shape the concluding apocalyptic vision in which the ocean rises up to destroy the city. For it is the whole city, including all adults, and not only the gangsters, that inspires fear and rage – feelings reinforced by the words spoken before his return visit to the mountain by a 'friendly' gang member: 'Evil hides itself . . . . In the church, in banks, in town. That's why we have to destroy Cape Town. . . . That's how you fight evil. With evil' (Duiker 2000: 138).

Accompanying this growing self-confidence is an increasing tendency towards introspection. Of these moments his reflections on fear appear most significant. On his first visit to Table Mountain, he expresses his distance from the 'white people' he encounters, people who move across its surface as if they were its 'owners': 'They don't look at the ground. They only look ahead of them. That's why animals are always running away from them. ... White people don't know fear and animals know that' (Duiker 2000: 124–125). However, if, to his mind, a culture of owning, and especially owning 'nature', exempts white people from fear, those on the social margins can move with confidence by 'learn[ing] to live with fear', as happens in the gang world's violent control of the streets. Azure appears to reject both paths as he reflects: 'What does that mean [learning to live with fear]? It means grown-ups are evil ... they use anything they can use and when they get it they still want more' (Duiker 2000: 143). By the novel's end, he finds his own way of dealing with fear. Reflecting on the harshness of the world he is born into, a harshness he thinks of as matching the sun's, he comes to terms with fear through his own form of 'ownership', one that is visionary. For Azure, this vision is of nature rising up violently against the violent, hurtful city, destroying what is destructive (Duiker 2000: 162).

This visionary sense of nature can be noted from the narrative's beginning. Azure's response to the seagulls echoes in a different register his response to the pigeons. In both cases, he is interpreting animals as spirit-beings, as existing in the same existential plane as he does – the pigeons as sinister representatives of spirit subjugated by, and therefore in the service of, urban power; the seagulls as representatives of ocean, a spirit of healing that is mild but also potentially destructive. On the mountain he experiences spiritualised nature in terms that point back to ways of living before the appearance of a colonial modernity on the African continent (though, as Shaun Viljoen [2013: xvi] notes, the vision assembles biographical and popular-culture elements as well). Unlike the ocean, which has value for how it lies entirely beyond the human, the mountain has value for how it allows this vision by being a space for humans that exists nonetheless outside the city. Here, Azure, through trance and the medium of fire, encounters the spirits of the Cape's earlier inhabitants, first its animals and then a woman (she calls herself Saartjie, suggesting Sarah Baartman and recalling the historical depth of the cruelty in this boy's world).[11] The final apocalyptic vision of nature's power, a vision that affords him a sense of connection both with nature's power and old African ways of knowing, serves as a culminating moment. It offers Azure psychological liberation from fear and a sense of how, in this world as harsh as the sun, he owns himself, at least.

But, what is one to make of this ending? There is no consciousness outside the boy's that can be turned to for guidance: the moment's meaning for Azure is its meaning, a meaning the adult writing presents as valid, even if he may not endorse it. The solution that the vision provides to the boy's life situation, however disturbing for the homicidal rage it can be read as representing, makes sense within the terms set up by the narrative: the boy's marginal economic position (he cannot begin to articulate an industrial worker's perspective), his limited understanding of social history, his sense of aloneness, his sense that in this bewildering world it is only a self-reliance enacted as destructive violence that can help him survive. In the world that is left to him by 1994, the friendships and alliances he finds are too unstable to be relied on, and the uncertainty about the future that ends *The Heart of Redness* is also evident in this narrative. The social world in

South Africa, post-1994, offers no scripts for systemic transformation other than the official version in line with the needs of capital, both local and global, supporting an obviously problem-filled status quo. Duiker has nothing to draw on to offer his character other than a liberation that is internal, reinforcing his solitude and echoing the violence of the pasts that have produced his city.

Azure's attitudes reproduce, in extreme, the dominant neoliberalism, one maintained by those very gangster-bankers he seeks to escape. The historical moment of 1994 appears emptied of meaning and with it that history of social struggle embodied in modern revolution (traceable back to 17th-century Britain and its 'Glorious Revolution' of 1688). This history supplied the struggle against apartheid, and, as with much anti-colonial struggle, its language of democracy and rights. But in this post-1994 novel, South Africa appears as a world controlled by 'adults' who are 'full of shit' (Duiker 2000: 106). With no reference to existing struggles of communities and workers, there is no reason to think the world could be changed for the better. It is chilling to read these final pages (published in 2000) with al-Qaeda's 2001 destruction of New York's Twin Towers in mind. Thinking forward to such North American texts as Jared Diamond's *Collapse: How Societies Choose to Fail or Succeed* (2005) or the film *A Crude Awakening: The Oil Crash* (McCormack and Gelpke 2007) suggests that Duiker is shaping his narrative in accord with a postmodern temporality haunted by a post–Cold War version of apocalypse, in which, day by day, the global economy lumbers on, driven by aggressive self-interest, falling apart here, reconstituting there (thanks to this or that exciting, promising technological advance), but haunted by images of its own violent end. In such a vision, either people hostile to this global order will destroy it (and the increasingly intrusive electronic surveillance by world powers, justified by the need to guard against terrorists, speaks to this haunting) or nature will, as socio-economic imperatives modify the planet's ecosystems faster than they can recover.[12]

Duiker's narrative, in its social focus, gives sympathetic voice to one who seeks remedy in visions of apocalyptic violence and though these involve nature, they do not concern ecosystems – or Cape Town's relation to them. The novel's focus on a child, and one most dispossessed in this city,[13] produces a discourse far from the discourses of the city's professional and managerial classes. Moreover, its social focus powerfully displaces a thinking about Cape Town's life in its natural situation. Although it depicts astutely the class and race dynamics that are Cape Town's inheritance from its colonial pasts, its depiction of nature is driven by the boy's understandable need for a meaningful space that is 'outside' what Cape Town confronts him with. A moment on the mountain offers an emblem of this displacement. If the mountain offers Azure refuge and the possibility of self-discovery (intruded on, annoyingly at times, by others seeking pleasure there), it also reminds him of the structures of adult authority that he climbs the mountain to escape. He is chased away from the reservoir he swims in and this moment registers as simply one more imposition (Duiker 2000: 125). The complex history of water provision in Cape Town is alluded to (the fact that it was once deemed necessary to build dams to supply Cape Town with water) and then bypassed. Questions of conservation in this region, with its long, dry summers, of the need to find additional water sources in mountains distant from the city to ensure a steady supply of potable water, of expanding the use of 'grey' water, of protecting the city's waterways and wetlands from pollution that has multiple origins – questions of the kind faced by city planners and which are crucial for understanding this dimension of the city's metabolic life: our attention is drawn away from all of these issues (see City of Cape Town). And the narrative draws our attention away from other dimensions of this metabolic life, such as food and fuel supply, and sanitation and other waste-disposal requirements. Displaced, too, is the relationship between Cape Town's infrastructure and the fragile ecosystem within which it is built and which, inevitably, as the city expands, it disrupts increasingly.

A fuller reading of this novel would incorporate more of the social and natural reality with which Azure's narrative intersects and thereby feeds the readers' imagination with a sense of what is at stake in this city's life. Obviously, not all urban social problems have an ecological dimension: homelessness among children and sexual predation on children are examples of social problems needing urgent attention. While cities, to be effective, need to compartmentalise ('departmentalise') their work, literary study, through its critical explorations, can encourage a seeing with both eyes, as it were. Holding the social and ecological in mind simultaneously could contribute to promoting a culture that grasps reality as ecosocial, a culture that would then affect how specific problems are understood and addressed. Yet reading the novel also suggests some of what lies outside the scope of such 'objective' realities. Azure has a *need* for a nature 'outside' the city, for a nature that connects him with a precolonial culture, a culture that supplies a relation to the natural world that is very different from that fostered by the daily reproductive imperatives of global capitalism. Understanding this need in relation to all else in the narrative draws attention both to the novel's subjective dimension, and to the cultural and social dimensions shaping subjectivity. Such attention can add crucial material to objective accounts of ecosocial realities, enriching conversation in professional meetings and classrooms about our life in cities and towns, and in the nature that sustains us.[14]

Reference to the cultural and social dimensions shaping subjectivity recalls the point that *Thirteen Cents* is not simply about a homeless child. As noted above, Duiker, with Azure as the focaliser, is elaborating responses to his social world. Turning to nature in his narrative reproduces a move that Mda makes in *The Heart of Redness*. Duiker's novel, though, engages head-on with the aggressively acquisitive individualism to be found in modern and postcolonial city streets (masked, where possible, by orderliness, temporary alliances, and – as the episode with a wealthy banker suggests – by politeness and a veneer of 'high culture'). Whatever can be done for the ecosocial life of cities would need to recognise and counter the effects of this individualism (and its 'gang member' variants, of whatever class), an individualism rooted in modernity but exacerbated, as Duiker's historical vision suggests, by the neoliberal tendencies that South Africa was liberated into in 1994. Under such social conditions, it is reasonable to expect that urban life and its struggles will produce a distorted understanding of nature in its relation to urbanism, one that blocks, rather than enlarges, an awareness of the city-in-nature.

If Duiker's novel enacts this understandable distortion, so too does *The Heart of Redness*. In this novel the narrative moves away from Johannesburg to focus its intelligence on the rural Eastern Cape, exploring various issues there. These include the environmental health of the place as it confronts the forces of large-scale development and the value of reconnecting with an African cultural tradition. In this way, Mda's novel, like Duiker's, finds value in a nature outside city limits, one infused with cultural memory drawn from a time before colonial modernity. It, too, appears driven to do so in the rejection of an urban life tied to globalism; and it, too, in turning to locate value in the rural community, encourages a blindness to the present and past complex ways in which urbanism both affects ecosystems and generates inadequate images of nature–human relations (including those of rural life as somehow closer to nature.)

In developing this way of seeing the ecosocial life of cities, it is important to remember that the 'ecological' includes us who read and write. Humans do not exist independently of nature's flows. These flows constitute our bodily existence, whether we live as hunter-gatherers or as residents of Johannesburg, so it is crucial to augment abstract thought about urban metabolic life. Without human bodies, in all their complexity, there are no cities; without the natural systems to sustain these urban bodies, cities would be emptied of people.[15] As humans dependent now on globalised cities, we need to struggle to understand and come to terms with the intricate ways our bodies, and therefore also our minds, are involved in this urban life, constituted by constantly shifting global interconnections. As mentioned earlier, the narratives we read, even those that draw attention to the body, are likely to draw us away from attempting such ecosocial understanding, motivated as they will be by awareness of largely social and psychological problems, and the need for their resolution. Nonetheless, such narratives will speak to subjective issues crucial to an ecosocial understanding that includes our involvement in cultural dynamics. I end this section with a brief reference to Doreen Baingana's *Tropical Fish* (2005), which, through short stories featuring moments in the lives of three sisters coming into adulthood, explores the experience of middle-class women in Uganda – and suggests a yearning for the body's life in a very different ecosocial order.

However different in texture from *Thirteen Cents*, these narratives also depict struggles for an adult self in a post-independence world – one that is, again, depicted as dominated by men (local and Western). Their setting, though, places the central characters in worlds far from Azure's: in the family, school, university and the workplace. The attempt to integrate emotional and sexual satisfaction into that sense of self is, likewise, beyond Azure's experience, in that his body is mostly a site of commerce, not desire.[16] References to a natural environment in these stories with an urban setting tend to be of slight significance. Yet, in the final moment of the last story, the writer turns to nature for a resolution. The central character notes, with wistful hope, how people are transforming the urban landscape, replacing colonial-style lawns (reproduced fervently in the US, from where she has recently returned) with productive urban gardens, a form of interacting with natural processes that accords with African cultural memory (Baingana 2005: 146–147). In this postcolonial moment, the future she faces appears less fraught with the difficulties from her past. She faces it with the resolve of the newly returned, to 'dig deep down into this mud with her bare hands' (Baingana 2005: 147). Placed as it is, at the narrative sequence's end, this momentary observation of the gardens cannot erase a difficult past or remedy all that she will confront as she negotiates a return to her urban home. Yet it does offer her both hope and a metaphor for engaging with future difficulties, personal and social.

One can think of this moment as one more instance of a writer turning to nature (inflected by cultural memory) to resolve the stresses of urban social life, a moment that displaces a rich awareness of cities-in-nature with the personal vision of a character in need. What gives the moment special significance, though, is how it is gendered. It shows a woman finding a moment of satisfaction in what is traditionally women's work with natural processes – bringing to grow, around the homestead, what nourishes, then tending and harvesting the crop. It is not only her fraught family experience that this moment comments on implicitly, but also her sexual experience, as she focuses on the gardens' luxuriant unruliness. This social-sexual experience recounted in the earlier *Tropical Fish*, the central story in this collection, which tells of her sexual encounter with a European male and the pregnancy she aborts, suggests how a woman's most intimate life can be limited by interconnected patriarchal and colonising behaviours. Obliquely, her reflective moment provides her with a way to contextualise that experience, to give a brief imaginative glimpse of how she might have enjoyed her woman's body, her sexuality, in a society formed by a culture of tending, not domination, and one in which women's experience matters. This moment offers intuition of a different kind of relation between the human body's life, with its participation in natural processes, and the social order, a kind of relation that involves a different significance for gender. Gender issues and women's sexuality are more than social issues, this moment suggests. They have an ecosocial dimension that is as important to us, as readers and writers focused on cities-in-nature, as issues of water supply or food provision, for example.[17]

As with Duiker's novel, Baingana's fiction, when read in the way I propose, would draw on an understanding of what supports its cities (Entebbe and Kampala) with their material life and what gives them their social vitality. Such a reading would also draw on an understanding of the difficulties these cities face. In relation to such an awareness, the fiction's insights into the city's social worlds and its characters' experiences, objective and subjective, can be held in creative tension.

In closing, I return to general considerations. Urban places involve a rearranging of natural processes in accord with social intent – to produce, as much as possible, a beneficial kind of 'nature' as inhabitants supply themselves with food, water, fuel and material for infrastructure and transportation, etc. Yet nature is not simply inert or subject to human power, and cities have to deal with the unwanted consequences of their growth (for example, pollution, damaged ecosystems). Globalised urbanism now faces the consequences of its long use of fossil fuel, namely both climate change and depleted and acidified oceans, deforestation and the spread of invasive species (which include, increasingly, bacteria and non-living viruses). And human societies are not fixed but, either under the pressure of circumstances or independently, transform themselves – with increasing speed in this globalised urbanism. Clearly, there can be no formula for establishing a successful relation of city to nature, for both society and nature exist in flux as each strives to flourish. Under these conditions, good governance becomes even more of a social necessity, and citizen awareness of what needs to be done, and needs to be done well, is essential. Such an awareness can only rest on as rich an understanding of ecosocial circumstance as possible. Literary study can serve as one further means of crystallising this understanding, one that brings to the wider conversation about cities the kind of interpretation that illuminates the subjective forces set in motion by the social pasts – the histories of colonisation and resistance – that have produced this planet of globalised cities.

For these reasons, ecocritical work should not be reserved for literature focused on nature. Literary texts, regardless of their setting, incorporate and develop attitudes to the natural world, ranging from recognition of its power to affirming its subordination to human interests, to casual reference in passing. In the printed literature emerging from urbanised cultures, 'society' and 'nature' are therefore not in straightforward opposition, but serve to reinforce each other, with specific attitudes towards the urban making plausible specific attitudes towards nature, and vice versa. In many of the world's regions, and this is the case in Africa, where the presence of traditional cultures is felt strongly, especially in rural areas, narratives can draw on traditional attitudes towards nature, with all the ethical and political freight that these may carry, to reinforce attitudes towards the city. Hereby, they can help clarify critical attitudes towards modernity and the global forces that it rests on.

Yet, whatever insights into attitudes towards cities and nature can be drawn from the study of literary texts, such a study needs to be augmented by insights from the study of the objective life of cities, to recall us to all that literature, with its power to move, to influence imagination, might draw our attention away from.[18] In this way, the reading of literature can participate in the project of encouraging the kind of awareness our human ancestors needed to have if they were to survive (an awareness that the modern term 'ecosocial' attempts to stimulate). Whatever built environment our distant ancestors lived in (from the nomad's shelter to the settled hut), it encouraged a sense that the cosmos had a social dimension expressive of non-human energies – energies with which humans lived, on which (if they were beneficent) they relied, and among which they could mingle, leaving the ordinarily human behind.[19] The dominant world of airports, Wi-Fi, gated and guarded luxury communities, of highways and motorised transportation, and so on, develops subjective barriers to entering such ways of being, whether among the wealthy or among the most impoverished, who have to struggle daily to survive, while aware of what they are missing and what defines their life chances. In this world, priorities have shifted, in both objective and subjective dimensions.

Literary study can remind us of currents of need that run counter to modernity's dominant forces. What Duiker's, Mda's and Baingana's African narratives all suggest is the need felt within urbanised cultures for a sense of psychological balance that incorporates both social and natural worlds – one that modernity, in its restless innovation and constant commodification of both social and natural spaces, will continue to undermine. This need to wake to social and natural worlds in an active – interactive – balance, although utopian under modern conditions, does supply a vision to aspire to: a world in which urban places flourish in balance with natural systems, and so provide people with the objective conditions for psychological balance. The narratives looked at in this chapter underscore how utopian this vision is, and there is no plan of action to be conjured that will bridge the gap in living social time between reality and vision. Yet, in the meantime, there is the ongoing multidisciplinary conversation about our life in cities that can hold out the hope of a better life, of a future more optimistic than apocalyptic vision, whether that of the anxiously comfortable or that of the angrily disempowered.

What an ecocriticism of the kind outlined here can supply is a tension in the reader's mind between what the literary text urges us to imagine as real and the complex reality of urban existence – as well as (and this is the second site of desirable tension) the utopian goal of a modern civilisation that lives well 'in place', whether that place is a particular locale or the planet.[20]

References

'About Mshenguville'. Mshenguville Project, http://www.soweto.co.za/html/pro_mshenguville2.htm#aboutSoweto.co.za (accessed 23 July 2015).

Achebe, Chinua. *Arrow of God*. New York: Doubleday (1964), 1989.
Baingana, Doreen. *Tropical Fish: Stories Out of Entebbe*. Amherst: University of Massachusetts Press, 2005.
City of Cape Town. 'Water and Sanitation', https://www.capetown.gov.za/en/water/Pages/default.aspx (accessed 10 March 2013).
DeLoughrey, Elizabeth and Handley, George B. 'Introduction: Toward an aesthetics of the earth', in E. DeLoughrey and G. B. Handley (eds), *Postcolonial Ecologies: Literatures of the Environment*. New York: Oxford University Press, 2011.
Diamond, Jared. *Collapse: How Societies Choose to Fail or Succeed*. New York: Penguin, 2005.
Dirlik, Arif. *Global Modernity: Modernity in the Age of Global Capitalism*. Boulder: Paradigm, 2007.
Duiker, K. Sello. *Thirteen Cents*. Cape Town: David Philip, 2000.
Freund, Bill. *The African City: A History*. New York: Cambridge University Press, 2007.
Lawhon, Mary. 'Situated, networked environmentalisms: A case for environmental theory from the South.' *Geography Compass* 7, 2 (2013): 128–138.
Martin, Julia. 'Situating "place" for environmental literacy.' *English Studies in Africa* 52, 2 (2009): 35–49.
McCormack, Ray and Gelpke, Basil. *A Crude Awakening: The Oil Crash*. Docurama (DVD), 2007.
Mda, Zakes. *The Heart of Redness*. Cape Town: Oxford University Press, 2000.
Miller, John. *Empire and the Animal Body: Violence, Identity and Ecology in Victorian Adventure Fiction*. New York: Anthem, 2012.
Myers, Garth Andrew. *African Cities: Alternative Visions of Urban Theory and Practice*. London: Zed Books, 2011.
National Institutes of Health Office of Strategic Coordination – The Common Fund. Program Snapshot Human Microbiome Project, https://commonfund.nih.gov/hmp/index (accessed 10 July 2013).
Said, Edward W. 'Reflections on exile', in Edward W. Said, *Reflections on Exile and Other Essays*. Cambridge, MA: Harvard University Press, 2000.
Schuttenhelm, Rolf. 'Urban population growth Africa – 300 percent between 2010 and 2050.' *Bits of Science*, 24 November 2010.
'"The Last Word": Sello Duiker', in Mbulelo Vizikhungo Mzamane (ed.), *Words Gone Two Soon: A Tribute to Phaswane Mpe and K. Sello Duiker*. Pretoria: Umgangatho, 2005.
Viljoen, Shaun. 'K. Sello Duiker's *Thirteen Cents*: An Introduction', in K. Sello Duiker, *Thirteen Cents*. Athens: Ohio University Press, 2013.
Vital, Anthony. 'Environmental justice on a postcolonial planet? Implications for literary studies: Considering Dangarembga's *Nervous Conditions*.' (under review).

Vital, Anthony. 'Situating ecology in recent South African fiction: J. M. Coetzee's *The Lives of Animals* and Zakes Mda's *The Heart of Redness*.' *Journal of Southern African Studies* 31, 2 (2005): 297–313.

Vital, Anthony. 'Toward an African ecocriticism: Postcolonialism, ecology and *Life & Times of Michael K*.' *Research in African Literatures* 39, 1 (2008): 87–106. (Corrected version, Anthony Vital, 20 July 2008, http://www.postcolonial-ecology.net.)

Wachsmuth, David. 'Three ecologies: Urban metabolism and the society-nature opposition.' *The Sociological Quarterly* 53 (2012): 506–523.

Chapter 8

NAVIGATING GARIEP COUNTRY: WRITING NATURE-CULTURE IN *BORDERLINE* BY WILLIAM DICEY

MATHILDA SLABBERT

'The plot would be written by the current of the river itself.'
—Jonathan Raban, *Coasting*, cited in George (1992: 258)

'... rivers and those who step into them are always in flux.'
—Blanton (2002: xii)

As a child growing up near the confluence of the Kraai and Orange rivers, I used to wonder what tales the brown water brought and gathered on its way to the sea. I remember the many dry seasons and occasional floods, when debris and the bodies of humans and animals would rush past. But the river not only evoked notions of far-off places or the coming and going of seasons, it also served as a constant reminder that we lived in a border zone: the North Eastern Cape of old on the one side, the Orange Free State on the other.

Apart from the railway bridge, the dusty little town's only link north remains a two-lane crossing with an old bridgehead and a toll house near the southern entrance – architectural reminders of the town's 19th-century past. Geographically, the river divides the land and brings water to a place where just a few kilometres inland sheep would stand in clusters in the shimmering heat, their heads hung low in one another's shade. Along the town's embankment, more structures recall histories of hardship and separation. East of the bridge is Aborsig, previously a white suburb for the more affluent. Further on stands a blockhouse, now a garden of remembrance, and on the bank of the Kraai River there used to be two cemeteries that held the graves of those who died in the concentration camp that was here during the South African War.[1] Left of the bridge, another burial ground embraces the remains of my parents and sisters. Past the railway line, downstream, reaching out into the dull, dry distance, enduring edifices of the black and coloured townships of the old South Africa remain, with a multi-columned granary etched against the horizon. This district, this seemingly inconsequential, bleak border town, which, by virtue of its geographical features and isolation, is not always worthy of the spectacular, is one of many places along the flow of the Orange River that signify the territory's history of suffering and marginalisation.[2] My personal connection with the region and interest in literatures of the environment are some of the reasons why I chose *Borderline*, by William Dicey (2004), for a postcolonial ecocritical reading.

Framed as an adventure (travel) narrative, *Borderline* traces the 1400-kilometre canoe journey down the Orange (Gariep) River[3] undertaken by the author and his two friends, Christopher and Lawrence, from above its confluence with the Vaal River to where it enters the Atlantic Ocean.[4] The trip lasted 34 days in 2001 and Dicey took two years to complete the narrative.[5] As the title suggests, the investigative nature of the travelogue transcends the theme of adventure and endurance. The narrative juxtaposes past and present in an examination of issues relating to the environment, race and culture, and especially perceptions about hybrid identity in a territory where a diversity of peoples have conflicting ideas about what it means to be categorised under the homogenising term 'coloured' or to be Griqua, Nama, Baster, etc.[6] By analysing the text through a postcolonial ecocritical lens, my aim is twofold. First, I am interested in how genre and narration in *Borderline* offer ways of thinking about 'corporeal subjects moving through material landscape' (Duncan and Gregory 1999: 5), thus reworking a *Heart of Darkness* and *Huckleberry Finn* theme, and how Dicey negotiates notions of literal and figurative boundaries to prompt engagement with socio-environmental issues. In the first part of the discussion, therefore, I draw on a range of travel-writing criticism to examine Dicey's stylistic and thematic border crossings, and to consider the ways in which he fuses the pragmatic and physical experience of the journey with the lyrical and autobiographical to call for enquiries about people and place. My enquiry develops from Michael Kowalewski's observation that it is 'the hybrid, "androgynous" qualities of travel writing that place it in an unusual critical position' and that 'deserve to be studied, for the question of form raised by this genre bears directly on its attempts to intermix a sense of freedom with social awareness, an itch to escape with candid respect for ... landscapes and culture' (Kowalewski 1992: 8).

Second, while I do not neglect my literary interrogation, I feel impelled by the narrative's interdisciplinary content and its attention to manifestations of marginalisation (exploitation, separation, poverty, etc.) to write about history, geography, politics, economy, gender, and so on – in short, to consider 'the interrelatedness of all things', as represented in the text (Buell 2005: 139). I proceed from the suggestion of Graham Huggan and Helen Tiffin that postcolonial ecocritical text analysis requires an exploration of 'how different cultural understandings of society and nature' are 'deployed in specific historical moments by writers in the making of their art' (Huggan and Tiffin 2010: 15), bearing in mind the view of Byron Caminero-Santangelo and Garth Myers that postcolonial ecocriticism 'emphasises', among other concerns, 'a sense of political commitment, interdisciplinarity, and the interrogation of capitalist development' (Caminero-Santangelo and Myers 2013: iii). To develop an exploration of how these issues emerge in Dicey's representation, I refer to contemporary examples where socio-environmental and political injustices prevail in the region under discussion, and, in the latter part of the chapter, I draw specifically on Rob Nixon's ideas in *Slow Violence and the Environmentalism of the Poor* (2011) to support my claim that Dicey engages productively with issues of displacement, violence and loss. Nixon (2011: 2) defines 'slow violence' as 'neither spectacular nor instantaneous, but rather incremental and accretive, its calamitous repercussions playing out across a range of temporal scales'. He relates these issues to 'the environmentalism of the poor ... those people lacking resources who are the principal casualties of slow violence' (Nixon 2011: 4). In conclusion, I argue that *Borderline* serves as an example of how the writer's 'imaginative agility and worldly ardour ... help [to] amplify the media-marginalised causes of the environmentally dispossessed' (Nixon 2011: 6), and in so doing implicitly link the regionalist concerns of the narrative to transnational debates about histories of displacement and global environmental injustices.

In Part I of *Borderline*, Dicey (2004: 29) notes: 'One can hardly better the lower reaches of the Orange as the backdrop for an inquiry into the San, the Nama, the Korana, the trekboers, the Griquas and the Basters, and the coloured people into whom they have merged.' Because the author foregrounds his interest in the history of place with notions of identity, and I seek to explore the layered representation of past and present forms of socio-environmental marginalisation in the text, I begin with a brief overview of the history of the northern territories.

Before the arrival of the Dutch in 1652, Khoisan societies inhabited the Cape interior, reaching north-west to beyond the Orange River.[7] In her quest narrative, *The Side of the Sun at Noon* (2014), Hazel Crampton investigates the legend of the Chobona people, mentioned in the records of the Dutch officials who came to occupy the Cape in the 17th century. Crampton (2014) notes that groups such as the 'Goringhaique', 'Cochoqueas', 'Chainouqua', 'Charigurique' and 'Gerigriqua' occupied different areas of the modern Western Cape province. The Goringhaique, though, were the first to suffer the consequences of land dispossession when Commander Jan van Riebeeck built the first fort at the foot of Table Mountain and 'prohibited [them] from living within a distance of eight to 10 hours' travel' (Crampton 2014: 69).

North of the Olifants River, in the regions bordering on the lower and middle reaches of the Orange River, lived various groups of Nama people. Like their counterparts from the south, they too 'practised seasonal transhumance' (Crampton 2014: 2), and had been part of an ancient and intricate prehistoric trading network, bringing into contact people, 'cultures and bloodlines' (Crampton 2014: 171) from across Africa and further afield, e.g. 'Arabic ... Indian, Persian and other Asian' peoples (Crampton 2014: 170). This network functioned along routes leading to ports on the eastern coast of Africa, notably Mogadishu, Kilwa, Sofala and, once the Portuguese had arrived, coastal villages in Mozambique (Crampton 2014: 171). This intermingling of bloodlines along with the history of miscegenation 'contribute to the genetic mix' (Crampton 2014: 318) of South Africa's current 'genetically diverse population' (Crampton 2014: 315).

On the issue of trade, however, as historian Nigel Penn explains in his seminal text, *The Forgotten Frontier: Colonist and Khoisan on the Cape's Northern Frontier in the 18th Century* (2001), with Dutch occupation, the entire zone, from the Cape to the Orange River, became progressively more important as a grazing area, a hunting ground, and for livestock trade, especially during the 18th century, resulting in a surge of human and animal migration to the area. The desire for land ignited violent conflicts among the diverse subcultural groups (indigenous, creolised and colonists) who came to inhabit the region. This situation 'approached the genocidal after 1770' (Penn 2001: 9), with devastating effects on human and animal life.

My own interest in the area, reinforced by Penn's argument that researchers have neglected this territory in favour of 'the drama of the eastern frontier' (Penn 2001: 1), impels me to write about the region and my appreciation of Dicey's text. The Orange River was viewed as the unofficial border long before Sir Harry Smith declared it as such in 1847, but 'the societies of its immediate hinterland would remain frontier societies' until the late 19th century (Penn 2001: 286). Currently, the river maps the border between South Africa and Namibia, and it has maintained its boundary status, still burdened by 'competing claims to belonging and entitlement' on both sides of its banks (Huggan and Tiffin 2010: 87).

'Frontiers,' Dicey writes, 'are places of uncertainty, of shifting identity. Who are you, as you ride over the horizon? Who do you want to be, as you appear to strangers? If you want support, you stress commonality; if you want to fight, you stress differences' (Dicey 2004: 61–62). But he also mentions that 'the border [seems to be] of little consequence to the people of the [Orange] river' (Dicey 2004: 234). But where exactly is the official line of a border in a river? The London *Mining Journal* defines the divide of the Orange River as running 'along the north bank', despite Namibia's ongoing attempts to negotiate a dissection 'along the middle course' for increased diamond-mining purposes (see 'Orange River diamond licences': 5). National borders in Africa are the remnants of colonial institutionalisation and, as Homi Bhabha (1994) suggests, zones 'where space and time cross to produce complex figures of difference and identity, past and present, inside and outside, inclusion and exclusion', and 'it is in the emergence of the interstices – the overlap and displacement of domains of difference – that the intersubjective and collective experiences of *nationness*, community interest, or cultural value are negotiated' (Bhabha 1994: i). Such negotiations between past and present – similarities and differences – and shifting perceptions about border spaces are not only mirrored in the constant flow and flux of the river, but also symbolised in the moving subject's engagement with territory and individuals, as well as in the layered representational strategies of *Borderline*.

Generic border crossings

In terms of genre and narration, Kowalewski's thoughts are pertinent here. 'Travel writing,' he states, 'involves border crossings both literal and figurative' (Kowalewski 1992: 7). While Dicey and his friends physically criss-cross South African and Namibian soil, the metaphorical and stylistic border crossings are more significant, especially in Dicey's enmeshed enquiry into ownership, control, race, identity and the environment. The genre has long been burdened by a fair level of critique. According to Blanton (2002: 128), 'Studies by anthropologists and literary critics alike have centred on the way travel writing, like its scientific double, ethnography, tends to be Eurocentric and even imperialistic.' So Mary Louise Pratt and others have argued perceptively about the use of tropes and how these 'disunify [and] unify ... a rhetoric of travel writing' (Pratt 1992: 11). For instance, the trope of 'monarch-of-all-I-survey' (Pratt 1992: 201) enforces notions of conquest and difference in 'the contact zone' (Pratt 1992: 4). But Kowalewski (1992: 9) counters that a 'postcolonial legacy of cultural ignorance or wilful distortion' has cultivated awareness among travel writers 'to narrow their eyes at signs of cultural chauvinism', and Bart Moore-Gilbert (2009: xxii–xxiii) takes the argument further:

> Postcolonial authors at times use travel-writing to challenge the resolution of conflicts of identity which is traditionally understood to structure western male autobiography, thereby in the end producing a stable subject position through which the Subject accedes to full self-knowledge. However, if they employ the genre to stress instead the processual and unfinished nature of identity-formation, in the manner often claimed for women auto/biographers, postcolonial life-writers also use travel-writing as a counter-discourse, in a way which exceeds the ambitions of their western counterparts. For instance, the genre provides grounds both for *auto*-ethnographical challenges to western representations of the non-West and for an ethnography of the West itself.

It is not within the scope of this discussion to include a concise overview of the historiography of South African travel writing, as this body of work spans more than five centuries, including accounts of 15th-century maritime voyages, travels into the southern African interior and more recent journeys captured in diverse media and hybrid forms (see note 8), including letters, diaries, journals, official reports, travelogues, and so forth. However, as Ben Maclennan (2003) notes in the preface to his anthology, *The Wind Makes Dust: Four Centuries of Travel in Southern Africa*, 'the most glaring' characteristic of the body of conquest writings is that 'the overwhelming majority of writers are [male] Europeans' (Maclennan 2003: 1). His collection of (unsettling) anecdotal excerpts, from texts written between 1497 and 1900, serves as a poignant example of the kind of imperialistic discourse and cultural chauvinism Kowalewski, Pratt and other critics discuss.

In narratives of travels to the region under investigation here, the first attempt to reach the Orange River from the Cape, in 1661, lauded as the first European expeditionary group to meet and trade with the Nama, is recorded in Pieter van Meerhoff's letters to Jan van Riebeeck, included in H. B. Thom's edited version of the *Journal of Jan van Riebeeck* (Maclennan 2003: 31, 377). Van Meerhoff's account forms part of a heralding multi-vocal narrative, documenting various excursions to the north. Despite the detailed nature of the text, the Dutch commander cannot be credited with authorship because it was 'not written by Van Riebeeck himself, but by the Company scribe or clerk' (Crampton 2014: 375). Nevertheless, the journal is one of the first in a large body of travel writings by colonists, settlers, adventurers, explorers, missionaries, and such – each laying claim to a 'first discovery' of some kind. This archive of pioneering travels and findings consists of topics such as first reaching and/or crossing the Orange River; finding metals, precious stones and minerals of different kinds; seeing the Augrabies Falls; encountering various indigenous groups; and discovering 'new' botanical and zoological species. Written either by the leader of a journey or a companion, the narratives relate the experiences of Simon van der Stel, Jacobus Coetzee, François Le Vaillant, Hendrik Hop, Robert Gordon, Hendrik Jacob Wikar, Sir James Alexander, Heinrich Lichtenstein, William Somerville, William John Burchell and Robert Moffat, to name but a few. Most of them are mentioned in *Borderline*.

Returning to Moore-Gilbert's point about 'postcolonial life-writers [who] also use travel-writing as a counter-discourse' (Moore-Gilbert, 2009: xxii), I argue that Dicey is alert to the pitfalls of the travel-writing genre, maintaining and reworking conventions in his investigation of the 'unfinished nature of identity-formation' in relation to territory. Therefore, I concur with Isaac Ndlovu's comment that *Borderline* 'tries to subvert the discredited patronising colonial travellers' gaze by jettisoning its totalising tendencies' (Ndlovu 2013: 115). Unlike so many adventure writings published by South Africans in the past decade, Dicey's examination has a regional focus (Caminero-Santangelo 2011: 6)[8] on the lives of ordinary people on both sides of the river in an area he is familiar with. 'In this landscape,' Dicey explains, 'I knew something of the people's situation, and I speak good Afrikaans' (Dicey 2004: 19). Seen as a process that 'defamiliaris[es] the familiar ... exploring what is under [his] nose' (Matos 1992: 217), Dicey's approach further demonstrates a resistance to neo-imperial practices that simulate 'colonial re-enactment [that] works to maintain boundaries, categories, and hierarchies established in imperial writing'

(Neumann 2011: 44). A scrutiny of national news media in any given week indicates that the region under discussion here receives very little attention. *Borderline* therefore confirms Kowalewski's view that travel writing with a local (and regional) focus is valuable in 'exposing and investigating conditions at home that most would prefer to ignore' (Kowalewski 1992: 13). As much as it is a 'book about the river' (Dicey 2004: 38), the author negotiates its 'interstices' (Bhabha 1994: i) to argue that 'the Gariep [can be seen] as metaphor for a non-racial South Africa, its several ethnic tributaries together constituting a new main-stream culture ...' (Dicey 2004: 273). By streaming together the private and the public, history and memory, in a metaphorically layered representation, these 'literary tropes' become 'crucial sites where postcolonial national and cultural identities are being formed and contested' (Woods 2012: 3).

Representing interrelated awareness

How do the structure and style reflect Dicey's revision of conventions, and his negotiation of history and memory in creative non-fiction? *Borderline* comprises eight parts, each tracing a specific stage of the journey. On the contents page, the inclusion of a series of topics under geographical headings is reminiscent of imperial travel-writing conventions that still pervade many contemporary works. To illustrate from a section *in medias res*, Part V, for instance, reads:

> AUGRABIES TO PELLA
> augrabies falls – patrick bosman – riemvasmaak – marengo – forced removals – giraffe hunting – the fishermen of red rock weir – onseepkans – bushmanland – scully – vanishing game and vanishing san – anthing's special mission – tgaams – richie falls – johannes jacobs (Dicey 2004: contents page)

In the developed chapter, however, Dicey subverts reader expectations induced by key topics, such as 'giraffe hunting', to merge related concerns stemming from encounters on that particular leg of the journey. For instance, he traces the consequences of colonial expansion on a species by recollecting the first sighting, shooting and naming of the giraffe by a European (Robert Gordon) 'in southern Africa ... in 1663' (Dicey 2004: 151). He recounts anecdotes from other travel texts to expand on this topic, while turning to cultural associations preceding the arrival of Europeans. Rock art, for instance, dating back more than 'three thousand years' (Dicey 2004: 151), indicates the importance of giraffes and other species to precolonial cultures. To conclude the topic, he conveys his own survey of the landscape in minimalist yet loaded terms. Giraffes, along with elephants, rhinoceroses, zebras and hippopotami, have all disappeared, leaving only 'the occasional kudu and ostrich still roam[ing] the Augrabies area' (Dicey 2004: 153). In this way, the history of place becomes infused with Dicey's references to intertexts from across disciplines – for instance history, ethnography, archaeology, literature, folklore and science. Embedded in this interdisciplinary approach is his own lively interest in human–nature interaction.[9] He is clearly alert to the ties between nature and the shifting cross-cultural dynamics of a specific area. The use of intertexts reveals his meticulous research. By citing other travel writings, he further confirms what Paul Fussell (1992: 79) describes as the practice of 'reading about someone else's travel ... which is to say that traveling' is 'ipso facto, literary traveling ...', 'making an exciting metaphoric relation between one's current travel and someone else's travel in the past' to establish an 'anthropological and historical framework' (Matos 1992: 223).

Dicey's overview of wildlife disappearance, read as an example of speciesism alongside the history of racism in Riemvasmaak, as recorded in the 'border-crossing activity' (Dicey 2004: 145) and 'forced removals' in Part V, emphasises the history of othering in this particular area. What emerges is a sense of Dicey's ecological awareness and humanism, straddling fields from both the humanities and the sciences. Riemvasmaak, 'a seventy-thousand-hectare tract of arid mountain on the northern bank' (Dicey 2004: 144), became home to Nama, Damara and Herero peoples, who had fled to the region during the late 19th century 'to escape protracted violence in Namibia'. By 1934, however, it was declared 'a temporary Native Reserve' (Dicey 2004: 148) despite its predominantly coloured population, who were then under pressure 'to apply for Bantu identity books' (Dicey 2004: 148). During the early 1970s, the inhabitants (including Xhosa-speaking residents) were moved and removed (to the Eastern Cape) under segregation legislation and the newly introduced homeland laws. Eventually, 'Riemvasmaak was given to the South African Defence Force, who used it for missile-testing, and to the Augrabies Falls National Park, who planned to introduce black rhino' (Dicey 2004: 149).

Dicey then turns to the present and persisting sociopolitical and economic problems. Shortly after the first democratic election, 'Riemvasmakers ... won the right to return to their land' (Dicey 2004: 149) but, as the local tourist officer, Norbit Coetzee, tells Dicey (one of the many examples of dialogue between the author and people he encounters and interviews en route), there are abiding concerns – for instance, the threat to the survival of the Nama language ('there is no institutional support for the language') and the lack of 'capital funding' (Dicey 2004: 150), which undermines development and employment opportunities, causing younger people to migrate to the cities. In *Riemvasmaak: Hartland, Harde Land* by Euodia Engels (2005), presumably the same Norbert Coetzee (his first name spelled differently in this text) summarises the history of the region, as recorded in *Borderline*, but he adds the recollection of a convention held in Upington in 1994, where the new government promised people housing, paved streets, electricity, running water and land along the river, where they would be able to farm and grow their own vineyards (Engels 2005: 13, paraphrased in translation). Alas, the government did not fulfil its promise.

Dicey sustains this strategy of interweaving diverse themes throughout, especially to elucidate the plight of marginalised communities. In Part I, for instance, he discusses the '!Xu and Khwe people who were chased out of Angola into Namibia by the MPLA [in 1972]' (Dicey 2004: 39). Many of these men joined the South African Defence Force (and Jonas Savimbi's UNITA), 'serving as trackers and combatants' (Dicey 2004: 39). When Namibia gained independence, however, the 'San were given the option of moving to South Africa, and in 1990 some seven thousand ... arrived at Schmidtsdrift,' a territory previously inhabited by the 'Thlaping (Tswana-speaking) group that had been forcibly evicted in the late 1960s' (Douglas 2013: 47). Stuart Douglas (2013: 46) notes that 'the South African state agreed, early in 1996, to furnish the bushmen who were living at Schmidtsdrift with a substantial financial grant, rumoured to have amounted to R61 million, to assist in the development of a permanent home'. In 2001, at the time of Dicey's journey, they were 'still ... living in military tents' (Dicey 2004: 39). Douglas's study prompts the question, drawing on Bhabha's arguments about hybrid identity, whether this persistent marginalisation of a group – in the apartheid and post-apartheid state – is a 'construction of a political object that is *neither One nor the Other*' (Bhabha, cited in Douglas [2013: 3], emphasis in original). The Schmidtsdrift community has since been 'resettled' at Platfontein, near Kimberley, where tourists can now visit them as one of the sites on a 'Footprints of the San' tour (see *Open Africa*).

Riemvasmaak, like Schmidtsdrift, is marketed as a remote tourist destination offering the experience of traditional cooking, dancing and storytelling, as well as four-wheel-drive excursions into the desert landscape. Such cultural tourism constitutes a pastime which, like game-reserve tourism, is mostly aimed at the privileged (and wealthy), and which poses its own set of debates about the consumption of environments and cultures. In *Borderline*, Dicey alludes to controversies related to game reserves, tourism and agriculture when, on the last leg of their journey, the group reach the Richtersveld. In a conversation with researcher Howard Hendricks, Dicey discusses a previous disagreement between local goat farmers and authorities who proposed a game reserve based on claims that overgrazing had damaged the ecosystem. Hendricks raises two crucial findings. Firstly, he points out that 'stock numbers ... sometimes exceed 6 600 in summer, but never by more than ten per cent. In winter, they drop below the limit. ... The ecosystem is as it is partly due to centuries of grazing.' And, secondly, 'the botanists and their 4x4s probably cause more damage than the goats' (Dicey 2004: 260–261). By emphasising such environmental issues and linking them 'to postcolonial debates surrounding belonging and entitlement' (Huggan and Tiffin 2010: 69), Dicey's text evokes interrogations about ethics and the consumption of nature-culture, as well as the reality of transformation in the post-apartheid state where the environment and communities at the margins both become commodities.[10] Cultural-studies critics, such as Jeanne van Eeden, have cautioned that game-reserve tourism and other forms of 'rediscovering' Africa enforce 'binary oppositions ... that draw attention to the distinction between culture/nature, power/powerlessness, male/female, technology/primitive' (Van Eeden 2006: 343).

What appeals to me as a reader is Dicey's synthesising technique, which demands engagement with serious issues through expressive passages of nature writing. Moreover, he draws the reader back into the quotidian experience of his journey by situating nature descriptions carefully to frame moments of solitude or personal introspection. For instance, towards the end of Part I, he writes:

> It was a warm evening and we had no need of splash-decks or paddle tops. We glided along the moonlit water, freed of accessories, purged of tenses. The voices of cicadas, crickets and frogs pierced the night. Half-seen trees flitted by on the banks. Then we were amongst ducks again and the growing crescendo of wings beating the air. And afterwards, silence. (Dicey 2004: 64)

What emerges from his narrative strategy is carefully crafted imaginative writing: investigative literature in which an 'advocacy for the demarginalisation of groups' blends with 'aesthetic' and 'socioenvironmental' (Nixon 2011: 32) concerns in 'politically engaged non-fiction' (Nixon 2011: 25).

Remaining with the topic of form and representation, I turn briefly to the textual and visual layout of the book. As is the practice in travel writing, a map of the region precedes the written work. The map, however, is minimalist in style (without topographical details), featuring only the line of the river and a few place names, tributaries and subregions. In addition, black-and-white images from various media are dispersed throughout (photographs, sketches, paintings, old maps, newspaper articles, journals and the odd mathematical table). These images are not captioned, thus challenging the reader to continue reading to contextualise the seemingly disconnected visuals. For example, a landscape photograph of the Orange River (Dicey 2004: 154) is followed by photos of Dicey and his friends (Dicey 2004: 155).

Within a few pages, the mood changes when the reader is confronted with a 19th-century photograph (by Ennis Edwards) of a springbok massacre (Dicey 2004: 158–59) and images of a *kokerboom*, or quiver tree (Dicey 2004: 236), a *halfmens* plant (Dicey 2004: 237) or wind pumps (Dicey 2004: 74). These evoke the iconography of the landscape but serve as a backdrop to the narrative unfolding in the written text, explaining the legends, botanical features, medicinal use, history, etymology and anecdotes related to each object. The text confirms the claim of James Duncan and Derek Gregory (1999: 4) that such an 'alternative strategy of attending to the physicality of representation imposes the obligation to read these different media together, and in so doing, to attend to their different valences and silences'. Textual and visual information (private and public) is reduced and reconfigured along similar patterns to 'create a literary, political and historical context' (Matos 1992: 228).

Regarding the adventure theme of the narrative, Dicey acknowledges those who have challenged the dangers of the Orange, ranging from the 'San, or Bushmen, ferrygliding across the river on swimming logs' (Dicey 2004: 37) to Louw van Riet and Mickey du Toit, who canoed from Aliwal North to the mouth, passing down the same route just three weeks before Dicey and his companions (Dicey 2004: 27). The thrills, challenges and accomplishments of their journey, as well as the moments of camaraderie and conflict, are recalled in a style that parallels the mood, themes or rhythms of the broader narrative. The times when the team paddles in silence provide opportunities for reflection, private moments in which Dicey allows the reader glimpses of himself – his memories, interests, philosophies and contemplations. At moments like these, Dicey sometimes humanises the landscape. For example, he addresses the river directly: 'Will you help us, I wondered. Will you carry us safely to the sea?' (Dicey 2004: 16). But, soon, the mathematician in him emerges: as 'a piece of driftwood floated past', he calculates, 'travelling in a current of, say three kilometres per hour, it would reach the Atlantic in under twenty days. … We were banking on thirty to forty days, given that we'd only be on the water for a quarter of any given day' (Dicey 2004: 16). In other instances, the lyrical, philosophical and metaphorical quality of the writing counters the pragmatic and critical content of the work:

> I needed the simplicity of the desert landscape, the vast open spaces, the nothingness. ... The clean air, the clear light, the primeval silence. The seductive contrast, no doubt, between these delicate things and the vicious heat. The brooding majesty of the landscape, the hardiness of the plants and animals, the scarcity of humans, the miracle of dripping water. And the cumulative effect of all these things: that sense of immutable peace one gets in the desert. A peace that comes, I think, from finding one's inner markers. The desert is bound to reveal your true needs; there's nowhere to hide – just you and sand and stone and sky. (Dicey 2004: 242)

The landscape is often romanticised in the style of conventional desert literature. It provides a space for solitude and meditation, while the rather nostalgic mood of the imaginative depiction conveys nature's affective impact on the author's senses and psyche. Melancholy, however, does not convert to 'imperial nostalgia' or what Renaldo Rosaldo describes as a 'mourning for what one has destroyed' in situations where 'someone deliberately alters a form of life and then regrets that things have not remained as they were prior to his or her intervention' (Rosaldo 1989: 107–108). Nevertheless, with terms such as 'seductive' and 'delicate' – as is the case in other instances where Dicey genders landscape, for example, by referring to 'the sensuous curves of the basalt', which 'made it seem as if [they] had been weeks already without women, without the mystery their presence breeds' (Dicey 2004: 26),[11] accompanied by a photograph of the rock formation resembling features of a naked female body – he lapses into 'male-centred mythologizing' (Driver 1992: 455), whereby a binary 'association of women with nature and men with culture' (Driver 1992: 458) is perpetuated. This association is underscored by the masculine nature of the text, drawing on imperial ideals that viewed adventure (travel) as predominantly a masculine pursuit calling for separation from female company (MacKenzie 1987: 180).

The introspective narrative voice constitutes one of the arresting features of *Borderline*. Significantly, there are instances when Dicey confronts crucial existential questions: 'Who am I? What am I doing here? How do I belong in this place and how do I write about this place?' For instance:

> I considered the riverscape before me. What was it about these mountains, this river? What gave them this exultant quality? The startling contrast between the wetness of water and the stoniness of stones, yes, but why did I find this so compelling? Was it the suddenness of the transition? A metre off the water you are already in desert. A few steps further and the onslaught of rock and hammering sun so overwhelms you, you can hardly conceive of water any more, you begin to doubt the Orange's ability to wet you. Perhaps that's where the magic of the Richtersveld resides, in the steep gradient between water and stone, in the tension it creates. (Dicey 2004: 233–234)

The poetic quality of the metaphoric language emerges suggestively in these moments of self-reflexivity while maintaining a balance between the objective/external and subjective/internal narration. Dicey inclines to the plural personal pronoun 'we', switching to 'I' in the narration of personal encounters or private thought. This narrative shift establishes a voice that attempts objectivity through careful deconstruction of event and an enquiry into how a sense of belonging in a space is perpetually shaped across different narrative scales while ecological, cultural and historical interrogation overrides potential self-heroising. Scholarly exploration combined with introspection reveals an author 'caught up in a complex dialectic between recognition and recuperation' (Duncan and Gregory 1999: 4). Because the critical enquiry supersedes the level of self-narration, it avoids the type of self-glorification and 'if-it's-me-it-must-be-interesting' approach, which can endanger memoirs of this kind (Nixon 2011: 25–26) and suggests that the moments of meditation are intimate and analytical. Early in the text, Dicey (2004: 14) defines himself and his friends as 'novice paddlers': athletic ability and achievement remain subliminal to the more serious concerns brought to mind as their bodies move through the territory. 'My deepest motivation for tackling the river,' he admits, 'was ten years of fatigue' (Dicey 2004: 75). This acknowledgement, presented in the narrator's individual voice, might be seen as an exposure of his privileged position as a subject who can afford to travel for entertainment or recuperation. Yet he also attempts to capture collective voices from the larger community to discuss the ways in which locals perceive(d) and navigate(d) the river and live(d) their daily lives near it. San tradition, he recalls (drawing on William Burchell's writings), used 'the swimming log' to cross the river, making the Orange 'probably the largest river on earth on which no craft more advanced than a floating log was used until the coming of the Europeans' (Dicey 2004: 37). The logs, Crampton explains, also guided by Burchell, were called '*bā:s* ... a branch with a peg driven into one end onto which the swimmer could hold' and 'several logs' tied together were used as '/*āmas*, or rafts' (Crampton 2014: 156).

In Part VII, Dicey briefly chronicles the history of white paddlers of the Orange (beginning in 1952), again underscoring the entertainment value of the river for the fortunate. But it is his encounters with locals that convey alternative perceptions and voices about the river. For most, he explains, it is a space or source to negotiate for survival. For example, Patrick Bosman, a hunter they encounter near Augrabies, patiently sits waiting on the bank for a kudu to surface after drowning. Namibian shepherd Isak Botes lives with the elderly on the northern bank where 'they draw their pensions' but he has to 'row across the river each month' to get his (Dicey 2004: 189). Dabis, another Namibian, makes a living by fishing from an 'inflated inner tube of a tractor tyre' (Dicey 2004: 234). Similarly, fisherman Johannes Jacobs 'walk[s] the banks of the Orange' to fish at night (Dicey 2004: 173).

Foreshadowing the idea that the primary focus is not the adventure or even a 'rediscovery of the natural world' (Gray 1992: 49) of the Orange, Dicey begins his story on land, and it is this beginning, and his recollection a few pages later of the previous day's visit to a nearby site, that shaped my introduction to this essay. The account commences in a place that is one of the lasting remnants of white conservative Afrikaner separatist ideology: the self-imposed homeland (*volkstaat*) Orania, which is 'fenced and, as a board at the entrance warns, strictly private'

(Dicey 2004: 13). By representing this bastion of racism and paranoia as a precursor to the history of displacement and marginalisation, Dicey skilfully signifies that the travelogue is not only about a river journey or about arriving at a specific destination, but rather about the process of travelling to examine the intricate relationship between people and the environment: how history is inscribed onto landscape.

Following the first paragraph of this account, and underscoring the notion of segregation (forced or chosen), is an image of Hendrik Frensch Verwoerd's clothes worn on 6 September 1966, the day the National Party's prime minister was stabbed to death by Dimitri Tsafendas (Dicey 2004: 33, 276). Dicey returns to the topic of Verwoerd and Tsafendas at the end of the narrative, on arrival at the mouth of the river. Tsafendas had worked there 'on a dredger' (Dicey 2004: 276) before his employment as a 'messenger in Parliament' (Dicey 2004: 276), where he assassinated Verwoerd. Classified as white but 'born half-Greek, half-African in colonial Mozambique', Tsafendas had applied to be reclassified as coloured (Dicey 2004: 276). Living a life 'defined by racial prejudice' (Dicey 2004: 276), Tsafendas had lashed out violently against what Dicey describes as 'the artificial boundaries of race' (Dicey 2004: 272).

And so, despite the linear nature of the physical journey in *Borderline* from 'Orania to Oranjemund' (Dicey 2004: 21), it is a circular narrative, framing history within these two figures, Verwoerd and Tsafendas, who are symbolic of the many victims and perpetrators who shaped the history of a territory where lives intersect in multiple ways along the literal and metaphorical axis 'of a great liquid god snaking away across a subcontinent' (Dicey 2004: 16). Although the adventure theme of the narrative ends in this tidal or 'littoral zone' (Mansfield 2013: 2) where the river meets the ocean, the historical theme, embodied in the real and symbolic connectedness between Verwoerd and Tsafendas, resounds in the space of the 'sea's social function as a transport surface connecting distant and dispersed landmasses' (Samuelson 2013: 10), echoing themes of loss and dislocation, and the transport of people, animals and resources central to the discursive field of literatures of the 'black Atlantic' (Gilroy 1993; Goyal 2010) and '"black water" … of the Indian Ocean' (Samuelson 2013: 2).

Moving from Orania, Dicey recalls his visit the previous day to another symbolically loaded site in the same area: the 'Orange River

Station Concentration Camp'. This is a remnant of the South African War, in which '28 000 Boer women and children and somewhere in the region of 20 000 black South Africans died in British concentration camps' (Dicey 2004: 22). As well as the blockhouse, a structural reminder of conflict and oppression, Dicey (2004: 20) notes the 'relics' that still litter the camp ground – the enduring 'minutiae ... baked bean and bully beef tins, a cooking screen, two kettles, pieces of ceramic water cask, a coffee grinder, a handful of buttons, several horseshoes, a blue medicine bottle and a bucket'. And he notes where 'the parade ground had been – in one hundred years the vegetation has still not recovered' (Dicey 2004: 21). By capturing these details, Dicey suggests that the abusive power of one ideology versus another and the lasting consequences of these conflicts are not only recorded in the history books, but also inscribed on the environment. Here, the desolate space, along with the rows of alien pecan trees, so crucial to the economy of Orania, signifies the many manifestations of slow violence in the territory.

In the final section of this chapter, I isolate examples in *Borderline* that relate explicitly to Nixon's arguments about slow violence and the environmentalism of the poor, in particular the politics of mining. In the early stages of the journey, Dicey and his friends visit Westerberg, a mining town near Koegas, about 25 kilometres downstream from Boegoeberg Dam. To their surprise, they find that what is defined as 'a reasonable settlement on [their] map' is nothing but 'a ghost town' (Dicey 2004: 76). Dicey does not elaborate on the history of the mining village, although he does examine the impact of the dam as 'the first significant barrier to restrict the Orange' and 'to silence' the river's voice (Dicey 2004: 84), beginning with a geological discussion of the region's strata formed during the 'break up [of] the super-continent of Gondwanaland 180 million years ago' (Dicey 2004: 83).

I turn to the silent aftermath of Westerberg's mining history, which is representative of similar mining practices in the territory and across the globe (for example, in India). In 1805 explorer Heinrich Lichtenstein discovered blue asbestos (crocidolite) in this area. Subsequently, asbestos was mined here and at various other South African sites. The health risks and dangers associated with asbestos became known during the late 1970s, and Westerberg mine was closed down; others, such as the

'Griqualand exploration mine near Kuruman', remained in operation until 1996 (see 'Westerberg Asbestos Mine [Closed]'). Despite the shutdowns, however, the aftermath (on bodies and the environment) will linger for years, as a 1998 government report confirms:

> The mine dumps and much of the adjacent area are heavily contaminated ... and must still be rehabilitated by levelling the spoil heaps and covering the area with a thick layer of gravel and top soil. The cost of the rehabilitation ... is one of the many issues which will be considered when assessing the feasibility of a new dam at Boegoeberg. ('Westerberg Asbestos Mine [Closed]')

To date, no new dam has been built and the current dam remains the source for agrarian irrigation in the region. Asbestos mining serves here as an example of what Nixon (2011: 211), in another context, refers to as 'environmental toxicity'. One can rephrase Nixon's question[12] to ask, who is counting the casualties of this form of slow violence, which is not mainline news any more?

Another mining commodity associated with the Orange River is diamonds. As Dicey (2004: 266–267) reports:

> Today diamonds are mined along the coast for hundreds of kilometres on either side of the Orange River mouth. Operators have spiralled off upstream to Sanddrif, Bloeddrif, Jakalsberg, Sendelingsdrif, Oenas near Pootjiespram, and Grasdrif. The madness of it all – the open-cast strip-mining, the devastated sandveld vegetation, the transformation of the coloured reserves into pools of cheap labour. San and Nama children, writes one historian, used to play with bright stones in the vicinity of the mouth. They never actively looked for diamonds, he comments, 'omdat hulle nie die waarde daarvan besef het nie' [they were unaware of the value]. Which, of course, entirely misses the point. Diamonds *are* just bright stones. (Italics in original)

Perhaps not on a par with the levels of corruption and exploitation – or newsworthiness – of the diamond industry in Sierra Leone, mining here nevertheless carries its own history of conflict on both sides of the river. Dicey's survey recalls past (and present) activities, but again raises questions about wealth and poverty, ownership, power and environmental degradation. At Grasdrif he notices the 'rubble hill' of the mine and 'the compound for Aussenkehr's eight-thousand-strong labour force' (Dicey 2004: 239). Just past the confluence with the Great Fish River, the paddlers see the 'deserted caravans and corrugated remains of failed claims ... the mining equipment abandoned' and they begin to call these remnants 'diamond ugly' (Dicey 2004: 258). Near Sendelingsdrif they spot 'Reuning's man-made mesas – great trapeziums of stripped overburden, which is to say the remains of a delicate ecosystem', along with the 'immaculately reeded [*matjieshuisies*] for tourists' (Dicey 2004: 259).

It is perhaps Dicey's conversations with two locals that best summarise lingering socio-environmental issues related to diamond mining. In the first, Willem de Wet, a parks official, remarks, 'Just look out that door at what Transhex [*sic*] are doing in their search for diamonds', to which Dicey responds in reflection: 'I'd seen the torn earth, the cones of raw rock ... The Nama, in over a thousand years of continuous occupation, have had a far smaller impact on the Richtersveld environment than mining concerns have in the past eighty' (Dicey 2004: 261). In the second, the director of an industrial theatre show attended by Dicey and his friends comments on power, inequalities and avenues to address indifference:

> Industrial theatre's the only way to go with a complex issue like this theft thing. I mean the workers feel the diamonds are theirs, that they're being robbed of them by the whites. You could never have a government or company person stand up there and hope to cover so much ground. (Dicey 2004: 270)

By linking issues about the divide between the wealthy and the poor, the powerful and powerless, and environmental degradation to a capitalist-driven commodity ('bright stones') *and* returning to the topic of Verwoerd and Tsafendas at the end of the narrative, Dicey's work seems to encapsulate Nixon's suggestion that violence 'needs to be seen—and deeply considered—as a contest not over space, or bodies, or labor, or resources, but also over time' (Nixon 2011: 8). The text 'convert[s] into image and narrative the disasters that are slow moving and long in the making' (Nixon 2011: 3). In this respect, *Borderline* seems to voice the intersection of environmental, social and cultural concerns related to this boundary territory in a literary form that has to reinvent its own history and perpetuation of marginalisation.

It is Dicey's closure to the travelogue, the skilful return to Verwoerd (and Tsafendas), and the consequences of discriminatory ideologies, that, once again, prompted another personal memory, leaving me astonished at how history (and violent history, at that) has intersected with my own experiences at the Orange River. Over the Easter weekend in 1993, I kayaked with friends from Vioolsdrift to the mouth. During that weekend, on Saturday 10 April, Chris Hani was assassinated by Polish immigrant Janusz Waluś. It was also 'effectively the day that Nelson Mandela became President of South Africa' (Vavi 2012). And so, I have come to learn some of the stories that are gathered by this river on its route to the sea. Moreover, post-apartheid literature such as *Borderline* intimates that a river is but one of many sources that contribute to a larger water body and archive – real or metaphorical – that link it to the histories of the oceans along the South African shoreline, and by implication to lands and people beyond their horizons. In this respect, my concluding argument is that Dicey's creative non-fiction, despite its regional focus, nevertheless succeeds in connecting socio-environmental concerns with transnational and imperial histories to stimulate an awareness of Africa's extensively interwoven history of nature and culture. At the same time, the local history of oppression and exploitation, bound up with current anxieties about injustice, poverty in the post-apartheid state, persistent racism and environmental degradation, forms part of global concerns that transcend divisions of class, race and nation.

References
Bhabha, Homi K. *The Location of Culture*. London and New York: Routledge, 1994.
Blanton, Casey. *Travel Writing: The Self and the World*. New York and London: Routledge, 2002.

Buell, Lawrence. *The Future of Environmental Criticism: Environmental Crisis and Literary Imagination*. Malden and Oxford: Blackwell Publishing, 2005.

Caminero-Santangelo, Byron and Myers, Garth. *Environment at the Margins: Literary and Environmental Studies in Africa*. Athens: Ohio University Press, 2011.

Caminero-Santangelo, Byron and Myers, Garth. 'Different shades of green: African literature, environmental justice, and the politics of scale.' Unpublished paper presented at Stellenbosch University, 4 September 2013. Book publication similarly titled.

Crampton, Hazel. *The Side of the Sun at Noon*. Johannesburg: Jacana Media, 2014.

Dicey, William. *Borderline*. Cape Town: Kwela Books, 2004.

Dicey, William. Email communication with author, 25 June 2013.

Douglas, Stuart. 'Reflection on state intervention and Schmidtsdrift Bushmen.' *Journal of Contemporary African Studies* 15, 1 (1997): 45–66.

Driver, Dorothy. 'Women and nature, women as objects of exchange: Towards a feminist analysis of South African literature', in Michael Chapman, Colin Gardner and Es'kia Mphaphlele (eds), *Perspectives on South African English Literature*. Johannesburg: A. D. Donker, 1992.

Dugmore, Heather. 'Fresh wind blows in the Kalahari for the Khomani San.' *Farmer's Weekly*, 6 February 2013.

Duncan, James and Gregory, Derek. 'Introduction', in James Duncan and Derek Gregory (eds), *Writes of Passage: Reading Travel Writing*. London and New York: Routledge, 1999.

Engels, Euodia. *Riemvasmaak: Hartland, Harde Land*. Hermanus: Hemel & See Boeke, 2005.

Fussell, Paul. 'Travel and the British literary imagination of the twenties and thirties', in Michael Kowalewski (ed.), *Temperamental Journeys: Essays on the Modern Literature of Travel*. Athens and London: University of Georgia Press, 1992.

George, Roger. 'A boat swamped with abstractions: Reading Raban's *River*', in Michael Kowalewski (ed.), *Temperamental Journeys: Essays on the Modern Literature of Travel*. Athens and London: University of Georgia Press, 1992.

Gilroy, Paul. *The Black Atlantic: Modernity and Double Consciousness*. Harvard University Press, 1993.

Goyal, Yogita. *Romance, Diaspora and Black Atlantic Literature*. Cambridge: Cambridge University Press, 2010.

Gray, Rockwell. 'Travel', in Michael Kowalewski (ed.), *Temperamental Journeys: Essays on the Modern Literature of Travel*. Athens and London: University of Georgia Press, 1992.

Huggan, Graham and Tiffin, Helen. *Postcolonial Ecocriticism: Literature, Animals, Environment*. London and New York: Routledge, 2010.

Jordan, Bobby. '"They call us the poor millionaires".' *Sunday Times*, 22 September 2013: 11.

Kowalewski, Michael (ed.). *Temperamental Journeys: Essays on the Modern Literature of Travel*. Athens and London: University of Georgia Press, 1992.

Lehohla, Pali. Census 2011: Provinces at a Glance. Report No. 03-01-43. Pretoria: Statistics South Africa, 2012.

MacKenzie, John E. 'The imperial pioneer and hunter and the British masculine stereotype in late Victorian and Edwardian times', in J. A. Mangan and James Walvin (eds), *Manliness and Morality: Middle-class Masculinity in Britain and America 1800–1940*. Manchester: Manchester University Press, 1987.

Maclennan, Ben. *The Wind Makes Dust: Four Centuries of Travel in Southern Africa*. Cape Town: Tafelberg, 2003.

Mansfield, Deb. 'The armchair traveller: Littoral zones and the domestic environment.' Alter*nation* special edition 6 (2013): 197–216.

Matos, Jacinta. 'Old journeys revisited: Aspects of postwar English travel writing', in Michael Kowalewski (ed.), *Temperamental Journeys: Essays on the Modern Literature of Travel*. Athens and London: University of Georgia Press, 1992.

Mbembe, Achille. 'At the edge of the world: Boundaries, territoriality, and sovereignty in Africa' (trans. Steven Rendall). *Public culture* 12, 3 (2000): 259–284.

Mbembe, Achille. *On the Postcolony*. Berkeley: University of California Press, 2001.

Moore-Gilbert, Bart. *Post-colonial Life Writing: Culture, Politics and Self-representation*. London and New York: Routledge. 2009.

Ndlovu, Isaac. 'Of shorelines, borderlines and shipwrecks in Justin Fox's *The Marginal Safari: Scouting the Edge of South Africa*.' Alter*nation* special edition 6 (2013): 109–129.

Neumann, Roderick, P. '"Through the Pleistocene": Nature and race in Theodore Roosevelt's *African Game Trails*', in Byron Caminero-Santangelo and Garth Myers (eds.), *Environment at the Margins: Literary and Environmental Studies in Africa*. Athens: Ohio University Press, 2011.

Nixon, Rob. *Slow Violence and the Environmentalism of the Poor*. Cambridge, MA and London: Harvard University Press, 2011.

Open Africa, http://www.openafrica.org/experiences/route/29-footprints-of-the-san (accessed 30 July 2015).

'Orange River diamond licences.' *Mining Journal* (London), 6 July 2001.

Pauw, Kalie, Punt, Celia and Van Schoor, Melt. 'A profile of the Eastern Cape province: Demographics, poverty, inequality and unemployment', http://wwwold.elsenburg.com/provide/documents/BP2005_1_2%20Demographics%20EC.pdf (accessed 6 August 2015).

Penn, Nigel. *The Forgotten Frontier: Colonist and Khoisan on the Cape's Northern Frontier in the 18th Century*. Athens: Ohio University Press and Cape Town: Double Storey House, 2001.
Pratt, Mary Louise. *Travel Writing and Transculturation*. London and New York: Routledge, 1992.
Rosaldo, Renato. 'Imperial nostalgia.' *Representations* 26 (Spring 1989): 107–122.
Ross, Robert Rev. *The Griqua Conundrum: Political and Socio-cultural Identity in the Northern Cape*, by Linda Waldman. *H-Net reviews*, November 2007: 1–2.
Sadler-Altena, Mary. 'Gariep: The Great Orange River', http://www.southerncape.co.za/geography/rivers/gariep.php (accessed 15 July 2010).
Samuelson, Meg. 'Sea changes, dark tides and littoral states: Oceans and coastlines in post-apartheid South African narratives.' *Alternation* special edition 6 (2013): 9–28.
SouthAfrica.info, Northern Cape Province, South Africa, http://www.southafrica.info/about/geography/northern-cape.htm (accessed 31 July 2015).
Van Eeden, Jeanne. 'Land Rover and colonial-style adventure.' *International Feminist Journal of Politics* 8, 3 (September 2006): 344–369.
Vavi, Zwelinzima. 'Zwelinzima Vavi's letter to Chris Hani'. SABC News, 10 April 2012, http://www.sabc.co.za/news/a/5728fa804ad59279b44bf480bd764233/Zwelinzima-Vavis-letter-to-Chris-Hani-20120410.
Waldman, Linda. *The Griqua Conundrum: Political and Socio-cultural Identity in the Northern Cape*. Bern: Peter Lang Publishers, 2007.
'Westerberg Asbestos Mine (Closed)', https://www.dwaf.gov.za/orange/Low_Orange/westerbe.htm (accessed 21 July 2013).
Woods, Tim. *African Pasts: Memory and History in African Literatures*. Manchester and New York: Manchester University Press, 2012.

Chapter 9

NEGOTIATING IDENTITY IN A VANISHING GEOGRAPHY: HOME, ENVIRONMENT AND DISPLACEMENT IN HELON HABILA'S *OIL ON WATER*

OGAGA OKUYADE

> The world into which I was born has changed drastically over the years. It has gone without being replenished ... But the major problem had to do with the discovery of oil in the Delta. The oil boom became doom for inhabitants of the region. (Ojaide 1996: 122)

> Crimes against humanity require new means of redress, a mechanism that records hidden histories of atrocity, didactically promotes collective memory, and gives victims a place of respect, dignity, and agency in the process. (Cole 2007: 171)

> The writer of fiction can be and must be the pathfinder.
> (Ngũgĩ wa Thiong'o 1986: 85)

What is left of Nigeria's Niger Delta today is its residual ecological image. Bearing in mind the total significance of what the habitat once represented for the inhabitants of this capriciously vanishing wetland, the need to salvage what is left is absolutely imperative. The aftermath of the mindless and soulless exploration and exploitation of crude oil in the area has led to the destruction of the major part of ecolife in the Niger Delta. Life has become precarious for the human inhabitants and other living beings that make up the ecosystem of this wetland as a result of the nightmarish consequences of oil exploitation, captured in the apocalyptic images of river oil slicks and hellish flares against the night sky. As a consequence, numerous creek communities, both human and animal, which form part of an interconnected natural web, have evacuated and continue to evacuate this area. Therefore, one often observes flocks of migratory birds circling the skies, struggling to locate their former habitat, then in frustration changing direction to alternative feeding sites. Animals are either burnt to death by uncontrolled gas flares or die of starvation. The most stunning of the ecological disasters in the area are the dead rivers, a product of constant blow-outs and oil spillages. It is important to note that the activities of multinational oil firms in the Niger Delta have completely destroyed local biodiversity and devastated local economies. Migratory birds are now seldom seen in this area. Many freshwater plant species have become extinct, and fishing – once a primary source of income for local people – has come to a tragic end. With the transformations to the creeks and wetlands, the climate also continues to change with the passage of time. In addition, the heavy government security build-up and the brutal efficiency with which it executes its objectives in the area equally constitute a serious threat to existence.

Two factors have led to the increasing invisibility of the problems in the Niger Delta region. The first is the rise to prominence of Boko Haram, the notorious Islamist religious sect operating in the northern part of Nigeria. Their attacks have received extensive media coverage both locally and internationally, which may lead one to conclude that the crises in the Niger Delta have disappeared. The second factor that may make one think that the social and environmental crises in the region have been resolved is the effect of the amnesty package offered to the Niger Delta militants by the Yar'Adua/Jonathan administration in 2009, which was aimed at a radical transformation of the Niger Delta. The amnesty package was geared towards creating a platform for meaningful dialogue among stakeholders, which would, in turn, create a peaceful environment for redressing the Niger Delta question. The transformation was supposed to be threefold: firstly, it involved disarmament; secondly, rapid infrastructural development of the Niger Delta; and, thirdly, the rehabilitation and reintegration of the 'lost souls' (militants) into society.

However, a critical appraisal of the amnesty package suggests a travesty of environmental and social justice. Since some Niger Delta militants have been removed from the area and relocated to cities around the world, ostensibly to acquire skills, the flow of oil, which their activities curtailed, now continues unchecked. In terms of the package, other activists have received allowances that have blunted the contradictions and privations that continue to be experienced by people who live in the area not favoured in this way. These activists have been effectively alienated from their communities and silenced. Another consideration to bear in mind is the fact that the immediate past head of government, Goodluck Jonathan, comes from this region, suggesting that he may have the best interests of the area at heart, which, in reality, may not be the case. The current silence on the question of the Niger Delta may very usefully serve the purposes of allowing the state to realise its developmental plans for the area.

The subject of this chapter does not, however, relate to the amnesty policy – although it would be a little difficult to appraise Nigeria's Niger Delta today without making reference to that policy. This essay deals specifically with how Helon Habila's third novel, *Oil on Water* (2011), captures the enchanting power of the natural world of the Niger Delta. It will demonstrate how different forms of violence inflicted on the Niger Delta environment and its inhabitants have provoked different responses from the people – resistance, silence and migration. The chapter, therefore, attempts to subject this violence to scrutiny in order to reveal the fact that there appears to be a major issue that has eluded researchers in literary and cultural studies on the question of the Niger Delta. That issue is the reality of displacement – a kind of displacement that is environmentally induced, bringing to the fore a kind of violence that is associated with dispossession of the Niger Delta people's ancestral home.

Habila's debut novel, *Waiting for an Angel* (2002), won the 2003 Commonwealth Literature prize for the best first novel by an African writer. *Measuring Time* (2007) is his second novel. *Oil on Water* foregrounds the rivers and mangrove swamps to highlight the relationship between the natural habitat of the Niger Delta and its inhabitants. But, apart from the sheer power of the environment, Okechukwu Ibeanu notes the world significance of this region. The Niger Delta's mesh of marshland, creeks, tributaries and lagoons forms a 'fragile mangrove forest, the second largest mangrove forest in the world' (Ibeanu 2007: 316). The relationship between the natural and the social in *Oil on Water*, arguably, becomes the cardinal principle in the process of identity formation of the inhabitants of the area. Although not from the Niger Delta, Habila has artistically deployed his narrative to figure the travails of rural indigenous communities in the delta creeks and to establish the fact that the Nigerian government continues to fail to protect this habitat and the people who negotiate their existence in the area. *Oil on Water* eloquently pits a real world characterised by an earlier subsistence against the trials and uncertainties of the present. Unlike his first two novels, *Oil on Water* focuses more on environmental issues. However, it equally significantly addresses 'some of the issues that have preoccupied African fiction since the 1960s: notably despotism in postcolonial Africa, its etiology, its effects on ordinary people and dissident intellectuals, and popular resistance' (Erritouni 2010: 144). The foregrounding of the environment in African literature may be linked to the particular historical, economic and social juncture in which the continent currently finds itself. Although nature has been represented in African literature since its origins, it is increasingly highlighted in the work of the most recent generation of writers. In a national context, Pius Adesanmi and Chris Dunton position Habila within the 'third generation' of Nigerian novelists, referring to:

> a new generation of writers born mostly after 1960, the emblematic year of African political independence from colonialism. This generation, the first in Africa to be temporally severed from colonial event ... came to be identified as writers of the third generation in Anglophone and Francophone critical traditions. (Adesanmi and Dunton 2005: 14)

Locating Nigeria's Niger Delta

What part of Nigeria exactly is designated by the term 'Niger Delta'? Joe Ushie (2006: 3) describes the Niger Delta region as an 'area covered by the six states of Akwa Ibom, Bayelsa, Cross River, Delta, Edo and Rivers. It stretches over a continuous rainforest characterised by a beautiful pattern of creeks, streams and rivers.' However, for the purpose of geographic delineation, the states that constitute the Niger Delta are sometimes reduced to the core states, including 'Rivers State, Bayelsa State and Delta State' (Ukaogo 2009: 55). Although this description may be contentious in some quarters, as there are other states that insist that they are part of the Niger Delta, since they share some of the geographical features and the economic and social problems of the core Niger Delta states. Hence, the territory termed the 'Niger Delta' has been extended beyond the core states because 'the political definition of the Niger Delta has recently been enlarged to include all nine oil-producing states, namely, Abia, Akwa Ibom, Bayelsa, Cross River, Delta, Edo, Imo, Ondo and Rivers' (Darah 2011: 4).

Studies on the Niger Delta question oscillate between two poles. By 'the Niger Delta question', I am referring to the ideological and dialectical positions that express the numerous conflicts that have arisen from the federal government's control of oil resources and the distribution of revenue among the constituent states of the federation. The two poles of the debate may be summarised as follows: on the one hand, the discourse generated by the Niger Delta is focused on the politics of violence. On the other hand, observations are made about the paradox for the delta inhabitants of negotiating existence where extreme poverty and great wealth are located side by side. Metaphorically, one could say that the Niger Delta is an area where the rich creeks house poor people. The Niger Delta question concerns communities who suffer the environmental impact of oil extraction but do not enjoy the benefits accrued because of the government's iniquitous distribution of wealth. Although the Niger Delta is rich in oil and funds the economic stability and survival of the nation, ironically, it is also the most marginalised and least developed region in the country. The contrast is staggering if one compares the wealth extracted from the region with the benefits accrued. As J. B. Ejobowah's analysis observes:

> Nigeria extracts about 93.1 million metric tons of oil annually from its soil to account for 2.9% of world production. The Niger Delta and the sea gulf off its shores, which host over a dozen oil companies, produce what accounts for 80% of Nigeria's annual revenue. (Ejobowah 2000: 33)

It is disturbing to note that people so well endowed in terms of natural resources are on the cliff-edge of existence compared with their compatriots. The dire living conditions of the people of the Niger Delta are made clear by Ibeanu (2007: 320–321):

> Only about 27% of people in the Delta have access to safe drinking water and about 30% of households have access to electricity, both of which are below the national averages of 31.7% and 33.6% respectively. There is [despite environmental degradation and pollution] one doctor per 82,000 people in the Niger Delta, rising to 132,000 per doctor in some areas, which is more than three times the national average of 40,000 per doctor. ... Education levels are below the national average and are particularly low for women. While 76% of Nigerian children attend primary school, this level drops to 30–40% in some parts of the Niger Delta.

As noted above, some of the studies on the Niger Delta privilege issues that foreground militancy and the violence that emanates from the confrontations between the various insurgent groups, multinational oil firms and the federal government in the Niger Delta. Other studies tend to concentrate more on the struggles and sufferings of the Ogoni, perhaps because they were the first among the micro-minority ethnic groups in the Niger Delta to have staged a sustained resistance against the blatant despoliation of their environment. This is combined with agitation for justice centred on the hanging of Saro-Wiwa by the

Nigerian military government on 10 November 1995 on trumped-up charges. Earlier studies on the Niger Delta that deal with the economic and political rift, the bureaucratic failure of government to remedy the situation amicably and those that emphasise the role of the Ogoni in the present violent confrontations in the Niger Delta include Osaghae (1995); Cayford (1996); Travis (1997); Narr (1997); Na-Allah (1998); Okome (2000); Osha (2001); Campbell (2002); Okunoye (2008); Ibeanu (2008); Nwahunanya (2011); and Simon, Akung and Bassey (2014). In relation to research on this area, Oyeniyi Okunoye (2008: 414) observes that:

> the scholarly responses to the Niger Delta situation have been remarkable but it has also been confined to assessing the social and economic realities that precipitated the collective revolt of the people after the late Ken Saro-Wiwa brought the plight of the Ogoni people to the attention of the international community.

A reappraisal of some of the theoretical and conceptual concerns of these studies brings to the fore the fact that the nature of the violence itself is hardly ever conceptualised. As noted earlier, this chapter attempts to subject the forms of violence in the Niger Delta to scrutiny to reveal the fact that a major issue that has continued to elude researchers on the question of the Niger Delta is the reality of displacement. Displacement is one of the major consequences of strategic and structural violence among groups struggling to vilify or demonise the other within this glocal oil enterprise. Displacement as a concept is almost too broad to be subjected to an easy definition or description, since it could be subsumed under the broad spectrum of the discourse of exile.

The Niger Delta, oil capital and displacement in *Oil on Water*

This chapter addresses displacements that articulate various forms of sociocultural dislocation engendered by oil exploration and exploitation in the Niger Delta, and how they underscore the gradual loss of the identity of micro-minority groups in Nigeria, an identity determined by the relationship between human beings and the places they call home.

Although the discourse anchors on environmental displacement, it equally falls within the latitude of what Rob Nixon (2011: 2) describes as 'slow violence'. Good fictional examples of the local consequences of the violence that environmental displacement engenders are the crises of identity and growth suffered by Michael, the boy in *Oil on Water*, whose school has been closed down because of the oil crisis in the area (Habila 2011: 36), and the protagonist of Kaine Agary's *Yellow-Yellow* (2006), who is forced to go to the city to begin a new life because her mother's only means of livelihood, the land, has been destroyed as a result of incessant oil spillages. Both these examples fall within the parameters of Nixon's concept of slow violence. The two characters referred to here are not injured physically in any way. However, the truncation of their education in their communities and the need to relocate them bear the stamp of violence, the kind that is not instantaneous or immediate, but the consequences of which are enormous. And their vicissitudes are practically visible in both narratives because the characters are not disoriented only as a result of the loss of their ancestral homes to oil firms and environmental-related crisis, but they equally suffer the pains of dispossession and dislocation from the communal web of kinship. Displacement receives media attention when it is sudden and involves large numbers of people, as Angela Subulwa notes in the African context: 'When it comes to information about African refugee movements and settlements, the vast majority of news coverage focuses on the crisis or emergency phase' (Subulwa 2013: 1). Subulwa also suggests that the effects of displacement over time hardly take the front burner in public discourses:

> With more than 10 million forcibly displaced people across the African continent, this coverage certainly tells an important part of the story – but in no way does it come close to uncovering or even exploring the specific social, historical, and geographic particularities in which these phenomena flourish. Though they may attract attention, these crisis narratives rarely capture the complex geographies of forced displacement. The tendency within the long history of refugee research was (is) to reify the refugee. (Subulwa 2013: 1)

In response to this inadequate study and problematic representation of the forced movement of people out of their homes, Habila's fictional narrative *Oil on Water* underscores the sociopolitical, developmental and cultural challenges of protracted displacement. Invariably, an exploration of the deeper social and spatial histories of oil-induced or environmental displacement in the Niger Delta, and the exclusionary practices around displaced people in the new areas where they seek refuge can increase knowledge of the glocal oil crisis in Nigeria. Therefore, assaults on the environment lie at the heart of displacement and its consequences.

Oil on Water recounts how a young Nigerian journalist is recruited to negotiate with kidnappers for the release of the wife of a British oil engineer from the hands of her abductors, a group of Niger Delta militants. A respected reporter, Zaq, is to lead the delegation of journalists in this search. Rufus, a less experienced fellow journalist, wants to prove himself to his managers as well as to Zaq, so he volunteers to be part of this life-threatening expedition. However, the story they hope to get drags them deeper into the den of the militants and things do not go exactly as planned as the two journalists end up on a long journey through the creeks in search of the British woman and her kidnappers. The journey, therefore, becomes the dominant trope of the novel – specifically because the journalists are in a quest that will help them not only unravel the mystery behind the disappearance of the wife of the British oil engineer, but also understand the nature of the violence in the Niger Delta. Significantly, journeying, therefore, offers both journalists the yardage to explore the environment and meet the different groups involved in this glocal oil racketeering. Hence, a critic notes: 'Mobility is fundamental in the construction of consciousness' (Okereke 1997: 91).

Habila inscribes the physical journey as an important dimension in the ideological consciousness of the psyche of an impressionistic young man, Rufus, struggling to come to terms with life as a journalist. Through the journey to the creeks of the Niger Delta in search of the abducted Englishwoman, Rufus for the very first time becomes exposed to the petro-capital and glocal oil enterprise. In *Oil on Water* the trope of the journey is also linked to the idea of a quest, so the major characters in the narrative – like those in Habila's debut novel, *Waiting for an*

Angel (2002) – are journalists. The search for truth becomes the essential narrative thread with which Habila weaves the tale of the deadly oil racketeering in the Niger Delta, focusing specifically on how oil has become a mixed blessing for its inhabitants. Since the journey turns horribly wrong and becomes life-threatening, Rufus's idea of the concept of truth becomes unsettled. He is radicalised as he struggles to come to terms with the mendacity of the Nigerian government, the brutal efficiency with which the task force dispatched to the area to keep 'peace' accomplish their task, the complacency of multinational oil firms operating in the area, the resistance of the militants and the grim realities of the socio-economic conditions of the indigenous people, whose communities host the oil firms and their installations in the habitat of the delta, which becomes increasingly submerged.

The narrative frame within which the quest is located provides a panoramic overview of the delta landscape, and the deadly and shocking oil encounters that detail how politics, economics and geography continue to connive in the contraction of the identity of the Niger Delta people. With the numerous flashbacks and the protagonist's reflections, the plot structure of *Oil on Water* is by no means linear, nor is it episodic. However, the organic wholeness of the narrative is only realised when Rufus's tales and those of other characters, like Zaq, Chief Ibiram and Dr. Dagogo, are read as separate pieces held together by Rufus's perspective. The main plot of the novel, the search for the abducted wife of the oil engineer, Ms Isabel Floode, is unconnected with the issue of environmental crisis associated with the creeks in the Niger Delta, since her initial abductors were driven by vengeance and greed, but it creates a window through which Habila takes the reader to the heart of rural locations that continue to disappear daily as a result of oil encounters in the Niger Delta. Habila's protagonist embarks on this journey specifically to search for the truth. Ironically, all the groups involved in these glocal oil encounters – the soldiers deployed to the creeks to check the growing insurgency in the area and ensure protection of the oil installations, the militants who deploy various insurgent tactics to resist and frustrate the multinational oil firms and the Nigerian government – insist that Rufus must tell the truth. Trapped among three groups struggling to tell their respective ideas of the truth,

Rufus gives the reader an opportunity to re-evaluate the logic of the journalist as a reporter of truth.

The oil trade in the Niger Delta vibrantly articulates the disastrous end to which capitalist industrialism can be put to the disservice of humanity, and the dangers of technomodernity that does not facilitate human development. Interestingly, therefore, 'oil and capital are linked inextricably, so much so that the looming demise of the petrochemical economy has come to constitute perhaps the biggest disaster that "we" collectively face' (Szeman 2007: 807). The oil war in the Niger Delta has always attracted the media and its reportage has been robust. *Oil on Water* pushes the discourse further, offering a graphic account of the oil encounters. Sometimes the narrative reads like a documentary and on other occasions like an adventure story or a film script. However, the most fascinating aspect of the narrative is how the relationship between the concrete and the imagined is addressed. Habila crumbles the binaristic notions of happening-truth and story-truth. *Oil on Water* is a narrative that recounts the debilitating and abysmal conditions in which the Niger Delta people negotiate their existence through the story of the degradation of the environment. The landscape Habila describes in the novel is one that is subjected to constant bombardment as a result of capitalist industrialism's insensitivity to nature. Through the journey motif, one follows the protagonist from one ravaged community to the other as the narrative depicts pollution and degradation of the ecosystem:

> The atmosphere grew heavy with the suspended stench of dead matter. We followed a bend in the river and in front of us we saw dead birds draped over tree branches, their outstretched wings black and slick with oil; dead fishes blobbed white-bellied between tree roots. (Habila 2011: 9)

What is described here is not dissimilar to the characters' encounter in another village:

> In the village centre, we found the communal well. Eager for a drink, I bent under the wet, mossy pivoted beam and peered

into the well's blackness, but a rank smell wafted from its hot depth and slapped my face. I reeled away, my head aching from the encounter. Something organic, perhaps human, lay dead and decomposing down there, its stench mixed with that unmistakable smell of oil. At the other end of the village a little river trickled toward the big river where we had left our boat. The patch of grass growing by the water was suffocated by a film of oil, each blade covered with blotches like the liver spots on a smoker's hand. (Habila 2011: 9)

Habila provides us with powerful, alluring and dramatic images. Since the novel does not tell, but shows the disasters brought upon the indigenous people of the Niger Delta, one of the questions it raises is not just whether it succeeds in its political and pedagogic aim – too blunt a question to be posed in relation to the vibrant imagery, in any case – but what we are to make of the visual imagistic mechanisms that Habila employs in his narrative and their capacity to name the central place of oil in our social imaginaries and ontologies.

The violent confrontations occasioned by the exploration of oil create room for widespread deforestation of the rainforest, which, in turn, prepares the place for subsequent ecological havoc. The most perplexing incident in the novel is the attitude of the people to the seismic devaluation of their habitation through gas flaring. As a provincial people, they hardly understand the health and environmental hazards that gas flares are associated with. Little wonder that they bask in the excitement of the orange fire that replaces the electricity they had been promised as host communities by oil-prospecting firms and their government. The orange flares of the local people may be contrasted with the beautifully lit locations of the multinational companies. The narrator notes that:

... the villagers feasted for weeks they got their orange fire, planted firmly over the water at the edge of the village. Night and day, it burned and now the village had no need for candles or lamps, all they had to do at night was to open their doors and windows and just like that, everything was illuminated. That light soon became the village square. (Habila 2011: 91–92)

The attendant health hazards that are associated with gas flaring are not only varied, but sometimes capable of wiping out an entire community. They include cancer, asthma, bronchitis and blood disorders. Besides these health problems, the environmental practices in these host communities are associated with global warming, deforestation, wildfires and toxic water, among others. Dr. Dagogo is a medical researcher in the novel. His findings on the effect of oil exploration and exploitation capture the growing fear of a possible environmental crisis and the vulnerability of the villages. Zaq's health is similar to Dr. Dagogo's; Dagogo appears to be suffering from dengue fever, an ailment that eventually kills Zaq. Dagogo informs Rufus of the grave danger of life in the creeks: 'Sometimes I wonder what I'm doing here; I tell you there's more need for gravediggers than doctors' (Habila 2011: 93). Dagogo's musings and fear of a possible end to human and environmental life in the communities become real if one considers the poisoned wells, the poisoned rivers and streams, the dead and diseased fish, the health issues faced by villagers, how villagers were tricked or forced off their land and how entire villagers are now nomadic, roaming from place to place in search of somewhere with no pollution where they can survive.

Shell, believed to be the most notorious[1] of the multinational oil firms operating in the Niger Delta, rationalises its complacency on the hazardous consequences of the gas flares. By flaring almost all of the associated natural gas produced for close to 50 years of oil production, Shell and other oil companies have burnt a vast quantity of natural capital. Beside this wastage of resources through gas flaring, it is embarrassing and insulting for Shell to remark that 'local residents benefitted from these flares because they could dry their foodstuffs for free by setting them near the burning gases' (Gedicks 2001: 44–45). These incidents in the narrative, which parallel reality, give expression to how oil exploration has completely altered the once calm and subsistent life of these provincial people. But, above all, they accentuate how humanity continues to fail to protect the environment – especially in the case of the Nigerian government – in spite of the negative environmental impact of crude-oil mining and refining in the Niger Delta. The narrative draws the reader's attention to how pollution arising from crude-oil spillage not only destroys marine life and crops, and makes water unsuitable for fishing, but also renders farmland unusable.

However, it is humanity – both corporates/multinational entities and locals who are most implicated in glocal oil racketeering. The fire that almost claims Boma's life, for which Rufus's father is serving a jail term, falls within the context of the unhealthy petro-capital trade – a situation whereby individuals, locals in particular, perhaps as a result of poverty and misery perform the functions of a gas station by retailing petroleum products in bottles and other small vessels, duplicitously obtained from burst oil pipes, which has left virtually all the characters blind to their moral-ethical duty of protecting the environment. Boma, Rufus's elder sister, becomes permanently scarred, both physically and psychologically, as a result of a fire disaster. In a more general context, Sarah Amsler gives two reasons for the failure of humanity to rise to the duty of protecting the environment: 'There are two prominent narratives of crisis in contemporary environmental politics. One is rooted in fears of ecological catastrophe, and the other in a sort of anthropological pessimism that human beings lack the will or capacity to prevent it' (Amsler 2010: 129). The only innocent party in the oil war crisis is the environment. The multinational oil firms, government and militants all contribute in different ways to the decimation of nature. The narrative in *Oil on Water* highlights the corrupt practices of government and the oil firms in the aggravation of the crisis, thus confirming William Slaymaker's suggestion that the 'disruption of the landscape is tied to political corruption' (Slaymaker 2007: 131). For over four decades, these deplorable environmental crises have prevailed and the people continue to endure this premeditated attempt at submerging their homes, with local chiefs from the Niger Delta conspiring with both the federal government and the oil firms in the gradual but persistent degradation of land, and aquatic and human life.

Considering the role played by government and multinational oil firms, which profit from this glocal oil capitalist enterprise in the Niger Delta, in ensuring 'barrenness and death instead of fertility and prosperity' (Taussig 1980: 224), politics may not pass as a credible option to remedy the situation, as most governments of the world, especially those in developing nations, depend heavily on oil capital. As Matthew Schneider-Mayerson (2013: 871) has noted, this seeming 'resignation is motivated by a sense of political alienation and a bleak evaluation of contemporary environmental politics'. Szeman describes eloquently this doubtfulness about the place of politics in terms of resolving the oil crisis by underscoring our capacity to imagine a world without it and our uncertainty as to whether politics can mobilise the relevant discourses:

> It is not that we can't name or describe, anticipate or chart the end of oil and the consequences for nature and humanity. It is rather that because these discourses are unable to mobilize or produce any response to a disaster we know is a direct result of the law of capitalism – limitless accumulation – it is easy to see that nature will end before capital. (Szeman 2007: 820–821)

Szeman describes the lingering petro-fever across the world as strategic realism, a fact that articulates why the world has failed over time to come up with eco-friendly policies capable of redeeming the submerging world. He defines strategic realism as

> a discourse that makes the nation-state the central actor in the drama of the looming disaster of oil, an actor that engages in often brutal geopolitical calculations in order to secure the stability of national economies and communities. While oil is hardly divorced from the operations of global finances, its political value as a commodity is such that it is apparently not permitted to slosh autonomously through markets that we have been repeatedly told take little note of borders today: the state must be present in order to ensure that every day the right amount of oil flows in the right direction. (Szeman 2007: 810–811)

However, international markets and politics, and global flows of capital and oil, are only part of the story. There is also a very local story about people and their sense of wholeness through place. For a space to be labelled a place, it needs to undergo numerous cartographical and cultural processes, which include naming, mapping, description, storytelling and mythologising. The naming of a place often gives expression to the topography of the area, which, in turn, becomes a potent identity marker for the group that occupies that space. Considering how identity is constructed, it therefore becomes imperative to note that the main threat to the Niger Delta people in Habila's *Oil on Water* is not just the assaults of the oil industry but, more specifically, the disintegration of the sociocultural and environmental fabric that makes them an indigenous group in Nigeria – in short, their relationship to their primordial base. This explains why a scholar like Daniel Omoweh insists on the cultural constitution of the Niger Delta area. Omoweh (2005: 130) defines the Niger Delta environment as 'the entire environmental resources of the Niger Delta, including the culture of the people and other natural things attached to it'. The relationship between humanity and their homeland often conditions the religious choices of the people and their sociocultural beliefs. In considering the symmetry between humanity and the occupation of space and place, Onookome Okome (2002: 157) suggests that 'attachment to geography, a place of origin, is of high importance to many artists. This attachment is often symbolised in the metaphor of the soil or the earth'. These are ideas that one also encounters in Sule Egya's (2013) overview of Nigerian anglophone poetry as well as in the analyses of Zimbabwean cultural forms in other chapters in this volume.

In the novel, the real effects of dislocation engendered by the oil industry are made clear. Chief Ibiram, the head chief of one of the creek communities in the narrative recalls how Chief Malabo, another prominent chief and environmental activist, was gruesomely murdered by the agents of the state while in detention, and how his community was fraudulently asked to vacate their habitation and confront the grim realities of losing their homes. These events point to the social costs of oil production, which enunciates the asymmetric power relationship between transnational capital and the populations of developing countries, particularly indigenous peripheral people. Chief Ibiram sums up his narration with a kind of lamentation that underscores the consequences of petro-capital on the Niger Delta people:

> They sold. One by one. The rigs went up, and the gas flares, and the workers came and set up camp in our midst, we saw our village

change, right before our eyes. And that was why we decided to leave, ten families. We didn't take their money. The money would be our curse on them, for taking our land, and for killing our chief. We left, we headed northwards, we've lived in five different places now, but always we've had to move. We are looking, for a place where we can live in peace. But it is hard. So your question, are we happy here? I say how can we be happy when we are mere wanderers without a home? (Habila 2011: 40–41)

As well as the forced evacuation of people from their homes, the oil companies, backed by federal power, have caused not only social marginalisation, but also the destruction of ecology and – significantly in the context of this essay – the liquidation of culture. Michael Cernea (2000) expresses this eloquently when he suggests that one of the most negative consequences of development-induced displacement, usually associated with mining and oil exploitation, is the devastation of the psyche of the displaced. The displaced often struggle with problems of permanent itinerancy, landlessness, loss of access to common property, homelessness, joblessness, food insecurity, social marginalisation, increased morbidity and social disarticulation. Unfortunately, until recently, as Terminski (2012: 2) states, 'according to many scientific studies, oil production in developing countries almost never contributes to improving the situation of local communities. Loss of land leads to loss of economic base functioning of the whole community.' Ibeanu pushes the debate further when he argues that these numerous forms of injustice have not only been going on for a long time, but the primary issues that generate these conflicts with disastrous consequences are hardly ever resolved. Therefore, people who remain in affected areas are obliged to live in a permanent state of humanitarian emergency. A potent marker of many oil-producing communities is that 'a strong presence of military and police detachments; and systematic state repression, sometimes taking the form of extra-judicial killings, has remained a fact of life' (Ibeanu 1998: 86).

To return to the question of environmental displacement in *Oil on Water*, chief Ibiram and his people, and other neighbouring communities, like Irikefe, are forever dislocated from places that offer them not only socio-economic security, but also a sense of belonging. Which explains Brinklow's observation that 'community and kinship webs were changed irrevocably as resettlement hauled people – many of whom had hauled their houses with them – into the industrial world of the twentieth century, leaving, for many, grief and loss in their wake' (Brinklow 2013: 41). For these indigenous people of the Niger Delta, the 'seamless progression of time (becomes) snapped' (Hay 2006: 33), leaving many of them to come to terms with the capricious loss of their homes, land, sense of socio-economic security, livelihoods, communities, religious belief systems and, above all, their identity.

If one applies exile and alienation theories in attempting to understand the psychological state of Ibiram and his people, the concept of displacement becomes invariably polyvalent and multifaceted. In 'Reflections on Exile', Edward Said defines exile as 'the unhealable rift forced between a human being and a native place, between the self and its true home: its essential sadness can never be surmounted' (Said 1990: 357). Sule Egya argues that, 'With the soils damaged, the waters polluted, the air invaded by permanent gas flares, and the debasement of the fauna and flora, the people become extremely vulnerable' (2013: 3). Besides the terrifying ecological disasters brought upon the human habitation, aquatic lives and winged creatures, like birds and insects, are also affected. The environment described here is devoid of people specifically because nature, the human support base, has been destroyed:

> UNHCR defines a protracted refugee situation as one in which 'refugees find themselves in a long-lasting and intractable state of limbo [where] their lives may not be at risk, but their basic rights and essential economic, social and psychological needs remain unfulfilled after years in exile'. (UNHCR 2004)

The role of ecocriticism in this context is vital. Ecocriticism draws our attention to ecologically sensitive creative writing and criticism, which, according to Michael Branch, is meant to promote 'ecological literacy' (Branch et al. 1998: viii). He further elaborates on the importance of the concept: it is not only meant to make readers aware of the global environmental crisis but also for literature to suggest 'means by which we might read literary texts with a new appreciation for what they reveal about the complex of relationships that mediate interactions between humans and their environments' (Branch et al. 1998: xiii). It is a call for a change in culture to a more 'biocentric worldview, an extension of ethics, a broadening of human conception of global community to include nonhuman life forms and the physical environment' (Branch et al. 1998: xiii). With awareness of ecocriticism – what Cheryll Burgess Glotfelty calls 'the relationship between human culture and the environment' – literature will lead towards 'an ecologically sustainable human society' (cited in Branch et al. 1998: 29). Since the environment will continue to play a significant role in African life and society, it becomes imperative for writers to constantly sensitise humanity to the need to be ecological in the use of natural resources. This is because environmental and 'human rights issues are necessary aspects of African experience that informs the literature' (Ojaide 2012: 65).

In sum, as one aspect of the public discourse concerning oil-induced displacement, literature continues to demonstrate a great deal about the perceived social and political importance of violent conflicts, and how they leave people who negotiate existence in the creeks of the Niger Delta vulnerable and almost hopeless. The public discourse on the Niger Delta question, in which different groups continue to be subjected to incessant displacement, gives expression to this observation, since there is now a corpus of imaginative composition described as Niger Delta literature or literature on the Niger Delta. Literature, without doubt, is a potent sociocultural vehicle for addressing ills of varied dimensions in society because it brings alive artistically the lived experience of a fictional world that parallels that of the real.

Oil on Water, through its journey motif, which creates an opening through which the reader can accompany the protagonist on his petro-capital voyage, historicises the burden of displacement on the psyche of rural people who negotiate existences in oil-producing communities by subtly detailing the process by which their homes are lost and life becomes almost unbearable because of the depletion of the human support base that is nature. *Oil on Water* will continue to remain an important narrative on the Niger Delta because it draws attention to issues that people treat as inconsequential – environmental displacement caused by petro-capital lost for natural resources to power the economy of the world; postcolonial hubristic blindness; and the myopic, developmental self-destructive tendency of the environmental policies of the Nigerian government. The insurgent groups' confrontations against government or the post-independence nationalist posture of the groups is, without doubt, the reason that government has paid some attention to the pains of the Niger Delta people. This incredible resilience, which eventually snowballed into insurgency where arms have become the weapon for agitation, would have been avertable had government understood the politics of eco-justice. Most of the imaginative composition on the Niger Delta hardly gives the local people a voice because of the foregrounding of violence. Habila not only gives them a voice, but he also re-humanises them by rewriting history from the perspective of the displaced and oppressed.

As the novel reaches its denouement, the conflicts are unresolved. Though the worshippers in Irikefe village return to their traditional worship by the riverside – an act that provides a means of spiritual, environmental and social regeneration after a partial ecological collapse of the village – the possibility of sustaining a world characterised by ecological balance remains far-fetched. However, as the novel ends one still notices the dystopian tone with which the conflicts are partially resolved, characterised by Rufus's gloomy farewell to his friends and sister, whom he leaves behind at Irikefe. Habila sustains the belief that things may return to normality only when humanity comes to terms with the fact that all of nature has its place. The idea that things may return to normality is accentuated by Boma's insistence on not returning to the city. Irikefe becomes a sanctuary for her, regardless of the fact that what is left of this rural habitat is its residual ecological image. Her insistence on remaining at Irikefe underscores the healing power that the creek signifies, a position Zaq constantly reiterates before his demise. The insistence on returning to their primordial base after the carnage amplifies the connection between humanity and places one regards as home, especially because the home forms part of what constitutes the identity of an individual. Invariably, the relationship between humanity and the natural habitat should not be perceived as wholly dependent upon biologically determined inclinations, but between human conscience and how the environment functions as resources – because humanity needs nature to survive, but nature hardly needs humans for survival.

References

Adesanmi, Pius and Dunton, Chris. 'Nigeria's third-generation writing: Historiography and preliminary theoretical considerations.' *English in Africa* 32, 1 (2005): 7–19.

Agary, Kaine *Yellow-Yellow*. Lagos: Dtalkshop, 2006.

Amsler, Sarah. 'Bringing hope "to crisis": Crisis thinking, ethical action and social change', in S. Skrimshire (ed.), *Future Ethics: Climate Change and Apocalyptic Imagination*. London: Continuum, 2010.

Branch, Michael, Johnson, Rochelle, Patterson, Daniel and Slovic, Scott. *Reading the Earth: New Directions in the Study of Literature and the Environment*. Moscow, Idaho: University of Idaho Press, 1998.

Brinklow, Laurie. 'Stepping-stones to the edge: Artistic expressions of islandness in an ocean of islands.' *Island Studies Journal* 8, 1 (2013): 39–54.

Campbell, Marion. 'Witnessing death: Ken Saro-Wiwa and the Ogoni crisis.' *Postcolonial Studies* 5, 1 (2002): 39–49.

Cayford, Steven. The Ogoni uprising: Oil, human rights and a democratic alternative in Nigeria.' *Africa Today* 43, 15 (1996): 183–197.

Cernea, Michael. 'Risks, safeguards and reconstruction: A model for population displacement and resettlement.' *Economic and Political Weekly* 35, 41 (October 2000): 3659–3678.

Cole, Catherine. 'Performance, transitional justice, and the law: South Africa's Truth and Reconciliation Commission.' *Theatre Journal* 59 (2007): 167–187.

Darah, G. G. 'Revolutionary pressure in Niger Delta literature', in C. Nwahunanya (ed.), *From Boom to Doom: Protest and Conflict Resolution in the Literature of the Niger Delta*. Owerri: Springfield Publishers, 2011.

Egya, Sule E. 'Eco-human engagement in recent Nigerian poetry in English.' *Journal of Postcolonial Writing* 49, 1 (2013): 60–70.

Ejobowah, J. B. 'Who owns the oil? The politics of ethnicity in the Niger Delta of Nigeria.' *Africa Today* 47, 1 (2000): 29–47.

Erritouni, Ali. 'Postcolonial despotism from a postmodern standpoint: Helon Habila's *Waiting for an Angel*.' *Research in African Literatures* 41, 4 (2010): 144–161.

Gedicks, Al. *Resource Rebels: Native Challenges to Mining and Oil Corporations*. Cambridge, MA: South End Press, 2001.

Habila, Helon. *Waiting for an Angel*. London: Penguin, 2002.

Habila, Helon. *Measuring Time*. London: Hamish Hamilton 2007.

Habila, Helon. *Oil on Water*. New York: W. W. Norton, 2011.

Hay, Pete. 'A phenomenology of islands.' *Island Studies Journal* 1, 1 (2006): 19–42.

Human Rights Watch. *The price of oil: Corporate responsibility and human rights violations in Nigeria's oil-producing communities*. New York: Human Rights Watch, 1999.

Ibeanu, Okechukwu. 'Exiles in their own home: Internal population displacement in Nigeria.' *African Journal of Political Science* 3, 2 (1998): 80–97.

Ibeanu, Okechukwu. 'Petroleum, politics and development in the Niger Delta', in Okello Oculi and Yakubu Nasidi (eds), *Brain Gain for the African Renaissance: Issues in Governance*. Zaria: Ahmadu Bello University Press, 2007.

Na-Allah, Abdul-Rasheed (ed.). *Ogoni's agonies: Ken Saro-Wiwa and the crises in Nigeria*. Trenton: Africa World Press, 1998.

Narr, Wolf-Dieter. Ken Saro-Wiwa and the global responsibility for human life.' *Dialectical Anthropology* 22 (1997): 399–408.

Ngũgĩ, wa Thiong'o. *Decolonizing the mind: The politics of language in African literatures*. Nairobi: East African Educational Publishers, 1986.

Nixon, Rob. *Slow Violence and the Environmentalism of the Poor*. Cambridge, MA and London: Harvard University Press, 2011.

Nwahunanya, Chinyere. 'The lachrymal consciousness in the literature of the Niger Delta: Its implications for conflict resolution', in Chinyere Nwahunanya (ed.), *From Boom to Doom: Protest and Conflict Resolution in the Literature of the Niger Delta*. Owerri: Springfield Publishers, 2011.

Ojaide, Tanure. *Poetic Imagination in Black Africa: Essays on African Poetry*. Durham: Carolina Academic Press, 1996.

Ojaide, Tanure. *Contemporary African Literature: New Approaches*. Durham: Carolina Academic Press, 2012.

Okereke, Eche Grace. 'The journey as trope for female growth in Zaynab Alkali's *The Virtuous Woman*', in Azubike Ileoje (ed.), *Currents in African Literature and the English Language*. Calabar: University of Calabar Press, 1997.

Okome, Onookome (ed.). *Before I am hanged: Ken Saro Wiwa, politics, literature and dissent*. Trenton, New Jersey: Africa World Press, 2000.

Okome, Onookome. 'Tanure Ojaide: The poet laureate of the Niger Delta', in Onookome Okome (ed.), *Writing the Homeland: The Poetry and Politics of Tanure Ojaide*. Bayreuth: Bayreuth University, 2002.

Okonta, Ike and Douglas, Oronto. *Where Vultures Feast: Shell, Human Rights, and Oil in the Niger Delta*. London: Verso, 2001.

Okunoye, Oyeniyi. 'Alterity, marginality and the national question in the poetry of the Niger Delta.' *Cahiers d'Études Africaines* XLVIII, 3 (2008): 413–436.

Omoweh, Daniel. *Shell Petroleum Development Company, the State and Underdevelopment of Nigeria's Niger Delta: A Study in Environmental Degradation*. Trenton, NJ: Africa World Press, 2005.

Osaghae, Eghosa. 'The Ogoni uprising, minority rights and the future of the Nigerian state.' *African Affairs* 94 (1995): 325–344.

Osha, Sanya. 'Shifting the Sands: The Ogoni crisis and the recrafting of the national question', in A. E. Eruvbetine (ed.), *The humanistic management of pluralism: A formula for development in Nigeria*. Lagos: Faculty of Arts, University of Lagos, 2001: 82–93.

Said, Edward. 'Reflections on exile', in Russell Ferguson et al. (eds), *Out There: Marginalization and Contemporary Cultures. Documentary Sources in Contemporary Art* vol. 4. New York: New Museum of Contemporary Art; Cambridge, MA: MIT Press, 1990.

Saro-Wiwa, K. *A Month and a Day: A Detention Diary*. Penguin, 1995.

Schneider-Mayerson, Matthew. 'From politics to prophecy: Environmental quiescence and the "peak-oil" Movement.' *Environmental Politics*, 22, 5 (2013): 866–882.

Simon, E. D, Akung J. E and Bassey B. U. 'Environmental degradation, militancy/kidnapping and oil theft in Helon Habila's *Oil on Water*.' *Mediterranean Journal of Social Sciences* 5, 2 (2014): 383–388.

Slaymaker, William. 'Natural connections; unnatural identities: Ecocriticism in the Black Atlantic.' *Journal of the African Literature Association* 1, 2 (2007): 129–39.

Subulwa, Angela, G. 'Settlement, protracted displacement, and repatriation at Mayukwayukwa in western Zambia.' *African Geographical Review* 32, 1, (2013): 29–43.

Szeman, Imre. 'System failure: Oil, futurity, and the anticipation of disaster.' *South Atlantic Quarterly* 106, 4, (2007): 805–823.

Taussig, Michael. *The Devil and Commodity Fetishism in Latin America*. Chapel Hill: University of North Carolina Press, 1980.

Terminski, Bogumil. *Environmentally-induced displacement: Theoretical frameworks and current challenges*. CEDEM, University of Liège, 2012.

Travis, Sarah. 'Seeking a common ground: Environmental degradation in Ken Saro-Wiwa's country.' *Dialectical Anthropology* 22, 3–4 (1997): 389–398.

Ukaogo, Victor. '"Strangulated federalism", resource rights agitations and the deepening crisis in the Niger-Delta.' *African Journal of History and Culture* (AJHC) 1, 3 (2009): 54–59, http://www.ademicjournals.org/AJHC (accessed 12 June 2013).

UNHCR (Office of the UN High Commissioner for Refugees). *Protracted Refugee Situations* (EC/54/SC/CRP.14). Geneva: UNHCR, 2004.

Ushie, Joseph. 'Challenges of the creative writer in the Niger Delta.' *Ker Review: A Journal of Nigerian Literature* 2, 1 & 2 (2006): 3–26.

Chapter 10

HUMAN MASKS?
ANIMAL NARRATORS IN PATRICE NGANANG'S *DOG DAYS: AN ANIMAL CHRONICLE* AND ALAIN MABANCKOU'S *MEMOIRS OF A PORCUPINE*

WENDY WOODWARD

Non-human animal narrators may seem more consistent with folk tales or narratives written for children, but a number of recent novels for adults have animals as the central narrators or focalisers, including Paul Auster's *Timbuktu* (1999), Kerstin Ekman's *The Dog* (2009) and Joseph Smith's *The Wolf* (2008). Other novels have dogs as partial focalisers or points of view: Orhan Pamuk's *My Name is Red* (1998), David Wroblewski's *The Story of Edgar Sawtelle* (2008) and John Banville's *The Infinities* (2009). Cameroonian Patrice Nganang, in *Dog Days: An Animal Chronicle* (2006) (henceforth referred to as *Dog Days*), and Congolese Alain Mabanckou, in *Memoirs of a Porcupine* (2011) (henceforth *Memoirs*), may seem to be conforming to an international trend with their animal narrators, but Nganang's dog and Mabanckou's porcupine are specifically African beings. Anthony Vital asks in Chapter 7 of this volume, 'What would need to enter [globally situated ecocriticism] to account for what makes African worlds distinct?'. This chapter asks a similar question in relation to literary human–animal studies, as it offers a reading that engages with the African particularities of these two novels. In doing so, it challenges conventional literary criticism, which favours, anthropocentrically, culture over nature, the human over the non-human.

Both novels are francophone translations into English, but the significance of their French provenance is difficult to determine. Animal figures do perhaps occur in French fairy tales more than in English ones, for example, but animal agents and/or tricksters also appear in traditional myths throughout Africa. Nganang's translator, Amy Baram Reid, insists that the novel derives from 'myriad connections to literature from around the world' (Reid 2006: 212), as well as from cartoons by Popoli, which had dogs and cats as political commentators (Reid 2006: 229). Mabanckou's story was inspired by his mother's traditional tales, and he refers specifically to her belief in harmful animal doubles, creatures whom he found especially frightening (Sullivan 2012). In Kofi Opoku's 'Animals in African mythology', he notes the significance of animals in the 'sacred wisdom' of Africa, which he ascribes to their sharing the world with humans, as well as their experiencing 'the same faculties, and the same experience of life and death' (Opuku 2006: 351). Through their narratives, Mabanckou and Nganang modernise and subvert such high seriousness in African mythology. Mabanckou represents the occult as a dynamic and resilient entity in contemporary village life. Nganang has Massa Yo alternate between admiring his dog and casting him out as an evil spirit onto the streets of the Cameroonian capital, where rumours and gossip express current fears of sorcery and witchcraft. Opoku, too easily, differentiates an idealised past from a vacuous present. More relevant to these novels is the non-differentiation of 'tradition' and 'modernity', fantasy and reality. For Zakes Mda, magical realism is especially relevant to African storytelling: 'In my culture the magical is not disconcerting … No one tries to find a natural explanation for the unreal. The unreal happens as part of reality' (in Fincham 2011: xxii). For Harry Garuba, the assimilation and appropriation of aspects of European modernity into 'traditional ritual and culture' (Garuba 2003: 263–264) constitute a process he ascribes to an 'animist unconscious' within a 'continual re-enchantment of the world' (Garuba 2003: 265). For Peter Geschiere, in his study *The Modernity of Witchcraft*, occult forces are powerful and prevalent in contemporary West African politics, including the case of President Paul Biya, in power in Cameroon since 1982, whose government ascribes the economic success of his ethnic rivals to 'vicious new forms of witchcraft' (Geschiere 1997: 18).

Dog Days, which is the less fantastical narrative of the two, critiques the politics and corruption of contemporary Cameroon. Mboudjak, Nganang's dog narrator, is tantamount to a double who shifts, in Massa Yo's eyes, between harmless and harmful, depending on the human's fortune. The dog is a chronicler and observer of human foibles, but, unlike the porcupine memoirist, he is deeply moral and politically engaged. He lives in populous Madagascar, a working-class quarter of Yaoundé, Cameroon. As an urban and political being, he critiques the social formation and joins revolutionary protests against the corrupt regime of Biya in the slum area he inhabits. In *Memoirs*, which plays surreally with the occult in contemporary life, the porcupine, Ngoumba, is the 'harmful double' of the psychopathic Kibandi, enacting murders at his bequest. He is also literate and familiar with Western literature of the supernatural, and develops a conscience, somewhat belatedly, of the crimes he perpetrates. Ultimately, he becomes increasingly unhappy at doing his master's bidding and longs to assert himself independently after Kibandi's death. The issue of 'who laughs at whom' (see Reichl and Stein [2005: 12]) across the human–animal divide is a significant one. Both novels are satires, with the laughter in *Dog Days* more 'conciliatory' and that of *Memoirs* more 'subversive'.

Hybridised narrators

To what extent the writers have imagined their narrators as 'real' animals varies. Rosi Braidotti (2009) favours the 'neoliteral approach' to animals, finding that the 'old metaphoric dimension' has been supplanted by fresh ways of relating to animals. No longer are animals 'the keepers of the gates between species', she maintains (Braidotti 2009: 528). Although, broadly, I concur with Braidotti's argument about recent trends in relation to animals, representations of non-human animals in *Dog Days* and *Memoirs* cannot be so clearly delineated, nor should the metaphoric aspects of animals be so negatively construed. Traditionally, according to Opoku (2006), animals are our '*useful* companions' (emphasis added) even as they 'constitute an indispensable source of wisdom without which our self-understanding would be incomplete' (Opuku 2006: 351). For Opoku, traditional constructions of animals have them as human adjuncts or, in Braidotti's words, as 'the signifying system that props up humans' self-projections and moral aspirations' (Braidotti 2009: 528). Garuba's proposal that 'the most rewarding approach to … much of African literature' includes a primary acknowledgement of an 'animist intertext' (Garuba 2003: 280), similarly has its limitations for my reading of animal narrators. His suggestion that the 'animist world-view' obtains in literature in 'a representational strategy that involves giving the abstract or metaphorical a material realization' (Garuba 2003: 284) serves to reduce animal narrators to ciphers without any potential for subjectivity. The dog, Mboudjak, and the porcupine, Ngoumba, are situated in both the neoliteral and the metaphoric. Although animals as narrators may embody convenient perspectives, quite literally from below, their characterisation, particularly that of Mboudjak, conveys a sense of animal subjectivity. Reid (2006: 214) refers to the 'universality of Mboudjak's concerns' in relation to the question that Mboudjak and others repetitively ask: 'Where is Man?'. This question also gestures to where humans stand in relation to animals.

A highly articulate, politically aware dog and a literate porcupine are, of course, fantastical creatures, who could be seen as entirely anthropomorphised, but they are also embodied subjects. Maurice Taonezvi Vambe defines the fantastic as an 'elastic conceptual term that can be stretched to accommodate and explain the literary qualities of fluidity, liminality and crossing of zones of occult instability' even as the fantastic 'diffuse[s] and decentre[s] dominant narratives' (Vambe 2012: 62). Although Vambe's definition applies to the novels under discussion, the narrating dog and porcupine incorporate a further aspect of liminality – anthropomorphism, which could be read as merely fantastical or, as I will suggest below, as empathetic, or even, potentially, ethical. Lorraine Daston and Gregg Mitman propose that instead of regarding anthropomorphism as negative, we regard 'thinking with animals' as having a double purpose, thus implicitly linking Braidotti's categories and echoing Opoku's sense that we can deploy animals to think through human experience and desires as well as being aware of the real animal, with whom we think in a 'community of thought and feeling' (Daston and Mitman 2005: 2). That both Mboudjak and Ngoumba are made to critique the figure of the 'master', for example, is suggestive not only of non-human–human dynamics, but also of human politics, so that the reader is enjoined to 'think with animals' in both of its meanings.

The animal narrators, then, are not just human ventriloquists but they are performative of the animal. While they may be, in Opoku's terms, 'an abundant source of wisdom' for us (Opuku 2006: 358), they are also, as Daston and Mitman argue, 'symbols with a life of their own ... We [humans] may orchestrate their [animal] performance, but complete mastery is an illusion. Eyes peer through *the human mask* to reveal another life, mysterious—like us or unlike us?' (Daston and Mitman 2005: 13, emphasis added). The choice to cast animals as narrators points to an ethical purview on the part of the writers who, either explicitly or implicitly, engage with the position of animals in human culture. Giving a voice to those generally regarded as powerless shifts animal vulnerabilities and apparent silences. Because the animal narrators are hybrid creatures who embody crossovers between human and non-human, and between nature and culture, we cannot regard them as the 'absolute other', in Jacques Derrida's words (Derrida 2008: 11) – their animal subjectivities are undeniable. To what extent the animals are embodied does, admittedly, vary. If Nganang depicts the 'animal sensorium', to use Cary Wolfe's phrase (Wolfe 2010: xxv), of Mboudjak, Ngoumba is less of an embodied animal in relation to his senses. He barely engages with the world through the lived experience of a porcupine. As a harmful double, he is a supernatural creature, often taking on human characteristics: he talks with his paw raised, for example, like a human taking an oath, and the only sexual desire he feels is for the sleeping adolescent, Kiminou, 'said to be the prettiest girl in Sekepembe' (Mabanckou 2011: 90), who is his first victim.

Issues of power inherent in the politics of naming and who gets to name whom recur colonially and in relation to animals. In the latter case, naming can signify ownership or the taming of an animal. Mboudjak is initially proud of his name, which means '"the outstretched hand"' (Nganang 2006: 8). He regards his name as signifying connection with Massa Yo, for whom he is an 'enlightened guide' and his 'infallible hand' (Nganang 2006: 8). In his narcissism, he is 'proud to point out to men truth's modest hiding place' (Nganang 2006: 8) but he cannot deny that he is constrained by 'a chain that binds me to his will' (Nganang 2006: 9); nor can he deny his master's cruelty. Ngoumba reveals his name only towards the end of his narrative. Resentful of his master's right to name him generically – for 'in our language', Ngoumba means porcupine (Mabanckou 2011: 145) – he is also critical of the motives behind Kibandi's naming. He surmises that

> he rather liked the idea that I was not just a porcupine, an ordinary everyday porcupine, well he would wouldn't he, he was a human being, and since I didn't like this ugly sounding name, I pretended I hadn't heard him when he called me by it, but he would insist. (Mabanckou 2011: 145)

Memoirs opens with the porcupine reminiscing belligerently about 'men', who describe him as 'just an animal, just a *dumb, wild animal*' (Mabanckou 2011: 3) and Mabanckou has him rail further – against Kibandi, who has recently died and who thought of him as 'a lowly bit player, a pawn in his hands'. Ngoumba is adamant, however, that the power did not reside in the human: 'Without me he'd have been a bit of rotten pulp, his life as a man worth less than a few drops of piss' (Mabanckou 2011: 3).

Although conflict recurs in the relationship between human and animal in the narrative, at the beginning of their lifelong kinship the young Ngoumba feels the pull towards the boy Kibandi as irresistible. When their affiliation begins, Ngoumba dreams of the boy, and 'from somewhere would come this vibration inside of me, only known to animals predisposed to fuse with a human being' (Mabanckou 2011: 36). The porcupine experiences Kibandi's initiation nausea and vulnerability, and is convinced that they are one hybrid being: 'I was him; he was me' (Mabanckou 2011: 37), he claims, and he submits to the notion that his 'destiny was to serve human beings, not for better, but for worse, for the very worst' (Mabanckou 2011: 35). His constant proximity to his master means that he has to reject his fellow animals and live near humans, aware always of Kibandi's other self (identical to him but lacking a mouth and nose), who acts as a go-between. As a harmful double, the porcupine is forced to 'eat' people for Kibandi. He kills them by shooting quills into their temples; once he extracts the quills, the holes close up so that there is no evidence of how they died. Because the alternative to being a harmful double is only feasible for the porcupine once Kibandi dies, his whole life has been murderous. In justification, he argues that he was 'just an underling, a shadow in Kibandi's life' (Mabanckou 2011: 126).

Mboudjak also struggles with alternatives to being his master's creature, but when Massa Yo loses his job as a civil servant he victimises Mboudjak, calling him a 'parasite' and a *'njou njou Calaba'*, or evil spirit (Nganang 2006: 10), so that the dog has no choice but to migrate to the streets. Nganang foregrounds the power relations in which the dogs are situated, as they have little choice between being a subservient pet or a deprived street dog. For Mboudjak, crossing 'class lines' (Nganang 2006: 10) opens up communication with street dogs, who raise the issue of 'canitude', which they regard as freedom from a master. A colonial dimension resonates with this discussion between the dogs when the three-legged 'communist' dog derides the 'white men's dogs', who submit to being leashed, like the dogs of 'their black lackeys' (Nganang 2006: 14). After Massa Yo is forced to run a bar, and his wife a fritter stand, to make ends meet, Mama Mado takes Mboudjak with her to a beauty parlour, so that together they can be admired like royalty. Mama Mado enjoys the admiration but 'there were some critics—Afrocentric intellectuals to be sure—who said, "That poor dog, alienated from his canitude!"' (Nganang 2006: 70). In the disassociation of the dog from his natural appearance, the politics of dogness echoes that of negritude in this homology of human/animal and white/black. As Reid points out, the reference to 'canitude' echoes Léopold Senghor and Aimé Césaire's notions of negritude – as well as Wole Soyinka's retort that 'Africans had as much need to proclaim their Negritude as did a tiger his "tigritude"' (Reid 2006: 227). In this serio-comic construction, Nganang plays in myriad ways with the shifting question of who laughs at whom. The question of how identities are constituted also recurs with Mama Mado intent on changing dog identities and lives. She is publicly adamant that Mboudjak is 'the dog of the future' (Nganang 2006: 70), a future in which there is no more starvation, illness or disfigurement in the canine population of Madagascar, Yaoundé. Her concern is not just superficial but envelops the embodied dogs who suffer on the streets.

Mboudjak, after Massa Yo's son tries to murder him by hanging, is fired by the imperative for a 'canine revolution while sharpening [his] race consciousness' (Nganang 2006: 23). He tells himself that 'to escape from men's crimes ... I needed to muster up the courage to return to the dangerous circle of their definitions and demand justice' (Nganang 2006: 23). But the grandeur of these motivations is reduced when he confesses that he actually returned to Massa Yo to test his master's 'humanity' (Nganang 2006: 23). He trains himself to become an observer, commenting on how poverty renders humans more atavistic while noting government corruption and irresponsibility. Even though he succumbs to being a 'watchdog' (Nganang 2006: 24) in Massa Yo's bar, The Customer is King, and to bolstering Massa Yo's masculinity, he remains critical of the lack of community spirit in the neighbourhood, of the victimisation of the weak and of the brutality of the police commissioner. When the commissioner unjustly arrests the cigarette vendor, one of the neighbourhood characters, Mboudjak 'bark[s] out [his] indignation' while the men in the vicinity wallow in their 'torpor' (Nganang 2006: 95). An enigmatic, silent man, nicknamed the Crow, is the only one who protests, but he becomes a martyr, as he, too, is arrested. Mboudjak, enraged at the passivity of the crowd, barks in protest, feeling 'outraged that all men in the quarter let themselves be dominated by one man, even if he did have a gun in his hand' (Nganang 2006: 97). The dog's quest for justice for his own species elides with his righteous rage at political injustice in the human sphere. Nganang might represent this scene satirically, with the dog unsure of the political discourse the Crow deploys, but, even so, he has Mboudjak embody an activist, ethical conscience: he bites the police commissioner and then 'bark[s] out his disappointment' (Nganang 2006: 99) at the cowardice of his master.

If Nganang represents the dog as a 'source of wisdom' (to use Opoku's phrase), Mabanckou does not have the porcupine as such a consistent ethical touchstone, nor is Ngoumba's context political. Instead, Mabanckou engages more directly with the occult as he shifts human centrality to give a voice to the harmful double. Again, although the mode is satirical and surreal, the subjectivity of an animal is foregrounded. As in *Dog Days*, the ideal of community is tested. For Malidoma Patrice Somé (1999: 22), 'the general health and well-being of an individual are connected to a community, and are not something that can be maintained alone or in a vacuum'. Somé's vision positively connects ritual with 'the forces of the natural world' and with people motivated by 'a clear healing vision and a trusting intent toward the forces of the invisible world' (Somé 1999: 22). The narrative of Kibandi and his harmful double contradicts such seamlessly positive notions of African indigeneity. Kibandi, who is solitary and individualistic, engages directly with the dark forces of nature through his harmful animal double. Always quick to take offence, his edgy paranoia and lack of standing in the Sekepembe village community spur him to 'eat' his victims (Mabanckou 2011: 99), who number 99 – from the young Kiminou, whose father had tricked Kibandi in his role as potential suitor, to Youala's baby, who, as a spirit, is instrumental in his downfall. Kibandi's life trajectory resonates with Geschiere's explication of the *djambe*, a creature within the belly of the individual that enables her/him to transform into a spirit or an animal for the purpose of material acquisition and power (Geschiere 1997: 16). The focus is on the aggrandisement of the individual at the expense of the family (Geschiere 1997: 42). While Geschiere studies the Maka in Cameroon particularly, he notes, via Jean-François Bayart, that the 'politics of the belly' (Geschiere 1997: 7) is endemic in African politics.

Like Mboudjak, Ngoumba is irrevocably tied to his master, although in the dark, spiritual realm. The porcupine justifies the murder of Kiminou: 'For one human to eat another you need concrete reasons, jealousy, anger, envy, humiliation, lack of respect, I swear we never once ate someone just for the pleasure of eating' (Mabanckou 2011: 92). Ngoumba is the perpetrator of all the murders, but over the years he develops some ethical reticence about his practice, feeling pity for his victims. When he is directed to 'eat' Youala's baby, initially his 'quills grew heavy and reluctant' (Mabanckou 2011: 119) as his conscience pricks him. Subsequently, however, he dispenses with such reservations, goading himself on by thinking of Youala's debt to Kibandi and his rudeness. As a harmful double, he has no choice but to obey his master, for he is 'stuck with [his] role as a double as a turtle is stuck with his shell' (Mabanckou 2011: 4). Yet he seeks inspiration from his past mentor, the old porcupine who liked 'preaching that all men were bad, including children, because "the tiger's young are born with claws"' (Mabanckou 2011: 119). The murder of the baby, then, is framed within a very particular species discourse, eliding the innate, embodied violence of the tiger with that of the human. Although Ngoumba tells himself he is making his own decisions and is agentive in his dismissal of humans and their ethics, he is, ironically, disempowered by these very ethics. Gradually, over the years, Ngoumba and his master begin to lose their potency, but Kibandi is adamant that they have to continue with their killings, castigating the porcupine and threatening to murder him. The porcupine resents the lack of acknowledgement of his 'devotion' (Mabanckou 2011: 124) but begins to understand that Kibandi is driven to continue with the killings because he has to feed his other self: '"He's been getting hungrier and hungrier ... this guy needs to eat, or you'll pay the price"', Kibandi tells his harmful double (Mabanckou 2011: 124).

Literacies

That Kibandi is able to perform extraordinary feats – he is able to read the Bible without tuition, for example – is a sign of his access to the supernatural. Mabanckou also has the porcupine become literate and eloquent without effort. The narrative is constituted by Ngoumba's confession of his life story to the Baobab, an addressee who is silent, accepting and part of nature, which points to the animal's desire for some natural community and some exoneration of his evil-doing. Highfield (in Chapter 1 of this volume) discusses the iconic status of the baobab tree in Africa and its significance in myths throughout Africa. John Mbiti (2008: 51) also notes the sacredness of the baobab tree, long associated with God and spiritual beings. Ngoumba feels that the tree will protect him and he longs for 'the benefit of [the Baobab's] ancestral experience'

(Mabanckou 2011: 24). Through this interchange, the porcupine allows himself a glimpse of a kinder, more ecologically balanced world, where nature is a source of healing with benevolent ancestral spirits, rather than a base for evil and destruction, or an enemy to be conquered. A self-preservational element also obtains, for he is telling his story after the death of Kibandi – a risky, transitional moment for a harmful double, who, traditionally, dies when his master does. The fearful Ngoumba therefore invests the 'spoken word' with almost magical properties because, as he tells his silent listener, 'it delivers us from the fear of death, and if it could help me stave it off for a little while, or escape it, that would make me the happiest porcupine in the world' (Mabanckou 2011: 21).

In depicting this reliance of an animal on human language, Mabanckou contradicts those traditional African beliefs that value nature as 'the home that holds the wisdom of the cosmos' (Somé 1999: 49). For the Dagara, the 'Source ... has no word ... because meaning is produced instantly, like a cosmic and timeless awareness' (Somé 1999: 49). Yet in *Memoirs*, an animal is in eloquent control of human language, which 'wise men and women in the indigenous world ... insist is an instrument of distance from meaning' (Somé 1999: 50). In this belief, the language of animals is 'closer to the Source, the world of intrinsic meaning' (Somé 1999: 50), thus contradicting the Western valuing of language as a sign of intelligence, which animals fail to possess. In representing animals as narrators, both Mabanckou and Nganang conform more to Western beliefs about language; that both dog and porcupine are adept in human language increases their standing. They tell the stories from their own points of view, foregrounding an animal perspective, performative though it might be. Mboudjak boasts that he 'take[s] in the world from below. This allows me to apprehend men at the very moment of their emergence from the primordial muck. In the same way, I apprehend the phases of humanity's annihilation' (Nganang 2006: 29).

The writers also satirise certain linguistic cultural forms. Mabanckou has Ngoumba critique the Bible with 'all the stories men have forced themselves to believe, on pain of not deserving a place in what they call *Paradise*' (Mabanckou 2011: 10). Yet Ngoumba enjoys the Noah's Ark story, where 'the whole of humanity, including us animals' is preserved (Mabanckou 2011: 11). The porcupine is also a literary critic who construes novels and stories, mostly of horror and violence, as narratives of harmful doubles. Western forms and tales are humorously reinterpreted, from Ernest Hemingway's *The Old Man and the Sea* to Edgar Allan Poe's 'The murders in the Rue Morgue'. Implicitly, however, the narrative of a harmful double who kills humans untraceably by means of his quills tops them all for horror.

Unlike Ngoumba, Mboudjak is not a reader, but he has 'made men's words [his] own' (Nganang 2006: 7) in his narration of picaresque stories of Madagascar, Yaoundé, and human machinations – stories that tumble over each other in their richness. Reid (2006: 217) suggests that 'Mboudjak's musings on the consequences of adopting another's language signal both the linguistic legacy of colonialism and the ongoing debates over language use in the Cameroon'. These 'musings' also signal issues of power, language and animality, as the dog is made to be painfully aware. The word 'dog' conveys his status as an 'object in the human universe' (Nganang 2006: 7), but that Mboudjak is represented as linguistically astute resonates with and potentially critiques the dualistic conceptualising of human and non-human, with the former regarded as superior because they are in command of language and the latter are seen as lacking. Mboudjak is also a sceptical interpreter of rumours, which are seductive to humans – 'reality's hallucinatory magic', he calls them (Nganang 2006: 79). Unlike the clients of Massa Yo's bar, for example, the dog is not taken in by the story circulating in the quarters of a man who '"mak[es] men's bangalas disappear"' and he keeps his 'sceptical, scientific, canine head' (Nganang 2006: 79, 80).

Both novels include central, intellectual human characters whose interpretations of the world are significant for the development of the narrators' linguistic sophistication. In *Memoirs*, Amédée, a 'young man of letters' (Mabanckou 2011: 112), is a charismatic figure, but given the negativity of Kibandi and his harmful double, Amédée is sacrificed to Kibandi's ego. Granted, Amédée is a smug narcissist, displaying his learning from the 'countries where it snows' (Mabanckou 2011: 102) along with his prejudice against tradition. As the 'village intellectual', he has read studies of the ritual of 'trial by corpse', which, as a man steeped in modernity, he does not believe in. In such trials, the corpse of someone who has died in mysterious circumstances reveals his or her murderer by slewing the coffin carried by the pall-bearers towards the culprit. (Kibandi has always circumvented detection by means of this ritual by inserting a palm nut in his anus, thus blocking any apprehension of his guilt.) Amédée is doomed partly for his disbelief in a tradition that frames the existence and efficacy of harmful doubles, and partly because he is an unsympathetic character. Amédée is lecherous, manipulative and critical of older people for being 'ignorant' (Mabanckou 2011: 103), but his worst sin is to mock Kibandi for being thin, to patronise him for reading 'an esoteric book' (Mabanckou 2011: 107) and to suggest that he, like '"an unfortunate character in *Stories of Love, Madness and Death*"' (Mabanckou 2011: 107), is being sapped by a blood-sucking beast who lives in his pillow. Amédée had used these stories by Uruguayan Horacio Quiroga to scare and seduce the young village women, but Kibandi is furious about being construed as a character in fiction and being seen as naive. Amédée is a rich source of satire. Not only is he insulting to the villagers of Sekepembe, but he also lacks understanding of the contemporary powers of the occult. Mabanckou ridicules his rationality in the face of harmful doubles, as well as his anthropological discourse, which is quintessentially colonial. Amédée's death at the quill of Ngoumba contradicts the rationality of his belief, which he has incorporated along with his studies in Europe. Yet his lavish funeral is anything but rational: he is buried along with two boxes of books, a Bible in his coffin and, to please his parents, a Latin-speaking priest officiates.

Ngoumba, in spite of himself, is 'intrigued' by the 'big show-off novels' (Mabanckou 2011: 103, 104) that Amédée reads and by the richness of their narratives. Yet they are also threatening to the porcupine. He tells his confidante, the Baobab:

> ... novels are books written by men to recount things which are untrue, they'll say it all comes from their imagination, there are some novelists who would sell their own mothers or fathers to steal my porcupine destiny, draw inspiration from it, write a story in which I'd have an [*sic*] rather less than glamorous role, make me look like low life. (Mabanckou 2011: 104)

The porcupine is as narcissistic as his victim, fearful of being negatively portrayed. Ironically, to what extent he can avoid representing himself negatively is a moot point, given the serial murders he commits at Kibandi's orders. Mabanckou also plays with reflexivity here, reminding the reader that the author is the ghostwriter even as he has Ngoumba narrating his life story to the silent, sympathetic Baobab.

Ethical endings?

If Amédée is sacrificed in *Memoirs* for his exploitative attitudes and his binary thinking about modernity/tradition, in *Dog Days* the intellectual character nicknamed the Crow is a writer who becomes an ally to Mboudjak. Initially, he seems to have an 'evil aura', to be 'ripped straight out of a rumor' (Nganang 2006: 81), and in The Customer is King, Mboudjak and the hens are fearful of him. He is silent, dressed in black and displays his 'usual studied arrogance' (Nganang 2006: 81) as he nurses a drink and takes notes. The other clients at the bar threaten him, as they suspect he might be a spy, but his notebook reveals the discourse of a philosopher, according to Docta, a vociferous customer, who reads out from the Crow's notebook: 'The neighbourhoods are the forge of mankind's creativity. The wretchedness of their surroundings is but an illusion. It conceals the profound reality of the unknown which remains to be discovered: the truth of History is its creation.' (Nganang 2006: 82).

The next day, the Crow brings a book he has written called *Dog Days*, which attempts 'to put the reins of History back into the hands of its true heroes' (Nganang 2006: 83). Human responses to him are mixed: some want to tell the Crow their stories, and one wants to tell of his talents as a poet, but the engineer, Docta, remains suspicious of his silence. Mboudjak 'was on the philosopher's side, if only out of pure professional solidarity among observers' (Nganang 2006: 87). Enigmatic though the Crow may be, he is embraced nevertheless by the dog narrator as a positive figure, partly because of the dog's derived sense of self-aggrandisement as a fellow observer.

The Crow is an ethical man who, by criticising the police commissioner for arresting the cigarette vendor for no reason, raises political issues. Mboudjak 'heard the word "justice," then the words "injustice," "dictatorship," and "new deal," the name "Biya," and finally the sentence, "Cameroon is Cameroon."' (Nganang 2006: 96). Mboudjak doubles for the Crow as an observer with political integrity yet, unlike the Crow initially, he is less romantic about the working-class inhabitants of the neighbourhood. The dog is disillusioned to realise that 'men are not brothers' (Nganang 2006: 100), as none is prepared to try to get the cigarette vendor and the Crow out of jail. Mboudjak's street wanderings take him to the party headquarters but instead of keeping to a human political agenda, Nganang has his dog observer perform his 'canitude' in the garbage dump nearby. The representation of the dog's joy in the filth alerts the reader to the 'animal sensorium' (to use Cary Wolfe's phrase) and to the dog's paramount sense of smell. As Vicki Hearne (1986: 79) observes, for a dog, 'scenting is believing'. Mboudjak tells how:

> I touched, I sniffed, I tasted ... I rediscovered my joie de vivre. All of a sudden it was like I had escaped from the prison of an overly small bar courtyard ... I let myself get carried away and wandered unknown in the Infinite of Art. I was once again a vagabond, a Bohemian, and I accepted the chaos. ... I had stayed among men too long. (Nganang 2006: 103)

Although Mboudjak rediscovers a life of the senses on the streets, he remains faithful to a new political awareness, at least for a while. He quarrels with dogs behind walls who 'said it was better to be a prisoner in a palace than to live in misery on an endless street. I told them it was a question of choice' (Nganang 2006: 108). But then he returns to Massa Yo's bar.

The Crow reappears, having been released from prison. Furious and disillusioned with the men he had so idealistically thought were heroes, he gets drunk, taunting the bar customers because they did nothing to aid his release: '"You're killing yourselves with alcohol, but you're bigger cowards than hyenas. How many have died in prison while you sat in bars getting drunk on indifference?"' (Nganang 2006: 113). Enraged with them for their lack of political awareness and their cowardice, he throws rolls of francs into the air – 'the money of their shame' (Nganang 2006: 115), in Mboudjak's words, but this does not stop bystanders from grabbing the notes in a pitched battle. That Mboudjak visualises the Crow symbolically as a 'lugubrious silhouette soaring ominously overhead, a bird-like portent of evil, watching from afar as man's fate played out in front of my master's bar' (Nganang 2006: 119) suggests that the man is both human and bird, a voice of conscience, even in his disillusionment. Although he may not seem to convey the 'sacred wisdom' of Africa, he embodies a deep political wisdom. For the dog, he is 'the true master of speech that drives people crazy' (Nganang 2006: 119). Through the Crow's silence and his new cynicism with its sinister edge, he speaks the truth not to power but to those who have been disempowered and impoverished, and who lack the inspiration or bravery to confront the corrupt government, which has them in apathetic thrall. When word gets around that the Crow's money is counterfeit, the street is covered in a 'silent shame' (Nganang 2006: 119). Mboudjak's final analysis is that 'it was as if the Crow's laughter had gotten even louder, and this time it shook everyone's soul down to the core' (119).

According to Elspeth Probyn (2005: xiii), shame is 'biologically innate', inherent in being human and can be 'productive in how it makes us think again about bodies, societies and human interaction' (Probyn 2005: xviii). Shame in both these novels, however, is felt by the animal narrators. Both narrators, in the final denouement of the novels, are overwhelmed by shame. This shame brings about dramatic shifts in their lives, but its relevance for Ngoumba is potentially immobilising. When he kills Youala's baby, his 99th victim, he overrides his remorse and reservations in order to shoot his deadly quill, but the shame he feels is persistent: 'I felt ashamed of my own reflection in the water, I went to the funeral, perhaps hoping for some kind of forgiveness, I heard the poor folk singing their funeral songs, and I wept' (Mabanckou 2011: 120). His emotions are not entirely disinterested, however, as he intuits that the spirit of the baby has a message for him: it was 'trying to tell me to revolt' (Mabanckou 2011: 121). But the connection with Kibandi is too strong and he remains with his master, although filled with presentiment that their 100th murder would culminate in their demise.

After the attempt to kill Ma Mpori, who suspects Kibandi and Ngoumba, is unsuccessful, Kibandi turns his attention to the twins of the Moundjoula family, who torment him because they claim they know he 'ate' a baby – a fact the baby has divulged to them in the graveyard. First, Ngoumba is attacked by the twins, Koty and Kote. With their rectangular heads, each 'the size of a brick' (Mabanckou 2011: 131), and their laughter 'like two dwarves at a fair' (Mabanckou 2011: 131), they are formidable enemies. In the supernatural cataclysm that follows, which is directed by the twins and the baby, Kibandi is rendered powerless when his other self is kidnapped and reduced to 'a puppet, a clown, a marionette' (Mabanckou 2011: 139). Ultimately, Kibandi cannot defend himself and collapses 'like an old tree felled with a single blow' (Mabanckou 2011: 140) as baby Youala brings back the darkness of night after the 'blinding light' that had enveloped them all. The baby 'raised his left hand to the sky, as though he could command all nature' (Mabanckou 2011: 140) and then turns his gaze on Ngoumba, who assumes he will be destroyed, but the baby signals to him to escape and he flees 'like a fugitive' (Mabanckou 2011: 141) as his master expires. The baby's supernatural force is surely for the good, and the fact that he permits Ngoumba to survive suggests that he takes pity on an animal as part of a redeeming nature, rather than destroying the harmful double along with his master.

Full of shame for the evil he has perpetrated, Ngoumba tells the Baobab that he must have been spared by 'some higher will' than his (Mabanckou 2011: 149). His mission henceforth will be to 'wage a merciless campaign against all the harmful doubles in this country' (Mabanckou 2011: 149) as a means of 'atonement' for the harm he did. Conciliatory aspects may seem paramount in this satire, with the prospect of nature being restored to equilibrium, and goodness prevailing with the eradication of harmful doubles. Ngoumba has a second mission, however, which is more self-serving, and that is to return to his native territory, find a mate, have offspring and then, possibly, to become a peaceful double. Death is not in his trajectory, as he hopes to become 'the Methuselah of the animal kind' (150) and he boasts of his potency with his ability to shoot his quills a fair distance. Clearly, the porcupine continues to nurture ambitions and desires to connect with the human. If he seems to embody the 'sacred wisdom' of an animal in a traditional legend, it is only for a moment. He had, earlier in his narrative, bemoaned the dullness of a peaceful double's life, premised, as it is, on goodness, generosity and healing, and suggested that he would have 'no tale to tell ... if [he'd] been a peaceful double, with no particular history, nothing out of the ordinary to speak of' (Mabanckou 2011: 1497).

In the Appendix, which is a missive to the publishers from Monsieur Stubborn Snail on the origins of *Memoirs*, Ngoumba explains that it was written by his late friend, Broken Glass, who believed that 'the world was just an approximate version of a fable which we will never understand as long as we continue to take account only of the material representation of things'. Mabanckou seems to be nudging the reader to take seriously the representation of the dark arts of Kibandi and the tradition of harmful doubles. In addition, he draws attention to the magic of a speaking porcupine, a performative animal. Ngoumba is far less of an embodied animal than Mboudjak – representations of his 'animal sensorium' barely feature in the novel, apart from his lethal quills. Because he is more a 'human mask', the eyes of the real animal do not obviously peek out, as they do in Mboudjak's narrative. Yet Mabanckou has the Stubborn Snail confess that reading the narrative 'changed his view of animals'. He asks: 'After all, which is really the beast, man or animal? A huge question!', thereby contradicting the conventional dualistic construction of human and animal as immersed in culture and nature, respectively. Implicitly, the Stubborn Snail collates the negative connotation of 'beast' as cruel, insatiable and instinctively 'red in tooth and claw' with the reference to 'man' and Kibandi. Ironically, his harmful double, to whom Mabanckou assigns a voice, is a far more ethical being than his master.

A similar question about species difference and ethical comportment resonates in *Dog Days*. Mboudjak is preoccupied with issues of self-assertion and independence, which correspond with political issues in Cameroon. Yet he is not above selling out, in spite of the Crow's inspiration. When the dog returns, chastened, from a four-month episode on the streets, the hens are incredulous that Mboudjak has missed The Customer is King. Mboudjak reports:

> They believed me even less when I said that life on the road is no life at all, and that in order to survive you have to give up your intelligence. They repeatedly raised their voices: 'Freedom has no price.' (Nganang 2006: 166)

Mboudjak tries to assure them that what matters is 'freedom of the *mind*' (Nganang 2006: 166), but they are unconvinced. Then, unexpectedly, even the inhabitants of Madagascar cannot ignore the protests against Biya. The dog perks up, incredulous that the '"starving masses were starting to shake their bodies!"' (Nganang 2006: 183). When rumours of deaths in protest marches circulate, however, Massa Yo still insists on ignoring politics, turning up his music, and the bar customers seem unconcerned that the Crow has been arrested for writing to Biya about poverty in certain neighbourhoods. What rouses them from their apathy is the police commissioner's shooting of the boy, Takou, the son of Docta. The inhabitants of Madagascar march behind a cart carrying the child's body to a nearby police station. Police repression is brutal and swift, but the inhabitants keep marching in spite of it, except for Massa Yo, who is without customers and with 'the humanity dying in his belly' (Nganang 2006: 204).

Like the porcupine, the dog is represented as having a more ethical vision than his master. Mboudjak keeps away from Massa Yo and remains open to the 'fever of change' (Nganang 2006: 202) rampant in Madagascar, in Yaoundé, in Cameroon and in the continent of Africa. As the demand that 'BIYA MUST GO' echoes without fear of 'death's creeping assault', human and animal seem united as the call is 'barked out' (Nganang 2006: 205). Mboudjak is ecstatic that the neighbourhoods have risen:

> United we were, man and me, in the spasmodic rush of our language: our barks. We marched, not only to bring somebody else's child back to life, but above all and foremost to chase out the crazed lion. We marched, hunters in an urban jungle. (Nganang 2006: 206)

Nganang, like Mabanckou, contextualises his narrative traditionally and correlates both human and animal with humans. Cross-species differences are undermined, with humans and dogs both having recourse to 'barks', as though they share a common language and rage. That Nganang chooses to represent this protest in terms that are reminiscent of traditional legends ('the crazed lion' and 'hunters in ... [the] jungle') suggests some continuity between this modern political action and the heroism required in the wild. (*Waiting For the Wild Beasts to Vote* by Ahmadou Kourouma [2004] also situates animals and humans together in contemporary politics but more graphically and sinisterly). The heightened perceptions of a dog's sense of smell constitute the final words of the novel:

> Each time I passed by the place where Takou died, I sniffed, re-sniffed, re-re-sniffed, and I re-re-re-sniffed the tar that, more than anyone, had witnessed the abrupt silencing of his infantile words. Yes, you can believe me, dear readers, the scent of his blood was still hot. (Nganang 2006: 206)

Both human and dog have been galvanised against injustice, as though both human and animal have claimed their agency simultaneously. The Crow's idealism about history in Madagascar is now enacted, with all the inhabitants of the quarter transformed into heroes.

Nganang brings the novel to closure with a political vision, and the tragic and needless death of a child. As Somé (1999: 53) reminds us, however, 'community becomes a form of immortality' if connections within that community are truly felt. The traditional notion of death as 'a different form of communion, a higher form of connectedness' (Somé 1999: 53) is also hinted at, with Takou's death serving as a profound influence on the Madagascar inhabitants, who now constitute a powerful community. *Memoirs* does not end so triumphantly or communally. Instead, Ngoumba hopes for an animal community beyond the human–animal connection, which has been, for him, conversely, a rich source of narrative as well as a source of shame. Occult trans-species overlaps, however, are dramatised gothically in the appearance of Kibandi's corpse, which, according to Ngoumba, has the massive head of a porcupine, although he admits that 'the fear of my own demise [might have] conjured up this illusion' (Mabanckou 2011: 17).

While both novelists have been thinking with animals as metaphors, they have also been thinking with animals communally. The real animal behind the 'human mask' tends to take precedence in the closure of the novels. Both dog and porcupine are, finally, subjects without fear of being mastered by a human. In the satire of who laughs at whom in relation to humans and animals, Ngoumba certainly has the last laugh. Mboudjak, conversely, has set aside adversarial politics between humans and animals, and laughs with them. The actual dog in *Dog Days* peeks out from behind his performance as a narrator, very much a dog who smells the world. In *Memoirs*, Ngoumba nurtures belated desires to live naturally like a porcupine, as though Mabanckou wishes to represent him peeking from behind his narrative mask. In both novels, the liminality of the fantastical is reduced. In *Memoirs*, the occult instability of the partnership between Kibandi and Ngoumba is over, and the elderly porcupine celebrates his independence and potency. In *Dog Days*, human and dog are both passionate about their political activism, which asserts the democratic rights of the populace of the Madagascar community in Yaoundé.

A human–animal studies reading of these two novels, then, has disaggregated the hybridity of the animal narrators, as it removes, if only for a moment or two, the human mask from the animal narrator. Both dog and porcupine, in varying degrees, as this essay suggests, draw the reader's attention to their animality and to the representational ethics of having animals tell their own stories, magically and satirically, as well as those of their human companions and collaborators.

References

Auster, Paul. *Timbuktu*. New York: Henry Holt, 1999.

Banville, John. *The Infinities*. Picador, 2009.

Braidotti, Rosi. 'Animals, anomalies, and inorganic others.' *PMLA* 124, 2 (2009): 526–532.

Daston, Lorraine and Mitman, Gregg. 'Introduction', in Lorraine Daston and Gregg Mitman (eds), *Thinking With Animals: New Perspectives on Anthropomorphism*. New York: Columbia University Press, 2005.

Derrida, Jacques. 'The animal that therefore I am', in Marie-Louise Mallet (ed.), *Perspectives in Continental Philosophy* (trans. David Wills). New York: Fordham University Press, 2008.

Ekman, Kerstin. *The Dog*. London: Little, Brown, 2009.

Fincham, Gail. *Dance of Life: The Novels of Zakes Mda in Post-Apartheid South Africa*. Cape Town: University of Cape Town Press, 2011.

Garuba, Harry. 'Explorations in animist materialism: Reading/writing African literature, culture, and society.' *Public Culture* 15, 2 (2003): 261–285.

Geschiere, Peter. *The Modernity of Witchcraft: Politics and the Occult in Postcolonial Africa*. University of Virginia Press, 1997.

Hearne, Vicki. *Adam's Task: Calling Animals by Name*. New York: Skyhorse (1986), 2007.

Kourouma, Ahmadou. *Waiting For the Wild Beasts to Vote* (trans. Frank Wynne). London: Vintage, 2004.

Mabanckou, Alain. *Memoirs of a Porcupine* (trans. Helen Stevenson). London: Serpent's Tail, 2011.

Mbiti, John. *African Religions and Philosophy* (2nd edn). Johannesburg: Heinemann (1989), 2008.

Nganang, Patrice. *Dog Days: An Animal Chronicle* (trans. Amy Baram Reid). Charlottesville: University of Virginia Press, 2006.

Opoku, Kofi. 'Animals in African mythology', in Paul Waldau and Kimberley Patton (eds), *A Communion of Subjects: Animals in Religion, Science and Ethics*. New York: Columbia University Press, 2006.

Pamuk, Orhan. *My Name is Red*. New York: Alfred A. Knopf, 1998.

Probyn, Elspeth. *Blush: Faces of Shame*. Minneapolis: University of Minnesota Press, 2005.

Reichl, Susanne and Stein, Mark. 'Introduction', in Susanne Reichl and Mark Stein (eds), *Cheeky Fictions: Laughter and the Postcolonial*. Amsterdam: Rodopi, 2005.

Reid, Amy Baram. 'Afterword: Reading around Nganang's Yaoundé', in Patrice Nganang, *Dog Days: An Animal Chronicle* (trans. Amy Baram Reid). Charlottesville: University of Virginia Press, 2006.

Smith, Joseph. *The Wolf*. London: Jonathan Cape, 2008.

Somé, Malidoma Patrice. *The Healing Wisdom of Africa: Finding Life Purpose Through Nature, Ritual, and Community*. New York: Jeremy P. Tarcher/Putnam, 1999.

Sullivan, Meg. 'Mind openers: New novel debunks old myth.' *UCLA Magazine*, 1 April 2012.

Vambe, Maurice Taonezvi. 'Fantastic subversion of the African postcolony in *Songs Of Enchantment*.' *Journal of Literary Studies* 28, 4 (2012): 57–86.

Wolfe, Cary. *What is Posthumanism?* Posthumanities 8 series. University of Minnesota Press, 2010.

Wroblewski, David. *The Story of Edgar Sawtelle*. New York: Barnes & Noble, 2008.

Chapter 11

NATURE, ANIMISM AND HUMANITY IN ANGLOPHONE NIGERIAN POETRY

SULE EMMANUEL EGYA

In *The Future of Environmental Criticism: Environmental Crisis and Literary Imagination*, Lawrence Buell (2005: 2) is of the view that 'if environmental criticism today is still an emergent discourse it is one with very ancient roots. In one form or another the "idea of nature" has been a dominant or at least residual concern for literary scholars and intellectual historians ever since these fields came into being.'

Buell reminds us here that nature has been there since the beginning of life as an object of engagement not only for literary scholars and historians, but also for writers who, in most cases, hardly conceal (and, in most cases, accentuate) their inspirational and intellectual reliance on nature. This fact seems to underline an interesting turn in the interdisciplinary study that has come to be known as ecocriticism, which is the revisionist foregrounding of nature (the earth, the flora and fauna, and other natural objects and phenomena) to draw attention to the phenomenal presence of nature in literatures, oral and written. In other words, ecocritical scholars have in recent times indicated interest not only in how what one might see as a sense of place is organically connected to the life and survival of a people, but also in what I would see as a phenomenology of place – namely that physical settings in literary works could be seen as beings (in the same manner as characters are regarded), having their own destiny in a literary text. For instance, in their introduction to *Postcolonial Ecologies: Literature of the Environment*, eloquently titled 'Toward an aesthetics of the earth', Elizabeth DeLoughrey and George B. Handley (2011) draw attention to Martin Carter's 'Listening to the Land' and Chinua Achebe's *Things Fall Apart* to emphasise, among other things, how land plays an ontological, existential and epistemic role in the lives of the communities captured in those literary works; how land and all the natural objects it contains should be regarded as a being relevant to the collective fate of the communities.

In what has been hitherto seen as the mere natural, physical, even spiritual settings of African literatures, scholars of literature and nature are looking deeper to see the interdependence of culture and nature, and the ontology of nature – the notion that natural objects, like humans, possess a life of their own. In this chapter, I intend to present the nature–culture interdependence in contemporary Nigerian poetry in English, looking at how poets have relied heavily upon nature to aestheticise their thoughts in poetic forms. I argue that one of the ways the poets rely on nature hinges on the concept of animism – the belief, still prevalent in Africa, that natural objects such as rivers/streams/ponds, rocks, hills, trees, even animals, have their own souls. Some of the poets believe – and they exuberantly poetise the belief – that their poetic inspirations come from natural objects, such as water, hills, rocks and trees. Other poets clearly deploy the animist belief in natural objects to thematise critical issues in the life of their nation. These two forms through which Nigerian poets engage animism will be discussed here, and a number of selected poems will be read closely to buttress the points raised. In the end, it will be observed that what Harry Garuba (2003) calls the 'animist unconscious' underlines the invocation and thematisation of nature in contemporary Nigerian poetry.

Animism and poetic imagination

Animism, both as a concept and as a body of religions, has, until recently, been unpopular, as European Enlightenment culture and civilisation, enforced by colonialism, had a tight grip on human society. Thinkers often regarded animism as something, possibly a form of religious practice, that belonged to a 'primitive' people, so that a belief in the soul of non-human beings is often relegated, in the words of Christopher Manes (1996: 17), to 'the realm of superstition and irrationality, where [it] can easily be dismissed'. But, as Manes further stresses, animism is not totally removed from modernity; it is not something found in 'tribal societies' alone. Manes (1996: 18) writes:

> Even in modern technological society, animistic reflexes linger on in attenuated form. Cars and sports teams are named after animals (as if to capture sympathetically their power). Children talk to dolls and animals without being considered mentally ill, and are, in fact, read fairy tales, most of which involve talking animals.

If animism is not dismissible in technological societies, such as Western nations, then one can safely assume that it not only exists, but that it is also a spiritual phenomenon to reckon with in societies perceived to be less technological, such as African nations. Indeed, my claim here is that animism underlines most beliefs and practices in African societies, including cultural practices, such as writing. The force of animism on human thinking and activities in African societies is perhaps best captured by Harry Garuba in his engaging piece 'Explorations in animist materialism and a reading of the poetry of Niyi Osundare'. Garuba (2003: 41) begins that text by describing 'a larger-than-life statue of Sango, the Yoruba god of lightning' in front of the building of the headquarters of Nigeria's National Electric Power Authority (NEPA) in Lagos. Quoting Wole Soyinka, Garuba (2003: 42) explains that among the Yoruba people of Nigeria, it is 'a form of socio-cultural practice' to appropriate a god for specific human activities. Sango is the god of lightning, so he is easily appropriated as the spiritual pillar of electric power provision. The logic is that the statue of Sango in front of the NEPA building is inspirited with the powers of the god who gives light and lightning to the people. It therefore stands as an insignia for NEPA. The NEPA authorities have clearly taken advantage of the people's belief in Sango. Or they are simply duplicating, reiterating, through the statue, an existing belief that supports their profession.

The appropriation of gods and other inspirited objects in Nigerian society for economic, cultural and sociopolitical purposes is what Garuba sees as an animist unconscious. Crucially, Garuba's piece centres on the deployment of animism or animist beliefs or animist thoughts 'within the terrain of culture and society' (Garuba 2003: 47) to contextualise more usefully the relationship between humans and their environments, between natural beings and cultural activities. For Garuba, the most pertinent feature of animism is its 'almost total refusal to countenance unlocalized, un-embodied, un-physicalized gods and spirits' (Garuba 2003: 47). He further explains:

> Animism is often simply seen as a belief in objects such as stones or trees or rivers for this simple reason that animist gods and spirits are *located* and *embodied* in objects: the objects are the physical and material manifestations of the gods and spirits. Instead of erecting graven images to symbolize the spiritual being, animist thought spiritualizes the object world thereby giving the spirit a local habitation. (Garuba 2003: 47)

While the objects housing or embodying the animist spirits are in themselves important, and while the concept of embodiment is itself central to animism, I would like to stress here that the relationship between the inspirited objects and humans is central to the argument presented in this chapter, in the sense that it crucially produces the nature–culture discourse that is exemplified in contemporary Nigerian poetry. This discourse is itself a product of the process of the poets recognising the significance of a place, a place being, for the poet, an interface between nature and culture.

Let us consider the significance of the idea of place to a poet. No doubt, a poet's sense of place – indeed any writer's sense of place – is profound. Like the animist spirit that seeks an object in which to locate itself, the poet, no matter how footloose, no matter his sense of dispersal, is ever yearning to locate himself in a place, to bind himself to nature through place. Poet Nourbese M. Philip writes:

> Literature, and in particular poetry, only begins to belong to a place when the poet belongs; the poet belongs when the language

belongs; the language belongs when it arises from and reflects the essence of all that combines to produce place. In this process, the bond between the poet and place remains indispensable. (Philip 1997: 173–174)

Place offers the poet an identity and adds to his art a local flavour that helps in constituting his personhood. There is a spiritual, ontological, dimension to place. As Neil Evernden (1996) points out, all poets, all humans, desire a sense of place because the 'establishment of self is impossible without the context of place ... there is no such thing as an individual, only an individual-in-context, individual as a component of place, defined by place' (Evernden 1996: 101–103). In Evernden's view, animism forms one of the most formidable contexts through which an individual can realise his sense of place:

> What *does* make sense, however, is something that most in our [Western] society could not take seriously: animism. For once we engage in the extension of the boundary of the self into the 'environment,' then of course we imbue it with life and can quite properly regard it as animate – it is animate because we are part of it. And, following from this, all the metaphorical properties so favored by poets make perfect sense: the Pathetic Fallacy is a fallacy only to the ego clencher. Metaphoric language is an indicator of 'place' – an indication that the speaker has a place, feels part of a place. (Evernden 1996: 101)

It is pertinent to note how Philip and Evernden, in talking about the poet's sense of place, emphasise the central role of language, which we all know is the primary passion of the poet. All poets are passionate about language. Their sense of place profoundly inheres in their language, and in most cases a poet's locality is easily extrapolated from the poet's diction.

Most Nigerian poets, as we shall see, not only have a profound sense of place, but they also make quite conscious efforts – one of which is through the deployment of animist thought – to assert their sense of place. When, for instance, the poet Christopher Okigbo aligns himself with the water goddess, Mother Idoto, implying that his poetic imagination is from the goddess (he says in an interview that he is from a lineage of priests – see Whitelaw [1970: 31]), he is consciously connecting his poetry to the life of nature. Like most poets in Nigeria, he is implying that his art, his vocation, is rooted in mythic beliefs in nature. A cursory look at anglophone Nigerian poetry shows that Nigerian poets are fascinated by the flora and fauna of their immediate communities. 'In modern African poetry,' the Nigerian poet Tanure Ojaide (1996: 28) writes, 'these fauna and flora become sources of symbols, images, figures of speech, and fables.' Mindful of the fact that the flora and fauna have a life of their own, the poets deploy them to make political statements about the condition of their nation. The poets' use of these beings – animals and natural objects – is, I argue, a result of what Garuba (2003: 49) calls the animist unconscious – the often taken-for-granted 'manner in which an animistic mode of thought is embedded within the processes of material, economic activities and then reproduces itself within the sphere of culture and social life'.

It is important to stress that the difference between poets who deploy animism in their nature poetry to express their affiliation to gods and goddesses, to stage their poetic inspirations, and those who use animism to engage in counter-discourse is not clear-cut. It is rather a matter of degree. Nigerian poets such as Gabriel Okara, Niyi Osundare, Onookome Okome and Tanure Ojaide have written poetry that could be located on both sides of this divide. In some of their poems, they romanticise nature for providing them with poetic inspiration; in others they thematise the plight of nature (and of humans organically linked with nature) in the face of adversity caused by governments and multinational corporations, as is the case in the oil-rich but devastated Niger Delta region of Nigeria, which Ogaga Okuyade discusses in this volume in his analysis of a novel by Helon Habila. It is also important to stress that poets writing about nature and the environment are often influenced by their oral tradition. African traditional aesthetics rely heavily on nature and thus provide an aesthetic convention for contemporary poets – in most cases, the aspects of nature the poets versify are embedded in the local lore of their birthplaces, as demonstrated in the works of the poets studied here.

Poets and gods: The poetics of filiation

Beginning with pioneer poets, Nigerian poets have tended to attach themselves to certain mythical powers embedded in the animist beliefs of their communities. Whereas some of them cast themselves as disciples of gods and spirits embodied in natural objects, such as water, trees and hills, others foreground their affinity for, or, indeed, organic connection with, such inspirited objects, and clearly indicate that their poetic inspirations emanate from the connection. Their sense of filiation becomes a locus for an aesthetic exuberance that underscores their poetic production.

We return to Okigbo, whose connection to the water goddess, Mother Idoto, marks something of an inspiration in his career as a poet. A segment of 'Heavensgate' called 'The Passage' reads:

> Before you, mother Idoto,
> naked I stand;
> before your watery presence,
> a prodigal
> leaning on an oilbean,
> lost in your legend.
> Under your power wait I
> on barefoot
> watchman for the watchword
> at Heavensgate;
>
> out of the depths my cry:
> give ear and hearken ... (Okigbo 1971: 1–12)

What appears here as a picture of a penitent worshipper who has returned as a prodigal to his water goddess is indeed a dramatisation of Okigbo's filiation to Mother Idoto, his ancestral goddess. Okigbo and Soyinka, among early Nigerian poets, are perhaps the most conscious of their affiliation to their traditional deities. Okigbo, in fact, thought of himself as a priest of Mother Idoto, which was something of a family deity to him. This self-awareness would come to inhere in his poetic imagination, as he told Marjory Whitelaw in a 1965 interview: 'I have tried to evolve my own personal religion. The way that I worship my gods is in fact through poetry ... each poem I write is a ceremony ... The creative process is a process of cleansing' (Whitelaw 1970: 31).

For Okigbo, who had had a Western education and was brought up in the Catholic faith, and who probably compared Catholicism with the traditional belief of his society, the figuration of a prodigal who has strayed away from Mother Idoto and now returns to the goddess, as depicted in the poem above, is, we may conjecture, autobiographical. Standing naked before Mother Idoto is an act of surrendering, of repentance, of confession; and pronouncing the power of the goddess, as the penitent persona does, is an act of worship that points out how crucial the goddess is to the life of the persona. He is lost in her 'legend' and waits under her 'power' and implores her to 'hearken' to his cry. All of these imprecations are made while he stands before her 'watery presence'. That the goddess is represented by water and that the persona (more than likely a poet-persona) believes that the water is not ordinary because it represents Mother Idoto suggest that water is assumed to be imbued with a powerful spirit.

Poet and playwright Wole Soyinka is noted for adopting Ogun, the Yoruba god of iron, metallurgy, wine and war, as the spiritual inspiration for his creativity. In two lengthy poems, 'Idanre' and 'Ogun Abibiman', Soyinka casts Ogun as a saviour of and a revolutionary essence for humanity, imbued with exceeding energies to build and destroy. In 'Idanre', Ogun displays his savage strength, emerges as the most powerful in the Yoruba pantheon, and ushers in bounteous harvest and creativity for humans in the world. The poem begins with the worship of the god:

> The flaming corkscrew etches sharp affinity
> (No dream, no vision, no delirium of the dissolute)
> When roaring vats of an unstoppered heaven deluge
> Earth in fevered distillations, potent with
> The fire of the axe-handed one
>
> And greys are violent now, laced with
> Whiteburns, tremulous in fire tracings
> On detonating peaks. Ogun is still on such

Combatant angles, poised to a fresh descent
Fiery axe-heads fly about his feet

In these white moments of my god, plucking
Light from the day's effacement, the last ember
Glows in his large creative hand, savage round
The rebel name, ribbed on ridges, crowded in corridors
Low on his spiked symbols. (Soyinka 1967: 6–20)

Such is the grand entry of Ogun, 'the axe-handed one', into the world in the time of harvests, according to Yoruba mythology, where he distinguishes himself in the Battle of Ire. Ogun's rare bravery in dealing with villains and overwhelming zeal to liberate human society are thematised throughout the long poem. But the poet-persona in 'Idanre' is not only interested in showing how Ogun displays his prowess, but also in his affiliation to the powerful god, which he proudly regards as 'my god' throughout the poem, in addition to showering moving appellations on the god. Soyinka's deep regard for Ogun is captured in his essay 'The fourth stage', in which he attempts to place Ogun, his personal god, above all other deities in Yorubaland. In Soyinka's words (1988: 22), 'Ogun [is] the creative urge and instinct, the essence of creativity.' The god, Soyinka insists, is the 'first suffering deity, first creative energy, the first challenger, and conqueror of transition' (Soyinka 1988: 24). To this god, Soyinka owes his creative energies. He is quick to point out that he is a disciple of Ogun, and most of his fans have always regarded him as such.

In the case of Niyi Osundare, the consummate political poet, his animist belief in the water goddess, Osun, goes back to his birth. The goddess's home is a river called River Osun. Osundare's mother had dedicated her son to Osun at birth and had constantly invoked the powers of the goddess while blessing him. As a child, Osundare was barred from washing his body or swimming in rivers or streams because he was regarded as a child of water ('*olomi*'). A self-professed Marxist-humanist, Osundare had been rather silent about the powers of Osun during his life and creative work until he published *City Without People: The Katrina Poems*, a collection about the 2005 Hurricane Katrina, which ravaged New Orleans, during which he and his family almost perished. In a lengthy poem titled 'What mother said', Osundare, through the voice of a female persona, obviously his mother, celebrates his connection to the water goddess in terms of survival and creativity. The poem is, in short, a eulogy to Osun, also known as 'Eyekaire' and 'Yeye'. According to the mother-persona in the poem, Osundare is:

> Osun's precious gift
> Her tall, abiding grace
> Osun gave you to me
> Yes, Osun gave me you
> She of the soothing voice
> And liquid laughter
> Eyes like fresh-laid eggs
> Lips like well sculpted lobes
> She whose beauty is bounty
> Skin ebony-black, teeth cotton-white
> Wardrobe generous like her supple motions
> She of the patient passion, the billowing gaze
> Who conquers raging fires with liquid mercies
> Parrot feather in Eyekaire's hair. (Osundare 2011: 61–76)

The two vital thrusts of the lines quoted above are that, first, the poet Osundare is a gift from the goddess Osun (hence the name 'Osundare' is adopted) and, second, the goddess is described as a being of beauty and bounty. That is to say, Osundare is descended from a fine and strong lineage, and this runs deep into making him a poet. It is overtly suggested in the poem that Osundare's creative prowess emanates from the goddess Osun. From the beginning, the goddess told Osundare's mother that the son she brought to her would become famous as a wordsmith. That is why the mother-persona in the poem consistently asserts, in addressing her son, that 'You sang the rainsong anywhere you went / You never broke your covenant with Water' (Osundare 2011: 147–148). Osundare's poetry is the 'rainsong' – aptly suggestive of the abundant imagery of nature for which his poetry is noted.

Osundare regards himself as 'Farmer-born peasant-bred' (Osundare 1986: 43) and is quick to point out that his poetic inspiration is rooted in nature: he is the son of a farmer and oral artist, with an upbringing in bucolic society and a keen interest in the natural landscape of his birthplace and the folklore of the Yoruba, his ethnic group. His poetisation of two landmark rocks, called Olosunta and Oloore, in Ikere, his birthplace, dramatises the animist belief informing the strong bond between the people of Ikere and these rocks, especially Olosunta, which, as myth has it, is a deity that protected the people of Ikere and helped them to victory in the internecine wars they faced in the past. In the highly evocative poem 'The rocks rose to meet me', Osundare eloquently apotheosises the rocks, foregrounding the reliance of the Ikere people on the rocks as spiritual and humanist beings, and locates his creative endeavour in the powers of nature, which the rocks exude. In his imaginative conversation with the rocks, Osundare intones:

> *Olosunta* spoke first
> The eloquent one
> Whose mouth is the talking house of ivory
> *Olosunta* spoke first
> The lofty one whose eyes are
> Balls of the winking sun
> *Olosunta* spoke first
> The riddling one whose belly is wrestling ground
> For god and gold.
> [...]
>
> *Oloore* came next
> his ancient voice tremulous
> in the morning air
> (harmattans here whip with the flaying fury
> Of a slavemaster,
> But how can we banish them
> Without a season of unripened peas?). (Osundare 1986: 5–58)

In these lines, as in the rest of the poem, Osundare cashes in on the people's belief in the rocks, and their lore surrounding the rocks, to produce perhaps his most moving eulogy for the natural objects of his birthplace. As is clear from the poems in *The Eye of the Earth*, the collection in which this poem appears, Osundare sees his creative essence as springing from the creative powers residing in the natural objects of his birthplace and the reservoir of artistry in his Yoruba ethnic nationality.

Invoking gods: Poetics of nation

Whereas some Nigerian poets, like those discussed above, invoke the spirits of gods and goddesses deemed to be residing in natural objects to stage the inspiration and source of poetic practice through what one might call mythopoeia, others deploy their animist beliefs to express their feelings about the political condition of their society and, crucially, to confront the political institutions responsible for the state of their society. Poets in Nigeria, as in other parts of Africa, have felt the need, since independence, to historicise sociopolitical realities around them, thereby turning poetry into a demotic art. The Nigerian Civil War (1967–1970) and the almost three decades of military rule in Nigeria, terminating in 1999, have been, in the view of many literary historians and critics, responsible for the political dimension of modern Nigerian poetry (Alu 2001: 198–203; Amuta 1988: 85–92). In the 1980s and 1990s, for instance, Nigerian poets had to see the art and act of writing poetry as part of the cultural and political struggles sweeping through the country to dethrone military oppression and enthrone democracy. The general tone of Nigerian poetry, then, was that of anger and threnody, and each poem, it seemed, had a grouse against what was perceived as the oppressor figure. Besides other traditional aesthetic means, the belief that natural objects have a soul of their own was deployed by some poets to drive home their points in the struggle against repressive regimes.

Tanure Ojaide's *Invoking the Warrior Spirit* (1998), as the title suggests, is programmatic in its deployment of animist beliefs established in Africa. Ojaide centres on five African myths (Mbira, Ivwri, Edon, Ivwie and Urhoro) which, in his view, could be used to tackle present-day problems in Africa. Ojaide (1998: ix) states his intention as follows: 'I'm interested in the current generation of Africans gaining inspiration from traditional African institutions, practices, and philosophies that can help overcome contemporary adversities.' What he succeeds in doing with this collection is to radically re-contextualise the beliefs of people, mainly animist beliefs, and the use of animism in confronting the oppressor figure responsible for the current travails of Africa.

The poem 'Ivwri: Invoking the warrior spirit' traces the exploits of the powerful battle god of the Urhobo people in the Niger Delta region. According to the poet, the god Ivwri is physically represented by 'a carving, part human, part animal with many icons that defined the fighting spirit of the people' (Ojaide 1998: x). The Urhobo people's belief in this god is strong – supported by Ivwri, the people were able to fight and withstand the incessant raids and harassments they faced during the slave-trade period. The god protected his people effectively. Consequently, Ojaide is of the view that '[no] period after the slave-raiding centuries has needed *Ivwri* more than now to eliminate the many obstacles in Africa's way' (Ojaide 1998: x). The persona in this lengthy poem speaks on behalf of his society; his is a long-drawn lamentation about the hardship and oppression threatening society. Consistently, the poet persona laments the gulf between the poor and the rich, blaming the political elite for oppressing the people. This we-versus-them dialectic dramatised in the poem is such that the majority 'we' – the persona himself is implicated in the victimhood – is condemned to raise a national dirge, articulating the people's plight at the hands of a powerful few. Ojaide, who is from the Niger Delta region, draws attention to the brutalisation of the region by multinational oil companies in collaboration with the Nigerian national government. The oil-rich Niger Delta region has been the revenue base for running the Nigerian economy, but it has paradoxically suffered from years of neglect. (Chapter 9 in this volume, by Ogaga Okuyade, maps the eco-sociopolitical context of the Niger Delta region more fully.) Oil exploration has rendered the biotic community in the region almost useless. Spillages of crude oil have adversely affected the lives of the local people, who are mainly farmers and fishermen; gas flaring has denied the people any fruitful relationship with nature.[1] Ojaide, like almost all poets who have written about the plight of this region, indicts Shell BP:

Before overbreeding
tore the tangles with machetes and matches,
before Shell BP flared

> the forest into a wasteland,
> the hyrax cried *aghwaghwa*
> all night – who knew what
> spirit kept it sleepless?
> in the shrubbery, moist
> from copious downpours,
> ritualists stalked bushfarers
> to behead the weak and unwary
> for skulls to toast prowess. (Ojaide 1998: 180–189)

The crushing of the 'weak and unwary' by powerful institutions such as Shell BP has been a daily experience in the Niger Delta, as it was in other regions of Nigeria during the decades of military oppression. The struggle is still on to get Shell BP and other oil companies to pay full compensation to the people of the region for degrading their environment. But, in this poem, the poet is more concerned with deploying the animist belief in the carved image of Ivwri to tackle the Niger Delta problem and other problems in Nigeria. The poet persona's tone is triumphant at the end of the poem, having invoked the battle god to intervene. The invocation of the god is predicated on the belief that:

> Ivwri waits at the bottom of the precipice
> To cushion us against a hard fall,
> Ivwri fortifies the threatened with *uteri*
> That blunts the blades of machetes,
> Ivwri keeps the gun from firing at his devotees,
> Ivwri snatches his favourites from peril
> And throws them into safety. (Ojaide 1998: 294–300, emphasis in the original)

With the intervention of this powerful god, society will come to have peace as the people are given adequate protection. The poet persona is full of hope that, with the power of Ivwri, he has become an 'irrepressible rebel' (Ojaide 1998: 315), with an uncommon might, since 'All ropes that tied me to myself / have snapped and my restless soles / chase the horizon on its blue heels' (Ojaide 1998: 318–320).

Onookome Okome's second poetry volume, *The Mammiwata Poems* (Okome 1999), is a sustained rendition of the animist powers residing in water, precisely the River Ethiope, which runs through the homeland where Okome grew up, and how such powers could be harnessed to tackle contemporary crises. In Africa, most people who live near rivers and other bodies of water have the belief that there is a water mermaid, half-human and half-fish, who is powerful enough to rule over all other creatures of the water, and who, in dealing with humans, exercises an incredible control over them. Okome regards Mammiwata as not only his goddess of inspiration, but also one powerful enough to liberate his society. His Mammiwata poems thus both express his filiation and his view on Nigeria's political condition. The poet's supplication to the goddess is against the backdrop of his society facing a repressive regime. Okome's volume, like Ojaide's, attempts to foreground the military-dictatorship regimes that oppressed Nigeria from the 1970s to the 1990s, culminating in the coup by Ibrahim Badamasi Babangida, which resulted in a protracted political crisis engendered by the cancellation of the June 1993 general elections. This crisis gave way to the terrible dictatorship of the late General Sani Abacha, regarded as the worst ever to have beset the country. The thrust of Okome's invocation of the water goddess is that only the goddess can bring succour to the people in such a time of anomie. But, like older poets, such as Okigbo and Soyinka, Okome begins by foregrounding his organic connection to the goddess, who evidently is his poetic inspiration:

> I put my mind in the river
> Where all markets meet.
> [...]
>
> In the twilight of the bank's waters
> I see.
> In the little piece of this river
> I cover my wetness.
> In the legend that you, my river, wrapped around
> This town of my tears, I live.
> From you everything comes and goes.

> You speak when *Aridon* stammers.
> You hear when *Omonigbo* rains.
>
> I take the stone around which you wrapped me
> For a thousand year,
> I take the blisters.
> I take the bones.
> I take all, learning to
> Live the purity of your ever-present waters.
>
> So I return to the river
> Where all things meet,
> Where I stand before your laughters. (Okome 1999: 'Prologue', 5–29)

These words are praise for the goddess, in whom, as the poet makes clear throughout the volume, there is an enormous reserve of power that can be used to combat the cruelties of the military dictatorship. But, beyond that, the poet is explicit about his being the goddess's subject: in her, he acquires the strength to poetise the realities of the repressive regime; and it is only the goddess who has power against the dictator, despite his political strength. The goddess is seen as embodying uncommon powers and perceived as the only one who can liberate society. After pouring before the goddess the litany of woes that the society encounters, the poet persona brings up the voice of the goddess, who promises that she will intervene:

> The season does not smile.
> After the lash, I promised an eruption.
> After the lash promised is the final vowel of renewal.
> The lips of the leaves will open up smiles.
> The smile of the tongue will chew up the fire in the wind.
> Up in the street,
> Near where history was murdered,
> The sleeves of a hidden name will tear-up the dust-cover
> Of the book of your nation and

A name that is pure, pure,
Like a child's presence, will erupt from the bowel of the sea
Deeper than any human thought.
[...]
Go, my son, search the debris.
Search the creeks.
Meaning and life are stationed in the stain where you live...

This, my son, my believer
Is the beginning of your midmorning dreams.
(Okome 1999: 7–28)

Given his sustained praise for the goddess and his enduring belief in the powers of the goddess, the poet persona has no doubt that the promised renewal will be experienced in society. All the crises generated by the ineptitude of the military dictators will end and the pro-democracy struggles of the people will bear fruits.

Nigerian poetry concerned with nature and the environment can take the form either of the poet's self-fashioning, whereby nature is invoked as poetic inspiration, or of a poetic counter-discourse that foregrounds the suffering of the environment and people. In either case, the poets are also conscious of nature imagination in African orality, which often serves as a resource base for them. Although poetry is a cultural practice, it could positively derive inspiration from, and have its source in nature, thereby providing an avenue for the nature–culture relationship. This assertion forms the basis of the discussion above, which centres on how contemporary anglophone Nigerian poetry achieves the nature–culture relationship through the aestheticisation of certain animist beliefs. The central argument here is that animism has come to inform the aesthetic mode of the poetry in two ways: first, the poetry's organic connection to certain inspirited natural objects relied upon by the poets for inspirational powers, and, second, the deployment of such powers in inspirited objects to dramatise and historicise contemporary sociopolitical realities with the aim of invoking such powers to confront the establishment. Crucial above all in this engagement with animism is the overall goal of giving humanity a better social vision.

In a sense, the poet's vision, artistic and social, prefers being rooted in what one might call traditionalism – the notion that contemporary Nigerian poetry, an art emanating from modernity (in the sense that it came with Western education), is not far away from the cultures and orality of the peoples of Nigeria. Therefore, beyond the influence of traditionalism in contemporary Nigerian poetry is the artistic latitude that lets us into a nature–culture poetics that foregrounds the interdependence of acquired arts and native wisdom, practices, beliefs and philosophies. Animism, in essence, offers Nigerian poetry a philosophical, religious and cultural consciousness (and identity) that it needs not only to bring itself into being but also to tackle the existentialist problems of Nigerian peoples.

References

Alu, Nesther A. 'Echoes of commitment in modern African poetry', in Macpherson Nkem Azuike (ed.), *Studies in Language and Literature*. Jos, Nigeria: Mazlink, 2001: 198–203.

Amuta, Chidi. 'Literature of the Nigerian Civil War', in Yemi Ogunbiyi (ed.), *Perspectives on Nigerian Literature: 1700 to the Present*. Vol 1. Lagos: Guardian Books, 1988: 85–92.

Buell, Lawrence. *The Future of Environmental Criticism: Environmental Crisis and Literary Imagination*. Oxford: Blackwell Publishing, 2005.

DeLoughrey, Elizabeth and Handley, George B. 'Introduction: Towards an aesthetics of the earth', in Elizabeth DeLoughrey and George B. Handley (eds), *Postcolonial Ecologies: Literatures of the Environment*. Oxford: Oxford University Press, 2011: 3–39.

Evernden, Neil. 'Beyond ecology: Self, place, and the pathetic fallacy', in Cheryll Glotfelty and Harold Fromm (eds), *The Ecocriticism Reader: Landmarks in Literary Ecology*. Athens: University of Georgia Press, 1996: 92–104.

Garuba, Harry. 'Explorations in animist materialism and a reading of the poetry of Niyi Osundare', in Abdul-Rasheed Na'Allah (ed.), *The People's Poet: Emerging Perspectives on Niyi Osundare*. Trenton: Africa World Press, 2003: 41–60.

Manes, Christopher. 'Nature and silence', in Cheryll Glotfelty and Harold Fromm (eds), *The Ecocriticism Reader: Landmarks in Literary Ecology*. Athens: University of Georgia Press, 1996: 15–29.

Ojaide, Tanure. *Poetic Imagination in Black Africa: Essays on African Poetry*. North Carolina: Carolina Academic Press, 1996.

Ojaide, Tanure. *Invoking the Warrior Spirit*. Ibadan: Heinemann, 1998.

Okigbo, Christopher. *Labyrinths*. Ibadan: Heinemann, 1971.
Okome, Onookome. *The Mammiwata Poems*. Calabar: University of Calabar Press, 1999.
Okonta, Ike and Douglas, Oronto. *Where Vultures Feast: Shell, Human Rights, and Oil*. London: Verso, 2003.
Osundare, Niyi. *The Eye of the Earth*. Ibadan: Heinemann, 1986.
Osundare, Niyi. *City without People: The Katrina Poems*. Boston: Black Widow Press, 2011.
Philip, Nourbese. 'Earth and sound: The place of poetry', in Kofi Anyidoho (ed.), *The Word Behind the Bars and the Paradox of Exile*. Illinois: Northwestern University Press, 1997: 169–182.
Soyinka, Wole. *Idanre and Other Poems*. London: Methuen, 1967.
Soyinka, Wole. *Art, Dialogue and Outrage: Essays on Literature and Culture*. Ibadan: New Horn Press, 1988.
Whitelaw, Marjory. 'Interview with Christopher Okigbo.' *Journal of Commonwealth Literature* 9 (1970): 31.

Chapter 12

ANIMALS, NOSTALGIA AND ZIMBABWE'S RURAL LANDSCAPE IN THE POETRY OF CHENJERAI HOVE AND MUSAEMURA ZIMUNYA

SYNED MTHATIWA

Chenjerai Hove and Musaemura Zimunya belong to the second generation of Zimbabwean writers – a generation of writers who were born between 1940 and 1959 (Veit-Wild 1993: 7). In their poetry, Zimunya and Hove show that they 'feel attached to nature and [the] landscape' of their country and its people (Veit-Wild 1988:11). A landscape, however, is also a culturescape (Wylie 2005: 149) and, as such, the two poets' construction of and response to the landscape provide a lens through which to understand rural cultures in Zimbabwe. Besides, animals, plants, birds or insects are 'inscripted (or even encrypted)' in poetry for 'aesthetic or iconic import' (Wylie 2005: 149). Paying attention to the animals in the poetry reveals not only their symbolic import, but also the attitudes of the poets to nature in general, and animals, in particular.

This chapter is a critical analysis of the ways in which animals and Zimbabwe's rural landscape (both physical and moral) are represented in the poetry of Hove and Zimunya. My focus in the chapter is on the way nature and animal imagery are mobilised to express the poets' conceptualisation and construction of rural Zimbabwe and the Shona people's nature-culture. I argue that the presence of animals and other aspects of nature in the poetry reveals and highlights the Shona people's embeddedness in their ecology, and exposes the relationship between the people, their land, and flora and fauna – a relationship spoilt by colonial and postcolonial exploitation of both humans and nature. The representation of animals and description of the landscape in the poetry also reveal the poets' ecological awareness and displeasure at the abuse and destruction of nature. The rural landscape, on the other hand, works as a metaphorical map of the poets' childhoods, real or imagined, and of their attempts at self-exploration and discovery, given that both poets subsequently chose to leave the rural world for Western education and the city.

To contextualise my argument, a brief overview of the Shona worldview regarding land and nature is necessary here. In Shona religious belief, land, whose (ultimate) owners are 'the tutelary spirit, *Mwari*' (Taringa 2013: 195), the creator, and the spirits of the ancestors who were buried in it, is considered sacred. Mickias Musiyiwa's chapter in this book gives more insight into what he refers to as the Shona land mythology, or Shona people's beliefs about the land, as expressed in popular songs. The sanctity of the land among the Shona also obtains from the umbilical cords of the people buried in it. By virtue of 'his supposed connections with mythological founder-ancestors of his chiefdom' (Taringa 2013: 195), the Shona believe that the ancestors bequeathed the land to the chief, who acts as a trustee and manages the land for all generations of people, the dead, the living and the unborn. This, therefore, presupposes group ownership of the land. That is, all generations of people (the living, the dead and those yet to be born) in a particular chieftaincy own the land, whose overseer is the chief. It is not surprising, therefore, that, as Nisbert Taringa (2013: 204) observes, among the Shona 'land has no marketable value' and 'cannot be sold or transferred to another', given that the rights to the land are 'vested in cooperative groups that have overriding right over those of individuals'. This belief in the sacredness of the land means that certain taboos must be observed. Failure to do so is believed to anger the ancestors, which will lead to calamities being unleashed, such as droughts and epidemics (see also Jacob Mapara's chapter in this book). The taboos and prescribed behaviour have the effect of instilling an ecological sensibility in the people and conserving nature.[1]

However, Taringa cautions against romanticising the Shona attitudes to nature (and the past to which these attitudes mainly belong) as ecological, arguing that a critical examination of Shona worldviews reveals that the people's attitudes to nature are ambivalent and discriminative, and are 'primarily about power and relation with spirits than with ecological issues in the scientific sense' (Taringa 2013: 194). Whereas some aspects of nature are respected and conserved among the Shona, others are abused and exploited. For Taringa, this exploitation and abuse also affects animals, in spite of the existence of the totemism principle among the Shona.

In analysing Hove and Zimunya's representation of nature and rural landscape, I use what I refer to, after Dana Mount (2013: 21), as ecopostcolonialism or postcolonial ecocriticism. By definition, ecopostcolonialism 'is the study of the representation of nature and the environment in dialogue with postcolonialism' (Mount 2013: 2). Ecopostcolonialism rejects the tendency of first-wave Euro-American ecocriticism to see environmental consciousness as the preserve of a Euro-American mindset and to construct the global South and its literatures as 'an exotic new arrival on the scene of environmental consciousness' (Mount 2013: 2–3). Contrary to this perception, environmental consciousness has always been an overlooked aspect of African literature and criticism. This is the subject of Coral Wu's chapter in this book. Wu provides evidence that African environmental literature and criticism in fact pre-date Anglo-American ecocriticism. She also shows that it is the methodological and conceptual parochialism of the practitioners of first-wave ecocriticism that has led to the unfounded claim of indifference among Africanist scholars and African literary authors to environmental issues and criticism.

However, ecopostcolonialism sees ecocriticism and postcolonialism 'not as antagonistic, but [as] dialogic' (Mount 2013: 5; see also Nixon 2005), where questions of ecology and the environment are tackled in relation to, or together with, questions of poverty, underdevelopment and exploitation (both human and environmental) (Iheka 2011; Huggan and Tiffin 2010). In other words, postcolonial ecocriticism is both ecologically and politically/socially committed, as it also engages with the politics of decolonisation, especially in an African context. This way, postcolonial ecocriticism avoids the pitfalls or parochialism of first-wave ecocriticism. In my analysis of Hove and Zimunya's poetry, I pay attention to both the environmental consciousness in the poetry and the poets' engagement with colonial injustices in Zimbabwe, formerly Rhodesia.

In their poetry, Hove and Zimunya make a mental journey to the lost world of their childhoods to shape memories of their rural lives and childhoods, and evoke the beauty of the rural landscape. Here the seasons, forests, and birds and their songs are all woven into the fabric of rural life, spirituality and belief systems of the people. But memories of rural beauty sit side by side with memories of the peasantry suffering due to inclement weather or prolonged drought – as nature is not always benevolent – and of painful poverty, as well as suffering, loosed upon the people by colonialism. For both authors, too, rural life and the beauty of the landscape are constantly vanishing owing to the ravages of colonial injustice. The land is being scarred by the bulldozer; hills and mountains are being denuded as the axe goes to work, tearing down trees; and sacred caves are desecrated by people from far-off lands – in short, home is fast becoming home no more.[2] As Musiyiwa points out in his chapter in this book, colonialism and colonial experiences dislocated and overturned the Shona people's *mwana wevhu* (child of the soil) land philosophy as they were alienated and uprooted from the ancestral lands that formed the core of their existence.[3] Later, however, independence did not bring the hoped-for transformation or change. Some of Hove's poems published in the late 1990s and in 2003 indicate, as I will show later, that independence did not bring freedom and happiness, as the people had expected, but more pain and suffering, as a result of the dictatorial tendencies of postcolonial leaders such as President Robert Mugabe.

Hove and Zimunya's representation of the rural landscape and nature, as analysed in this chapter, evokes both the Shona land mythology – the subject of Musiyiwa's chapter – and memories of the European peasant experience, similarly embodied in the poetry of John Clare and William

Wordsworth. Like Clare and Wordsworth, Hove and Zimunya are lovers and observers of nature who highlight the connectedness of the human and natural worlds. As is the case with the works of the two English poets, the poetry of Hove and Zimunya 'is primarily a celebration and affirmation of life' (Summerfield 1990: 13) in all its natural forms, that is, plants and animals. It is also a celebration of the soil, the seasons and the weather. But, as Summerfield observes in reference to the poetry of Clare, 'it is also, inescapably, a song of sorrow and mourning, of loss, deracination and disenchantment' (Summerfield 1990: 13).[4]

In their poetry, Hove and Zimunya both emphasise what they see as the beauty and revitalising nature of the rural world. Broadly speaking, rural Zimbabwe in Zimunya's poetry is, in Robert Muponde's words, 'about the beautiful and fragile, children, flowers, love and freedom. It is a grand canvas depicting pastoral innocence and serenity. It is an animated landscape that explodes with colour and sound' (Muponde 2005: 11). It is important to note, however, that the motif of admiration for the beauty of nature, especially the obsession with flowers, may be a romantic import or a carry-over from 'first generation' Zimbabwean poets. In Shona ecocultural imagination, as Munamato Chemhuru and Dennis Masaka (2013: 128) observe:

> Certain natural vegetation and wildlife are revered because they are believed to be hosts of some spiritual forces. It is, therefore, taboo to visit [say, for purposes of merely admiring flowers] or defile certain sites that are regarded as sacred.

Unlike Zimunya, Hove does not dwell much on the beauty and idyllic nature of rural life, but exposes the transitions taking place in the country, and the pain, suffering and dislocation of rural life and culture occasioned by colonialism and postcolonialism. In the process, he offers in some of his poems, especially those dealing with the colonial period, glimpses of what may be considered the ecologically sound relationship of rural people with their environment. In his poetry about post-independence Zimbabwe, Hove focuses on the personal and cultural distress of the wider Zimbabwean society as a result of the violence and ruthlessness perpetrated by those in power.

Country life, environmental degradation and violence in Hove's poetry

In the poem 'Mazes that yawn' (Hove 1982: 43–44), Hove protests against the progress and development model of civilisation, especially when progress and development mean altering the landscape by erecting huge buildings, paving roads and avenues, and a professional life that entails obeying timetables. For Hove, such a civilisation is antithetical to life, as it deadens the soul and even leads to physical death. In an interview with Flora Veit-Wild, Hove observes that 'in my poems [in] *Up in Arms* I question a lot of what we do in the name of civilization ...' (Veit-Wild 1988: 41). 'Mazes that yawn' is an example of one such poem. In it, Hove protests:

> Don't civilize me with walls,
> forests of lines, lanes and edges
> or in roofed mazes that yawn
> for my sudden death. ('Mazes that yawn': 1–4)[5]

The 'walls' here are a metonym for the buildings of the city, while the 'forests of lines, lanes and edges' refer to the road network criss-crossing the city landscape. The 'roofed mazes that yawn / for my sudden death' could, apart from office buildings, also refer to factories that suck the individual's labour until he becomes useless, or metaphorically – even physically – dies. This is hardly surprising, as in his poetry Hove conceives of rural and city/urban landscapes and spaces as sharply divided, for he sees rural spaces 'as more "authentic" than urban' spaces (Primorac and Muponde 2005: xiv).

Disliking the stifling life and space of the city, the poet-protagonist prefers life in the country. In the poem he undertakes a mental journey back to the unspoilt rural past, to the green forests, trees and grass that 'fan' or revitalise the soul. He declares:

> Out I wade to forests, green,
> where trees airy, grasses free,
> my soul is fanned. ('Mazes that yawn': 5–7)

The emphasis on the word 'green' highlights the fact that, unlike the city, with its stifling walls, 'forests of lines' and 'mazes', the country is full of life. Further, in the green forests of home,

> the jungle squirrel calls
> answering the go-away mystery
> upon a rough unhewed bush.
> The hornbill muses in dance,
> pricked by unknown drives that last.
> The eagle dives, the forest lives
> and blood stirs to wrestle with death.
> The owl, disturbed, unnerved, wings by
> with streams in pursuit
> to punch with beaked hate
> that long fed master. ('Mazes that yawn': 9–19)

The vitality of life in the country is represented here by the activity of the animals and birds in the green forest. This section, like other parts of the poem, contains many suggestive images and metaphors that characterise most of Hove's poetry. However, the imagery also has the negative effect of obscuring meaning in the poems.[6] It is difficult to say unequivocally what Hove means in the metaphors in the quotation above, but one can, nevertheless, attempt to unravel their meaning.

In this extract, 'the jungle squirrel calls / answering the go-away mystery'. The 'go-away mystery' could be Hove's interpretation of a particular birdsong. As Leonard Lutwack (1994: 12) observes, 'all bird song is open to a variety of human interpretations'. The 'go-away mystery' in Hove's poem could therefore be a reference to a bird song that Hove interprets as saying 'go-away'. Besides, 'go-away' here could be an allusion to the call of any one of the birds that, in Shona folklore, help people escape the dangers of the forest by issuing warnings of encroaching snakes and predatory animals, or that help lost people find their way out of the forest. But 'go away' could also be a reference to the call of the grey go-away bird, or grey lourie.

The fact that the bush in which the squirrel calls is said to be 'rough' and 'unhewed' indicates that it is untouched or untampered with by destructive humans. The hornbill's musing 'in dance' is a reference to the bird's gait as it walks, a manner of walking that, to poetic eyes, is akin to dancing. The phrase 'unknown drives that last' refers to the bird's primordial desires that have endured the test of time and have guided the life of the species over the years.

The *dendera* bird (hornbill) that 'muses in dance' in the poem is viewed positively in Shona culture, and features in cultural songs and dances. Unlike the hornbill, however, Hove negatively constructs the owl in the poem, depicting it as fearful and running away from retribution. In so doing, he reflects the negative conceptualisation of the bird from a Shona eco-cultural perspective, where it is associated with witchcraft (Taringa 2006: 200–201).

In the poem the people living in the country attach meaning to birdcalls. We hear that 'When the dove mourns / maybe granny is dead' (Hove 1982: 20–21). This not only shows the people's embeddedness in their environment, but also underlines Emmanuel Obiechina's observation that rural people 'recognize bird-songs and build them into the consciousness as a way of telling the time or interpreting reality, since the songs of some birds are ominous' (Obiechina 1975: 43). The dove's song for the poet-protagonist is certainly ominous because, as well as predicting death, it could also be a sign that a snake is in the vicinity, waiting to inflict 'fanged death' (Hove 1982: 24). Thus, the life of humans in rural Zimbabwe is integrated with the lives of animals and their behaviour.[7]

The idyllic picture portrayed of country life here is probably one of precolonial Zimbabwe because, in most of his poems that deal with the country, Hove laments the loss and destruction by colonialism of what used to be home. Precolonial Zimbabwe is a period that, as Mickias Musiyiwa mentions in his chapter in this book, is nostalgically mythicised in Shona orature as *pasichigare*, meaning a period akin to nature in the Romantic imagination or Arcadia in pastoral poetry. However, it seems that Hove deliberately avoids identifying the idyllic and harmonious picture of rural life here with precolonial Africa.

This is perhaps because, as we shall see below, Hove seeks to offer a wider vision of that historical period – a vision that is different from the reductionist 'paranoid reading of history' (Mbembe 2002: 252) that characterises the anticolonial vision of Africa. And Hove's wider vision of precolonial African societies comes through in the poem 'Country life' (Hove 1982: 69–71), which, although it offers glimpses of integrated precolonial country life, does not depict that rural past as full of glory, purity and harmony but as a period with its own contrasts and ambiguities.

In 'Country life' Hove again makes a mental journey to the past to offer his reconstruction of life in the country. He writes:

> Our hut puffs streaks of hope
> in smoke that waves.
> Inside, granny lies skeletal on the mat,
> while her snuff-box dangles
> in flashes of hope.
> Her walking-stick waits
> on stand-by
> like the crafty workman.
> Chicks may peck at her scars
> and the wince tells floods of tales:
> unless Takura comes to the rescue,
> the hen calls for the whole invasion. ('Country life': 1–12)

What we encounter in these lines is an ironic and sceptical version of hope. Although we may be tempted to believe that hope, rather than despair, governs the people's lives in this rural setting – the hope that food might result from the smoke in the hut and, for 'granny', hope for another day – the imagery that Hove uses to characterise the hope contests such a reading. In the poem we are told that the 'hut puffs streaks of hope / in smoke that waves'. The association of hope with smoke here signals anticipation of food, as smoke suggests food being cooked in the kitchen. Ordinarily, the sight of smoke streaming through the hut's grass-thatched roof symbolises an operational homestead, and the granny's snuffbox highlights the symbolic import of the kitchen in Shona culture as the venue for the homestead's religious rituals. However, the association of hope with smoke also evokes the destruction of that hope by fire. The hope here is therefore lost hope – hope that no longer exists because it has been destroyed.

Although the figure of the old woman here could represent a celebration of the longevity associated with rural people, as opposed to urban dwellers, it also highlights the poverty and suffering in this rural setting. In the second stanza, Hove writes:

> Outside, a path to the field
> where little Tendai treads in bright song,
> head flat aside
> as the fields yawn in dismay
> with the laziness of elders
> who trudge along to the journey's end. ('Country life': 13–18)

Here the 'bright song' of the young ('little Tendai') contrasts with the image of 'elders / who trudge along to the journey's end', that is, to the grave. The reality of death amid the people is exaggerated here by the hyperbole of the personified fields yawning 'in dismay'. As in 'Mazes that yawn', in 'Country life' human life is integrated with the land. One way in which the integration between humans and the land/soil is also signalled in the poem is through dance, which forms a major part of recreation in the country. During the dance,

> Bare soles patter the soil
> to cement the relationship,
> a slap of union in man and home. ('Country life': 55–57)

The 'bare soles', as opposed to shod feet, ensure close physical contact with the soil to confirm the bond between humans and the earth (home), from which, according to the biblical story of creation, humans were made. More importantly for the Shona, though, as I explained earlier in this chapter, the (psychic) connection with the earth or the land is also a connection with the ancestors, the living dead, who dwell in it and who are invoked or consulted to intervene in the affairs of the living (Owomoyela 2002: 40).

Although Hove shows rural people's contact or closeness with nature, he does not offer a romanticised, idyllic and pure picture of rural life. Rather, he offers an ambiguous picture that includes ugliness, suffering and death. The poet, like his counterpart, Zimunya, as I will show later, is well aware of the challenges and suffering that rural life entails. The rain, for example, which is very important for the livelihood of people in an agrarian society, is a mixed blessing because it also causes suffering for the people. The failure of the rain to fall spells doom for the people, as Hove indicates in his short poem 'To father at home' (Hove 1982: 64), where the fate of the people if the rain does not fall is captured with a calmness that does not belie the sadness in it or the weight of the message:

> If it doesn't fall
> then, father,
> it's we
> Who have to fall. ('To father at home': 4–7)

Hove plays with the word 'fall' in this poem. Whereas the word refers to rain in the first line, in the last line it means death.

In the poem 'You will forget' (Hove 1985: 3), Hove also shows the hardships associated with rural life, while at the same time critiquing 'traditional' gender roles. This poem catalogues the challenges of life in the country, particularly for women – challenges that someone who stays 'in comfort too long' is likely to forget: the weight of a water pot on a bald head, the weight of bundles of grass on a sinewy neck and the pain of childbirth without a nurse, among other things. The suffering and pain of rural life here are shown to affect women more than men, possibly because the men might have migrated to the towns and mines, leaving women to fend for themselves and their children in the new capitalist economy.

The negative effects of colonialism and the capitalist economy on the people and the land are also a concern in Hove's eponymously titled poem 'Red hills of home' (Hove 1985: 1–2). In this unambiguously ecopostcolonial poem, Hove combines postcolonial and environmentalist perspectives to create a piece that exposes the deleterious effects of colonialism on both the environment and African rural livelihoods. In this poem, Hove captures the disintegration of social life and ecological communion in the country as a result of the colonial encounter. In the first stanza the speaker tells of how his father grew up in the rural countryside (possibly before colonisation):

[…] tuning his heart
to the sound of the owl from the moist green hills
[while] beyond, the eagle swam in the air
[and] mother-ant dragged an unknown victim to a known hole
printed on the familiar unreceding earth. ('Red hills of home': 1–7)

The expression 'tuning his heart / to the sound of the owl' refers to his recognition of the animals and nature around him, building their songs into his 'consciousness as a way of … interpreting reality' (Obiechina 1975: 43). The description of the hills as 'moist' and 'green' highlights the fact that the hills are a healthy ecosystem conducive to life that thrives in their midst. The eagle is said to swim in the air to suggest the smoothness of her movements as she glides in the sky and the harmoniousness of the scene being described. This harmoniousness, however, is interrupted/ruptured in the next line by the mention of 'mother-ant drag[ging] an unknown victim'. The verb 'drag' suggests the heavy weight of the victim and the struggle as the victim resists being taken into the ant's hole. Here nature emerges as violent and cruel, although some of its aspects are nonetheless reassuring, such as the seeming permanence and reliability of the earth as anchor, highlighted by the expression 'familiar unreceding earth'. In the extract above, as Muponde (2000: 53) rightly observes, 'there is spiritual communion between man and insect, and man and bird, quietly living in their own ways and governed by their own laws'.

When we get to the second stanza, we learn that the father had died seven years before, 'underground', which suggests that he died in a mine. Hove then proceeds to contrast two periods – then (the days of the father) and now (the speaker's own time) – when he writes:

> Now the featherless eagle, like roast meat,
> recites the misery of the dusty sky.
> Mother-ant never surfaces
> for father is enough meat, underground.
> The green hills of home died,
> Red hills cut the sky
> and the nearby sooty homes of peasants
> live under the teeth of the roaring bulldozer. ('Red hills of home': 12–19)

The phrase 'for father is enough meat, underground' reveals that in the poet-protagonist's imagination, the ant never 'surfaces' because she is feasting on the remains of his dead father, who is buried underground. From the quotation above, we notice that the ecological contact/interaction that characterised the days of the father is no longer, for the eagle that once 'swam in the air' is featherless, 'like roast meat', and 'recites the misery of the dusty sky'. The bateleur eagle is regarded in Shona traditional culture as a bird of ill-omen, and this is underscored by the negative images in its description in this poem. The dusty sky is perhaps a reference to the dust rising from the dry, overcrowded reserves (Machingaidze 1991), where Africans found themselves following the land dispossession drive by the settler colonialists.

Unlike the days of the father, the present (the speaker's day) is characterised by 'red hills cut[ting] the sky', following the death or disappearance of 'the green hills' from the landscape. The hills change from green to red as they are denuded following the clearing of vegetation, exposing the red soil that characterises the hills around the area where Hove was born.[8] The jutting hills, rising into the sky, are compared to cutting/pricking the sky, while the peasants' homes are described as 'sooty' – either to emphasise their ugliness and uninspiring appearance or, perhaps, in an allusion to the derogatory British slang for a black person. The reference to the 'teeth' of the bulldozer suggests the predatory and menacing nature of the bulldozer devouring or destroying the homes of the peasants as they are evicted from land appropriated by the colonialist.

We hear in the poem that 'the sacred hill bleeds / robbed even of her decent name' ('Red hills of home': 39–40). The bleeding of the hill is a metaphorical reference to the red soil, which invites the description 'red hills', the suffering of the people and the abuse of the environment through agricultural activity, especially by white farmers, which involved clearing and preparing large tracts of land for commercial agriculture. Commercial agriculture, like mining, played a significant role in causing forest degradation and soil erosion in colonial Zimbabwe (Kwashirai 2006; Musemwa 2012). The reference to the 'red hills' also evokes the Shona land myth *Zimbabwe ndeye ropa* (Zimbabwe is of blood), to which Musiyiwa also makes reference in his chapter in this book. This mythic construct is inspired by the fact that black Zimbabweans have had to struggle and shed blood fighting for the return of the land they lost to the colonisers. (The blood spilled in the struggle is also graphically evoked by the image of bloody hands on the collection's cover.) The hill's 'decent' name refers to the hallowed reputation of the hills and the land in the eyes of the locals. They were places of worship and the abode of the ancestors, respectively – a reputation that the newcomer colonialists completely ignore.

When we get to the last stanza, the rural home is no longer what it used to be. Exile for the villagers looms in the air – it is an exile either to the reserves or the mines, to sell their labour cheaply to colonial capitalism:[9]

> Red hills, and the smell of exile
> Exile breathing over our shoulder
> In a race that already looks desperate.
> Red hills, and the pulse of exile
> Telling us this is home no more. ('Red hills of home': 53–57)

Exile here is personified as a fiend who breathes over the people's shoulders, reminding them of the impending dislocation and signalling its inevitability. The inevitability of exile adds to the desperation of the black people, who have already lost their freedom and land. But this is freedom and land that they never regain after independence.

Commenting on Robert Mugabe's despotism and the violent land repossession against white farmers, or the third Chimurenga, led by the war veterans in Zimbabwe,[10] Hove laments:

> That the so-called war veterans are allowed to run the country like their own chicken farm is shameful. Have the politicians, for reasons of power, forgotten that every Zimbabwean contributed to the liberation struggle in their own way? Those who were working in the city did what they could to keep the villagers supplied with money in order to support the war effort with food and clothes for the guerrillas. The city provided a safe haven when the countryside became too hot. And city-dwellers have not asked for compensation. Support for the struggle was a duty dictated to us by conscience. (Hove 2002: 7)

He goes on to say:

> In the rural areas villagers were left without a chicken to their name. They sacrificed their all to feed and shelter 'the children of the soil'. The rural businessmen, agricultural officials, nurses and teachers were often pillars of the struggle. And yet, today, they are rubbished by the so-called war veterans. (Hove 2002: 7).

The old Shona land mythologies are overturned as the rich and powerful control that which should belong to all: the land. Again, we hear Hove lament: 'We were all once beautiful dreamers, we had hopes for our country, but now we have woken up to the ugliness of nightmare. We live in an ugly political system devoid of human dignity and conscience.' (Hove 2002: 8)

In his poems that appear in *Rainbows in the Dust* (Hove 1998) and *Blind Moon* (Hove 2003), collections published more than a decade after independence, images of violence, blood and death predominate – blood spilled by those in power and their cohorts. In a poem titled 'I will not speak' (Hove 1998: 9–15), Hove, who realises the dangers of speaking out against oppression in a dictatorial regime, declares:

> i will not speak
> when i see things sore to my eyes
> when i hear bitter words
> i will not speak
>
> i will not speak
> when the presidential speech spills blood
> on the streets where i walk
> when women ululate at the sight of blood —
> the blood of their own children,
> i will not speak. ('I will not speak': 7–16)

The images of blood in these lines emphasise the ruthlessness perpetrated by those in power, a fact underlined by the reference to the 'presidential speech [that] spills blood' ('I will not speak': 12).

Further, in 'The soil' (Hove 2003: 53), a poem that laments the desecration of the land/country by those in power through ruthlessness and violence, Hove writes:

> i cry for you
> as i see old men of power
> wielding blood-plastered fists,
> as i see old women of power
> wielding grinding stones made of skulls.
>
> land, i cry for you
> as you lose your voice
> to the echoes of the sky,
> your beauty sinking,
> your breath turning into mist,
> your vision blurred in the mist. ('The soil': 10–20)

The ruthlessness and violence of the rich and powerful, and the loss of vision by the leaders, which Hove refers to in *Palaver Finish*, when he says, 'Lost visions. Lost opportunities. Another junction missed in our walk to freedom' (Hove 2002: 22), are also clear in these lines.

The poems above and others in his *oeuvre* show that Hove does not see independence as a panacea to the ills of colonialism in his country. Pain and suffering among the people continue unabated. In his earlier poem 'Red hills of home', the bleeding of the sacred hill (the land) was, among other things, a metaphorical reference to the colonial suffering of the people and the abuse of the environment through agricultural activity, especially by white farmers. Later, in his poetry dealing with post-independence Zimbabwe, the bleeding land (where, as we see in 'The soil,' the persona digs the potato he planted and finds it red with blood ['The Soil': 4–5]) highlights the blood thirst and ruthlessness that characterise the ZANU-PF leadership in Zimbabwe.

The images of blood in Hove's post-independence poetry also continue to evoke the Shona land myth *Zimbabwe ndeye ropa* (Zimbabwe is of blood). This way, Hove pushes the inspiration behind this mythic construct beyond the fact that black Zimbabweans had had to struggle and shed blood for the return of the land they lost to colonisers, to underscore the fact that ordinary Zimbabweans continue to struggle and shed blood for the return of their land – this time, from the untrustworthy and thieving politicians of the post-independence era.

Nostalgia, loss and suffering in Zimunya's poetry

Unlike Hove's poetry, most of Musaemura Zimunya's poems about the country are unashamedly pastoral. But he, too, combines aspects of ecopostcolonialist thinking in his engagement with rural Zimbabwe. Zimunya grew up in the Eastern Highlands of Zimbabwe, where rolling hills and mountains covered with rich grasslands and forests, and mountains, such as Nyanga to the north, Vumba or Bvumba, near Mutare, and Chimanimani to the south, offer great scenic beauty. When asked by Veit-Wild whether there was a connection between his celebration of 'the beauty of Zimbabwe's landscape and nature' in his poetry and the place where he was 'born and brought up', Zimunya answered in the affirmative:

I was born at the foot of the Vumba mountains in Zimunya communal land which is very near Mutare. It is a very dramatic landscape. And in those days there was still a lot of bush and forest – now it is no longer the case, the whole countryside has been denuded of vegetation – but in those days it was very, very beautiful. (Veit-Wild 1988: 56).

In his poetry Zimunya shows how this natural beauty has influenced his poetic sensibility. In 'I like them' (Zimunya 1982a: 4), Zimunya writes nostalgically about the hills and mountains of his home:

I like the northern mountain of my home
crouching like a monstrous lion—
with a brown bald head
that shines with summer's water patches
and upon whose muzzle
stands a huge rhino-horn of stone—
always ready to pounce upon the western. ('I like them': 1–7)

Whereas the northern mountain (i.e. Nyanga) is menacing and fearful, despite its beauty – although the 'brown bald head' that shines after the rains in summer exposes its vulnerability – the western mountains are compared to a Chevrolet 'tearing its way towards the south'. The invocation of the lion and the rhino (through the reference to the rhino-horn) is meant to highlight the menacing appearance of the northern mountains, which look like they are 'ready to pounce upon the western' mountains. However, instead of inspiring terror and danger, Zimunya's mountains come across as caricatures, as the image of the lion 'with a brown bald head' and 'a huge rhino-horn' upon his muzzle also triggers contempt and amusement, as well as bewilderment, for lions have neither 'bald heads' nor horns. The rolling and undulating features of the eastern mountains, on the other hand, evoke the image of waves on the sea, which makes their depiction striking and vivid, and the landscape beautiful and memorable. Not surprisingly, the poet-protagonist's being is entangled with these geographical features, the love for which he confesses.

'Valley of Mawewe' (Zimunya 1982a: 93–96) is another poem that shows the poet's appreciation of the scenic beauty and ecological harmony in the valley of the poem's title at a time before the ravages of colonialism – 'before the wagon came with plunder' ('Valley of Mawewe': 21). In the precolonial valley of Mawewe, birds welcome daybreak with a burst of song that echoes throughout the valley, while baboons do so with barks and snarls. However, this pristine environment is threatened with destruction by greedy and selfish colonialists prospecting for gold, who see the land as a source of self-enrichment. A rock rabbit that spies a 'gold-digger with blood in his Saxon eyes' chatters in protest at the intrusion ('Valley of Mawewe': 34). Here animals and humans alike are potential victims of the greedy and violent intruder.[11]

Zimunya captures the Edenic quality of life for the human residents of Mawewe:

> As day came, Mawewe was the joy of Zimbabwe
> and the earth flourished and exalted creation;
> the cows mooed unto the mountains and bellowing
> bulls rebellowed;
> there were heard bleating sheep and crowing cocks
> and the bones of the hills and the mountains
> and the suns in the leaves lived in Mawewe. ('Valley of Mawewe': 36–42)

On reading these lines, one immediately becomes aware of the fact that the suggestiveness and combination of metaphors one encounters in Hove's poetry are missing here. Instead, we are confronted by a poem that sounds clichéd and lacklustre. This is perhaps because, unlike Hove, who tries to ensure that his poetry is 'overloaded with meaning' and his words 'burst with meaning' (Veit-Wild 1988: 39), Zimunya aims at simplicity and readability.[12] But, as can be seen from the poem 'Valley of Mawewe', the simplicity compromises an important quality of the form and style of Zimunya's poetry.

'Valley of Mawewe' shows that besides livestock, Mawewe was also rich in foodstuffs, such as melons, cucumbers, pumpkins, pears, maize and millet. The Shona people's precolonial way of life as successful agriculturalists is referred to.[13] Zimunya makes it clear in the poem that the pristine beauty and harmony of Mawewe is destroyed by the colonial encounter and the revolutionary struggle that followed when he reiterates that 'I sing of an age before the torch and the bulldozer / and I sing of the life lost in the napalm' ('Valley of Mawewe': 56–57). The bulldozer stands out in the poem as a symbol of the ecologically unfriendly agricultural methods of the colonialists, who ripped and tore great tracts of land to open up commercial farms.

Colonial destruction did not stop with the land alone, which, unlike for the Shona or Ndebele, held no sacred memories for the newcomers. The arrogant colonialist, who held no respect for the spiritual values of the local people, also interfered with spiritual values, as we are told in 'Valley of Mawewe':

Thus, when Rhodes came to Matopo, he made home in
the rock
with a blast of the dynamite where the native made
their shrine
and the Gods had a view of the world. ('Valley of Mawewe': 64–66)

Making his 'home in / the rock' is a reference to Rhodes's decision to have his remains buried in the Matopo Hills after his death, thereby interfering with the spiritual values of the Kalanga, Ndebele and Shona, who held, and still hold, 'the hills and caves of the Matopo region as sacred' (Sheehan 1996: 8). However, while lamenting the colonial scourge on the people's way of life and on the landscape, the poem 'Valley of Mawewe' also depicts the beauty of the Zimbabwean landscape in precolonial times.

As well as describing the beauty of the landscape, Zimunya's poetry provides glimpses of recollections of 'the simple joys of the poet's early childhood' (Mutswairo 1991: 105) in rural Zimbabwe. Happy memories of a sweet and carefree childhood are the subject of Zimunya's

'Children's rain song' (Zimunya 1982a: 3). In this poem children fling away their clothes, and hop and dance in the rain, singing:

> Rain fall fall
> we will eat berries
> rain fall for all
> we will eat mealies
> we will eat cucumbers
> rain fall fall. ('Children's rain song': 6–11)

Here Zimunya expresses nostalgia for the childhood he will never enjoy again. This poem shows how the country people's livelihood is interwoven and connected with the seasons. If rain does not come, it means the food that the children mention will not be available. The children celebrate the rain for its utilitarian value. As agriculturalists inhabiting a drought-prone country, for the Shona the coming of the rain was cause for celebration (Mutswairo 1991: 105). But the poem is also tinged with a sense of loss. Watching the children sing and dance in the rain reminds the poet of the childhood he has lost with age:

> Children in the rain
> they don't feel the pain
> of longing all the time
> to streak through the years
> and dance in the rain again. ('Children's rain song': 22–26)

Zimunya's 'Rain and fire' (Zimunya 1982b:7) also celebrates the rain, which brings joy and happiness to children and adults alike in the rural areas, showing the beneficent role of the rain to the agricultural endeavours of the people. The poet observes:

> Rain suckles the earth
> where seedlings grow and grow green
> and the mealies and groundnuts and the millet
> will soon be ready. ('Rain and fire': 5–8)

The poet later writes nostalgically of how pumpkins would steam in the pot and how the people would roast corn. Like 'Children's rain song', this poem reads like a song, relying on repetition for its rhythm.

In *The Country and the City*, Raymond Williams expresses the view that the pastoral genre is, among other things, perhaps 'a well-known habit of using the past, the "good old days," as a stick to beat the present ...' (Williams 1975: 21). Nostalgia and the memory of childhood inspire writers to select and idealise only those aspects of rural life that fit 'the myth of the happy past' (Williams 1975: 54) or the myth of a lost Eden. In this selective process, writers gloss over the variety and complexity of the actual history of the country with its problems of class and gender, for example.[14] Hove and Zimunya's representation of the countryside in Zimbabwe invites this same charge of selectiveness. One rarely, if ever, encounters the tensions, conflicts and injustices perpetrated by fellow Africans in the poets' accounts of the past. To their credit, however, the two poets' narratives of the past, as I have already mentioned, do include stories of suffering, painful rural existence and poverty.

For instance, although the rain is celebrated in the lines analysed above, Zimunya is all too aware of the suffering that comes with the rain for poor people. In 'Cattle in the rain' (1982a: 5–6), we come face to face with the suffering rain brings to a herdboy trying to herd cattle while it is raining. Cattle held, and still hold, great symbolic capital for the Shona (Vambe 1972: 2–3). In the poem, the poet, who is prompted by the sight of rain, muses:

> Nothing has no end,
> it is true.
> This rain used to sock [*sic*] us in the pastures
> and the cattle would not stop to graze,
> they would not be driven to the kraal,
> it made me cry and curse sometimes
> and I used to wish I were born differently. ('Cattle in the rain': 1–7)

The poet-protagonist remembers the coldness and discomfort the rain used to bring as he herded cattle out in the bush. Besides the rain, some of his painful experiences included being stung by wasps, covering himself with a smelly jute sack to keep the rain out, and having 'wet thorns snap … at random in your benumbed feet' ('Cattle in the rain': 17). The poet also suspects that the behaviour of the cattle was calculated to exacerbate his suffering. Gatooma, the ox, features as the perpetrator of more suffering for the herdboy:

> This ox, tail high,
> in two sniffs and a cajole
> all meant to humiliate
> would crash through the thin bush
> leaving me running weakly
> sobbing at each step. ('Cattle in the rain': 28–33)

The anthropomorphised cattle emerge as calculating and insensitive to the plight of the suffering boy. However, the cattle in the poem are tangential and are used as mere props against which the suffering of the hapless herdboy is depicted.

Besides rural suffering, Zimunya also laments the Shona people's loss of tradition, mainly as a result of the colonial encounter, which introduces new ways of seeing the world. In 'No songs' (Zimunya 1982a: 10–11), the people's alienation from their spiritual ways of life – from their ancestors' shrines, sacred caves and gods of rain – could be the cause of the drought that now afflicts the land. In this drought-hit landscape an eerie silence descends on the land:

> No songs of cicadas—
> only a sighing silence
> where, once,
> as I walked below the yellow leaves
> of fresh foliage,
> a spray of urine
> moistened my face
> and a shrill symphony
> waned into my ears. ('No songs': 1–9)

For the poet-protagonist, the 'urine' here is not a bad thing but a positive symbol of thriving life. These lines symbolically express the existential despair caused by the drought, real or metaphorical, triggered by the people's abandonment of spiritual ways following the colonial encounter.

The poem is a call to self-rediscovery, to return to the old religious ways of the ancestors. Lamenting the people's loss of the ecological ways of the ancestors, the poet-protagonist wonders:

> Where shall we find the way back?
> Opaque darkness guards our exit
> we have groped and groped until
> our eyes were almost blind and
> it was hard to rediscover. ('No songs': 24–28)

Hopelessness and pessimism for the possibility of rediscovery characterise the poet-protagonist's feelings here, as highlighted by the 'opaque darkness' guarding the only possible exit for the people and their near-blindness, and hence the difficulty in finding their way back. Besides, the poet-protagonist believes that by the time the people realise how far they have strayed and seek to retrace their footsteps it will be too late and 'the lion tongue of death will be licking / the last gush of blood from our souls' ('No songs': 36–37) – the people will almost be dead, culturally.

The poem 'Let me go' (Zimunya 1985: 27) is Zimunya's attempt to experience the beauty of the pristine, unspoilt landscape of his home and preserve its memory before it is completely wiped out by greedy capitalists. The poet begs:

> Let me go to the eastern mountains, my fellow citizen,
> for I hear strange news of things afoot
> of villages flourishing where once forests stood
> and fields where once cattle grazed and watered
> that I may breathe the last of ancient sunsets. ('Let me go': 1–5)

In the poem, the beautiful landscape of the poet's Eastern Highlands is being destroyed. Forests die as they are cleared to pave the way for human settlements; old places of worship are desecrated; and the poet seeks to experience the former glory and beauty of the landscape before it is completely wiped out – to kneel again 'and worship the gods of my forefathers / before the saw and the axe make bald heads of hills / laying naked the spirits of the land as never before', ('Let me go': 7–9) and reducing the mountains to mere skeletons. The poet's desire to go back to the rural country is inspired by the fear of forgetting the beauty of the mountains and 'the world of [his] boyhood up there once' ('Let me go': 19). But the journey back home is also a quest for rejuvenation and revitalisation from nature, as the poet also wishes to be 'reborn in a baptism of the last ancient sunset' ('Let me go': 24). This poem, appearing in *Country Dawns and City Lights*, which was published in 1985, five years after independence, could be interpreted as highlighting post-independence injustices to the land. That is to say, five years after independence, Zimunya noted the continued abuse of nature, such as the wanton felling of trees that threatened to lay bare the beautiful mountains of his childhood.

Muponde (2000: 55) argues that whereas Hove rejects the rural home, as it 'is not home at all but an aftermath of an invisible war', Zimunya 'still holds that there is something of value in the rural home despite the deep cracks and disruptions occasioned by colonialism'. Contrary to this view, as the above poem shows, Zimunya is aware that the value of the rural home is fast disappearing through the transformations that render it unliveable and unlovable. In this poem, too, Zimunya shows his ecological sensibility as he despairs about the destruction of forests and the denudation of the beautiful mountains of his home. Nevertheless, the picture of the persona here is of an impotent and helpless individual who, instead of acting against the destruction of the pristine land, only wishes to see the mountains, hills and valleys in their majestic beauty once more before the agents of destruction fully succeed.

From the foregoing, we notice that Hove and Zimunya are ecologically conscious poets who are nostalgic about rural life, the beauty of which was destroyed by the ravages of colonial rule in Zimbabwe. The two poets expose and lament the destruction of the land and the transitions taking place in the countryside, as well as the pain, suffering and dislocation of rural life, mainly occasioned by colonialism, which not only robbed the people of their much prized land, but also led to a spiritual death and exile, to the loss of culture and old ecological ways of seeing and imagining the world. Both poets also show a concern for nature – the seasons, the forest and its creatures – and acknowledge the beauty and revitalising nature of the rural world. However, memories of country life are not always beautiful or pleasant in the poetry. The poets are well aware of the challenges and suffering that rural life entails. They therefore reveal a broader vision of rural Zimbabwe, a vision that does not see rural societies only as idyllic and alluring, but as encompassing suffering as well. But beneath this vision of rural Zimbabwe perhaps lies 'the attitude of romanticising the past' that is observable in literature and other disciplines, an attitude 'which assumes that an eco-golden age existed at some point in the past' (Taringa 2006: 192).

References

Bourdillon, M. F. C. *The Shona Peoples: An Ethnography of the Contemporary Shona, with Special Reference to their Religion*. Gweru: Mambo, 1982.

Callicott, J. Baird. *Earth's Insights: A Survey of Ecological Ethics from the Mediterranean Basin to the Australian Outback*. Berkeley: University of California Press, 1994.

Chemhuru, Munamato and Masaka, Dennis. 'Taboos as sources of Shona people's environmental ethics.' *Journal of Sustainable Development in Africa* 12, 7 (2010): 121–133.

Hove, Chenjerai. *Up in Arms*. Harare: Zimbabwe Publishing House, 1982.

Hove, Chenjerai. *Red Hills of Home*. Gweru: Mambo, 1985.

Hove, Chenjerai. *Rainbows in the Dust*. Harare: Baobab Books, 1998.

Hove, Chenjerai. *Palaver Finish*. Harare: Weaver Press, 2002.

Hove, Chenjerai. *Blind Moon*. Harare: Weaver Press, 2003.

Huggan, Graham and Tiffin, Helen. Postcolonial Ecocriticism: Literature, Animals, Environment. London and New York: Routledge, 2010.

Iheka, Cajetan N. 'Postcolonial ecocriticism and African literature: The Nigerian Civil War example.' MA thesis, Central Michigan University, 2011. Available at CMU Online Digital Object Repository.

Ikeke, Mark Omorovie. 'The forest in African traditional thought and practice: An ecophilosophical discourse.' *Open Journal of Philosophy* 3, 2 (2013): 345–350.

Kanengoni, Alexander. 'The long way home: One man's story', in David Harold-Barry (ed.), *Zimbabwe: The Past Is the Future*. Harare: Weaver Press, 2003.

Kwashirai, Vimbai C. 'Dilemmas in conservationism in colonial Zimbabwe, 1890–1930.' *Conservation and Society* 4, 4 (December 2006): 541–561.

'Land issue – fact sheet: Pre-independence legislation on land, race and history', www.raceandhistory.com/Zimbabwe/landfacts.html.

Lutwack, Leonard. *Birds in Literature*. Gainesville: University Press of Florida, 1994.

Machingaidze, Victor E. M. 'Agrarian change from above: The Southern Rhodesia Native Land Husbandry Act and African Response'. *The International Journal of African Historical Studies* 24, 3 (1991): 557–588.

Mbembe, Achille. 'African modes of self-writing' (translated by Steven Rendall). *Public Culture* 14, 1 (2002): 239–273.

Mount, Dana C. 'Enduring nature: Everyday environmentalisms in postcolonial literature.' PhD thesis, McMaster University, 2012, DigitalCommons@McMaster.

Muponde, Robert. Zimbabwean Literature (Poetry): Module ECS 402. Harare: The Zimbabwe Open University, 2000.

Musemwa, Muchaparara. 'Miner-farmer struggles and the rise of conservation practices in colonial Zimbabwe, 1940–1961.' Draft of paper presented at the Ninth International Mining History Congress, Gold Reef City, Johannesburg, 17–20 April 2012.

Mutswairo, S. M. 'A Zimbabwean poet writing in English: A critical appraisal of Musaemura Zimunya's Thought-Tracks.' *Zambezia* XVIII, ii (1991): 105–118.

Nixon, Rob. 'Environmentalism and postcolonialism', in Ania Loomba *et al.* (eds), *Postcolonial Studies and Beyond*. Durham N.C.: Duke University Press, 2005.

Nkala, Denis. 'Tackling agricultural development with land dearth', in Carlos Lopes (ed.), *Balancing rocks: Environment and Development in Zimbabwe*. Harare: SAPES, 1996.

Obiechina, Emmanuel. *Culture, Tradition and Society in the West African Novel*. Cambridge: Cambridge University Press, 1975.

Owomoyela, Oyekan. *Culture and Customs of Zimbabwe*. Westport and London: Greenwood, 2002.

Primorac, Ranka and Muponde, Robert. 'Introduction: Writing against blindness', in Robert Muponde and Ranka Primorac (eds), *Versions of Zimbabwe: New Approaches to Literature and Culture*. Harare: Weaver Press, 2005.

Rakodi, Carole. *Harare: Inheriting a Settler-Colonial City: Change or continuity?* Chichester: Wiley and Sons, 1995.

Raymer, A. J. 'Virgil and Wordsworth: The poetry of Romanticism'. *Greece & Rome 9*, 25 (October 1939): 13–25.

Sheehan, Sean. *Zimbabwe*. Singapore and Kuala Lumpur: Times Editions, 1996.

Summerfield, Geoffrey. 'Introduction', in Geoffrey Summerfield (ed.), *John Clare: Selected Poetry*. London: Penguin, 1990.

Tangwa, Godfrey B. 'Bioethics: An African perspective'. *Bioethics* 10, 3 (1996): 183–200.

Taringa, Nisbert. 'How environmental is African traditional religion?' *Exchange* 35, 2 (2006): 191–214.

Vambe, Lawrence. *An Ill-Fated People: Zimbabwe Before and After Rhodes.* London: Heinemann, 1972.

Veit-Wild, Flora. *Patterns of Poetry in Zimbabwe.* Gweru: Mambo, 1988.

Veit-Wild, Flora. *Teachers, Preachers, Non-Believers: A Social History of Zimbabwean Literature.* Harare: Baobab, 1993.

Williams, Raymond. *The Country and the City.* St. Albans: Paladin, 1975.

Wylie, Dan. 'Mind has mountains': Poetry and ecology in eastern Zimbabwe', in Robert Muponde and Ranka Primorac (eds), *Versions of Zimbabwe: New Approaches to Literature and Culture.* Harare: Weaver Press, 2005.

Zimunya, Musaemura. *Thought-Tracks.* Essex: Longman, 1982a.

Zimunya, Musaemura. *Kingfisher, Jikinya and Other Poems.* Harare: Longman, 1982b.

Zimunya, Musaemura. *Country Dawns and City Lights.* Harare: Longman, 1985.

'Zvishavane, Zimbabwe.' *Wikipedia, the Free Encyclopedia*, https://en.wikipedia.org/wiki/Zvishavane, accessed 17 October 2010.

ABOUT THE AUTHORS

Byron Caminero-Santangelo is Professor of English and Environmental Studies at the University of Kansas.

Sule Emmanuel Egya is an Associate Professor in the Department of English at Ibrahim Badamasi Babangida University, Lapai, Nigeria.

Jonathan Bishop Highfield is Professor of Literary Arts and Studies at Rhode Island School of Design.

Jacob Mapara is a lecturer and inaugural Chair of the Centre for Indigenous Knowledge and Living Heritage, at Chinhoyi University's Institute of Lifelong Learning.

F. Fiona Moolla is a Senior Lecturer and the Graduate Coordinator in the English Department at the University of the Western Cape, South Africa.

Syned Mthatiwa is a literary scholar and fiction writer who teaches Literature at Chancellor College, University of Malawi.

Mickias Musiyiwa holds a PhD in popular songs obtained from Stellenbosch University in 2013 as well as an MA in African Languages and Literature from the University of Zimbabwe.

Ogaga Okuyade teaches popular/folk culture, African literature and culture, African American and African diasporic studies and the English novel in the Department of English and Literary Studies, Niger Delta University, Wilberforce Island, Nigeria.

Mathilda Slabbert lectures in the Department of English Studies at the University of Stellenbosch.

Anthony Vital is a professor of English at Transylvania University, a liberal arts college in Kentucky.

Reinier J.M. Vriend works as a lecturer at the Media and Culture department of the University of Amsterdam.

James Maina Wachira holds a Bachelor of Education (Arts) and Master of Philosophy of Literature from Moi University.

Wendy Woodward teaches southern African Literature, Animal Studies and Creative Writing in the English Department at the University of the Western Cape, South Africa.

Chengyi Coral Wu is a PhD candidate in English at the University of Nevada, Reno, USA.

ACKNOWLEDGEMENTS

This edited volume owes its existence to the generosity and support of a number of people. Thank you to my colleagues Julia Martin and Wendy Woodward in the English Department at the University of the Western Cape (UWC), whose lack of scholarly territoriality allowed my entry into a field that they have actively and imaginatively occupied for a number of decades. I appreciate your generosity in sharing academic networks (and ideas). Heartfelt thanks also to Hermann Wittenberg, whose investment in the pursuits and success of colleagues, and the department in which they grow, extends beyond scholarly and moral support. Thank you, Hermann, for being a professional pillar. Postdoctoral fellow in the UWC English Department, Kate Highman, acted as scrupulous copyeditor of a number of chapters in the volume. Kate's depth and breadth of knowledge, and sensitivity to the nuances of language meant that her actual remit went well beyond simply copyediting – thank you for your fine reading and discretion.

Deepest gratitude is also owing to those excellent scholars of niche areas who agreed to act as internal reviewers of first drafts of chapters at a very busy time in the academic year. One of these academics got back to me to say, 'Do you know what you are asking?!', but provided detailed and very critical feedback despite time constraints. (You know who you are – and an even bigger thank-you to you.) Sincere appreciation to Harry Garuba, Louise Green, Marika Flockemann, Julia Martin, Chris Ouma, Rethabile Possa, Kelwyn Sole, Asonzeh Ukah, Hermann Wittenberg and Dan Wylie for feedback on chapters.

Finally, thank you to Roshan Cader of Wits University Press, a discerning and extremely rigorous publisher, who, to the advantage of the volume, has set the highest standards, but who has also been very supportive of the project since its inception.

NOTES

Chapter 1

1. The epic and its hero are known by many names. I have chosen 'Sunjata' because it seems fairly common and it is phonetically between the 'Sundiata' of D. T. Niane's (1965) transcription/retelling and the 'Son Jara' of John William Johnson's (1986) transcription. Both Gordon Innes (1974) and David C. Conrad use 'Sunjata', as does Ralph Austen's (1999) collection on the epic. Dani Kouyaté uses 'Keita'. To differentiate between the title character and the narrative itself, I have italicised the epic.
2. Mali is the name of the traditional Manding, or Mande, homeland. Manding or Mande refers to both a specific group of people found across a large part of West Africa and the language group they speak. See Bird (1982).
3. 'Keita' is another transcription of 'Djata' or 'Jara'. In the film, it is both the patronym of Mabo's family and the name the griot Djéliba uses to reference Sunjata.
4. 'I am fortunate to belong to the age of cinema: it is a fabulous instrument for a griot' (author's translation).
5. As Patrick McNaughton points out in *The Mande Blacksmiths: Knowledge, Power, and Art in West Africa*, 'these two population segments are both engaged in vocations and possess special intellectual and spiritual capacities whose ramifications are enormous' (McNaugton 1993: 71). Hunters obtain their power from herbal collection and knowledge from the animals that provide their subsistance and which they compete with. The power of the blacksmiths is associated with forging tools and their resulting agricultural mastery.
6. See also AmbrosiaLab; 'Cosmetic preparations with an additive from the baobab tree – US 20090324656 A1'; 'Patent application of Baobab Fruit Company' (see Manfredini 2002); and 'Use of parts of the baobab plant as animal food or as additive in animal food – US 20090258112 A1'.

7. 'Our quinoa will become part of the junk food, and we will be dependent consumers: this is the reason why farmers mourn silently for they know that in the future they will never again be the owners of quinoa seed, and they are aware that some historical varieties with different uses will disappear entirely.' (author's translation).

Chapter 2
1. Oral artistic forms include myths, legends, folk tales, oral poetry (particularly traditional panegyric poetry); cultural practices include a host of religious ceremonies, such as rain-making ceremonies.
2. These are protest and war songs sung in resistance to the colonial establishment. They were also sung during the liberation war. Sometimes they are referred to as revolutionary or nationalist songs. The term *'chimurenga'* in the context of Zimbabwean nationalism refers to the war waged against British colonisation by the Shona in 1896–1897, a war now historically known as the First Chimurenga, and the struggle for independence of the 1960s and 1970s, which is referred to as the Second Chimurenga. In the same context, the term is used to refer to a revolution and in general terms to any struggle. At the turn of the millennium, it has been used to refer to the land invasions, which were officially dubbed the Third Chimurenga.
3. However, literacy is becoming more widespread and the mythology is also now found in written form, especially the literary texts that are being studied as part of this research.
4. In oral cultures these expressions are much more mnemonically and mentally based. However, the rise of imaginative literature in Shona and English from the 1950s has added literature as another expressive mode of Shona mythology. The recording of songs has also seen the mythology being conveyed through recorded music.
5. In some translations this appears as 'sons of the soil', as, for example, in the title of Wilson Katiyo's novel *Son of the Soil*. The same translation is used by David Lan in his anthropological work, *Guns and Rains* (1985), in which he analyses the relationship between guerrillas in the Second Chimurenga. However, this is a patriarchal translation consistent with the colonial period. The Shona noun *mwana* simply means 'a child' (irrespective of gender).
6. The rise of African nationalism has also seen the *mwana wevhu* mantra being extended to other ethnic groups in Zimbabwe, such as the Ndebele, who now speak of *umntwana wemhlabathi* (child of the soil).
7. Shona society is a conglomeration of various chiefdoms, usually identified from one another by territorial boundaries and distinct totems and praises. During certain periods, the chiefdoms could fall under one powerful

paramount chief, as was the case with the states of Great Zimbabwe (1250–1450), Mutapa (1450–1800) and Rozvi (1780s–1838).

8. This is a Shona word that means a lion that is host to a chiefly spirit. The lion is believed to be harmless. The term also refers to a person used as a medium by such a spirit.

9. Nisbert Taringa's reference to a Shona chief as the *muridzi wevhu* (owner of the land) (Taringa 2006: 195) is misleading because in practice it was difficult for a chief to claim personal ownership of all the land in the chiefdom. He held it in trust and would distribute it to any member of his chiefdom, and was even obliged to allocate land to outsiders seeking to live in his chiefdom.

10. Since the translation of the Bible into Shona in the 1960s, the term Mwari now also refers to the Christian God.

11. The ownership of the land was attributed to both female and male territorial spirits, which confirms my earlier argument about the gender neutrality of the *mwana wevhu* myth (see note 5). The founders of a chiefdom usually consisted of a man and a woman (a brother and sister).

12. The Shona terms *Mbuya* and *Sekuru*, while they literally refer to grandmother and grandfather, respectively, in the context of Shona religion, as is the case with this song, they refer to great male and female ancestors.

13. For instance, Nehanda is the best-known spirit in Zimbabwe because of nationalist reconstructions of the land mythology during the Second Chimurenga and Third Chimurenga. Nehanda presented the most radical resistance to British colonisation, which nationalists took advantage of to inspire ordinary Zimbabweans to fight for independence. Before her execution, Nehanda flatly rejected being baptised into Christianity and is also said to have told her tormentors that her bones were going to rise again. According to the myth, twice the guillotine failed to work until the executioner was told to take away Nehanda's snuff box.

14. Composed to promote the post-2000 land reform, the message of this song was directed to the opposition Movement for Democratic Change and their Western backers, who had condemned the land seizures and wanted the land invaders to vacate settler farms.

15. See, for example, Ranger's *Voices from the Rocks* (1999), an analysis of how the Matopos Hills, Mwari's religious shrine, was desecrated. In 1902 Rhodes was buried there, and later his friend Leander Starr Jameson and the first Rhodesian prime minister, Sir Charles Coghlan. In 1962 Africans were evicted from the area to create a national park around Rhodes's grave.

16. For example, the Tafara-Mabvuku Chimurenga Choir has a song entitled '*Negidi*' (By the gun).

17. At Zimbabwe's independence the song was recorded by the Harare Mambo Band and became an instant hit.
18. I have made some alterations to the English version of the song's lyrics for purposes of clarity.

Chapter 3
1. In *Dark Green Religion: Nature Spirituality and the Planetary Future*, Bron Taylor (2010: 10) defines dark green religion as one that believes that nature is sacred, has intrinsic value and is therefore due reverent care. It comes out of a profound sense of belonging to and attachment to nature, while recognising the earth and its living systems to be sacrosanct and interconnected. Dark green religion is usually deep, ecological, biocentric, or ecocentric, and considers all species to be innately prized, that is, treasured apart from their usefulness to human beings (Taylor 2010: 13).

Chapter 4
1. The Samburu people, who are mainly pastoralists, are one of Kenya's ethnic communities. They are largely found in Samburu County but the community has also spread to the counties of Laikipia, Marsabit and Isiolo.
2. Moranhood is a stage between boyhood and elderhood. The morans' major role is to protect the community against external aggression. Morans live together and remain in this status until admitted into elderhood by the elders. The elders determine how long they remain in this status.

Chapter 5
1. The term 'global North' is used here in opposition to the 'global South' and denotes north-western Europe, North America and Australia. The global South denotes large parts of Africa, Asia and Latin America (Steger 2009).
2. The term 'southern Africa' is used because, although the large majority of the voluntourism destinations are in South Africa, there are also programmes elsewhere in the region.

Chapter 6
1. The theme of the indigenous African relationship between people, their ancestors and the land is recurrent in early African literature, particularly in anglophone African novels, including Cyprian Ekwensi's *Burning Grass* (1962), Grace Ogot's *The Promised Land* (1966) and Sahle Sellassie's *The Afersata* (1968).
2. For a more detailed critique of ecocriticism's justification for using ecology to bring up environmental ethics in interpreting literature, see Dana Phillips's (1999) 'Ecocriticism, literary theory, and the truth of ecology'.

3. Essays that focus on environmental issues revealed in African literature include Gorgui Dieng's 'Environmental issues in Buchi Emecheta's *Naira Power*' (1997–1998); Noel Dossou-Yovo's 'Village and city environments in Ekwensi's major works' (1997–1998); and Ibrahima N'diaye's '*The Interpreters*: A study in urban, social, and scatological Imagination' (1997–1998).
4. For environmental justice's critique of ecocriticism, see essays in *The Environmental Justice Reader* (2002), including Mei Mei Evans's '"Nature" and environmental justice', and Devon G. Pena's 'Endangered landscapes and disappearing peoples? Identity, place, and community in ecological politics.' For recent postcolonial ecocriticism's critique of traditional ecocriticism, see DeLoughrey, Gosson and Handley's *Caribbean Literature and the Environment: Between Nature and Culture* (2005); Rob Nixon's 'Environmentalism and postcolonialism' (2005); Susie O'Brien's '"Back to the world": Reading ecocriticism in a postcolonial context' (2007); and Graham Huggan and Helen Tiffin's *Postcolonial Ecocriticism* (2010).
5. For example, see Ben Okri's *The Famished Road* (1991) and Chris Abani's *Graceland* (2007).
6. For example, see Cyprian Ekwensi's *Burning Grass* (1962).
7. See note 1 above.
8. For example, see Bessie Head's *When Rain Clouds Gather* (1968) and Ngũgĩ wa Thiong'o's *Petals of Blood* (1977).
9. For more discussions of 'environmentalism of the poor', see Ramachandra Guha's *Environmentalism: A Global History* (2000); Joan Martinez-Alier's *Environmentalism of the Poor* (2002); Deane Curtin's *Environmental Ethics for a Postcolonial World* (2005); and Rob Nixon's *Slow Violence and the Environmentalism of the Poor* (2011).
10. See Toyin Falola's *Britain and Nigeria: Exploitation or Development?* (1987)
11. See Alfred Crosby's *Ecological Imperialism: The Biological Expansion of Europe, 900–1900* (1986); Christine Ombaka's 'War and environment in African literature' (1998); and Olaniyan and Quayson (eds) *African Literature: An Anthology of Criticism and Theory* (2007).
12. See Ken Saro-Wiwa's *Genocide in Nigeria: The Ogoni Tragedy* (1992) and Michael Renner's *The Anatomy of Resource War* (2002).
13. See Graham Huggan's '"Greening" postcolonialism: Ecocritical perspectives' (2004); Rob Nixon's 'Environmentalism and postcolonialism' (2005); Susie O'Brien's '"Back to the World": Reading ecocriticism in a postcolonial context' (2007); Cara Cilano and Elizabeth DeLoughrey's 'Against authenticity: Global knowledges and postcolonial ecocriticism' (2007); and Graham Huggan and Helen Tiffin's *Postcolonial Ecocriticism* (2010).

14. See Richard Grove's *Green Imperialism: Tropical Island Edens and the Origins of Environmentalism, 1600–1860* (1995), and Tom Griffiths and Libby Robin's anthology *Ecology and Empire: Environmental History of Settler Societies* (1997).

Chapter 7
1. This essay represents a shorter version of a chapter to be published by Lexington Books, Lanham, MD, USA. For editorial guidance with this essay, I thank Fiona Moolla. For supporting the research, I thank Transylvania University's Kenan Fund for faculty and student enrichment.
2. I resist the label 'urban ecocriticism' simply because all ecocriticism, as academic activity, is urban for expressing the concerns of modern civilisation. Of course, not all environmental concern – and activism – occurs in urbanised worlds: it can emerge among those on modernity's margins, with different cultural traditions, who resist modernity's encroachment. The focus on modern cities inevitably draws in histories of colonialism and their impact on natural systems (no London or Amsterdam – and their 'exchanges' – then no East India companies). Thinking of ecocriticism as rooted in urbanism does not preclude exploring the textualising of rural or 'wild' places – frequently, in African worlds, in language that pre-dates the impact of colonial modernity.
3. Dirlik (2007) offers valuable analysis of the interrelationship of colonialism, modernity and capitalism. He distinguishes between a 'colonial modernity' (evident during the era of formal colonies and empire) and a 'global modernity', dominant in the present postcolonial era. In this latter form, different societies, with different cultural and political histories, express modernity differently and with regional unevenness. Yet all societies, to different extents, encounter 'the dynamic role played in [modernity's] universalization by capitalism' (Dirlik 2007: 163). Wanting to keep this sketch brief and focused on these three key terms, I do not work with any of the abundant scholarship on cities. This work, in both social and natural sciences, would 'join the conversation', giving detail to our understanding.
4. The focus that DeLoughrey and Handley (2011) provide, together with the essays they have collected, draws on a wide range of writing (by Chinua Achebe, Pablo Neruda and Edward Said, for example). Their interpretive frame has value for supplying postcolonial ways of thinking about how a society's apprehension of its living land could enable a resistance to colonial domination. This frame allows a similar way to chart opposition to global modernity.

5. For a discussion of urban metabolism, see Wachsmuth (2012), who notes that Karl Marx first drew the idea of metabolism into the social sciences.
6. I use the term 'literature' to include story and song crafted in oral cultures, which those of us reading become aware of mostly through the practices of urban cultural transmission (though family memory can still form an important channel).
7. More and more people across Africa experience urban life directly. Rapid urban growth has occurred since the 1950s, and according to a recent study by UN Habitat, the urban population is expected to triple between 2010 and 2050. See Schuttenhelm (2010). For an introduction to African cities, see Freund (2007); for an excellent recent study, see Myers (2011). Although my focus on *globalised* cities does appear to privilege northern frames of reference – and both Myers (2011) and Lawhon (2013) (in addressing how to think about South African environmentalism) explore the problems with such privileging – it suggests a dialectic characteristic of postcolonial thinking. See Vital (2005: 298–299) for my comments on a postcolonial interplay of the local and the global.
8. Comments on Mda's novel in this essay rest on a fuller reading, presented in my essay 'Situating ecology in recent South African fiction' (Vital 2005).
9. Shaun Viljoen (2013) provides an excellent introduction to the novel and its characterisation of Azure.
10. Viljoen (2013: xxii) suggests, rightly, that this generic approach to the novel would supply valuable results.
11. In these moments, the narrative enters worlds explored by Wendy Woodward in this volume (see Chapter 10) – worlds evidencing epistemologies very different from those enabling modernity and its processes. Duiker's novel, while not dismissing such epistemology (which has crucial value for the protagonist), nonetheless keeps a narrative focus on the physical actuality of a ruthless modernity, described in terms of a modern realism, with its sociological and psychological foci.
12. The book and film titles are, of course, strongly suggestive. An up-to-date study exploring the shifting forms of a Euro-American postmodern temporality and its relation to apocalypse has yet to be written. Although World War II and its aftermath mark a distinctive moment of origin, the waning of 'liberation' cultures in the 1970s, coinciding with worry over limits to growth, exacerbated by the rise of globalisation in the post–Cold War era – and, before the Cold War ended, the worry over the 'nuclear winter', and now the fear of terrorism, all suggest the complex interplay of social and planetary collapse that figure in this haunting. Another issue, entirely, is the relation of African thinking to these northern imaginings.

13. It is surely not coincidental that this orphan grew up in Mshenguville, Soweto, and his age suggests his birth date coincides with Mshenguville's inception, when homeless people invaded a golf course to erect their shacks there. See 'About Mshenguville'.
14. I acknowledge, here, Julia Martin's (2009) account of her classroom practice, one that encourages a revisioning of the flows at work in a city's life.
15. Humans can survive the winters of Antarctica because they are provisioned from elsewhere. In the globalised world, the natural systems sustaining cities are often far from a city's place – but they exist, as do the necessary transportation systems. It is important to note, too, that our individual bodies, provisioned within this network, are themselves communities of organisms, including bacteria, with which we live in symbiosis. In human bodies, bacterial cells outnumber by a factor of ten the human cells. The US government is conducting research into links between this human biome and health. See National Institutes of Health Office of Strategic Coordination 'Program Snapshot' (2013).
16. Viljoen (2013: xiii) notes accurately that, when the circumstances are made comfortable by wealth, Azure does feel pleasure during this bought sex – even if he does not feel driven to find it.
17. Baingana's collection, while valuing women's solidarity – and satirising women incapable of it – is heteronormative, which this association of gardening and sexuality reinforces. Linking sexuality and nature, though, does not need to reinforce existing social norms. Sexuality in nature, as biology reminds us, is 'wildly' various, while gardening, of course, is a form of domesticating nature – 'socialising' it and, historically, in ways that reinforce specific familial and social structures. Yet the binarism is misleading. Gardening need not be seen as restrictive – there is nothing necessary about the social structures it can be associated with. Moreover, it has always involved engaging with 'wild' species, creating hybrids.
18. Woodward's chapter in this volume, which explores the modern reworking of traditional animal tales, can illustrate this dialectic – one that builds a conversation between a literary work's critical insights and its perceived limits. The novels that Woodward examines indicate how a modern African response to urban environmental problems, drawing on both objective understanding and the intelligence embodied in African cultural traditions, will differ from the North's modern responses to its own urban problems.
19. Chinua Achebe's *Arrow of God* (Achebe 1964 [1989]) illustrates the drama of living within such a world, and encountering a society with a very different understanding of nature and humans, who carry with them an empire's sense of built environment.

20. This 'utopian goal', I argue elsewhere, can be given content in the present by drawing on an expanded sense of environmental-justice culture. See 'Environmental justice on a postcolonial planet? Implications for literary studies: Considering Dangarembga's *Nervous Conditions*.'

Chapter 8
1. Also known as the Second Anglo-Boer War (1899–1902). In 1980 the remains were excavated and reburied in a mass grave at a new memorial site on the other side of town.
2. I use the terms 'region', 'territory' and 'place' interchangeably, keeping in mind Achille Mbembe's explanation that place 'implies stability', whereas 'territory ... is defined essentially by the set of movements that take place within it. Seen in this way, it is a set of possibilities that historically situated actors constantly resist or realize' (Mbembe 2000: 261). These definitions are significant: perceptions about the Orange River region as a stable place are counterbalanced by its territorial status as a 'visible, material and symbolic boundar[y]' that has 'constantly expanded and contracted' (Mbembe 2000: 261), as I discuss later in this chapter.
3. According to Mary Sadler-Altena, 'Gariep was the Nama/Korana name for that part of the Orange River downstream from the confluence of the Vaal River' (see Sadler-Altena, 'Gariep: The Great Orange River': 1). The term 'means the river of the wilderness (!Garib from !Igaro, to be desert, !garob, desert, wilderness)' (Sadler-Altena, citing Pettman: 1). Robert Jacob Gordon named it the Orange River on his visit in 1778 (2).
4. The Orange River originates in Lesotho, where it is known as the Senqu River, and charts the southern boundary of the Free State, then flows through the upper regions of the Northern Cape. The final stretch of 450 kilometres – from Augrabies National Park to the Atlantic Ocean – maps the border between South Africa and Namibia. Despite being the largest river in the country, it remains inaccessible for commercial trade over long distances. The Northern Cape includes parts of the Great Karoo, the Kalahari, Bushmanland, Namaqualand and the Richtersveld, which have important mining and agricultural industries. As the largest province in South Africa, covering a 'land area of 372 889 km^2' (SouthAfrica.info), it has the smallest population, at around 2.17 million people (Lehola 2012: 3), and one of the highest rates of poverty and substance-abuse in the country (Pauw, Punt and Van Schoor 2005: 1–21). At the time of Dicey's journey, the proportion of the country's coloured population was highest in the Northern Cape (51.6 per cent). These are configurations seem significant to Dicey's exploration of identity and location (Pauw, Punt and Van Schoor 2005: 2).

5. Dicey, email communication with author, 25 June 2013.
6. See, for example, Linda Waldman's *The Griqua Conundrum: Political and Socio-cultural Identity in the Northern Cape* (2007) and Robert Ross's review of that book. He writes: 'The title of this book is in a way a tautology. No one, including the Griquas themselves, has ever been able to work out what it is to be Griqua' (Ross 2007: 1).
7. I use the 'generic' term 'Khoisan' to refer to hunter-gatherer (Bushman) and pastoral groups 'of indigenous societies' (Khoikhoi and San) who inhabited the region, mindful of Penn's discussion of terminology, identity and meaning shifts 'in the pre-colonial context and ... the colonial context' (Penn 2001: 6–9).
8. A comparative analysis lies outside the scope of this chapter, but I refer here to a range of adventure publications with underlying neo-imperial conquest themes, in which authors rediscover the African continent, which prevails in these works as 'the very figure of "the strange"' (Mbembe 2001: 3), to emerge as heroes with abilities to endure discomfort, etc. These narratives draw explicitly on tropes like the Cape-to-Cairo theme, the Stanley-Livingstone-Speke or 'I-did-it-first' syndrome, and/or humanitarian (philanthropic) ideals.
9. Currently a farmer, Dicey holds an MPhil in environment, society and development from Magdalene College, Cambridge, and has lectured in mathematics at the University of Cape Town (Dicey, email communication with author, 25 June 2013).
10. See, for example, land claim settlement cases of the ‡Khomani San community of the Kalahari (Dugmore 2013) and the Nama of the Richtersveld (Jordan 2013).
11. A feminist investigation lies outside the scope of this analysis but is part of my comparative research project on recent South African travel writing (see note 8).
12. Nixon (2011) examines 'environmental toxicity' in relation to 'military technologies', such as Agent Orange, atomic warfare and nuclear waste. He asks: 'Who is counting the veterans slain or disabled by environmentally transmitted "friendly fire" and the deferred casualties among refugees returning to poisoned, radiated landscapes, both groups harbouring the illusion that the war is safely behind them?' (Nixon 2011: 12).

Chapter 9
1. See Saro-Wiwa (1995); Omoweh (2005); Okonta and Douglas (2001); and *Gbemre* v. *Shell Petroleum Dev. Co.*, [2005] No. FHC/B/CS/53/05, at 29–30 (F.H.C.) (Nigeria), available at http://www.climatelaw.org/cases/case-documents/nigeria/ni-shell-nov05-judgment.pdf (holding that the Nigerian

constitutional right to life includes the right to a clean, pollution-free environment and that Shell's failure to halt gas flares violates that right). Shell has often been deliberately slow in its response to spillages because it rationalises the consequences of such spillages, as it is of the opinion that much of this damage has been occasioned by acts of sabotage. Although this point is not in doubt, it is not a fully adequate response for several reasons. Observers have argued that the proportion of oil spillage caused by old pipes and poor maintenance is much greater than Shell acknowledges (Okonta and Douglas [2001]; Human Rights Watch [1999: 6]). Most of the studies and reports on the issue foreground the fact that, as Shell conducted its business in Nigeria for about five decades, it operated in ways that produced enormous wealth but left the host communities and people living in the immediate vicinity of their operations more miserable and poorer in monetary, natural and social capital.

Chapter 11
1. For a detailed account of why and how Shell BP and other oil companies are accused of degrading the environment in the Niger Delta region, see Okonta and Douglas (2003).

Chapter 12
1. This is why, as Taringa (2006: 191) observes, 'African traditional religion, and Shona religion in particular, is generally regarded to be intrinsically environmental friendly.' Taringa cites the example of Terrance Ranger, who observes that 'African religious ideas were very much ideas about relationships, whether with other living people, or with spirits of the dead, or with animals, or with cleared land, or with the bush' (Taringa 2006: 192). This is contrary to J. Baird Callicott's controversial claim that African religions are anthropocentric. According to him, 'African thought orbits, seemingly, around human interests. Hence one might expect to distil from it no more than a weak and indirect environmental ethic ...' (Callicott 1994: 158). One suspects, however, that Callicott's overly generalised claim is a result of selective reading, given that there are African scholars who have described African attitudes to nature as ecocentric, or, according to Godfrey Tangwa (1996), 'eco-bio-communitarian'. Although the 'eco-bio-communitarian' outlook recognises differences between humans, plants and animals, unlike anthropocentrism, 'it does not give human persons any special privilege or unlimited right to subdue, dominate, conquer and exploit nature, rather human persons are to live with nature in a spirit of co-existence and friendship making moderate use of the things of nature' (Ikeke 2013: 349).

2. The concept of 'home', as used, here should be understood simply as a place of deep personal and social-cultural attachment.
3. Regarding land dispossession in colonial Zimbabwe, Alexander Kanengoni (2003: 48) observes that

> between the Rudd Concession of 1888 and the Lancaster House Agreement of 1979 lay a plethora of legal and statutory instruments that had one overriding intention, to consolidate the white man's grip on the land. The black person was systematically marginalised, pushed further and further from the fertile lands in the centre of the country to the arid and barren soils along the borders. These acts included the Land Apportionment Act of 1931 [*sic*], the Native Land Husbandry Act of 1951 and the Land Tenure Act 1969.

The Rudd Concession of 1888 that Kanengoni mentions was a written mining agreement secured through deceit and dishonesty by Charles Rudd (a business associate of Cecil John Rhodes) from Lobengula, king of Matebeleland on 30 October 1888 (Vambe 1972). The agreement led to the eventual takeover by white people of the land that was later named Rhodesia. The Lancaster House Agreement, on the other hand, was an agreement signed between the warring parties in Zimbabwe in London on 21 December 1979 to end the war of liberation and pave the way for the independence of Zimbabwe in 1980. The Land Apportionment Act of 1930 was aimed at formalising 'separation by law, land between blacks and whites [following] the deliberations and recommendations of the Morris Carter Commission of 1925' ('Land Issue–Fact Sheet'). The act 'divided the whole country into Native Reserves, Purchase areas and European areas, allocating the fertile lands to the Europeans and the poor areas to the reserves' (Veit-Wild 1993: 23). Further, the Native Land Husbandry Act of 1951 'meant to enforce private ownership of land, destocking and conservation practices on black small holders' ('Land issue – fact sheet') 'in the interest of capitalist economic development, particularly of the white minority' (Machingaidze 1991: 588). And, finally, the Land Tenure Act of 1969, according to Denis Nkala (1996: 4), 'was aimed at applying land use to effect conservation'.

4. In some ways, Hove and Zimunya's accounts of colonial injustice and African victimhood fall within what Achille Mbembe calls a Marxist and nationalist (or Marxist-nationalist) current of thought in Africa, which he characterises as 'a mechanistic and reified vision of history' where 'causality is attributed to entities that are fictive and wholly invisible, but are nevertheless said to determine, ultimately, the [African] subject's life and work' (Mbembe 2002: 243). In Mbembe's view, this 'paranoid reading of history' (Mbembe 2002: 252),

which leads to the invention of 'a narrative of liberation built around the dual temporality of a glorious – albeit fallen – past (tradition) and a redeemed future (nationalism)' (Mbembe 2002: 249–250), obscures Africa's responsibility 'for the catastrophes that [befell and] are befalling it' (Mbembe 2002: 243). Indeed, Africans themselves may be to blame for some of Africa's problems, but I am sure that even Mbembe knows that the colonial encounter had a negative impact on African ecology and culture, and that these deleterious effects of colonialism cannot simply be wished way.

5. Where numbers appear after a collection of poems, they refer to pages; where they appear after a quotation from a poem, they refer to lines.

6. Veit-Wild makes reference to this effect when she observes that 'many of [Hove's] poems about the war [of liberation, for example] are not always easy to approach in detail because [he] tends to overload them with an accumulation of metaphors and paradoxical images' (Veit-Wild 1988: 8). In reaction to this criticism, Hove maintains that 'poetry, any poetry, has to be overloaded with meaning, to make words burst with meaning, with human experience' (Veit-Wild 1988: 39). But overloading a poem with images can also have the unintended effect of stifling meaning, of making the words fail to 'burst with meaning'.

7. The reference to the mourning dove could also be an allusion to the emerald-spotted dove (also called the 'mourning dove' in Zimbabwe), whose call has been interpreted – at least by (mainly white) birders – as being a cry of sorrow.

8. Chenjerai Hove was born in 1954 near Zvishavane, a mining town in Zimbabwe's Midlands Province. '"Zvishavane" is a Shona name, which is said to be derived from "zvikomo zvishava", which means "red hills". The precise meaning of "Zvishavane" is said to be "reddish or reddened hills", referring to the many surrounding low hills that are characterized by red soil' ('Zvishavane, Zimbabwe').

9. This exile was preceded by the disruption and destruction of peasant agriculture, which, like the imposition of taxes on the black population, was a carefully orchestrated measure to induce men to seek work in the mines and on white-owned farms (Bourdillon 1982: 103; Rakodi 1995: 4).

10. 'Chimurenga' means war or revolution. The struggle for land reform, which started around 2000 in Zimbabwe, is known as the third Chimurenga, as it comes after the second Chimurenga (i.e. Zimbabwe's liberation war of 1966–1979), which, in turn, followed the first Chimurenga (the 1896–1897 Ndebele-Shona revolt against colonial rule).

11. In *An Ill-Fated People*, Lawrence Vambe (1972: 211) remembers some gold prospectors who came into his village to ask for directions, food or beer

as 'unwashed, unshaven, unkempt and often ... ill-clothed' men, whom the villagers despised or pitied.

12. In reply to a question on his poetic style posed by Veit-Wild, Zimunya says, 'In *Country Dawns and City Lights* I attempted to exploit something like street conversations and also some folkloric devices. Why? Because I found that most African poets have a problem: Unreadability. I have been a culprit in that regard myself. People love a poem but they don't know what it means' (Veit-Wild 1988: 64). However, the lines above from the much earlier collection *Thought Tracks* show that Zimunya started to avoid 'unreadability' or obscurity earlier in his career.

13. In reading this poem and other precolonial-based poems, one should, however, remember that the picture offered here is a sanitised and romantic version of what precolonial Mawewe actually was. The life of the Shona was not always Edenic, as we are made to believe here. Harsh climatic conditions made life difficult for the people, as droughts triggered famine and suffering among the people (Rakodi 1995: 3). Nevertheless, these kinds of suffering did not lead to the violent disruption of cultural and spiritual life of the Shona and other peoples of Zimbabwe as the changes brought about by colonialism did.

14. Commenting specifically on the work of Wordsworth in ways that echo Williams's misgivings about the pastoral genre, A.J. Raymer says 'in his passion for returning to nature for that primal simplicity of thought and speech he considered essential to his principles, Wordsworth assumed that rustic life and civilization were the purest and best. This, to any one at all familiar with rural pig-marketing, cottage life, or parochial meetings, is a rash assumption.' He goes on to say, 'It is difficult to reconcile the Lombardy shepherd or Wordsworth's crofter men, still less the modern farm hand on his motor tractor, with beings in whose condition "the passions of men are incorporated with the beautiful and permanent forms of nature".' (Raymer 1939: 15).

INDEX

A
Abacha, Sani 3, 271
acacia tree, value of 109–111, 114
Achebe, Chinua 6, 143–144,
    154–155
Things Fall Apart 9, 79, 141–142,
    258
African cultural production/
    expression vii, ix, xiii, 5, 10–11,
    13, 79
  ecological knowledge in ix, xi, 13,
    16, 103, 113, 115–116,
  see also African ecocriticism;
    African environmental writing/
    literature
  problem of universalism in 143
African ecocriticism vii–viii, ix, xii,
    1–3, 5–8, 11–12, 15, 23–24,
    229–230, 312n3:1, 319n12:1
  anti-colonial/imperial xi, 142,
    157–159, 168, 215, 279–280,
    286–292, 294–295, 297–301,
    320n4
  'cities-in-nature' focus xi–xiii, 14,
    20–21, 23, 167–172, 175–176,
    178–184, 314n2
  East African 7
  and foodways 16
  human-animal focus 9, 18, 159,
    236, 238, 255
  inter-/multidisciplinary 8, 13, 15–16,
    156–158, 167, 171, 189, 238, 257
  issues of justice/injustice 160
  literary aesthetics/creative
    imagination of 158–161, 172,
    190, 195, 199, 208
  Nigerian 2, 141, 230, 257, 262,
    269–270
  regional alterity of xiii–xiv, 5, 20,
    144–156, 160–162, 171, 236
  rural-urban divide 20, 180, 281–
    282, 285
  South African 6, 188
  transnational 7, 21, 190, 208
  travel narratives xiii, 15, 21, 188–190
  see also under African nationalism;
    foodways; postcolonial
African environmental writing/
    literature xi, xiii, 6, 8, 13, 20,
    141–142, 144–150, 215, 258
  apocalyptic vision in 3, 21, 175–177,
    184, 213
  satire in 22, 237, 242–243, 245,
    247, 251, 254–255, 316n17

African indigenous knowledge/
    cultures, ix–xi, 8, 13, 15, 44–45,
    100, 103–104, 113, 142, 157,
    161, 243, 309n5
African indigenous religions 18,
    53–54, 77–79, 84, 142
  ancestral spirits in 90, 142, 245
  anthropocentric 14, 155, 236,
    319:12n1
  biocentric/pro-life 79, 89–95,
    319:12n1
  environmental taboos in 114
  mutability of 79
  ritual sacrifice of animals in 79, 89
  see also animism; green religion;
    Shona indigenous religion
African mythology 22, 33, 52, 236
  concept of 'sacred wisdom' in xii,
    236, 250–251
  'harmful doubles' in 236–237,
    239, 241, 243–247, 251–252
  subversion of 22, 237
  see also Shona land mythology;
    Yoruba mythology
African nationalism x, 17, 56–57, 67,
    70–71, 231, 310n2&6
  influence on ecocriticism 149–150,
    152
  and reconstructions of land
    mythology 51, 53, 59, 61–63,
    65, 74, 310n6, 311n13
afroecophilosophy 146–147
Anglophone Nigerian poetry x
  filiation with gods 259–260, 262–273
  influence of oral tradition on 262,
    273–274
  interdependence of nature-culture
    in 258, 260, 262–268, 273
  poets' sense of place 227, 257–258,
    260–262, 320n2
  sociopolitical dimension 268–274
  see also under animism

animal narrators 8, 15, 235,
    245–246, 250
  hybridity of 237–240, 252, 255
animals, representations of xiii, 4–6,
    5, 8–9, 13, 23, 122
  metaphoric 237–238, 254
  in tourism advertising
  see also animal narrators; human-
    animal relationships; Samburu
    animal praise poetry; Shona
    indigenous religion: totemic
    animals in; Shona poetry:
    animal imagery in
animism x–xii, 14–15, 23, 84, 237–
    238, 259
  in Anglophone Nigerian poetry
    22, 257–263, 265, 267–269, 271,
    273
anthropocene era 10–11
anthropological discourses 8, 12, 247
anthropomorphism 238–239, 298
anti-colonial/imperial resistance viii,
    x–xi, 56, 63–64, 168, 177, 314n4
  postcolonial 9, 284
  see also African ecocriticism: anti-
    colonial/imperial; Zimbabwe:
    Chimurenga land wars
apartheid 12, 177, 198
  post-apartheid transformation
    6–7, 172, 177, 198, 208
  homelands 197, 203
Atlantic Ocean 14, 21, 30, 40, 188,
    200
Atlantic slave trade 28, 78, 269
Ayuk, Ojung 148, 150, 152

B

Baingana, Doreen: *Tropical Fish* 172,
    180–182, 184, 316n17
baobab tree x, 45
  mythological/symbolic status of
    16, 28–29, 33–38, 41–42

usefulness of 16, 34, 39, 42–44
see also biopiracy
Bede, Jacques L. 148–150
Bhabha, Homi K. 192, 195, 198
biocentrism 79, 230, 312:3n1, 319:12n1
biodiversity ix–xi, 44, 89, 94
  destruction of 213
biopiracy x, 16, 27, 42, 44–46
  quinoa 45, 310:1:7
bioregionalism 14, 23, 28
  precolonial 28
Bookchin, Murray 82–83
Born Free Crew 60, 64, 66–67
Braidotti, Rosi 237–239
Branch, Michael 229–230
Britton, Robert 123, 125
Buell, Lawrence 189, 257
bushmen *see* Khoisan/San people

C
Cameroon 157, 235–237, 243, 246, 249, 252
  President Paul Biya 237, 249, 253
'canitude' 241, 249
Cape Town 173–174, 177
  Table Mountain 21, 125, 175–176, 178, 190
capitalism x, 8
  colonial context xi, 9, 18, 61, 286, 289, 299, 314n3
  industrial 143, 168, 222, 225–226
  postcolonial critique of 11–12, 144, 189, 286–287
  see also global capitalism
Cartesianism 9, 11, 161
Chakrabarty, Dipesh 10–13
Chinx, Cde 59, 64, 72
Christian missionisation 142, 144
Christianity 34, 61, 77–78, 311n13
  African 93, 95, 142, 311n10
  Catholic 264
  green/pro-nature 83, 90–91

Clare, John 279–280
climate change 10–12, 14, 20, 83, 90, 154, 161, 167, 182, 213
Coetzee, J.M. 3–5
colonial
  biological control 157, 161
  exploitation of natural resources ix, xi, 44, 59–61, 143, 158, 161
  knowledge production viii, 38, 130
  land expropriation/dispossession x, xiii, 3, 14, 17–18, 21, 28, 60, 62, 98, 143–144, 158, 161, 189–190
  perceptions of African culture/cultural chauvinism viii, 78, 129, 142, 192–193
  present, concept of vii
  see also under capitalism; modernity
colonialism 7–9, 32, 120, 123, 129–130, 134, 138, 141
  cultural 27–28, 80–81
  Dutch 190–191, 194
  empty land myth 131
  see also violence, colonial/neocolonial; Zimbabwe: British colonisation of
colonisation *see* colonialism
commodification 19, 45, 124, 206–207, 226
  of nature ix, 184, 198
  see also voluntourism
Conrad, David 30–31, 33
conservation viii–ix, 3, 5, 161–162, 178
  imperial/colonial practices ix, 62, 71, 168
  role of traditional communities in xi, 14, 19, 83, 85–87, 90–92, 94–95, 103, 113–115

consumerism 45, 120–121
  anti-consumerism 9
cultural/ethnic identity xi, 21–22, 97, 190–191, 193
  and concept of 'culturescape' 23, 276
  destruction of 227
  flexible/changing 97–99, 102–103, 115–116
  importance of place/belonging to 23, 142, 149–150, 153, 160, 202, 218, 227–229, 231 *see also under* Anglophone Nigerian poetry
  influence of colonial institutionalisation on 192
  precolonial 141
  see also under foodways
Cunningham, Anthony 85–86

D
dark green religion, concept of 81–83, 312:3n1 *see also* green religion
Daston, Lorraine 238–239
De Loughrey, Elizabeth 4, 141–143, 145, 152–153, 159–160, 168, 258, 314n4
decolonisation 136, 148, 279
  of knowledge vii–ix, xi
democracy 177, 268, 273
  environmental 9, 12
despotism 215, 290
development viii–ix, xi, 4, 123, 157, 180, 189, 197, 214
  theory 121, 134–136
  see also environmental degradation: impact of development on
Dicey, William: *Borderline* xiii, 187–188, 200–208, 318n9
  interdisciplinarity of 15–16, 21, 188–189

  introspective narrative voice 202–203
  layered representational strategies of 189–192, 195–201
  regional focus of 194–195, 203
  textual and visual layout 199–200
  topic of Verwoerd and Tsafendas 204, 207–208
Dirlik, Arif 168, 314n3
Douglas, Stuart 197–198
Duiker, K. Sello: *Thirteen Cents* 20–21, 166, 177–180, 315n11
  Azure as narrator/character 172–177, 181
  ethical/political implications of 172–174, 176–178, 181–182, 184
Duncan James 188, 200, 202

E
East Africa ix, 7, 81, 149–150
Eastern Cape 180, 187, 197
eco-activism 5, 12, 14, 147 *see also under* Niger River Delta disaster
ecocentrism *see* biocentrism
ecocritical activism *see* eco-activism
ecocriticism, global/Anglo-American 2, 6, 8, 10, 18, 20, 142–144, 148, 150–152, 155, 257, 278
  anthropocentric focus 155, 236
  'black Atlantic' 146, 204
  critique of modernity144–145, 154, 157, 168
  localised/essentialist 145–146, 154
  universalised 143, 153–154, 162
  see also African ecocriticism: regional alterity of
ecofeminism xiii, 153
  African 14
ecology viii, x, 8, 51, 145, 278, 312:6n2
  deep 83, 155, 312:3:n1
  destruction of 228

ritually directed 17, 58, 61, 64, 277
see also green religion
ecopostcolonialism 278, 287, 292
ecosocial realities 153, 169–172, 179–180, 183
  concerning gender 181–182
  environmental degradation 20, 62, 67, 83, 142–144, 149, 152, 198, 207, 217, 293, 299–300
  impact of development on 12, 61, 180, 228, 231, 281
  urban 148–149, 161, 281
  see also socio-ecological issues/disasters
environmental displacement xiii, 3, 14, 21–22, 71, 190, 204, 214, 230
  and sociocultural dislocation xii, 228, 189, 218–220, 228–229
  see also Niger River Delta disaster
environmental ethics ix–x, xii, 5, 18, 141, 162, 198, 230–231, 278
  African 37–38
environmental justice/injustice xi, 151, 153, 158–160, 190, 214, 217, 228, 231, 317n20
environmentalism viii, 82, 90, 126, 146
  African xi, 6–8, 10, 14, 142–144, 159, 161–162
  black African scepticism of 151–152
  of the poor 4, 147, 154, 189–190, 205
  see also African ecocriticism; green religion
European Enlightenment 11–12, 258

F
Fabian, Johannes 104–105
folklore/myths 58, 61, 104, 196, 267, 282

symbolic meanings of 54–55, 104
see also Shona land mythology
foodways
  and cultural identity 36–38, 46, 310:1n7
  intersection with ecocriticism x, 3, 27–28, 33
  role in folk tales/mythology x, 33–34, 39, 84
  sovereignty x, 46
  see also under Sunjata oral epic
forests ix, 5, 9, 36, 54, 108
  conservation of 85–86, 91–92, 141
  exploitation of/deforestation 62, 86–87, 94, 142, 161, 299–300
fossil fuels, global dependence on 4, 11, 182 *see also* petro-capital
Fromm, Harold 149–150

G
Gambia 32–33
Garuba, Harry 236–238, 258–260, 262
Geschiere, Peter 237, 243
Ghana 30, 146
Gillespie, Alex 134, 136–137
giraffe 195–196
global capitalism 4, 45, 143, 158, 179
  and multinational corporate exploitation of natural resources 44, 157, 158, 161, 213, 217, 221, 223–225, 262, 269, 279
global economy 18, 82, 132–133, 138, 156, 168, 171–172, 222, 286
global environmental issues/crises 10, 12, 83, 144–145, 149–150, 158, 162, 229
  impact of development on 12, 228
  and survival of species 13
  urban focus 167
  see also climate change; environmental degradation; socio-ecological issues/disasters

global modernity 21, 145, 156, 161, 314n3&4
  impact on nature-city relationship 154, 168–170, 172, 183
  see also environmental degradation: urban; urbanism: globalised
global North 19, 121, 128, 132–134, 168
global South 5, 94, 132, 134, 147, 168
global warming *see* climate change
globalisation 9–10, 22, 126, 138
  humanist histories of 11–12
glocal oil racketeering 220–221, 225
Glotfelty, Cheryll 2, 149–150, 230
Gordimer, Nadine 3, 5
Gosson, Renée K. 143, 145, 160
Green Belt Movement xi, 7, 14
green religion x, 17, 77–79, 81–85, 91 *see also* dark green religion, concept of; Shona indigenous religion
Gregory, Derek vii, 188, 200, 202

H
Habila, Helon
  Oil on Water xii, 21–22, 212, 215, 218–228, 230–231
  Waiting for an Angel 214, 220–221
Hale, Thomas 31–32
Hall 129–130
Handley, George B. 4, 141–143, 145, 152–153, 159–160, 168, 258, 314n4
Hansen, Anders 121, 125–126, 133
Hatcliffe Chimurenga Choir 68, 72
Haught, J. 90–91
Heise, Ursula K. 145, 159–160
Hove, Chenjerai 4, 23, 276, 278, 294, 320n4, 321n6&8
  representations of nature-culture 282–288
  theme of colonial injustice/political transition 279–280, 286–292, 297, 300–301, 320n4
  theme of environmental degradation/poverty 281–282, 289
Huggan, Graham 3, 158–159, 189, 191, 198, 279
human-animal relationships x, xii, 3, 6, 8, 18–19, 23–24, 87, 92, 157, 236–237, 240–241, 253–254
  animal subjectivity and agency in vii, 22, 101, 238–239, 243, 254
  conflict prevention in 108–111
  see also animal narrators; Samburu animal oral
human-nature relationships *see* nature-culture relationships
human-non-human dynamics *see* human-animal relationships
humanitarianism 121, 126, 134
Hunt, Alex 3, 152–153, 159

I
Ibeanu, Okechukwu 215, 217–218, 228
imperialism vii, xii–xiii, 7–8, 21, 45, 192–194, 208
  resistance/challenges to viii, 158
  see also colonialism; modernity; travel writing
individualism 21, 38, 179
industrialism 1, 143–144, 154, 222
inequality, social/systemic viii, 20, 153, 172, 207
Iron Age 58, 81
Islam 30, 33–34, 78, 91
  Boko Haram sect 213

J

Jonathan, Goodluck 213–214

K

Kenya xi, 86, 97, 115, 168n1
  Samburu community, Wamba County 18–19, 98, 102–103, 105, 108–110, 114, 312:4n1
  see also Samburu animal praise poetry
Khoisan/San societies 190, 197–198, 200, 203, 318n7
Kouyaté, Dani 44
  Keita! L'héritage du Griot 37–42
Kowalewski, Michael 189, 192–193, 195
Kraai river 187–188
Krige, Norma J. 50, 70–71

L

land 50–51, 53
  indigenous/'kincentric' attachment to 51, 142–143, 150, 152, 154, 157, 161, 191, 227, 258, 276, 312:6n1
  see also Shona land mythology
Latour, Bruno 9–10, 12
Lodikir, Mzee John 107, 111

M

Maathai, Wangari x–xi, 5, 7, 147
Mabanckou, Alain: *Memoirs of a Porcupine* xi, 22, 235, 239–241, 243–248, 250–255
  engagement with magic/occult in 236–238, 241, 243–247, 251–252, 255
  human-non-human dynamics in 237–239, 243, 246–248, 252–255
  shame of narrator in 250–251
  Western beliefs about language in 245–246

Madagascar 237, 242, 246, 253–255
Mali 29–30, 32–33, 36, 43, 309n2
Mande/Manding people 16, 28, 31, 33. 35–36, 309n2
Martin, Julia 12, 316n14
Mashonaland *see* Zimbabwe
Mbare Chimurenga Choir 57, 64, 68, 72
Mda, Zakes 3, 5, 236
  Heart of Redness 4, 172, 174, 176, 179–180, 184
mining, politics of
  asbestos 205–206
  diamond 206–207
Mitman, Gregg 238–239
modernity xii, 11–12, 259, 315n11
  African 156, 172
  assimilation into traditional culture 236–237, 246–247, 274
  colonial/imperial vii, xii, 23, 143, 157
  divisions between cultural tradition and xi–xii, 4, 161, 246–248
  see also African mythology: assimilation of modernity into; ecocriticism: critique of modernity; global modernity
Moore, Gerald 149–150, 152
Mozambique 53, 66, 68, 80, 191, 204
Mugabe, Robert 17, 72–73, 279, 290
Muponde, Robert 280–281, 287, 300

N

Nama people 188, 190, 193, 196–197, 206–207
Namibia 191–192, 196–197, 203
nature
  as backdrop to human activity 9–12
  human alienation from 67, 143, 145, 154, 229, 279, 298

nature (*continued*)
    meanings of/Anglo-American
        concept of 121–122, 126, 128,
        145, 153
    visionary sense of 174–176
nature-city relationships xii, 14,
    20–21, 166–170, 172, 174–179,
    182
    see also African ecocriticism
        'cities-in-nature' focus
nature-culture, land-based/rural
    17–19, 51, 53, 58, 60, 84, 92,
    180, 215, 245
    Zimbabwe 23, 276–277
    disruption/destruction of 60, 74,
        227–228, 277 *see also* Niger
        River Delta disaster
nature-culture relationships xi–xii,
    13, 16, 21, 23–24, 28, 46, 133,
    153, 157, 180, 196, 230, 232
    see also under Anglophone
        Nigerian poetry
nature-human relationships *see*
    nature-culture relationships
Ndebele, Njabulo 5, 131
Ndebele peope 56, 80–81, 295
negritude 14, 241
neocolonial theft *see* biopiracy
neocolonialism ix, xii, 38, 46, 132,
    154, 158–159, 161
Nganang, Patrick: *Dog Days: An
    Animal Chronicle* xi, 22, 235,
    252–254
    engagement with magic in 236,
        238
    human-non-human dynamics in
        237–243, 245–246, 248–250,
        252–255
    political critique in 237, 241–242,
        246, 248–250, 252–255
    role of Crow in 242, 248–250,
        252–254

shame of narrator in 250
Western beliefs about language in
    245–246
Niger River Delta disaster xii, 2, 6, 9,
    212–215, 262, 269–270
    activism/resistance 3, 14, 214,
        217–218, 231
    amnesty package 213–214
    destruction of biodiversity and
        wetlands 213, 221–223, 225,
        229
    displacement/refugee crisis xii,
        21–22, 212, 214, 218–220,
        226–229, 231
    human health issues 224–225
    role of government and
        multinationals in 213, 217, 221,
        223–225, 230, 262, 269, 318n1,
        319:11n1
    see also politics of violence, Niger
        River Delta
Nigeria 2, 5–6, 30, 148,
    Igboland 141–142
    oil industry in 213, 216–217, 221
    political corruption in 225
    see also Anglophone Nigerian
        poetry
Nixon, Rob xii, 4–5, 189–190, 199,
    202, 205–208, 219, 278, 318n12

O

Obiechina, Emmanuel 283, 287
oil exploration/extraction *see*
    petro-capital
Ojaide, Tanure 6, 22, 212, 230, 262,
    268–271
Okigbo, Christopher 22, 261,
    263–264, 271
Okome, Onookome 22, 227, 262,
    271
Okri, Ben 6
    The Famished Road 142, 144

Opoku, Kofi 236, 238–239, 243
oral traditions/cultures 15, 59, 61,
    101, 262, 273, 310n4, 315n6
  importance of performative
    ethnography in 104–105
  see also orature
Orange (Gariep) River xiii, 21
    187–188, 190–193, 199–200,
    205–206, 208, 317n2&4
  Augrabies Falls 194–197, 203
Orania 203–205
orature ix–x, xiii, 3, 15–16, 22, 50,
    52, 98, 100, 142
  adaptable nature of 40
  oral poetry 101–102
  role of audience in 31, 33, 45,
    100–102
  see also folklore; Samburu animal
    praise poetry *Sunjata* oral epic
Osundare, Niyi 22, 259, 262,
    265–268

P

pastoral genre xii, xi, 14, 20, 23, 59,
    103, 153, 280, 322n14
  nostalgic 154, 283, 292, 297,
    299–301
patriarchy 23, 57, 182, 310n5
p'Bitek, Okot 7, 13
petro-capital 3, 161, 216–217, 222,
    225–227, 231 *see also* Niger
    River Delta disaster
Philip, Nourbese M. 260–261
politics of violence, Niger River
    Delta 213–214, 216–218, 220,
    223, 227, 230
polygamy 93–94
poverty 19–20, 189, 242, 253,
    Nigeria 225
  post-apartheid South Africa 12,
    125, 127, 132, 207–208, 317n4
  Zimbabwe 278–279, 285, 297

power, colonial/Western
    viii, 130
power relations, human-animal
    239–241, 246
power relations, uneven viii, xii, xiv,
    21, 128–130, 132, 134, 168,
    171–172, 207
  urban-rural 133
precolonial narratives x, 3–4, 28,
    32–33, 59, 80, 148, 179, 196,
    284, 294, 322n13 *see also*
    Sunjata oral epic

R

racism, history/legacy of 173–174,
    178, 196, 204, 208
Ranger, Terrence 17, 59, 62–63, 66,
    319:12n1
Reid, Amy Baram 236, 238,
    241, 246
Rhodes, Cecil John 60, 63, 295,
    311n15
Richtersveld 198, 202, 207
Riemvasmaak 195–198
Roos, Bonnie 3, 152–153,
    159

S

Sadomba, Zvakanyorwa W. 50, 59,
    65–66, 69
Said, Edward 23, 130, 170,
    229
Salazar, Noel 124, 127
Samburu animal praise poetry
    ix, 13, 15, 18–19, 101, 104
  Dorobo 99–100, 105, 107–108,
    111, 113–114
  Talas song to elephant 100, 105,
    107–111, 114–115
  Lebarta song to ostrich/lioness
    100, 105–107, 114, 116
  to livestock 98–101

Samburu animal praise poetry (*continued*)
   Morans/Moranhood and 99, 101, 111, 114, 312:4n2
   to rhino 99–100, 105, 107–108, 111–114
   as safeguard to survival 97–100, 102–103, 105–106, 115–116
   symbolic meanings of 104
Saro-Wiwa, Ken 3, 5, 155, 217–218
Shell Petroleum Development Company 224, 269–270, 318n1
Shishima, D. 78–79
Shona indigenous religion
   alien spirits (*mashavi*) in 81, 84, 88
   ancestral spirits (*midzimu*) in 54, 56, 79, 81, 84–86, 88–92, 94, 277–278
   ecological/green nature of x, 55–56, 58–59, 61–62, 64, 73, 77–78, 84–86, 89–91, 277–278, 280, 319:12n1
   environmental taboos in x, 58, 61, 85–89, 94, 277–278
   influence of agriculture on 59, 286, 296–297
   Musikavanhu 55, 77
   Mwari 55, 58–59, 66, 81, 277, 311n10
   pro-life practices in 92–93
   totemic animals in 23, 41–42, 53–54, 81, 85, 278, 310:2n7
Shona land mythology x, 11, 16–18, 23, 51–53, 71, 74, 58, 290, 295, 310n3
   and *Chimurenga* songs/folklore 15–17, 49–50, 53, 56–57, 61–62, 64–68, 71–74, 277, 310n2
   mwana wevhu philosophy 53–55, 61–62, 72, 279
   land-is-blood myth 67–69, 292
   land as sovereignty in 60, 64–66, 295

see also African nationalism: and reconstructions of land mythology; Shona indigenous religion; Shona territorial spirits
Shona language 79–81
Shona poetry 61
   representations of nature in 23, 276–279, 292–294
   animal imagery in 276–277, 282–283, 287–288, 293–294
   see also Hove, Chenjerai; Zimunya, Musaemura
Shona territorial spirits 311n11
   Chaminuka 56–58, 60, 63
   Kaguvi 56–58, 63–64, 67
   Nehanda 56–58, 60, 63–67, 69, 311n13
   ngozi 64
silk-cotton tree 39–41
Slaymaker, William 6, 146–148, 150–151, 154–155, 225
socio-ecological issues/disasters xii
   resistance to x
   'slow violence' of xii–xiii, 4, 151, 157–158, 189–190, 205–207, 209, 219
   see also Niger River Delta disaster
socio-environmental marginalisation 188–190, 197–198, 204, 208, 216, 228, 320n3
   demarginalisation of groups 199
Somé, Malidoma Patrice 243, 245
South Africa ix, 1–2, 5–7, 12, 148, 191, 193, 195
   neoliberalism in 177, 179
South African War 188, 205, 317n1
South African Tourism 125, 127, 130
Soyinka, Wole 2, 22, 241, 259, 263, 264–265, 271
Stearman, Gary 82–83, 90
Stoll, Mark 82–83

Sunjata oral epic x, 15–16, 29–33, 40, 43, 45–46
   representation of food/foodways, in x, 3, 16, 27, 30, 33–39
Szeman, Imre 222, 226

T
Taylor, Bron 81–83
Tiffin, Helen 3, 158–159, 189, 191, 198, 279
travel writing 133, 189, 192–193
   imperial xiii, 192–196, 201
   see also African ecocriticism: travel narratives
tourism
   cultural 198–198
   ecotourism 4
   mass 127, 138
   safari viii–ix, 131, 199
   'tourist gaze' 134–137
   see also voluntourism
tourismification of people/places 124, 127

U
urbanism/urbanisation 14, 158, 161, 169–170, 174, 179–180, 183–184, 314n2, 315n7
   globalised 182–183
Urry, John 134–135

V
van Riebeeck, Jan 190, 193–194
Viljoen, Shaun 176, 315n9
violence, colonial/neocolonial ix, xiii, 143, 151, 157, 175–177, 189, 196, 280–281, 290–292 *see also* politics of violence, Niger River Delta
voluntourism ix, 118–120, 128, 137, 139
   altruism 122–123
   definition of 121–122, 126

voluntourism websites, representations of nature in xiii, 5, 15, 19–20, 120–122, 129, 131, 139
   colonial historical/white-guilt narrative 123, 129–134
   development theory perspective 123, 132, 134–136, 138
   representation of racial 'other' 129
   rural-urban opposition 132–133
   tourism studies perspective 123–128, 134–135
   see also commodification: of nature

W
wa Thiong'o, Ngũgĩ 3, 7, 212
West Africa ix–x, 8–9, 16, 27–28, 30, 38, 40, 46, 146
   role of griot in 29–32, 34, 36–37
wild fig tree x, 84
Williams, Raymond 122, 126, 297, 322n14
Wolfe, Cary 239, 249
Wordsworth, William 279–280, 322n14
World War II 135–136, 315n12
Wylie, Dan 7–8, 23, 276

Y
Yoruba mythology 9, 259, 268, 271–272
   Ivwri 268–270
   Mother Idoto 262–264
   Ogun 264–265
   Olosunta 267
   Osun 265–266
   Sango 259

Z
Zambia 65, 80
Zimbabwe x–xi, 4–6, 18, 80–81

Zimbabwe (*continued*)
   British colonisation of 59–62, 64, 67, 71, 74, 80, 279–280, 283, 286–289, 292, 294–295, 298–301, 320n3, 321n9
   Chimurenga land wars 50, 53, 56, 62–64, 66–69, 72, 74, 290, 310n2, 311n13, 321n10
   land invasions/reform 17, 49–50, 59–60, 65, 68–74, 86–87, 290, 310n2
   postcolonial land expectations 70–71
   precolonial 59–60, 63, 65, 87, 283–284, 294–295
   ZANLA 67–69
   ZANU-PF 65, 68, 71, 74, 292
   see also Shona land mythology; Shona poetry
Zimunya, Musaemura 4, 23, 276, 278–280, 286, 322n12
   theme of colonial destruction 294–295, 298–300, 320n4
   theme of precolonial nostalgia 292–294, 296–298, 300, 322n13
zoocriticism 3, 8

www.ingramcontent.com/pod-product-compliance
Lightning Source LLC
Chambersburg PA
CBHW031056080526
44587CB00011B/703